Time Ahead

Investor's Guide to Prosperity and Impact

Ryan Zabrowski

Time Ahead

ISBN 978-1506-912-52-3 HC_CL
ISBN 978-1506-912-53-0 PBK

June 2024

Published and Distributed by
Alliance for Independent Authors, LLC

Disclosure

Although the author and publisher have made every effort to ensure that the information in this book was correct at press time, the author and publisher do not assume and hereby disclaim any liability to any party for any loss, damage, or disruption caused by errors or omissions, whether such errors or omissions result from negligence, accident, or any other cause.

The information contained in all featured documents are opinions only and are not intended as a solicitation, an offer, a recommendation to buy, hold, or sell any securities, products, service, investment or participate in any particular trading scheme in any jurisdiction.

The content of this book is for informational purposes only and is not intended to diagnose, treat, cure, or prevent any condition or disease. You understand that this book is not intended as a substitute for consultation with a licensed practitioner. Please consult with your own physician or healthcare specialist regarding the suggestions and recommendations made in this book. The use of this book implies your acceptance of this disclaimer.

Important People in My Career

The most important people in my career are my investors; nothing happens without them. They are the lifeblood of our business, and I'm forever grateful to them for trusting their life savings to our care. They are the reason I get the opportunity to do this every day. Their trust allows our dreams to come true together. And as Warren Buffett has said, they are the reason I tap dance to work every day.

I was able to write this book because of the many supportive people on our staff and colleagues who do their jobs so well. While they were not directly involved in the creation of the book, their dedication and competence made it possible for me to spend the time needed to complete the project.

To Krilogy Founder and CEO Kent Skornia, who established the firm's exceptional culture and core values of dedication and leadership, and for believing in our team and allowing us to bring our investors to Krilogy.

To Krilogy CIO John McArthur for his amazing work ethic and for inviting me to join the investment and portfolio strategy committees.

To both Kent and John for their empathy and support while writing my book.

To Jane Leech, a consummate professional and devoted colleague who continuously makes the interests of our customers her priority, often working nights, weekends, even while on vacation to make their lives just a little better.

To the many individuals and team members who collaborate so effectively to provide personal service to our investors, helping us fulfill our fiduciary responsibilities:

Michael Barbercheck, Taylor Dade, Stacy Flanagin, Charles Flecke, Kristin Fomon, Kyle Goepel, Matt Haywood, Nathan Holt, DeAnna Kaber, Jaime Knaeble, Megan Lockhart, Sean McKenzie, Matt Mercer, Patrick Monahan, Sheila Moran, Ben Orris, Matt Perlow, Kelly Rector, Jenna Schiller, Jeff Skornia, Deb Smiley, Nicki Stackelbeck, Morgan Tejcek, and Jake Thornton.

To Jason Turkin, who believed in me and gave me an opportunity early in my career in the Wall Street shark tank.

To Mike Going for trusting me to manage his clients after he moved on to institutional finance.

ACKNOWLEDGMENTS

No book, particularly one of this magnitude, comes together without the help of devoted collaborators.

To Jamie Saettele, CMT and author of "*Sentiment in the Forex Market: Indicators and Strategies To Profit from Crowd Behavior and Market Extremes,*" a friend and colleague whose charting, technical analysis and editing in support of the *Market Health* chapter was invaluable.

To John Eberth, MS PhD in the Department of Physiology at the University of Kentucky College of Medicine, for his indispensable technical knowledge and contributions to the "Breakthroughs and Market Implications" chapter.

To Tom Lewis for his proofreading expertise supporting compliance.

To Mike Dubes. Without you this book would have never been possible. Twenty years of starting and failing to write a book until you came into my life. I never thought when we started this journey together three years ago that I would learn so much from you. Your wisdom, humor and world class creativity made this book possible and hopefully enjoyable for readers. I look forward to many more life and written chapters together.

Time Ahead

Investor's Guide to Prosperity and Impact

CONTENTS

Section Two

Section Four

PROLOGUE

Time Ahead

Time is a critical component of every decision made in life, capitalism and investing. It's often the most important factor. As we grow older and hopefully wiser, we learn that time is not some intangible construct but rather life's most precious asset. The wealthiest cannot buy it and we all run out of it. Time is the greatest gift you can give to someone…unless they are poor, in which case it's money.

The book's title, Time Ahead, has two meanings that refer to two of the most important facets of capitalism: having a lead or advantage, and looking into the future. The same two words symbolize two different concepts, each of which is a vital element of succeeding in capitalism.

The investor or business that starts with a lead has a tremendous competitive advantage. The ability to look into the future and recognize the opportunities and threats helps sustain that competitive advantage.

Think about an NFL football game where one team has a two-touchdown lead. That lead represents more than a points advantage. It gives the team the flexibility to run any plays they want. They can run the ball, pass or even try trick plays, like a statue of liberty or fake punt. They are under no pressure to abandon their game plan because it's working. Meanwhile, their opponents have been put in the uncomfortable position of having to force the issue to get back in the game. They have to take chances. They have to forgo their original game plan and scramble just to stay in the game. Being behind creates pressure that often leads to mistakes. That's how the game gets out of hand and a team winds up getting blown off the field, even though there may not be a significant disparity in talent or opportunity.

As an investor, you want to start out with this kind of a lead. You want to own businesses with a competitive advantage that is sustainable. Whether that advantage is being the low-cost leader like Walmart, having universal brand recognition like Starbucks or Coca-Cola or being competitively invulnerable like Amazon. Businesses that have what Warren Buffett calls "wide moats" enjoy a sustainable competitive advantage.

Investors that own these companies are already ahead. They can remain patient, stick to their game plan and take measured risks when opportunities arise. It's like having a two-touchdown lead on the competition.

Prosperity and Impact

Prosperity has different meanings for different people. A formal definition is "the state of success, wealth and good fortune." For some, that translates as the accumulation of material goods, i.e., "The one with the most toys wins." But for me, prosperity is winning at capitalism so you can do more for others, whether that's charitable giving or leaving more to loved ones. Those who accumulate the most wealth have the greatest opportunity—and I believe the greatest obligation—to make the world a better place and, in the process, create a legacy with humanitarian impact.

Why Four Sections?

This book was written in sections. It's essentially four different books but the four sections are nonetheless interrelated.

Section I: Don't Blink: Understanding When to Take Risks

Competition exists wherever there is a prize, whether in sports, business or investing. To be successful in any competition, there are things that must be done well and consistently, fundamental principles that determine the winners and losers.

Winners achieve success through hard work, preparation, readiness and the ability to identify opportunities while avoiding blunders. They surround themselves with quality people, world-class analytics and efficient methodologies to take advantage of their opportunities.

They anticipate critical decision points, recognize when they occur and know how to respond, given their operating environment. In our field of investing, one of the biggest decision points is understanding when to take risks. That ability is a common denominator among the best and brightest in any field.

Warren Buffett and Tom Brady are examples of two people engaged in completely different activities that nonetheless share similar characteristics. They understand when to be aggressive and when to be restrained. When circumstances were favorable, Brady would abandon the conservative dink and dunk strategy, change the run/pass ratio, become more aggressive and push the ball down the field. Buffett does something similar when investing. He will remain patient, dinking and dunking small chunks of stocks, until he observes a lucrative opportunity, whereupon he unhesitatingly seizes a huge position.

Successful businesses display similar composure, unhurriedly executing their competitive advantage at a high level. They will suddenly emerge and complete a significant acquisition that has a massive impact on the organization. Just like Brady suddenly unleashing a 50-yard touchdown bomb after a series of short runs and passes, every competition has these common threads that continuously work and lead to wins. Investing is no different.

Section II: Learning How to Accelerate Financial Goals

I think of the investing public as being in two categories: passive investors content to accept average returns, believing they are avoiding risk, and investors that expect to achieve more, enjoy greater prosperity and make an impact with their money.

These are two disparate approaches to investing, but if you expect to achieve success, you must get the fundamentals correct. They're not easy to attain but the rewards are unbelievable and can make an enormous difference in the acceleration of your financial goals. You can do more for your children, retire sooner, have more money and a more fulfilling retirement and leave an impactful legacy.

One of the truly rewarding aspects of my field is that every decision is magnified over time. Merely making consistently sound small decisions has a huge financial impact because of how compound interest works. Those precisely correct little decisions become more and more meaningful over time. And the opposite is also true. If you mess up or miss an opportunity, the compounded impact of those errors is magnified over an extended period.

This section uses lessons from Buffett and other strategies to make sure you don't get wiped out in a bear market. It goes on to explain the importance of finding a competent, trustworthy advisor. It concludes with an examination of the two basic investing approaches so you can assess which path gives you the higher probability of accelerating your financial goals.

Section III: Lemmings, Liars, Loopholes and Free Lunches

Lemmings are the people that listen to the media and naysayers. They are usually the financial naifs that fall prey to the liars and scammers. Wall Street pigs feast on these unsuspecting innocents, leading them off the proverbial cliff.

Liars refers to the small but lethal percentage of financial advisors that prey on their clients. These include everyone from the brokerage pigs who misrepresent investment performance or charge outlandish fees to the outright con men like Bernie Madoff and the fraudsters that operate phone, sports betting, pump and dump and other scams.

The Loopholes are the legal maneuvers the wealthy take advantage of to maintain and grow their wealth and leave a memorable legacy.

The Free Lunches are sophisticated strategies like bond ladders and arbitrage. The system is structured to allow savvy investors to utilize leverage and get tax advantages. This can also be accomplished with real estate, including 1031 exchanges.

While the first two sections of the book are more financial and investment oriented, the third section is primarily about people: the players in the industry, including the misleaders and outright liars in the media and the "advisors" who cheat and steal. There are patterns to these behaviors. They are not doing something revolutionary in terms of lying or criminal activity. The message from the media is unchanging; fear tactics to sustain viewership. The message from the scammers seeks to take advantage of investor fear and greed. They are essentially the same scams that Charles Ponzi plied in the last century.

The chapter on Fiduciary Duty will help you recognize and avoid these detriments to your financial health by finding a trusted ally to guide your financial future. This is someone whose integrity and career takes precedence over making a few more dollars or taking advantage of the uninformed.

The final two chapters are instructional in terms of emulating the financial behaviors of the wealthy, who do things differently than the general population. This includes taking advantage of estate law and techniques that safeguard their wealth while providing substantial tax advantages.

Section IV: Looking Ahead to a Bullish Future

As an investor, you must constantly be looking ahead. Buffett is generally regarded as a value investor and while true, I think that's an overly confined characterization. While Buffett does value calculations, for the past half century he has been telling people that the most important thing in business or capitalism is the ability to look ahead 10 to 20 years and make cashflow forecasts. As Buffett says, you must be reasonably confident regarding the amount of money you can take out of a business.

As an investor, you must accurately assess what the future is going to look like, specifically how it's going to look different than today. Using that appraisal, you must avoid investments that are going to be quantifiably disadvantaged by change.

> *"It is not the strongest of the species that survives, nor the most intelligent, but the one most responsive to change."*
>
> Charles Darwin

You must cultivate the foresight to anticipate the big secular shifts and ensure that the massive capitalistic winds created by those shifts are at your back. The future promises to be an even more opportunistic time to be a business owner in capitalism. We are at an unprecedented point in history. Man's ability to innovate is at its highest-ever level of creativity because of technological advancements and the incredibly rapid pace of their development. What these transformations mean to us as a society and as individuals and investors is almost unfathomable in terms of a safer and better world.

Thanks to breakthroughs like gene therapy, AI, robotics and brain computer implants, we will be healthier, live longer and be infinitely smarter. As the final chapter alludes, we will be relieved from conventional learning; we will just know it.

INTRODUCTION

In 1952, a PhD student in Economics at the University of Chicago developed a thesis on portfolio theory. That student was Harry Markowitz and his groundbreaking theory was published that year in *The Journal of Finance* under the title of "Portfolio Selection."

The article introduced the concept of modern portfolio theory (MPT), which resulted in Markowitz receiving the Nobel Prize for Economics in 1990, along with fellow economists Dr William Sharpe and Dr Merton Miller, who further developed the theory.

MPT is a mathematical formulation, the full explanation of which would either put you to sleep or leave you gasping for breath in its complexity. Here's an abbreviated version of the equation:

$$\sigma_p^2 = w_A^2\sigma_A^2 + w_B^2\sigma_B^2 + w_C^2\sigma_C^2 + 2w_Aw_B\sigma_A\sigma_B\rho_{AB} + 2w_Aw_C\sigma_A\sigma_C\rho_{AC} + 2w_Bw_C\sigma_B\sigma_C\rho_{BC}$$

The equation provided the mathematics that allows sophisticated investors to construct a portfolio with the highest expected return and the lowest amount of risk. It facilitates a calculation that discloses where to put money and in what amounts. Seventy years later, it remains the most important equation in the field of investment and forms the foundational mathematics of virtually every endowment and pension fund in the world.

Prior to 1952, professionals managing money would construct investment portfolios with the traditional assets of stocks, bonds and real estate but would have to guess how much of each to hold. Before Markowitz, everybody guessed. After Markowitz, we knew.

The same immutable principles applied during the past century continue to work today and will still be valid when my great grandchildren begin investing. They will not change. They are a really big deal.

A Spark Ignites Decades Later

A few decades after Markowitz published his groundbreaking theory, a young man studying for his BS in Finance was introduced to this magical equation. Within a few seconds of seeing the equation, he experienced an "aha" moment: the realization that an investor could put riskier noncorrelated investments[1] into a portfolio and the risk of that portfolio would actually go down.

He reasoned that there must be other equations that would lead to even better performance. If he could find them, he could apply mathematics to test a virtually unlimited number of portfolio options to create better investment outcomes. It was the most logical thing he had ever seen.

That young man was me, and that day changed my life. The complexity of that equation was incredibly difficult to understand. Most of the students in my college class struggled mightily with it but for some reason, I understood it straightaway. That's when I began to realize that I had an inherent gift for investing. I knew this was my career path.

It's the reason I'm in the field of portfolio management, and also the reason I'm writing this book. It opened a door and gave me a roadmap to travel. Markowitz had given me the formula to identify optimal portfolios, the *strategic allocation.* His equation lit the fire in my belly to keep me searching and researching for alpha or superior investment performance.

The same decade MPT was introduced to the investment community, a similarly significant advancement occurred in aviation, when Boeing released its revolutionary swept-wing jet airliner, the 707. Overnight, the public viewed piston engine airliners as antiquated. Today, while historical enthusiasts may view the 707 with reverence, it's a relic compared to modern passenger aircraft. Yet the foundational principles that permitted airplanes to fly 50 or 100 years ago still apply today. The pioneers who provided the aviation basics were followed by generations of engineers who used that foundational knowledge to achieve aircraft with higher performance.

It was the critical transition from the foundational knowledge of flying—much like Markowitz's equation—to the science of modern aerodynamics using computing power—much like the evolution of modern tactical asset allocation.

Modern Tactical Allocation

The recognition that I had an innate talent for investing allowed me to expand the foundational knowledge of MPT. Like the aviation engineers who sensed they could achieve higher performance, I believed other calculations had to exist that would provide additional data, giving me a further investment edge.

I developed a collection of those calculations and they worked. I was able to take a single variable, such as the money supply, building permits or the Treasury yield curve, put it into deciles and measure its effect on stock market performance. I could test any number of economic and financial variables this way to determine which were materially important and predictive of asset price direction.

For example, in back testing the history of the money supply I found that when it is growing, the stock market tends to do well, so I would want my portfolio to be long stock and have more risk. Conversely, when the money supply is contracting, it's historically been a bad time to own stocks and I'm better off reducing that risk. Giving the variable of money supply growth substantial weight in the risk algorithm was partly responsible for our outperformance in 2020 during the pandemic.

So, by isolating an economic variable like money supply growth, putting it into a series of deciles and back testing it, I was able to make consistent, successful tactical asset allocations. My thought progression was not, "This is how I get rich," but rather the amazing realization that I could take my investors' life savings into the Wall Street shark tank and be a winner.

NFL teams with the most up-to-date analytics and best scouting departments are able to draft the best players. They hire the best coaches who make the optimal game decisions and get the best out of their players by putting them in positions to be successful.

Those NFL franchises enjoy success year after year after year in a highly competitive sport, largely as a result of their analytics.

Similarly, investing is a science, not an art. Investing, like football, is competing against others for profits. The investment goal, like the goal of the great NFL dynasties, is to consistently make the playoffs, giving them an opportunity to win a championship every year.

Like those rare, predictably dependable NFL franchises, I can win year after year because I am calculating while others are speculating.

That's what this book is about. It is not whether you should have a portfolio allocation of 60/40 or 80/20 stocks to bonds but rather whether you should have a static or dynamic asset allocation. If you see dark clouds and lightening on the horizon, you don't wait to get your kids out of the swimming pool. Like the weather, the investment environment is not static. It changes constantly and your portfolio should change in response, based on measuring the factors—both positive and negative—that cause the changes.

Ultra-high net worth investors have their money managed this way by leading institutional investors and hedge funds. You are going to learn exactly how they do it.

SECTION ONE

Don't Blink: Understanding When to Take Risks

CHAPTER ONE

First Steps to Success: Measuring Your Environment

It's your vacation. You've endured months of foul weather, all the while dreaming about the day you could jump into your swimsuit, plop into a lounge chair on the beach and just unwind.

Today is that day. Here you are, relaxing on that sandy beach, soaking up rays on a picture-perfect day under a cloudless sky. There is a whisper of a caressing breeze as you watch pelicans happily diving for their dinner in a near-motionless ocean. You forget the stack of work piling up on your desk back home and just chill. For the first time in months, you are aware of breathing—a good thing. Before you know it, you're nodding off in peaceful bliss.

Suddenly, you are awakened by a chill. Your eyes pop open and you can hardly believe what you see. The sky has turned a nasty shade of gray, the wind has kicked up and the temperature has dropped 20 degrees. The first few drops of rain spatter on your forehead.

Do you ignore what you see and pretend nothing has changed? Do you remain in your swimsuit and sunglasses, shivering as the drizzle turns into a downpour and the surf surges over your feet? Or do you react to the altered conditions?

Assuming your common sense has not abandoned you, I'll wager you get up, throw on the jacket you wisely brought with you and scamper back to the hotel to wait out the storm.

Remaining on the beach and getting soaked when weather conditions change dramatically makes no sense, any more than going for a walk in February in a blinding snowstorm and howling winds.

A frequently overlooked but fundamentally critical consideration for any investor is whether to continuously assume the same level of portfolio risk regardless of market conditions or to change the amount of risk based on market opportunity.

Under federal law, an investment adviser is a fiduciary. The Investment Advisers Act of 2016 specified that an investment adviser's fiduciary duty comprised a duty of care and a duty of loyalty. This fiduciary duty requires an adviser "to adopt the principal's goals, objectives or ends." This means the adviser must, at all times, serve the best interest of its client and not subordinate its client's interest to its own. This combination of care and loyalty obligations has been characterized as requiring the investment adviser to act in the "best interest" of its client at all times.[2]

An SEC interpretation of the Act[3] described the adviser obligations thusly: "The duty of care requires an investment adviser to provide investment advice in the best interest of its client, based on the client's objectives. Under its duty of loyalty, an investment adviser must eliminate or make full and fair disclosure of all conflicts of interest which might incline an investment adviser— consciously or unconsciously—to render advice which is not disinterested such that a client can provide informed consent to the conflict."

Given the fiduciary requirement, I believe the question of maintaining a constant level of risk in a client portfolio—or taking on more or less risk in response to market movements—is a compulsory discussion between advisor and investor. If the investor decides to assume more risk when there is more opportunity and less risk when there is less opportunity, how is that accomplished?

Understanding when and when not to take risks is what the first part of this book is all about.

Investors that do not wish to vary the level of portfolio risk have much cheaper options available (Vanguard, Fidelity, Schwab) than paying an advisory fee for a simple asset allocation that never changes. The reason for hiring and paying an investment advisor is that it will provide value beyond what an investor could get from low-fee ETFs or index funds. If an advisor can't fulfill that requirement, or if the investor refuses to allow the manager to vary the level of portfolio risk in response to changing market conditions, there's no earthly reason to pay a management fee. This consideration is one of the book's fundamental questions.

Defining Risk

A logical question, then, is "what defines risk?"

There is the generic, academic definition of risk: assessing the variance of a portfolio to determine how much that portfolio's value is going to fluctuate from some average. Another way to define risk is Warren Buffett's exquisitely simple definition: Risk is "the probability of losing money."

Using that definition, risk becomes a bifurcated equation. First, what percentage of the portfolio do businesses (stocks) represent? Second, taking the same action can have two totally different levels of risk, depending on market conditions.

The question of risk is not unique to investment management. It permeates virtually all fields of endeavor, from sports to medical research. There always exists opportunities to take more or less risk, with the choice typically being a significant determinant on the outcomes.

In my experience, most knowledgeable investors understand and embrace the concept of increasing or decreasing risk, based on market opportunities. As fiduciaries, we then must assume responsibility for delivering that. So again, how do we do it?

Most advisors I've encountered do not have a repeatable system in place capable of fulfilling what clients want. Instead, they do their best to talk clients out of active management, or use "rebalancing" as a justification for perpetuating an unvarying level of risk. For their clients, that typically means always having 60 percent of their money at risk, regardless of market conditions or latent investment opportunities. To me, that makes no sense.

Antiquated Business Model

As mentioned earlier, the traditional advisory model has become antiquated, partially due to technological advances, the emergence of robo advisors and the higher level of awareness among the investing public, thanks to the availability of knowledge via the internet.

Charging one percent or more for providing an asset allocation template offers little value to investors. It literally guarantees underperformance to the benchmark and thus, is rapidly becoming obsolete. For the amount of fees, it's like playing golf, making bogie on every hole and shooting 18 over par every round. It's no fun and why would you continue to accept the same unsatisfactory result without changing something?

Is it logical to continue doing the same thing repeatedly if you are not getting acceptable results? A pitcher wouldn't last long in the big leagues if he threw the same fastball every pitch. How long would you want to eat the same thing for dinner every night? Would you maintain the same 45-mph speed driving whether you were on the freeway, in a school zone or driving on icy pavement? Paying an investment-level fee for an asset allocation template similarly makes no sense.

If you are satisfied with passive investing, major brokerage firms now offer asset allocation and basic passive investment advice for virtually nothing. Financial advisors attempting to cling to the dated practice of trying to charge high fees for services readily available elsewhere, for no charge, have been put on notice. Passive portfolio management linked to a one percent fee is a failing strategy for investors, who are effectively guaranteed to lose one percent annually.

Investors have obviously awakened to this realization. If they want passive management, they ask themselves, "Why am I paying my advisor a fee when the same service is available for virtually no cost?" For investors who realize buying a benchmark index or using other passive strategies is not the risk profile they prefer and are willing to pay for superior active management, their advisors must provide tremendous value to justify their fees.

The process of interviewing an advisor should include a demand to see actual investor performance, not merely some fact sheet reflecting overall fund performance. It's an important distinction that, in my experience, most investors are unaware of. Today, when potential investors ask me about performance, I show them a disclosure of the authentic performance of my investors, audited and verified by Global Investment Performance Standards GIPS®, a registered trademark owned by CFA Institute. GIPS is a set of voluntary performance reporting standards you will learn about in a later chapter. It's one of the components that separates me from investment managers who use fact sheets to sell irrelevant past performance. The GIPS process has time consuming annual audit requirements, took more than a year to complete and, over a period of years, will personally cost me more than $100,000 in brokerage, employee, software and auditor fees.

Higher public awareness and the fiduciary standard are forcing advisors to authenticate their value. Chapter 12 will dive more deeply into this active/passive discussion. Advisors charging a lot of money will have to demonstrate they are providing commensurate value: active portfolio management, sophisticated financial planning, working harmoniously with other client advisors (CPA, estate planning attorney, etc.) and a system in place to provide proactive risk management. If they cannot, they have a cloudy future.

Decisions Using Algorithms

An algorithm is set of rules for accomplishing a task in a certain number of steps. Highly sophisticated algorithms incorporate mathematics and proven valuation approaches which take into account numerous factors that might affect an investment's price. Algorithms can be used to design investment strategies that avoid human tendencies and weaknesses.

As humans, we are pre-programmed to be horrible investors. It's burned into our DNA that the perimeter is dangerous and the center is safe. Our early ancestors learned there was safety in numbers and staying close to camp was safer than roving the plains hunting food. Unfortunately, that "stay in the middle" mentality has survived thousands of years of human evolution and manifests itself today in the way most people behave as investors: They stay in the center with the crowd and avoid the perceived dangers of the perimeter.

Back when the pioneers heading west in wagon trains were attacked, they would circle the wagons and gather those unable to bear arms into the center of the circle for safety. But when investing in capital markets, there are many times when the least amount of danger is on the perimeter and the greatest peril is in the middle of the pack.

The capital markets are created to hurt the greatest number of investors. It takes consistent new capital to push up the price of investments. If everybody is in the center, maintaining the same investment mentality, their perceived safety is an illusion. They may feel comfortable being surrounded by a bunch of other people making the same investment decisions, but the perimeter is the place to be when market conditions create investment opportunities in underpriced investments. Their DNA may be screaming "get back to where it's safe," but following a mathematical investment approach using algorithms allows them to overcome their fear of being on the periphery so they can outperform the crowd.

A study of a 30-year period showed that while individual investors averaged 3.69% annual return, the S&P 500 index averaged 11.1% returns annually.[4] A contributing factor to this discrepancy is the predisposition of individuals to overreact to market movements as a result of their learned behaviors and innate biases.

Algorithms don't suffer from human behavioral biases or the emotions of jealousy, fear and greed. Algorithms don't panic when the market roils, nor are they swayed by the media or the advice of friends. Algorithms don't buy high and sell low. In short, algorithms are not susceptible to any of the human frailties that cause individuals to make emotionally driven investment decisions that erode their portfolio returns.

A properly constructed algorithm can measure the full range of human behaviors and biases and profit from the critical information gained from the analysis.

In any endeavor, measuring and analyzing the competition can provide the critical information needed to gain a competitive advantage.

Today, anyone paying attention realizes people now know that data analytics have substantially transformed virtually every industry from healthcare to technology. In finance, algorithms allow us to conduct the vital measurement and analysis to gain an investment advantage over other investors who fall prey to behavioral biases, market sentiment and other deceptive influences.

> *"Take calculated risks.*
> *That is quite different from being rash."*

General George Patton

CHAPTER TWO

Reading Your Competitors: Measuring Market Sentiment

> *"It is impossible to produce superior performance unless you do something different from the majority."*
>
> Sir John Templeton

Prior to making an investment decision, there are four main indicators or data sets, each containing a group of factors, that should be evaluated and compared. The indicators are Market Sentiment, Market Health, Economic Health and Valuation.

By weighing these indicators and comparing them to their historic counterparts, an investor can assess whether the probability of a significant market decline is lower or higher than normal.

A fundamental difference between average investors and sophisticated investors is the ability to measure their competitors in capital markets. We spend a great deal of time measuring how our competitors view the future and how those feelings translate into what they are doing with their money. Are they fearful? Are they overconfident? Are they greedy? Do their responses to survey questions sound like sheep fearfully awaiting a shearing, cattle being mindlessly forced through a chute or wolverines looking for their next prey?

While retail investors are watching television or reading newsletters to gain investment cues, we are measuring and analyzing their sentiments—as well as those of professional institutional investors—to gain a competitive advantage.

When making investment decisions, we want to be buying into a crowd that's fearful of taking risks. We want to be selling into a greedy crowd focused on a collective belief rather than value. The last thing we want to do is to sell our productive businesses when there is panic in the market.

Much like the top echelon of NFL organizations that consistently make the playoffs by compiling better analytics than their competitors, we consistently measure the sentiments and actions of our investment competitors and use that information to outperform, sometimes utilizing a contrarian approach.

The market sentiment factors that we evaluate include:

- Options Market
- Surveys
- Comparative Yields
- Flight to Safety
- Flows & Volumes
- Insider Activity
- Margin Debt
- Short Interest
- Portfolio Cash Levels
- Cyclical vs. Defense Ratios

Factor 1: Options Market

The options market is where investors can go to buy portfolio insurance. Just as homeowners buy insurance to protect their property against damage or theft, investors can go into the options market and purchase portfolio insurance, such as a put option to protect against a market decline. Buyers pay a premium for the option to protect their portfolio similar to a homeowner, but the probability of a house burning down is miniscule compared to the probability of a portfolio going up in flames. Portfolio insurance is far more expensive—prohibitively expensive over extended periods of time.

Investors buy call and put options to express their view of the market or a particular stock. They buy calls when they expect the market to go up and puts to protect themselves when markets go down.[5]

In the options market, traders acquire contracts that give them the right to buy (call) or sell (put) a stock or other underlying security at a pre-negotiated price—the strike price—by a certain date. They are not obligated to exercise the contract to buy or sell the security by the time that date arrives, however. They have the option to simply let the contract expire, hence the name. The up-front premium they pay for options is forfeited if they allow the contract to expire.[6]

The Chicago Board of Option Exchange Put/Call Ratio is an indicator that shows put volume relative to call volume. The Put/Call Ratio is above 1 when put volume exceeds call volume and below 1 when call volume exceeds put volume. Sentiment is deemed excessively bearish when the Put/Call Ratio is trading at relatively high levels and excessively bullish when at relatively low levels.[7]

The Chicago Board of Option Exchange Volatility Index (VIX) is a real-time market index that represents the market's expectation of 30-day forward-looking volatility. Derived from the price inputs of S&P 500 index options, it provides a measure of market risk and investors' sentiments. It is also known by other names like "Fear Gauge" or "Fear Index." The VIX Index is a calculation designed to produce a measure of constant expected volatility of the U.S. stock market. On a global basis, it is one of the most recognized measures of volatility.[8]

Based on the same concept as the VIX, *The Chicago Board of Option Exchange Nasdaq Volatility Index* (VXN) is a measure of market expectations of 30-day volatility for the Nasdaq 100 index, as implied by the prices of options listed on the index.[9]

The Chicago Board of Option Exchange 3-Month Volatility Index (VIX3M) is designed to be a constant measure of the 3-month implied volatility of the S&P 500® Index Options.

The Chicago Board of Option Exchange SKEW Index is derived from the price of S&P 500 tail risk. Similar to VIX, the price of S&P 500 tail risk is calculated from the prices of S&P 500 out-of-the-money options. SKEW is a global, strike-independent measure of the slope of the implied volatility curve that increases as this curve tends to steepen.[10]

The International Stock Exchange Sentiment Indicator (ISE) measures investor sentiment by comparing the number of opening long call options to opening long put options purchased on the International Stock Exchange. The measure only considers purchases made by retail customers, thought by some to be the best measure of market sentiment. Purchases made by market makers or institutional clients are not included.[11] The higher the reading in the ISE, the bigger the discrepancy between optimistic activity (calls) and pessimistic activity (puts).[12] In short, when brokers and "the man on the street" are buying put options with both fists, it's an indicator that the market is bottoming.

Factor 2: Surveys

As previously mentioned, a defining distinction between average and sophisticated investors is the ability and willingness to measure the sentiments and actions of their competitors. Properly constructed algorithms include survey elements that provide this information on a preemptive basis.

For decades, surveys among both retail and professional investment audiences have asked the identical set of questions. The responses to these questions give us a tremendous amount of information as to what our competitors think about the current and forthcoming investment environment. Most importantly, the survey responses reveal how their current views differ from historical survey norms.

Garnering beneficial information is contingent upon having a sufficient number of survey responses, culled over decades, from which to draw conclusions. Often, what people say and what they do are two different things. But having years and years of survey respondent perspectives gives us a benchmark or norm from which to measure deviation.

Here are the surveys we use in the algorithm:

Consumers

The Consumer Confidence Survey® reflects prevailing business conditions and likely developments for the months ahead. Published monthly, it details consumer attitudes, buying intentions, vacation plans and expectations for inflation, stock prices and interest rates.[13]

The Survey of Consumer Expectations is a monthly survey of U.S. households by the New York Federal Reserve Bank. Consumers are asked how much they expect to spend, how high they expect inflation to be, their employment situation and whether they are searching for a job. Roughly 4,500 consumers have been surveyed each year since 2013. Survey results are calibrated to be demographically representative of U.S. households.[14]

The International Center for Finance at Yale University publishes United States Stock Market Confidence Indices, including the *One-Year Confidence Index* which measures the percent of the population expecting an increase in the Dow in the coming year. The *Crash Confidence Index* measures the percent of the population who attach little probability to a stock market crash in the next six months. The *Buy-on-Dips Confidence Index* reflects the percent of the population expecting a rebound the next day should the market ever drop 3% in one day.[15]

The U.S. Index of Consumer Sentiment (ICS) is provided by the University of Michigan. The index rates the relative level of current and future economic conditions, compiled from a survey of around 5,000 consumers. A higher-than-expected reading indicates a bullish consumer sentiment, while a lower-than-expected reading portends a bearish sentiment. The surveys have long stressed the important influence of consumer spending and saving decisions in determining the course of the national economy.[16]

The American Association of Individual Investors Sentiment Survey measures the percentage of individual investors who are bullish, bearish or neutral on the stock market over the next six months.[17] The AAII is a member society with a unique demographic: fifty percent of the members hold graduate level degrees and have an average net worth over $500,000.

If these surveys indicate that consumers intend to spend more money, it's a positive sign. As an investor, you want to have neutral or above average amounts of risk in your portfolio. When surveyed investors expect to spend more money because prices are going up and they feel they have to get ahead of future price increases, that sentiment accelerates economic activity and portends a healthy consumer environment.

On the other hand, if consumers are postponing purchases because of a deflationary environment, believing prices will go down and they will be better off waiting to spend money, that is generally a toxic environment in which to be taking higher than normal amounts of risk.

Financial Professionals

The Market Vane Bullish Consensus® measures the futures market sentiment each day by following the trading recommendations of commodity trading advisors. Trader sentiment determines the price directions of markets. If enough traders are bullish, regardless of the reason, prices will rise. Historical data from Bullish Consensus is available as far back as 1969, which makes it especially valuable for comparative historical analysis.

The Chartcraft Investors Intelligence Sentiment Index seeks to ascertain the balance of power between the bulls and bears. It is based on the opinions of 100 or more of the most widely read market newsletters whose writers' issue independent advice and commentary.[18]

This is a highly reliable contrarian indicator for market tops and bottoms. When we see an unusually high ratio of one to the other, it's an indication that the markets are going to start moving in the opposite direction. When the vast majority are writing bullish articles, it's likely that the market is approaching its top. When the opposite occurs and the ratio of bearish to bullish articles is high, it's even more apt that the market is about to bottom out.

The Consensus® Bullish Sentiment Index, published weekly, is a contrarian sentiment index for 32 major markets, including stocks indices, financial instruments, currencies, metals, energy, agriculture and others. Contrarian opinion holds that when a predominant number of market analysts are bullish, it's likely that the market is approaching an overbought condition and that a reversal is imminent. When a similar number of analysts are bearish, the market is apt to be approaching an oversold condition.[19]

The National Association of Active Investment Managers Exposure Index is a weekly summary of equity positioning of active investment managers. The Index is another contrarian indicator. A high net long position is bearish for stocks because these investors have already gone long during the uptrend, whereas short net exposure may be bullish because it can force traders to chase a bullish reversal by the market.[20]

Our Analysis

Because the data tracks trends among every market participant sector from Joe the retail investor to hedge funds, we gain a unique perspective of the market's representative sentiment. When the Joe's are bullish and the professionals are bearish, we know it's time to reduce risk. When sophisticated institutional investors that have been investing money through multiple market cycles are reducing risk while the general public that has never attended an investment class is increasing risk, we recognize it's a time for cautious investing.

We know what is "normal" in these survey responses, so when survey responses differ substantially from the historical norm, we immediately recognize that the approaching investment environment is either more fearful or greedier than is normal. That's the value of having responses to the identical questions over a significant period of time. The historical comparison of responses forms a database of reliable information on which to base investment decisions.

While we understand that survey responses may be right or wrong, what we are measuring is not the accuracy of the responses but rather the variance between what people are feeling today versus how they were feeling in previous surveys. So, while the responses reflect an accurate representation of their current feelings, if people are basing their investment decisions on those feelings and outlooks, it often leads to poor performance.

If, for example, investors are worried, we would typically see a confirmation of that fearfulness reflected in high cash balances in 401K plans and in do-it-yourself investment accounts. We would also likely see large purchases of gold, Treasurys and high demand for put options.

And while the financial markets would likely reflect current thinking, it doesn't mean that thinking represents the optimal way to invest at the time. It's more of a contrarian factor. The further away from normal the survey responses get, the higher the probability of having a regression back to normal. Isolating and investing on just those variables alone should allow an investor to outperform over long periods of time.

> *"Be fearful when others are greedy and greedy when others are fearful."*
>
> Warren Buffett

Factor 3: Comparative Bond Yields

Bonds are fixed-income instruments, typically issued by corporate or government entities to raise money to finance operations or projects. These securities pay interest on the bond's principal to purchasers, known as debtholders or bondholders.[21]

Bondholders lend money to the company or government agency that issues the security, which in return, pays interest—called the coupon rate—to the bondholder for the term of the loan. Bonds have maturity dates, when the principal amount must be paid back to purchasers. A credit rating is used to determine the interest rate, with a lower credit rating indicating a higher risk of default.[22]

The primary types of bonds include:

- Corporate bonds—debt securities issued by private and public corporations.
- Investment-grade or High-Quality bonds—higher credit ratings and less credit risk than high-yield corporate bonds.
- High Yield bonds—lower credit ratings and riskier than investment-grade bonds.
- Municipal bonds (munis)—debt securities issued by states, cities, counties and other government entities.
- U.S. Treasurys—issued on behalf of the federal government, including:
    - Treasury Bills—short-term securities maturing in a few days to a year.
    - Notes—longer-term securities maturing within ten years.
    - Bonds—long-term securities that typically mature in 30 years.
    - TIPS—Treasury Inflation-Protected Securities whose principal is adjusted based on changes in the Consumer Price Index, issued in maturities of five, ten, and 30 years.[23]

Barron's Confidence Index is a ratio that measures investor confidence by comparing the average yield to maturity (YTM) of Barron's best-grade bonds to average YTM of intermediate-grade bonds. A rising ratio indicates investors are demanding a lower premium in yield for increased risk, thus expressing confidence in the economy and the securities markets. A rising index is considered bullish for stocks; a falling index is considered bearish for stocks.[24]

Investors feeling uneasy about the economy's direction tend to seek safety in a flight to quality. Those with the opposite perspective are more inclined to buy lower-rated bonds offering higher yields. As such, the spread between high and low rated bonds reflects overall investor confidence in the economic outlook.

The BofA ML High Yield Bond Spread represents the difference between the yield in junk bonds and the yield in treasury bonds.

If spreads are high, specifically if high yield spreads are high, it indicates that lenders—people buying high-yield bonds or junk bonds—are worried about default. When junk bond yields are unusually high relative to their historical averages, it's an indication that investors are apprehensive and being cautious with their money. And once again, the opposite is true. When high yield bonds have a very narrow yield above treasury bonds, it's indicative of lenders or purchasers of high yield bonds having little concern about getting their money back and are highly optimistic about the future.

The thinner the spread, the more bullish investors become, a signal that they are willing to take higher risks than normal to get diminished returns. That's generally the precursor of disappointing investment returns. It's a contrarian indicator.

The vast majority of defaults have occurred among junk bonds. According to a S&P study, the 31-year average for high quality bonds (rated AAA and AA) were 0.0% and 0.2%, respectively. By contrast, the default rates among the two lowest-rated issuers (B and CCC/C -rated issuers were 3.44% and 26.63% respectively.[25]

Amateur investors salivate over the potential for profit with higher-yield securities, ignoring the elevated potential for default. Those who chased yields when the 2008-2009 Great Recession thundered in learned about defaults the hard way.

> *"Amateurs think about how much money they can make. Professionals think about how much money they could lose."*
>
> Jack Schwager

Factor 4: Flight to Safety

An inverse correlation exists between gold demand and investor sentiment. Gold prices are quashed when investors have a positive sentiment and are bullish about equities. When markets encounter stress, gold prices rebound. Gold is a popular landing spot for investors seeking safety and is also inversely correlated to the dollar over longer time periods. When the dollar falls in value, it makes gold more affordable and allows investors around the world to purchase more gold while the dollar remains weak. What is being measured here is demand.

Gold Spot Price Trend plots the trend in the gold spot market. The spot price is the price at which gold—or any commodity—can be delivered immediately, as opposed to futures or forward contracts.[26]

Gold Stocks Relative Strength calculates the current strength of gold stocks relative to the stock market. If gold stocks are up 10% and the overall market is down 10%, it's an indicator of bearish sentiment. Investors are bidding up the value of gold stocks while essentially liquidating their positions in cyclical stocks.

The opposite effect occurs when the relative strength of gold stocks is declining. That's a sign that market participants don't believe they need as much or any gold in their portfolio.

Factor 5: Flows and Volumes

Flow refers to the amount of capital going into investments on a securities exchange. Volume refers to the number of shares transacted. The ratio of current versus historical flows into speculative (high risk) investments versus conservative (blue chip) investments can be a reliable indicator of investor sentiment.

If investors are putting a lot of money into highly speculative investments, it's an indication of a bullish market potentially overheating and ready to peak. More importantly, the opposite is true: an unusual amount of flows going into very safe investments indicates a bearish trend. You can find bullish sentiment in virtually any stage of a bull market, but when sentiment is extremely pessimistic, there's a high probability that the market has bottomed out. And so flows, like some other sentiment indicators, is better at predicting troughs than peaks.

Liquidity Premiums in investments reflect the additional time required to find a buyer or seller. Investments that are easy to buy and sell, such as like high-quality stocks and bonds, have low liquidity premiums. Investments that are more difficult to liquidate, such as privately owned businesses, low-quality bonds and real estate have a high liquidity premium. In the algorithm, we compare current liquidity premiums to their historical counterparts.

If market makers are transacting in a security, it's evidence of a successfully functioning market—a low-friction market—and liquidity premiums are narrow. A market that starts to experience friction and wider liquidity premiums indicates that market makers are demanding a wider premium.

A classic example would be what happened to bond ETFs at the beginning of the 2020 pandemic where liquidity premiums ballooned because market makers were concerned about receiving good execution in those markets. When liquidity premiums expand, it's usually a bearish sign that some dislocations are occurring in the markets.

When comparing liquidity premiums on investments, some will obviously have greater liquidity than others. A share of the S&P 500 will always have a low liquidity premium as compared to, say, a real estate investment property, where liquidity is hampered by having to find a buyer, undergo inspections and all the other details that must be attended to before that property can be sold. As such, that liquidity premium is going to be wider. However, what we are measuring is the liquidity premium today relative to history. In a market that has experienced stress and friction, liquidity premiums would be wider than normal.

NASDAQ/NYSE Volume Oscillator (or McClellan Oscillator) compares the current volume of the two different markets and creates a ratio. The oscillator measures how much volume is coming into each of the two markets. If more money is coming into the New York Stock Exchange, it's an indication that investors are being cautious and moving to the relative safety of the blue chip-heavy NYSE. If more money is moving into the NASDAQ, it's an indication that investors are exuberant and greedy.

Factor 6: Insider Activity

The Securities and Exchange Commission (SEC) defines an insider as an officer or director of a public company or an individual or entity owning more than 10% of a company's stock.[27] The SEC requires these individuals to report purchases, sales and holdings of their company's securities by filing Forms 3, 4 and 5. Since these forms are public record, a database of insider activity can be compiled and compared to historical insider activity as an indicator of sentiment. When large numbers of executives at different companies are exhibiting similar behavior, that is, executing insider big block transactions, it can be valuable sentiment information.

Factor 7: Margin Debt

Margin debt is money borrowed to buy securities. The primary indicator here is margin debt for the average investor rather than the professional or institutional investor. When individuals are borrowing heavily to buy securities, margin debt can increase dramatically in a short period of time, an indication that a top is near. And the opposite is true. When virtually no one is borrowing money to buy stocks, it's usually indicative of markets starting to bottom. It also shows that there is liquidity sitting on the sidelines that could come into the market and push prices up.

What we are trying to do as an investor is to separate other investors into two categories—professional and uneducated—and track both their activities. By watching those activities and surveys of the two groups, we get an indication of what the markets might do.

A model that incorporates more than a dozen indicators with a track record of cycling to extremes is called "Dumb Money Confidence." It tracks the ebbs and flows in sentiment among broad categories of non-professional investors.[28] Capital markets are designed to hurt the most amount of people. Because these investors essentially don't know what they are doing, when their confidence and participation is highest, it's reflected in stock prices and that's when losses can occur. So, when individuals who lack financial training are fully invested into the capital markets, losses are likely to happen because in a capital market, a continuous injection of capital is required to make prices rise. If the investing herd is bullish, is fully invested and has borrowed heavily to invest, it's an indicator that the market has a higher probability of heading down.

Factor 8: Short Interest

Short selling is an investment or trading strategy that speculates on the decline in a stock or other security's price. In short selling, a position is opened by borrowing shares of a stock or other asset that the investor believes will decrease in value. The investor then sells these borrowed shares to buyers willing to pay the market price. Before the borrowed shares must be returned, the trader is betting that the price will continue to decline and they can purchase them at a lower cost.[29]

Short interest refers to the number of shares that have been sold short but have not yet been repurchased or covered. There is an average amount of short interest held by investors for most stocks. When that short interest increases, it indicates that sentiment is negative and that investors expect the stock price to decline. On the other hand, when it decreases, it's an indication that sentiment is positive.[30]

The *New York Stock Exchange (NYSE) short-interest ratio* is a metric that can be used to determine the sentiment of the overall market. The ratio is the same as short interest except it is calculated as monthly short interest on the entire exchange divided by the average daily volume of the NYSE for the previous month.[31]

The *NYSE Group Short Interest File* contains the reported uncovered short positions of securities listed on NYSE, NYSE Arca and NYSE American. Historical data is available from Jan 1988 to the present.[32]

Factor 9: Portfolio Cash Levels

Some investors believe by putting significant portions of their investment portfolio into cash or cash equivalents, such as CDs and bank accounts, they have eliminated market risk. Well, they may be free of market risk, but they are mistaken about being free of risk. Inflation is the elephant in the room when it comes to eroding future purchasing power. The cash they set aside may not change but it's ability to pay for things like groceries, gasoline and medical care in coming years is continually deteriorating.

An acquaintance talked about how his grandparents, who lived through the Great Depression, actually kept cash in their mattress, presumably a psychological holdover from that period when the banks were unable to meet withdrawal requests. Their money may have felt safer to them at the time, but inflation ultimately exposed that illusion.

A study by The Society of Actuaries found that even a low inflation rate of 2% annually would cause a gallon of milk that costs $3.75 to cost $6.79 in 30 years. A small boost to 3% annual inflation would mean that milk would now cost $9.10.[33] A friend of mine recounts how he purchased a luxury car in 2000 for just over $50,000. Replicating that car in 2024 would cost over $120,000, more than double in just two decades!

Graphic 2.1 depicts the erosion of the dollar's purchasing power over time. In just a recent 20-year period (2004-2024), the dollar has lost nearly 40% of is purchasing power.

With inflation soaring to over 7% during 2021 before receding to 3.5% in 2024, the dollar's purchasing power was eroding even faster.

Cash is not only a bad investment, it's really not an investment at all; it's merely a place to park money. Savvy investors understand this, so when we see institutional and other professional investors parking cash in large quantities, it's an indication of a short-term fear sentiment. When investors are nervous and feeling uncertain about what to do, they tend to stockpile high cash levels as a percentage of their investable assets relative to historical norms.

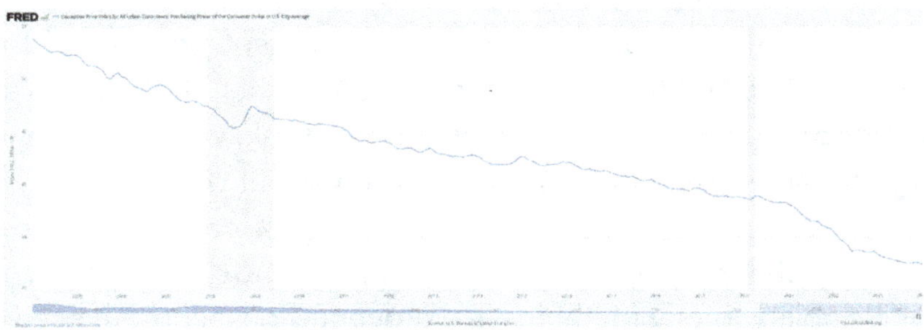

(Graphic 2.1: Erosion of Dollar's Purchasing Power)

Cash is a contrarian indicator. When mutual fund investors and 401k participants are sitting on large amounts of cash, that's an indication of the stock market's future direction. When investors are nervous and feeling uncertain about what to do, they will have huge cash levels as a percentage of their net worth and investable assets relative to history. When the majority believes the stock market is going to soar in the coming year, portfolio cash balances will be very thin, signaling the probability of a stock market decline is substantially higher because everyone has already pushed in all their chips and there's no one to infuse new capital to keep stock prices rising.

A note about cash reserves. When we talk about cash being a lousy investment, we are referring to including cash in one's investment portfolio, not cash set aside for emergencies, a planned major purchase or a tax obligation. Every financial planner worth their salt will recommend that their clients have a cash emergency fund. How long that cash reserve should be able to cover basic expenses largely depends on the individual's financial temperament and the scarcity of their job. A plumber, carpenter or car salesman probably only needs a few months cash reserve because finding a replacement position is relatively easy, whereas the CEO of a biotech company has far fewer options for replicating his situation.

Factor 10: Cyclical vs. Defense Ratios

Cyclical stocks are those that perform well when the economy does well; defensive stocks are those that can weather the storm regardless of market conditions. Investor sentiment about these stocks is usually determined by the condition of the economy. When the economy is down, investors tend to avoid sectors like retail, automotive, industrials and lodging that are by nature cyclical while defensive stocks like utilities, consumer staples and healthcare garner investor favor.[34]

When capital is flowing into cyclical sectors and not defensive sectors, it signifies investors are optimistic and have a high expectation of returns. When a huge amount of capital is flowing into defensive sectors relative to cyclical sectors, it implies investors are uneasy about the future.

This sentiment is especially useful on the downside as a contrarian indicator. When investors are snapping up utility stocks, consumer staples, healthcare stocks and other defensive sectors and avoiding growth sectors, that's the time sophisticated investors want to own the growth sectors with a bright future because that's typically a time when the markets will improve.

In the following chapter, I'll explain how we measure the health of the market and apply it as an indicator in making investment decisions.

CHAPTER THREE

Market Health: Measuring Markets with Technical Analysis

> *"Bull markets are born on pessimism, grow on skepticism, mature on optimism and die of euphoria."*
>
> John Templeton

Measuring the health of the market is, in many ways, like getting an annual physical exam. Seeing your doctor for a checkup helps you understand what is going on inside your body, determine whether you need to make changes to maintain a healthy lifestyle and assess risk for future health issues.[35] Similarly, evaluating the wellbeing of the market is an integral part of portfolio strategy, although market health assessment must be done continually, not once a year. And unlike people who quit smoking or drinking a few days before their physical in a fruitless attempt to fool their doctor, investors measuring the condition of the market want an unvarnished perspective.

Technical analysis provides that perspective by observing price movements within the market. Like the results of annual physicals, technical analysis of the market does not always result in a conclusive diagnosis. It can, however, provide an accurate overview of market and index movements, and for gauging activity in stocks, commodities, futures and any tradable instrument where the price is influenced by human behavior.

Public markets tend to operate inversely. That is, the faster a stock price rises, the more enamored the public becomes. It is, perhaps, the only place in the world where something goes on sale—the price of a stock is reduced—and almost no one recognizes the bargain and buys. It's the classic example of herding behavior, where people blindly follow the lead of others.

For clarity, all the charts in this chapter refer to the S&P 500.

Support & Resistance

Technical analysis is contingent upon an understanding of the market and price movements. One of the main aspects of technical analysis is understanding that markets are often not random: there are recognizable patterns that develop in response to important events. Prices react to the laws of supply and demand, that is, buying and selling pressure. But prices also have a memory, partially the result of support and resistance. Prices oscillate between the support and resistance levels within a trading range.

Support is a trough, a reaction by the market that buying activity is sufficiently robust to overcome selling pressure. It occurs when a price movement reaches its nadir, essentially finds a floor, the decline stops, and prices reverse direction, moving back up again. Graphic 3.1 is an example of a support level.

(Graphic 3.1 Support Level)

> *"I do not believe in the collective wisdom of individual ignorance."*
>
> Thomas Carlyle

Conversely, resistance happens when selling pressure surmounts buying pressure and the upward price movement encounters a barrier to moving up further and retreats.

Graphic 3.2 depicts a resistance level.

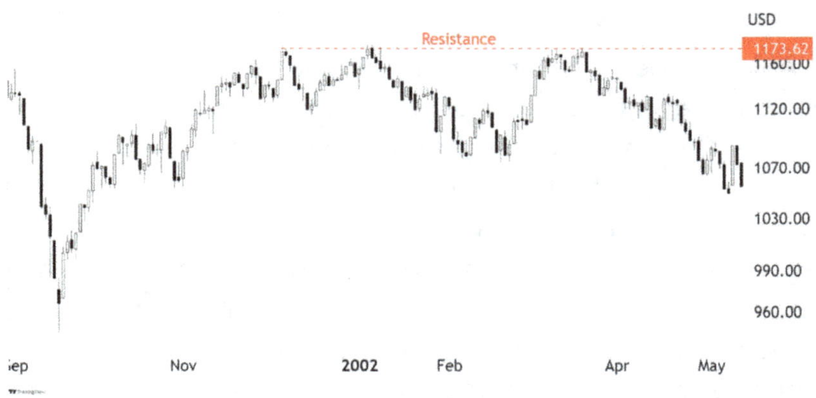

(Graphic 3.2 Resistance Level)

If there is a significant amount of buying or selling at a price level, it stands to reason that there's a vested interest at that level in the market, often due to concerns of investors that either bought or sold at that level. When the market gets back to that level, it can be an important indicator. Whenever there is a lot of activity in the market, it creates selling or buying pressure, one of the reasons why support and resistance exists.

Graphic 3.3 depicts how a price eventually broke through the trading range, moving above the resistance level. Then, when it came back down and tested the old resistance level, it held price and acted as support.[36]

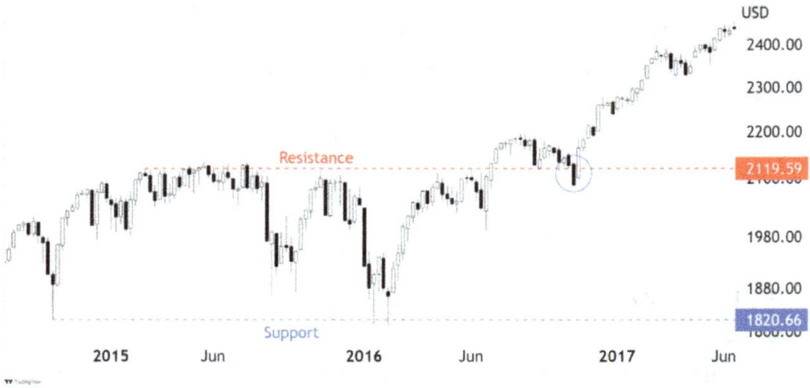

(Graphic 3.3 Support and Resistance Levels)

Any number of things can trigger price movements: an economic event, something the Fed does or the invasion of Ukraine. The reason for the upsurge really doesn't matter; the fact that there is a pattern of elevated buying and selling at a specific level on the price chart is what matters. It is the result of human behavior on the part of investors creating a pattern of resistance or support, a pattern which I believe is more reliable during a period of increased volatility because greater volatility is indicative of greater emotion in the marketplace. That's why we typically see clearer patterns in down markets than in a market that's grinding higher.

For example, the 2023 failure of Silicon Valley and Signature Banks took most investors (and analysts) by surprise, although regional banks were underperforming the market for quite some time prior to the defaults. While technical analysis might not have revealed that something cataclysmic was about to happen, the lack of buying interest in that sector should have suggested avoiding it. Insiders may have had some doubts, given what was happening, and they weren't buying.

These may seem like deceptively simple concepts but many investors that chart price movements confuse support and resistance with trends, which are indicators of where price levels may encounter support or resistance.

Trends

During your physical, your doctor will typically ask about any new trends—symptoms or changes in your physical or mental health, and whether they're big or small. For instance, a new lump, pain or returning symptom or something that is causing you concern.

Market movement often occurs in the form of a trend—an upward, downward or sideways movement in direction, as depicted in graphic 3.4.

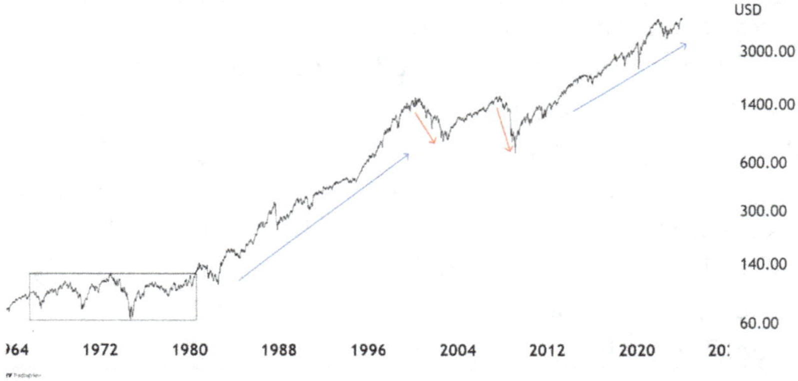

(Graphic 3.4 Market Trends)

Often an up-trend is represented in the form of a sequence of higher highs and higher lows. Similarly, a down-trend is represented as a sequence of lower lows and lower highs. A trend is said to reverse when the sequence is broken.[37] Graphic 3.5 illustrates a trend reversal.

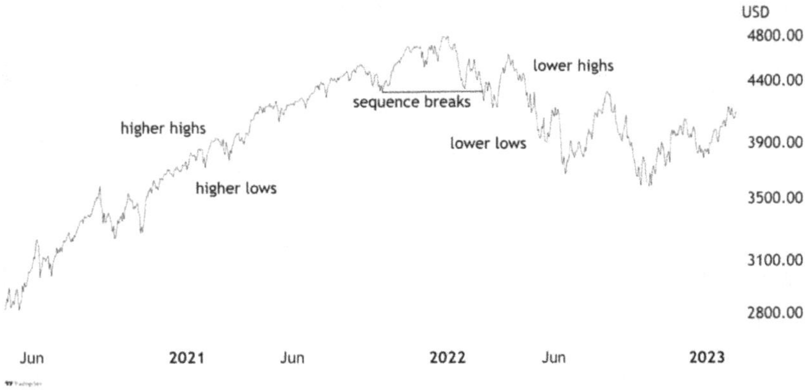

(Graphic 3.5 Trend Reversal)

Pivot highs and lows are indicators that help determine the overall trend of the market over different time frames.

Graphic 3.6 displays high and low pivots for the S&P 500 for the last 24 months. A price that establishes higher highs and higher lows indicates a bullish trend. A bearish trend is one in which price establishes lower lows and lower highs. The pivots are defined with a left and right strength of 20. Each high and low has 20 days left and right, so a pivot cannot be defined until 20 days after it is formed. The S&P 500 currently sports higher highs and higher lows. As long as price stays above the 3/13 low of 3808, another higher pivot low will form at that low on 4/11. That level will then become the new "line in the sand" for any bullish position.

(Graphic 3.6 Pivot High/Low)

As an analyst, there's no way to know whether the new high will be a sustained high, but plotting the movements over an extended period renders a series of higher highs and higher lows. Once one of these is broken, it indicates in real time that the trend has changed.

The underlying reason why markets trend has to do with fundamentals. Nothing happens because of technical analysis; it's a visual representation of trying to discern what is happening. But markets go through different trending phases, one of which is a corrective phase, known as a chopping sideways market. When a market is in a corrective phase, it tends to hover around the same price during that period. That's a bit of an anomaly as trends are typically marked by sharper price movements. That's not to say the highs and lows necessarily overlap but an uptrend, by definition, means the market is moving in one direction, rather like a series of stair steps. In a corrective phase, the pattern tends to be choppier, reacting to transitory events. Corrective price behavior is irregular and often totally random.

Most people think of trends in a binary way: uptrends and downtrends, bull markets and bear markets. In reality, however, there also exists a sideways trend—a horizontal price movement—where the price seesaws within a narrow range for an extended period without displaying a significant move up or down. The sideways trend usually occurs as a result of support and resistance being roughly equal.[38]

A market that consistently trends in an up or down direction is said to have persistence, an indicator of its overall strength. As market confidence increases or decreases, the capital directed towards it changes, generally moving in the same direction. As investors sense that a market has persistence, they will add increasing amounts of capital, and additional market participants will endeavor to profit from it as well. All that activity tends to incrementally increase the upward trend. The same is true on the opposite side of the coin, when the market wavers.

When it comes to the financial markets, most people have an inverted perception of supply and demand economics. As the market goes up, there's more demand and more investors participating. When markets go down, there's less. Yet, in almost every other economic environment, when something goes on sale, that is, when the price goes down, there's more demand and more people participating.

If, from a fundamental perspective, you believe in an asset at a specific price and that price goes down, you would logically buy more of it. The way trends work in the financial markets, however, is that price reductions cause people to sell out, mainly out of fear. It's completely counterintuitive thinking, but upside-down human behavior is what drives the market and creates trends.

Human behavior, or misbehavior in the case of the market, is also a force that drives the need for astute technical analysis. Whether we are discussing support and resistance, trends or any of the other factors influencing market movement, technical analysis is intended to help craft reliable judgments on market movements and patterns.

Charts

X-Rays or MRIs become necessary to look for signs of disease, fractures and other potential internal issues. They are a visual representation of what's going on inside the body. Technical analysis uses various types of charts to study changes occurring inside the market.

Financial markets display patterns that tend to repeat over time, not always exactly the same way but similarly. Charts manifest these patterns as well as the mood of investors, whether in indices, stocks, commodities, currencies or bonds.[39] Charts display the canvas where the story is painted. They plot the prices where trades have been executed. The most commonly used charts are bar, candlestick and line charts.

A bar chart typically uses vertical bars to represent the open, high, low and close prices in the market. The chart is useful for showing the overall trend over a specified time period.

"History doesn't repeat itself but it often rhymes."

Mark Twain

A candlestick chart is similar to a bar chart in that it also shows the open, high, low and close prices. The primary difference between the two charts is the manner in which the data is displayed. The candlesticks represent the data using dark or hollow (sometimes red or green) filled rectangles. The intensity or color of the rectangle indicates whether there was a rise or decline during the period.[40]

Candlestick charts were developed in the 1700s by Japanese rice trader Munehisa Homma to track the prices of rice futures. His methodology has been modified through the centuries and today is the standard on almost all investment platforms that plot prices of financial instruments or indices. The depth of information, component simplicity and ability to chain candlesticks together to reveal an underlying pattern makes candlestick charts a valuable indicator for observing past and present price action.[41]

Graphic 3.7 displays the basic candlestick construction.

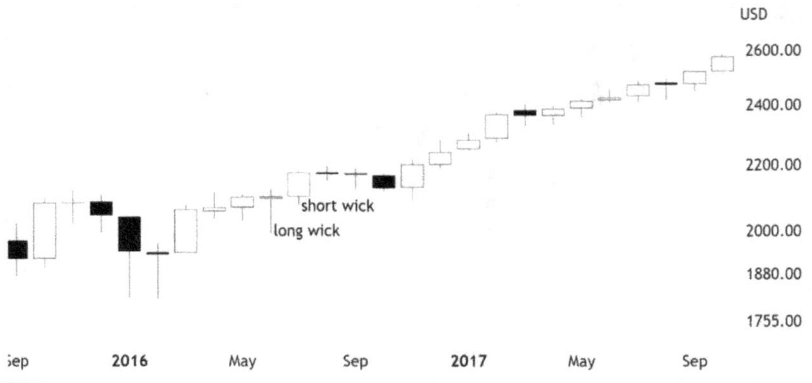

(Graphic 3.7 Candlestick Construction)

A candlestick consists of a rectangular body and two wicks or shadows. A hollow candlestick means that the opening price on that day was lower than the closing price that day, that is, the price moved up during the day, signaling a bullish candlestick. A dark candlestick means that the opening price was higher than the closing price that day, that is, the price moved down during the day, signaling a bearish candlestick.[42]

As a rule, the longer the body, the more intense the buying or selling pressure during regular trading hours. Conversely, short candlesticks indicate little price movement and represent consolidation.[43]

The two vertical lines above and below the body indicate the extreme from the open to the extreme from the close and are called wicks or shadows. They mark the high and low of that price for the period. The candlestick range is defined by the extreme high of the top wick above the body and the extreme low of the bottom wick. A short wick indicates trading was mostly held between open and close prices of that period. A long wick signals the price action has crossed the borders of the open and close prices. Graphic 3.8 depicts a typical candlestick chart of the S&P 500 Index.

(Graphic 3.8 Candlestick Example)

One way to comprehend candlestick analysis is to imagine the price movements in financial markets as a battle between the buyers and the sellers. Buyers speculate that prices will increase and drive the price up; sellers bet on falling prices and push the price down with their selling interest. The configuration of the candlesticks will reflect these patterns.[44] (see graphic 3.9)

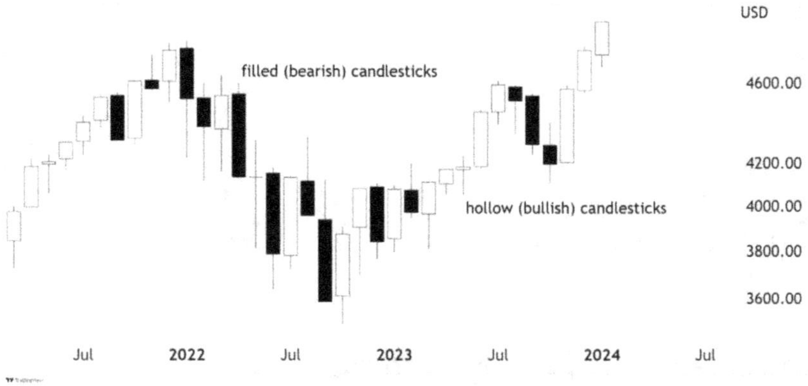

(Graphic 3.9 Bullish vs Bearish Candlestick)

The application and value of candlesticks is based on the assumption that when a set of factors that have played out in the past reoccurs, the same or similar outcome can be expected.[45]

> *"Nothing new ever occurs in the business of speculating or investing in securities and commodities."*

Jesse Livermore

Line charts (graphic 3.10) reveal the closing prices over a specified period. They are commonly used to discern momentum or Relative Strength Index (RSI) non-confirmations and divergences.

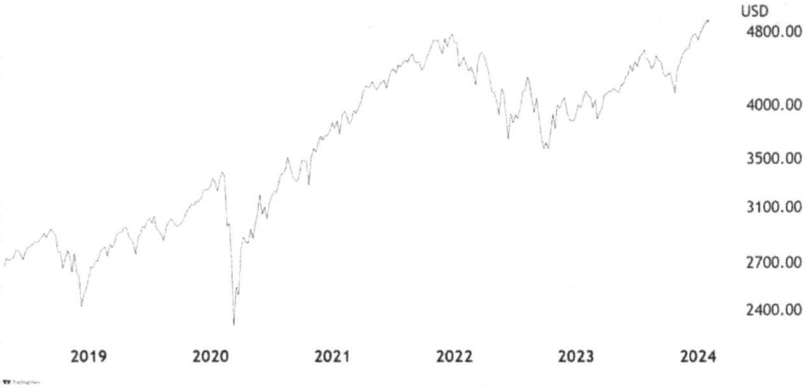

(Graphic 3.10 Line Chart)

Other Technical Analysis Indicators

Technical analysis weighs a variety of indicators, all of which are comparative. In addition to support and resistance, patterns and trends, there are also price-based and movement-based indicators.

Price-based indicators all have a closing price as their input and include:

- Momentum
  - Relative Strength Index (RSI)
- Simple Moving Averages (SMA)
  - Moving Average Convergence Divergence (MACD)
- Bollinger Bands
- Average True Range (ATR)

Movement-based indicators include:

- Advance Decline Ratio (ADR)
- Market Sector Breadth
- Volume

Price-Based Indicators

Momentum

Visits to your physician typically include a blood pressure check. Blood pressure measures the force of your blood pushing against the walls of your blood vessels. If your blood pressure is high, it means your heart is working too hard and the force of the blood flowing through your vessels is elevated. The increased velocity can cause your arteries to harden and your blood vessels to weaken, which can lead to serious health conditions.[46]

Just as blood pressure measures changes in velocity, momentum indicators measure the velocity of price changes. Momentum is measured by continually taking price differences for a fixed time period. A 10-day momentum, for example, would subtract the closing price from 10 days ago from the current day's closing price, the result plotted around a zero line. A momentum value above zero indicates that prices are moving up, and below zero indicates moving down.[47]

Essentially, market momentum is what creates a market trend. Since momentum is a result of the variations in prices, it also reflects the current market sentiment. Chart analysts use technical analysis indicators to measure market momentum and try to spot market trends. Principal examples of these indicators are the Moving Average Convergence Divergence (MACD) and the Relative Strength Index (RSI).[48]

The MACD indicator is a less-frequently used momentum hybrid that's computed from two different moving averages. The primary method of interpreting the MACD is with moving average crossovers. When the shorter-term 12-period exponential moving average (EMA) crosses over the longer-term 26-period EMA, it signals a market upturn.[49]

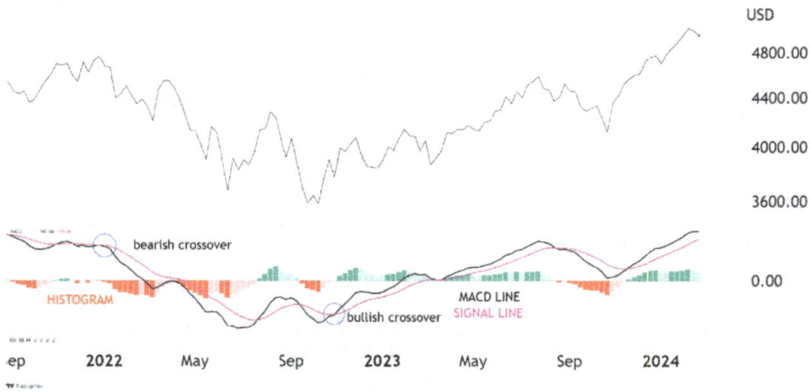

(Graphic 3.11 MACD Indicator)

Another of the momentum indicators is the RSI Indicator, which indicates whether an overbought or oversold condition exists. It measures the speed and velocity of price movements over a specified period of time. The goal is to measure the change in price momentum and it's often used to spot a general trend.

Developed by J. Welles Wilder, RSI oscillates between zero and 100, essentially measuring how well a market has performed compared to itself.[50] According to Wilder, RSI is considered overbought when above 70 and oversold when below 30. Signals that focus on a range of prices can also be generated by looking for divergences, failure swings and centerline crossovers.[51] Graphic 3.12 is an example of an RSI chart.

The Stochastic RSI indicator (Stoch RSI)—developed by Tushard Chande and Stanley Kroll—is essentially an indicator of an indicator, which makes it the second derivative of price. It provides a stochastic or haphazard calculation to the RSI indicator. This means that it is a measure of RSI relative to its own high/low range over a defined period of time. The Stoch RSI is an oscillator that calculates a value between 0 and 1 which is then plotted as a line and used like RSI to identify overbought and oversold conditions.[52]

Graphic 3.13 is an example of a Stochastic RSI chart.

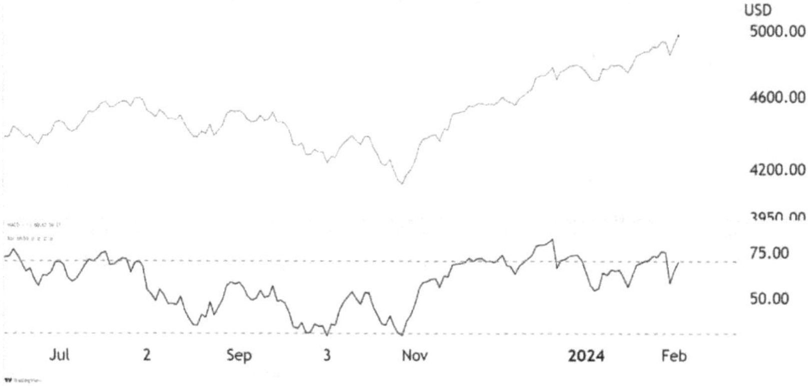

(Graphic 3.12 RSI Chart)

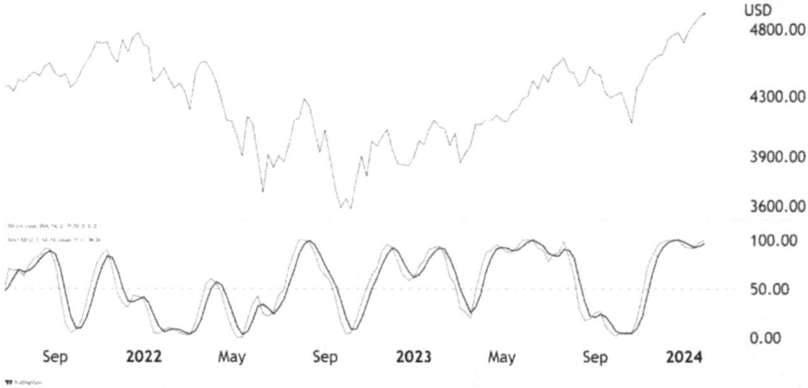

(Graphic 3.13 Stochastic RSI)

The Stoch RSI centerline is at 50. Stoch RSI reflects an uptrend when consistently above 50 and a downtrend when consistently below 50. Because this indicator is quite volatile, some smoothing with a moving average can help for short-term trend identification.[53]

Simple Moving Averages

The annual physical allows your doctor to evaluate your overall health and in what direction it's trending. How many of the elements of your fitness level are better or worse than they were at a different point in time? It's a simple but critical analysis of your anatomy's moving averages.

Simple Moving Averages (SMA) is an indicator that helps determine a trend's direction. In technical analysis, virtually every indicator can have a SMA. It totals the data points of the market and divides the total by the number of data points over a specific time period to arrive at an average. It is referred to as "moving" because it is continually recalculated based on the latest price data. Graphic 3.14 is a chart of the SMA of the S&P 500 Index.

(Graphic 3.14 SMA)

Moving averages smooth out price action and filter out the irrelevant to form a trend-tracking indicator. They also form the foundation for other indicators, such as Bollinger Bands (described below). Most moving averages are based on closing prices. A 10-day SMA, for example, reflects the 10-day sum of closing prices divided by 10. Old data is dropped as new data becomes available, causing the average to move along the time scale.[54]

In addition to the SMA there is also an Exponential Moving Average (EMA), which places greater weight and significance on the most recent data points. Graphic 3.15 is an illustration of an EMA.

(Graphic 3.15 EMA)

A working example of this action would be to take the closing amount of the S&P 500 every day for the previous 30 days and average it. That becomes our moving average. Let's say tomorrow is May 30th. Tomorrow, we will add on the day's closing amount and drop off the first day of our existing moving average (April 30th) to maintain a 30-day moving average. The SMA will thus change daily, based on the new day's addition and deletion.

We can apply this formula to different time frames and calculate a SMA for each. We can then continuously monitor the various moving averages to see if the market is healthy, that is, has a current price above the SMA. A characteristic of a bull market is an upward slope in the SMA. When the short-term average dips below the longer-term average to create an "X" shape, it is usually an ominous indication of a cyclical bear market, referred to in technical analysis as a *death cross.*

Death and Golden Crosses

A death cross occurs when a shorter-term moving average goes down and crosses under the longer-term average. Typically, 50-day and 200-day moving averages are used as the moving averages.[55] The death cross has been part of many of the worst bear markets: 1929, 1938, 1974 and 2008. In today's computerized investing environment, a death cross will inevitably cause hedge fund algorithms to kick in and trigger a sell off.

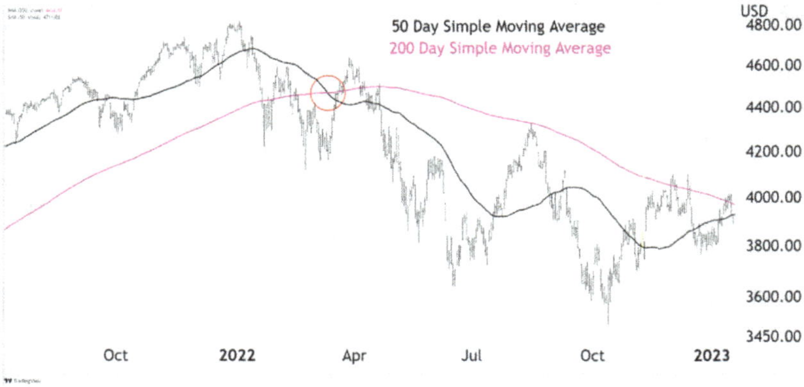

(Graphic 3.16 Death Cross)

Graphic 3.16 illustrates a moving average death cross represented by the S&P 500.

A golden cross (Graphic 3.17) is essentially the opposite of a death cross. It happens when a shorter-term moving average crosses above a longer-term average, portending an uptrend in the market.[56]

When interpreting the seriousness of a death cross or golden cross, sophisticated investors recognize that the pattern is most meaningful when combined with other technical indicators, such as volume. For example, higher trading volumes during a death cross usually indicate that more investors are selling into the death cross, trying to profit on the downward trend of the market.[57]

(Graphic 3.17 Golden Cross)

Bollinger Bands

Bollinger Bands is a volatility indicator. Created by John Bollinger, the indicator constructs three lines around price: a simple moving average (SMA) acts as the middle band while equally distanced upper and lower bands expand and contract in reaction to changing volatility.[58] The upper and lower band determine if prices are high or low on a relative basis. Bollinger Bands work best when the middle band is chosen to reflect the intermediate-term trend, so that trend information is combined with relative price level data.[59] Graphic 3.18 illustrates a typical Bollinger Band.

The outer Bollinger Bands reflect price volatility. The bands contract when volatility is low, indicating that volatility may increase, prompting a significant price movement up or down. When volatility is high, the bands expand, signaling that an existing price trend could be coming to a close. As a rule, price movements stay within the two bands. Once they touch one band, they are apt to start moving towards the other band.[60]

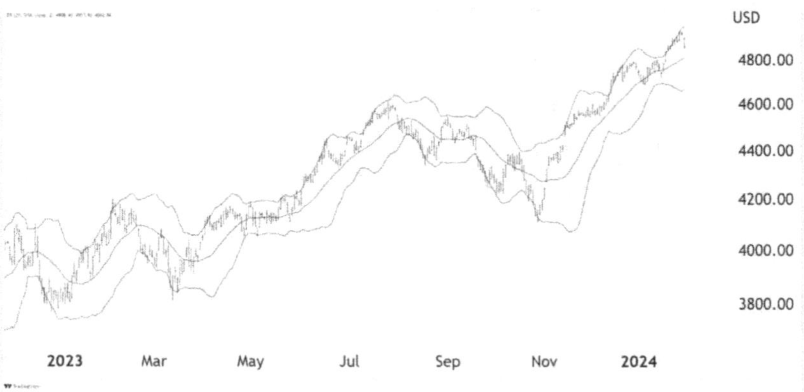

(Graphic 3.18 Bollinger Bands)

An important and commonly used measure of market volatility is called the standard deviation. It quantifies how much the market—or an individual asset's—return varies from its average return over a set period of time. A high standard deviation implies greater price swings.[61] By default, the Bollinger Bands are set to 2.0 standard deviations which means that statistically, roughly 95%

of all the price action happens between the bands. A move near or outside of the outer Bollinger Band indicates a significant price move.[62]

Analysts can choose the parameters for the middle band—representing the SMA—then can decide on the number of standard deviations needed for the volatility indicator by positioning the upper and lower bands on either side of the SMA band. The position of these outer bands provides information on how strong a trend is and the potential high and low-price levels that may be expected in the immediate future.[63]

Bandwidth is a measurement of the percentage difference between the upper band and the lower band. It decreases as Bollinger Bands narrow and increases as Bollinger Bands widen. Because Bollinger Bands are based on the standard deviation, falling Bandwidth reflects decreasing volatility and rising Bandwidth reflects increasing volatility. Bandwidth is calculated by subtracting the value of the lower band from the value of the upper band, revealing the absolute difference, which is then divided by the closing price, which normalizes the value.[64]

Average True Range

The Average True Range (ATR) is an indicator that measures market volatility. It measures the average variation of price movements during a given time frame.

(Graphic 3.19 Average True Range)

The range of a market is the difference between the high and low prices during a specified time period. The ATR indicator fluctuates in response to price moves that become larger or smaller. When the ATR is growing larger, it indicates increasing volatility whereas a lower ATR implies lower price volatility. The ATR is non-directional, so an expanding range can be an indication of either upward or downward market movement.[65]

Movement-Based Indicators

Much of what a doctor uses to interpret your physical progress or regression is based on an analysis of what's happened to your health since your previous physical. Has the level of your blood pressure, cholesterol, triglycerides and other factors advanced or declined since last year?

Advance Decline Ratio

Similarly, the advance decline ratio (ADR), a non-price-based indicator, compares the number of stocks in a market, such as the S&P 500, that increased or decreased in value on a trended basis, calculated over a specific time period. Looking at the ADR on a trended basis provides an indication as to whether the market is expected to show a bullish or bearish trend. A ratio that is increasing over time signals a bullish market trend while a ratio that is declining over time signals a bearish market trend. A ratio that is relatively high signals an overbought market while a ratio that is relatively low signals an oversold market.[66]

Graphic 3.20 is an example of an advance decline (ADR) chart.

The advance/decline line indicator (lower section) identifies a potentially fake spike in the security. This meant that the market was rising on falling participation and hinted ahead of time that the security was at risk of a correction.

The advance/decline line (A/D line) is an indicator that plots the difference between the number of advancing and declining stocks in a market on a daily basis and aggregates their values into a single reading. The A/D line tends to follow the S&P 500 but there are times when it falls despite the overall index hitting new highs.

This event is known as a divergence or non-confirmation and can be an indicator that market rally isn't supported by corresponding price action.[67]

(Graphic 3.20 ADR)

Sector Breadth

Most physicals include a blood workup. A routine complete blood count (CBC) checks for levels of 10 different components of every major cell in your blood. The test includes measurement of red and white blood cells and platelets as well as hemoglobin and hematocrit. Even if a person does not have heart disease, a blood test can show whether they may be at risk of developing the condition.

The sector breadth indicator, like a blood workup, examines major market sectors, among them utilities, consumer staples, consumer discretionary, financials, healthcare, technology, basic materials, real estate, energy and communications.

Sector breadth indicators analyze the number of sectors advancing relative to those that are declining. The percentage trading above a SMA is a breadth indicator that gauges the underlying indices' strength or weakness.[68] It's important to see broad sector participation. When only a few sectors are moving up, it's a signal that bad times may be on the horizon. An example of this was 2007, when the market as a whole was rising, but the buoyancy was being provided by just two sectors: real estate and oil. Everything else was declining. That's the sign of an unhealthy market and subsequent events proved so.

Certain breadth indicators also incorporate volume. Plotting a price chart with volume moves is called On-Balance Volume (OBV). This indicator reflects the market's buying and selling pressure by adding volume during rallies and subtracting volume on days when the market closes lower.[69] The volume aspect is important because price moves on larger volume are considered to be more significant than price moves on lower volume. Market breadth attempts to ascertain the underlying strength or weakness in the market's index. Assessing the strength or weakness, which isn't plainly visible by looking at a chart of the index, gains insight into what the index may do next. Most market breadth indicators are used to monitor for confirmation and divergence. Confirmation is when the indicator is moving favorably and the index is rising. Divergence is when the index and indicator move in opposite directions. This warns of an impending reversal.[70]

Like the psychological assessment of a patient's emotional swings, the High-Low Index (HiLo) is a form of breadth indicator that compares the number of stocks that are hitting their 52-week highs versus the number of stocks hitting their 52-week lows. It assesses the highest and lowest prices at which securities have traded during the previous 52 weeks, based on the daily closing prices for the securities.[71] From that calculation, a moving average can be created.

Fundamentally, if a majority of stocks are making new or more highs, it's a positive sign for the market; if more stocks are making new lows, it's a negative omen.

During 2022, the largest number of stocks in the S&P 500 making new lows occurred in June. Following a rally in August, the Index sunk to a new low in October. What was interesting is that there were fewer stocks making new lows in October than in June. Major companies like Tesla were making new lows in October but the majority of average-sized companies in the market had already made their lows four months earlier.

So even though the Index was lower in October than in June, it was apparent that the decline was less robust because fewer stocks were participating, indicating an impending reversal to the upside.

> *"Big movements take time to develop."*
>
> Jesse Livermore

A proliferation of new highs in the market typically occurs early on in a rally. The market tops tend to take much longer to unfold, and even if the number of new highs does not continue to increase as the market rises, that's not necessarily a bad sign. It's not until the market rally gets extremely narrow—almost flat—with perhaps just a few stocks making new highs that a reversal is indicated. This progression can go on indefinitely, for many months or even years.

Volume

Just as your weight reflects the total intake of food and drink over a day, week, month or extended period, market volume refers to the total amount of transactions conducted over a specific time period. The stock market volume is the total number of shares traded each day, also known as the trading volume.[72]

Volume is an important indicator in technical analysis because it measures the relative importance of a market move. The strength or intensity of a price movement depends on the volume of that movement over a defined time period. The higher the volume during the price move, the more significant it is.[73]

When a huge spike in volume occurs, it's usually an important signal that something is going to change. This is especially true at market lows and known as a capitulation—literally a surrender—where panicky investors, said to have "paper hands," rush to sell at almost any price. This triggers a steep drop in prices, at which point stronger investors, said to have "diamond hands,"[74] move in and begin to buy, which typically allows the market to rebound and move higher. My investors had diamonds hands in March 2009,

December 26, 2018, March 25, 2020 and June 17, 2022 when market panic was at its highest.

Capitulation of the entire market sometimes occurs in response to a singular economic event, such as the 2008 housing bubble burst that led to a massive selling frenzy. In 2020, the onset of the COVID pandemic set off a similar but less lengthy selloff.[75]

Individual stocks can experience voluminous spikes in response to unanticipated poor earnings reports or other negative news. Commodities, on the other hand, tend to work in reverse of equities, experiencing huge volume spikes not at their lows but at their highs, often in response to inflationary concerns. In either instance, the root cause of capitulation is the human emotion of fear, as described in chapter two on market sentiment. It's why an uncorrelated asset like gold tends to spike higher when fear permeates the market, causing a capitulation that drives prices lower and promotes a huge volume increase.

Summary

As investors, we want to own a market that has acceleration and positive momentum. To borrow a term from calculus, we want to see a positive second derivative, which is a positive change in the rate of change. In other words, we want to see the rate of change improving at a faster rate. If the rate of change is accelerating at a healthy rate, it's a positive sign. Bull markets tend to display an accelerating rate of momentum change. We have calculations in the algorithm that capture the momentum rate of change. If the rate of change in momentum is slowing, it's an indication of a market that is starting to lose steam. Once we see market momentum stalling out and moving negative, we know there's a higher probability of decline as a result.

Technical analysis is not a definitive science but rather a probabilistic discipline. While nothing works all the time, technical analysis identifies areas within the markets where points of inflection occur, particularly during periods of elevated activity. As an investor competing for profits with the profusion of computerized algorithms, technical analysis provides direction and is essential in a decision-making risk management framework.

Just as important as what technical analysis provides is what it prevents. It helps prevent reducing risk too early in a bull market and it helps prevent increasing risk too early in a bear market.

In a bullish environment, the market may appear overly expensive based on fundamentals. But if it has momentum above its moving average and is attracting fresh capital, technical analysis will suggest we hold on and let our winners run because sometimes, the fundamentals improve. Conversely, in a bear market, the fundamentals will occasionally be very attractive. But if there is downward momentum and heavy selling pressure, technical analysis will help us be patient. That's because in a bear market, stocks with attractive fundamentals but with beaten-down prices can sometimes continue to decline.

On a personal note, technical analysis proved to be invaluable for me during the Great Recession of 2008-09. Stock prices lost roughly 50% of their value between October 2007 and March 2009.[76] Fearful of losing most or even all of their investment capital, terrified investors flocked to the "safe harbor" of Treasurys.

In September 2008, the market fundamentals were attractively priced. A month later, there was widespread panic and the Treasury yield went negative, something that had not occurred since WWII. People were loaning money to the U.S. government, willing to let it hold—and ostensibly protect—their cash with the understanding that investors would actually get less money back than they had invested. The only thing that catches that link of historically unprecedented event is technical analysis.

In chapter four, we will take a look at leading economic indicators.

CHAPTER FOUR

Unexciting Economics: Measuring Leading Indicators

A discussion of measuring economic indicators influencing the risk parameters of an investment portfolio is a necessary, albeit enigmatic topic. It necessarily includes a lot of definitions and other uninspiring references, but it's an important indicator to understand so I'll do my best not to put you to sleep. Incidentally, the complexity is one reason why most investors avoid going down this path and why most managers fail to outperform their benchmarks.

British economist John Maynard Keynes is generally regarded as the founder of modern macroeconomics and the world's foremost economist. His influence was such that the movement adopted his name: *Keynesian Economics.* His 1930 book, *A Treatise on Money*, is widely regarded as a quantum leap forward in economic thinking. Prior to his publication, economics analyzed only static conditions. Keynes offered a more dynamic approach that converted economics into a study of the flow of incomes and expenditures, revolutionizing thinking on economic analysis.[77]

Keynes career and profound impact was the result of his efforts to make sense of the disruptions and crises that began with the First World War and continued through the Great Depression. Descended from a knight who had crossed the English Channel with William the Conqueror, Keynes was the son of a Cambridge University economist. Educated at Eton and Cambridge, he demonstrated early on an amazing intellect and singular mathematical dexterity. He once commented that his best ideas came from "from messing about with figures and seeing what they must mean."[78]

His career included an admirable record as an investor. During an eighteen-year period encompassing the Great Depression and WW II, his *Chest Fund* grew fivefold. Given the UK stock market fell fifteen percent during the same period, his investment performance was all the more remarkable.[79]

> *"The study of economics does not seem to require any specialized gifts of an unusually high order. Is it not a very easy subject compared with the higher branches of philosophy and pure science? Yet good, or even competent, economists are the rarest of birds. An easy subject, at which very few excel!"*

John Maynard Keynes

For investors lacking Keynes' innate genius, being able to weigh leading economic activity when making investment decisions is obviously important, but it requires a consistent, reliable method of measurement. One way to do this is to compare current economic conditions with those of the past, which gives us an idea if the current economic environment supports or threatens asset price growth and a stock market increase or decline.

The economic activity factors used in the algorithm include:

- Monetary/Liquidity
- Inflation
- Economic Activity
- Bond Market

Factor 1: Monetary/Liquidity

The Federal Reserve System (the Fed) is the central bank of the United States. It was founded by Congress in 1913 to provide the nation with a more stable monetary and financial system. The Board of Governors, also known as the Federal Reserve Board, is the national component of the Federal Reserve System. The board consists of the seven governors, appointed by the President and confirmed by the Senate. The Board's most important responsibility is participating in the Federal Open Market Committee (FOMC), which conducts our nation's monetary policy.[80]

Monetary policy refers to the Fed's activities influencing the quantity of money and credit in an economy. Fiscal policy refers to the government's decisions about taxation and spending. Both affect economic activity over time, either to accelerate or moderate growth and activity.[81]

The financial markets are sensitive to changes in the economy. Monetary policy is used to restore or maintain stability within the economy and can either be expansive or restrictive. The Fed manages interest rates and money supply as its monetary policy instruments.[82]

Market liquidity is an important factor because it directly affects both investment returns and related costs for both private and public sector borrowers. Illiquid markets tend to be more volatile and at the extreme, can trigger or exacerbate financial crises. Even the average level of volatility matters, as it is factored into the interest rates demanded by investors and paid by borrowers.[83]

The following are some of the principal monetary and liquidity indicators we monitor.

M1 and M2: M1 includes monies that are highly liquid, such as cash, savings accounts and other demand deposits. M2 money supply tends to be less liquid and includes M1 plus savings and time deposits, certificates of deposits and money market accounts, including institutional money market funds.

During some periods, money supply measurements have demonstrated a close relationship with nominal gross domestic product (GDP). Some economists—Milton Friedman being the most famous example—have argued that the money supply provides important information about the near-term course for the economy and determines the level of prices and inflation in the long run.[84]

M3 and M4: Whereas M1 and M2 are known as narrow money, M3 and M4 are regarded as broad money. The progressions are in decreasing order of liquidity, with M1 being the most liquid.

The M3 includes M2 money plus large time deposits, institutional money market funds, short-term repurchase agreements and larger liquid funds. M3 is more closely associated with larger financial institutions and corporations than with small businesses and individuals. The M4 money supply is a measure of notes and coins in circulation plus bank accounts. It is a broader definition because it includes bank accounts and not just notes and coins in circulation.[85]

Marshallian K is a measure of excess liquidity, that is, the ratio of liquid money to gross domestic product (GDP). It is calculated by dividing M2 by GDP. If the economy is experiencing excess liquidity, the supply of money is likely exceeding the demand for money as measured by GDP.[86] When the money supply is growing at a high rate, it tends to support asset prices.

The Fed Balance Sheet is like the balance sheet of any other bank: a list of current assets and liabilities. The bigger the Fed's balance sheet and the more it purchases securities, the greater its interest-rate risk exposure. In an unusually low interest-rate environment, such as the U.S. has experienced over the past decade, the Fed's balance sheet grows and the average return on the Fed's assets declines.

The Fed's assets are primarily comprised of Treasury securities, which typically represent 75%-90% of the Fed's assets. Its other assets include loans made to U.S. banks and other entities, mortgage-backed securities (MBS) and other Federal agency debt instruments. The Fed's liabilities include all circulated U.S. currency not held by the Fed and all the deposits of commercial banks and other financial institutions that the Fed holds in accordance with bank reserve requirements.

A quirk of the Fed balance sheet is that although currency in circulation is a liability for the Fed, when it prints additional money and then uses that money to buy additional securities, the purchased securities are assets on the Fed balance sheet.[87]

Graphic 4.1 tracks the Fed's assets over the previous 15 years. Graphic 4.2 tracks the Fed's liabilities over the same period.

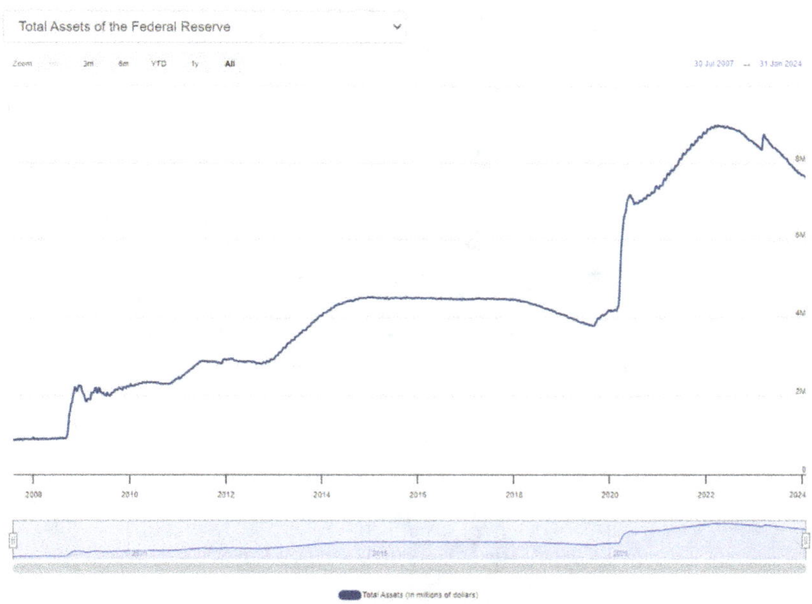

(Graphic 4.1 Fed Assets)

Prior to the financial crisis of 2007-09, reserve balances were less than $10 bn. As of January 2021, reserve balances were $3.2tn and on course to be $5.85 tn by the middle of 2022. The historically high level of reserve balances will ultimately lower banks' capital ratios and raise their capital requirements. In turn, those pressures will likely reduce GDP and raise longer-term interest rates. When that occurs, the high level of reserve balances will require the Fed to pay an elevated interest rate on reserve balances. It's impossible to accurately predict the Fed's added interest expense but some analysts expect it to be more than $20bn a year.[88]

Loan Demand represents how consumers and businesses borrow and spend money. When interest rates are high, bank loans cost more and the demand falls. When interest rates are lower, loan demand increases as individuals and companies borrow more, boosting economic growth. However, low interest rates can create inflation—too much money chasing too few goods. The Federal Reserve manages inflation and recession by controlling interest rates.[89]

(Graphic 4.2 Fed Liabilities)

Factor 2: Inflation

> *"Inflation is the time when those who have saved for a rainy day get soaked."*

Anonymous

Inflation is an overall increase in the prices of goods or services. It causes an erosion of the purchasing power of the dollar. Over time, the devaluation can be dramatic. There are many reasons for inflationary increases, including lower interest rates, wage increases, supply chain issues, global economic problems and others. A classic example was the government stepping in to create liquidity via a huge infusion of capital in response to the Covid pandemic.

There are various indicators that measure inflation, including the producer and consumer price indices and commodity prices.

The *Producer Price Index* (PPI) is a family of indexes that measures the average change over time in the selling prices received by domestic producers of goods and services. PPIs measure price change from the perspective of the seller versus that of the consumer. About 10,000 PPIs for individual products and groups of products are released each month. Since PPI measures the costs of producing consumer goods, and commodity and food prices directly affect retail pricing, PPI is seen as a good pre-indicator of inflationary pressures.

The PPI is important because it is a primary economic indicator of changes in what producers are getting for their products. This, in turn, influences decisions by the Fed and other government entities. In addition, other indicators, such as gross domestic product (GDP), will often be adjusted based upon the PPI. Commodity prices, such as food and natural gas, are determined by supply and demand. A spike in demand, for example, can affect the price producers charge, and in turn, the PPI.[90]

The *Consumer Price Index* (CPI) is a measure of the monthly change in the prices of approximately 80,000 goods and services, known as the market basket. If inflation rises, causing goods and services to cost more, the CPI will similarly rise. A decline in the CPI indicates a decrease in the prices of goods and services. A CPI of 120 means prices have risen 20% over the base period.[91]

The major expenditure categories tracked in the CPI are groceries, energy, consumer durables like clothes and automobiles, and services like rent and healthcare. Each category is assigned a relative importance based on its proportion of all expenditures, with services typically given the highest relative importance.[92]

Commodities are an asset class, most of which are raw materials or crops that originate in the earth. Agricultural commodities include corn, soybeans, sugar, oranges and coffee. Examples of energy commodities are crude oil and natural gas. Metals commodities include gold, silver, copper and uranium. Livestock commodities include hogs, cattle, pork bellies and the like. Most commodities trade on commodities exchanges, such as the Chicago Mercantile Exchange, Chicago Board of Options Exchange, New York Mercantile Exchange and the Chicago Board of Trade.

Commodity trading is usually carried out in the futures market. Commodity futures contracts are an agreement to buy or sell a specific quantity of a commodity at a specified price on a particular date in the future.[93]

An inverse relationship exists between commodities and the dollar. As a rule, commodity prices tend to drop when the dollar strengthens against other major currencies and rise when the value of the dollar weakens against other major currencies.[94]

Factor 3: Economic Activity

A leading indicator is a measurable set of data that can help anticipate trends and future economic activity.[95] Leading economic indicators precede economic events, such as the next phase of the business cycle. That becomes critical information, particularly when the economy is either coming out of a recession or heading into one.[96]

Leading economic indicators are calculated in the *Conference Board's Leading Economic Index®* (LEI), which is used to predict the future direction of economic movements. The LEI contains 10 components:

- Average weekly hours, manufacturing
- Average weekly initial claims for unemployment insurance

- Manufacturers' new orders, consumer goods and materials
- ISM® Index of New Orders
- Manufacturers' new orders, nondefense capital goods excluding aircraft orders
- Building permits, new private housing units
- Stock prices, 500 common stocks
- Leading Credit Index™
- Interest rate spread, 10-year Treasury bonds less federal funds
- Average consumer expectations for business conditions[97]

The *New York Fed Recession Probability* is a model used to calculate the odds of a recession during the next 12 months. It's predicted by the Treasury spread—the difference in yield between a U.S. Treasury security and any other debt security with a similar maturity. Because U.S. Treasury securities are considered zero-risk investments, the yield on the other security is almost always higher to compensate the investor for the added risk. The measure has breached the 30% threshold before every recession since 1960.[98]

The *Citigroup Economic Surprise Index* (CESI) measures the degree to which economic data is either beating or missing expectations relative to the consensus forecasts of market economists. CESI is a mean reverting index that cycles between highs and lows and is calculated over a three-month rolling window. The index weighs its constituent indicators based on how strongly positive or negative surprises in them have affected financial markets in the recent past. Positive surprises or disappointments can affect investors' willingness to buy assets. When the index is below zero, it means the constituent indicators have been coming in under anticipated levels, on balance, and vice versa.[99]

The *ISM Manufacturing Index*, also known as the purchasing managers index (PMI), is a monthly indicator of U.S. economic activity based on a survey of purchasing managers at more than

300 manufacturing firms. It is considered to be a key indicator of the state of the U.S. economy. A PMI above 50 would designate an overall expansion of the manufacturing economy whereas a PMI below 50 signifies a shrinking of the manufacturing economy.[100]

Unlike lagging indicators such as the GDP that track historical data, the PMI reflects current trends in manufacturing and services by encapsulating the outlook of corporate purchasing managers, who may be in the best position to assess economic activity within their respective industries. Because their decisions can be critical to their company's success in maintaining an efficient supply chain, purchasing managers have a unique insight as to what to expect versus what's already happened.[101]

Factor 4: The Bond Market

Whereas Factor 3 (Comparative Bond Yields) discussed in Chapter Two deals with bond yield spreads, Factor 4 in this chapter refers to bond yield changes at different points in time as illustrated by the yield curve.

A yield curve is a line that plots the yields of bonds having equal credit quality but different maturity dates. The slope of the yield curve suggests future interest rate changes and economic activity. The Treasury yield curve depicts the relationship between yields and maturities of Treasury bonds.[102] It is an indicator of economic activity and there is a high correlation between inverted yield curves and recessions. Graphics 4.3, 4.4 and 4.5 depict various types of yield curves.

In a normal yield curve (graphic 4.3), a positive upward slope indicates that short-term debt instruments provide lower yields than long-term debt instruments of the same credit quality due to the time horizon and investor risk perceptions.[103]

A flat yield curve (graphic 4.4) displays negligible difference between short-term and long-term rates for bonds of the same credit quality, typically Treasurys. This type of yield curve is often seen during transitions between normal and inverted curves.[104]

An inverted yield curve (graphic 4.5) has a negative or downward slope, which occurs when shorter-duration bond yields are higher than the yields on longer-duration bonds, an atypical situation that often signals an impending recession.[105] When a yield curve inverts, it's usually because investors lack confidence in the near-term economy and perceive the near-term as riskier than the future and so demand a higher yield for a short-term investment than for a long-term one.[106]

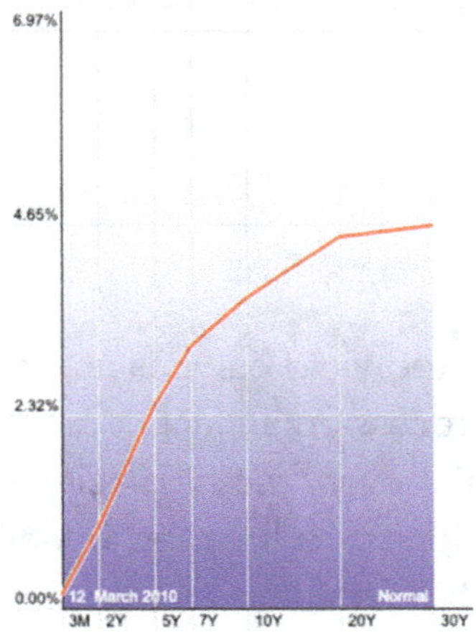

(Graphic 4.3 Normal Yield Curve)

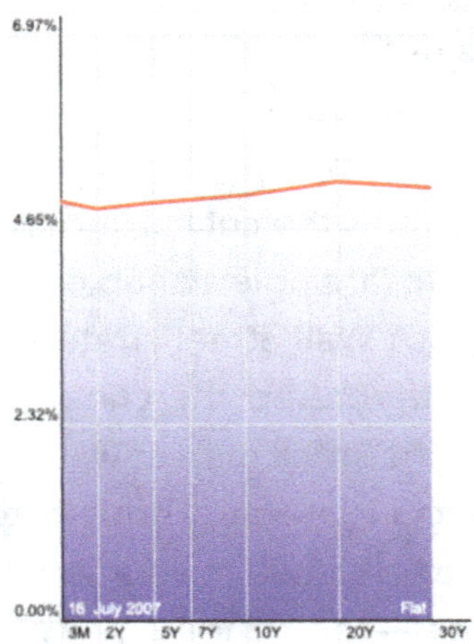

(Graphic 4.4 Flat Yield Curve)

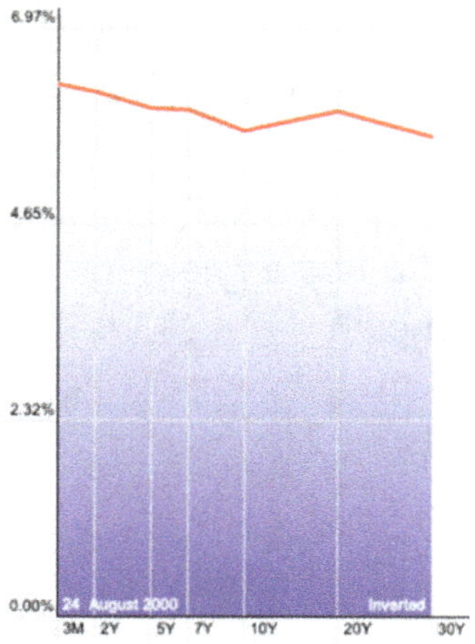

(Graphic 4.5 Inverted Yield Curve)

A continuing inverted yield curve is commonly interpreted as a reliable predictor of recession. In fact, it proved to be a false signal just once leading up to every recession since 1955.

The yield curve flipped to inverted in early July 2022 and has continued that inversion for the past two years. Despite that, we have not experienced a technical recession. To the contrary, the economy has experienced seven consecutive quarters of growth, and the S&P 500 has risen nearly 40%.

The fact that this indicator has failed to produce what an inverted yield curve normally produces—a recession—in the current cycle demonstrates the critical importance of not assigning an excessive weight to a single variable, an oversight routinely committed by numerous Wall Street strategists.

Because they misinterpreted the current inverted yield curve, believing it indicated the stock market was in trouble, they missed the recent rally, piling in late and hoping to save face for their investors. In fairness to all those misguided Wall Street "experts," a historically rare event—the pandemic—was a likely contributing factor to the yield curve inversion not leading to a recession, at least to date. But again, that's why it is so vitally important to analyze multiple indicators when assessing potential bear markets.

This is why we include 190 different variables in the algorithm. It's not that we are enamored with complexity but rather that we recognize that as humans, no matter how smart or experienced, we occasionally suffer myopia when it comes to reading financial tea leaves. In this case, being overly reliant upon or overreacting to a single indicator.

In conclusion, an inverted yield curve doesn't necessarily mean a recession will occur, and particularly not in the short term. Historically, yield spreads have not remained negative for very long, one reason why the current inversion appears to be an outlier. In addition, recessions don't usually happen while the yield curve is inverted. Rather, the yield curve tends to gradually revert prior to a recession occurring.[107]

In the next chapter, you will learn how to value businesses and stock prices.

CHAPTER FIVE

Valuing Opportunity: Modern Valuation Techniques

I realize the chapter you just completed discussing economic activity may not be the most stimulating topic in the book, but it was a necessary addition. I think you will find this chapter more stimulating, although it will require more deliberation. Understanding how to value businesses and subsequently a stock market is a critical element in successful investing, but unfortunately, there is no easy way to explain the process. Be prepared for some heavy lifting.

You are going to be introduced to some complex valuation techniques, including normalization, statistical analysis using regression, and analyses of ratios and discounted cash flow. As I said, some heavy lifting. But these, and some less esoteric topics, like apples-to-apples comparisons and breakeven periods, are all essential components of learning how to unerringly value a business and market.

If you have a background in analytics, when I start to discuss normalization on page 87, you may choose to move forward 20 pages to the apples-to-apples section.

I was challenged writing this book because some chapters, like this one, required a deep dive into certain topics. While readers have different backgrounds and some will move through this section faster than others, I wanted to keep it interesting for everyone, understanding that this is one of the most important and profitable pieces of information I have to give you. And, since the next chapters contain lessons from Warren Buffett—some delightfully compelling insights from the Sage of Omaha—there's some lighter and less demanding reading ahead.

A topic we hit on in the previous chapters and one we will scrutinize more closely later in the book is expectations, the principal driving force behind investor behavior. Expectations are important because they initiate the cycle that ultimately drives stock prices. Expectations propel human behavior, which drives economic activity which drives profitability which drives stock prices. It is a perpetual sequence that is as certain as rain the day after you wash your car, but it always begins with expectations. If you have doubts, consider that the Fed's first consideration in addressing economic issues such as inflation is an analysis of consumer expectations.

That said, let's get started.

Valuation factors are a really big deal. They explain more than 80 percent of portfolio return variance over a ten-year period. As a portfolio's time horizon is extended, valuation becomes increasingly crucial. If we get the valuation right and avoid taking excessive risk in an overvalued market, it's a virtual certainty that we should achieve superior investment results over the long term.

When the market is highly priced, the probability of decline caused by lofty valuations is dramatically increased, whereas the likelihood of a large decline is extremely low when valuations are cheap. We must get the valuation calculations correct in order to allocate investments profitably over the long run.

In all of my studies of investment research, the best graphic representation of the importance of valuation factors I have ever seen is a chart from Merrill Lynch research on the GFM Asset Management website. It is an eye-opening revelation regarding the importance of valuations, specifically in the area of normalized P/E ratios—which I will explain later in this chapter—and helps explain in graphic format why Warren Buffett has been the most successful investor in history. Graphic 5.1 is an example of valuation importance.

P/E ratio explains ~80% of the variability in annualized 10-year returns

Chart 9: Price to normalized earnings predictive power on subsequent holding period returns (since 1987)

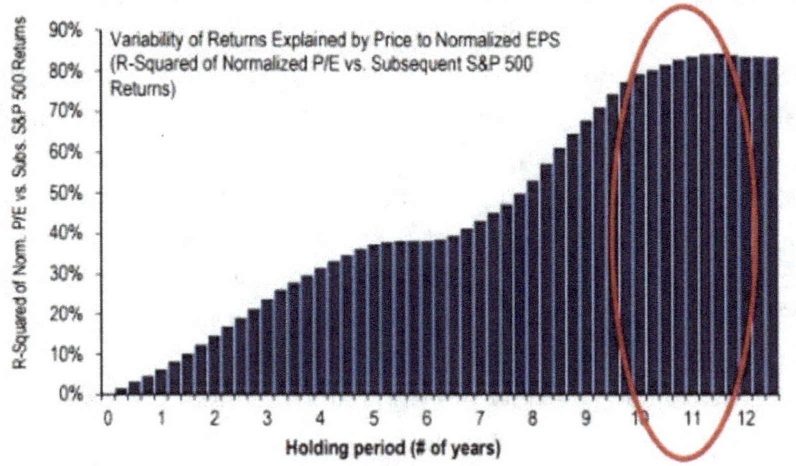

Source: BofA Merrill Lynch US Equity & US Quant Strategy

(Graphic 5.1 Valuation Importance)

Graphic 5.2 is another example of the growing impact of valuation factors over time.

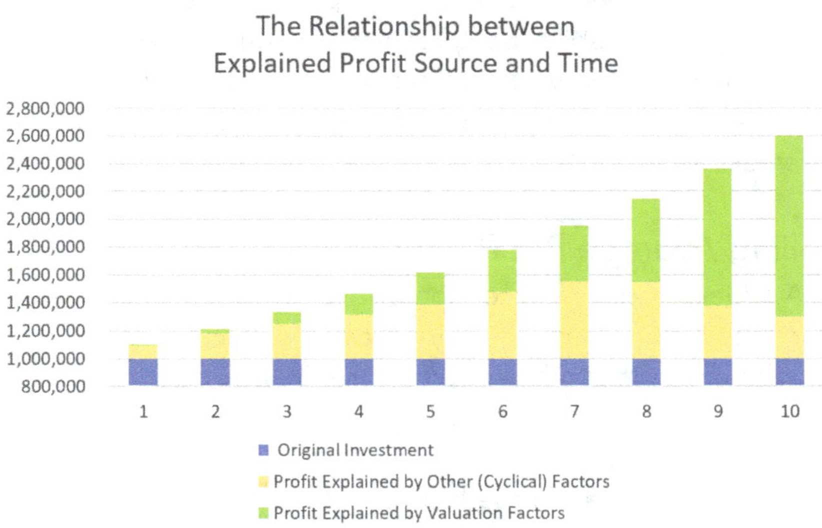

(Graphic 5.2 Profit by Valuation & Other Factors)

Using graphic 5.2, let's assume we own a portfolio worth 1mn dollars in year zero that grows 10% per year. By year three, it's worth $1.33mn, so the portfolio has grown $331k. Valuation factors (green bar) tell us that roughly 24%—or $79k of that $331k profit—is the result of what we originally paid for the investment. The other $252k is explained by other cyclical factors: economic health, market health, the sentiment picture, the number of companies beating earnings, business cycles, etc.

Now let's extend our investment horizon to ten years. Our portfolio is now worth almost $2.6mn, so it contains $1.6mn of profit. Looking at the chart, we see that by year 10, more than 80%—or about $1.3mn of that profit—is explained by valuation factors.

Here you can see how the original investment profits primarily from cyclical factors in the early years but, as time passes, valuation factors become the dominant profit factor...gradually at first, followed by a massive uptick that overtakes cyclical factors in year eight of the example. By year 10, valuation explains 81% of the investment growth!

The conclusion is obvious. The longer the investment horizon, the more important valuation factors become. In the short run, all the other indicators mentioned in the prior chapters play a role in explaining the variability and profitability of our portfolio. Over the long run, however, valuation factors are the most meaningful because while the price paid for an investment does not change, other factors are cyclical.

Rolling Average P/E Ratio Analysis

A widespread misconception about major market declines is that they are only caused by recessions, pandemics or other singular events, but that's not the case. Market downturns over a 12-month period—particularly large market downturns—are best explained by valuation factors.

How important are these factors? Of the 190 factors in the risk management algorithm, 36% are valuation factors because it reveals more about forward returns than any other factor. Valuation explains the historical frequency of a negative market and more importantly, it explains the historical frequency of a sharply negative market that causes a significant loss in portfolio value.

In my research, I formed a hypothesis that the largest declines in stock market history occurred when valuations were the highest. I reviewed several publicly available databases to see if my conclusion was correct, but none of the databases contained an apples-to-apples comparative analysis of whether there was an identifiable relationship between historic P/E ratios and market performance.

As you will read later in this chapter, relevant historical analysis is contingent upon comparing apples with apples, something surprisingly missing in stock market valuation studies. Typically, these studies compared today's apples with apples picked years ago. In effect, they are comparing apples with oranges. Significant accounting changes and other factors renders valuation conclusions drawn by comparing current stocks or earnings with those of other time periods irrelevant.

As I could find nothing to support or disprove my hypothesis in existing studies, I decided to conduct my own independent analysis. My first challenge was to figure out how to value companies within the same era, avoiding the factors that distorted other historical analyses. These distortions are caused primarily by huge changes in accounting and auditing methodologies over the past century. More about these changes later in the chapter.

The first step in the process was calculating a rolling average of U.S. stock earnings of every 12-month period in the last century, beginning in 1924. This study resulted in 1,171 separate observations. While the process was somewhat similar to what Schiller did with this cyclically adjusted price to earnings ratio, where Schiller took 10-year trailing earnings, I took five-year backwards earnings and five-year forwards earnings and averaged them, dividing by 10 to produce a rolling average earnings ratio for each year in each 10-year period (see graphic 5.3).

$$\text{Rolling Average Earnings} = \frac{\text{Trailing Five Year Earnings} + \text{Forward Five Year Earnings}}{10}$$

(Graphic 5.3 Rolling Average Earnings)

Next, I took the actual price of the stock market for that year and divided by the rolling average earnings ratio I calculated in the first step to arrive at a rolling average P/E ratio (as shown in graphic 5.4).

$$\text{Rolling Average P/E} = \frac{\text{Price}}{\text{Rolling Average Earnings}}$$

(Graphic 5.4 Rolling Average P/E)

I then took the P/E ratio for that year and divided it by the rolling average P/E ratio I created in step two, which created an entirely new ratio, the *Zabrowski Value Ratio* (ZVR) (as depicted in graphic 5.5).

$$\text{Zabrowski Value Ratio} = \left(\frac{\text{P/E}}{\text{Rolling Average P/E}} - 1 \right)$$

(Graphic 5.5 Zabrowski Value Ratio)

The ZVR creates a ratio between the numerator and denominator. I subtract one from that ratio. If the two are the same, the ratio would be a 1 and the ZVR would be 0. If the current P/E ratio is higher than the rolling average P/E ratio, the ZVR ratio would be more than 1, such as 1.2 or 1.5. Subtracting 1 from that ratio results in 20 percent or 50 percent. Conversely, if the current P/E ratio is lower than the rolling average P/E ratio, the ZVR ratio would be less than 1, such as .8 or .5. Subtracting 1 from that results in negative 20 percent or negative 50 percent.

I did that calculation for each month of every year of every 10-year period since 1924. I then sorted them—highest to lowest—into four groupings (as shown in graphic 5.6). The groupings refer to when the ZVR is either:

- Above 25% positive
- 0-25% positive
- 0-25% negative
- Below 25% negative

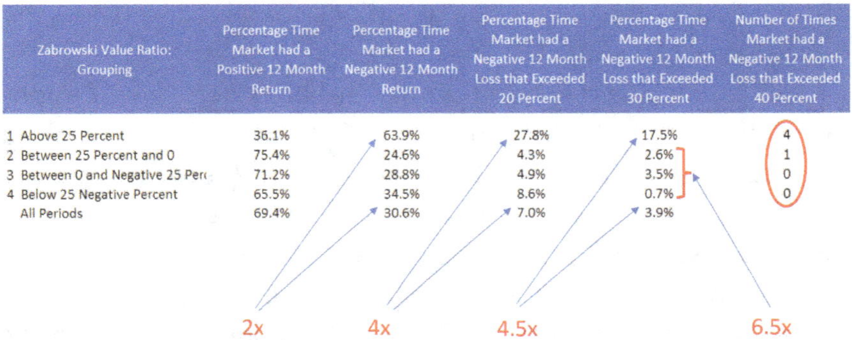

Zabrowski Value Ratio: Grouping	Percentage Time Market had a Positive 12 Month Return	Percentage Time Market had a Negative 12 Month Return	Percentage Time Market had a Negative 12 Month Loss that Exceeded 20 Percent	Percentage Time Market had a Negative 12 Month Loss that Exceeded 30 Percent	Number of Times Market had a Negative 12 Month Loss that Exceeded 40 Percent
1 Above 25 Percent	36.1%	63.9%	27.8%	17.5%	4
2 Between 25 Percent and 0	75.4%	24.6%	4.3%	2.6%	1
3 Between 0 and Negative 25 Perc	71.2%	28.8%	4.9%	3.5%	0
4 Below 25 Negative Percent	65.5%	34.5%	8.6%	0.7%	0
All Periods	69.4%	30.6%	7.0%	3.9%	

(Graphic 5.6 ZVR Groupings)

When I reviewed the graphic, what I discovered was nothing short of astounding.

When the ZVR was more than 1.25 or 25% above the rolling average P/E, the frequency of a major market decline was incredibly higher than all other observations.

During normal markets ("all periods" in the graphic), there was a 12-month positive return 69.4% of the time and a 12-month negative return 30.6% of the time. As expected, the market typically takes two steps forward and one step back over extended periods.

When the ZVR was more than 25% above the rolling average P/E ratio however, the stock market was positive only 36.1% of the time and negative 63.9% of the time. What this means is that during those periods, the market was more than twice as likely to have a 12-month negative return than during the average period.

As striking as that differential is, the next column, where the market had a 12-month negative return exceeding 20%, is even more telling. Of all the observations for grouping 1 under these conditions, 27% of the time, the grouping had a negative return exceeding 20%. Compare that with all periods, where a 20% negative return was observed only 7% of the time.

When the market had a negative return exceeding 30% for a 12-month period, 17.5% of the observations in grouping 1 lost 30% or more whereas less than 4% of the observations in all periods demonstrated that loss. Under these conditions, the percentage of observations of the other three groupings combined were less than half those of grouping 1.

Just as important, when the market had a negative 12-month loss exceeding 30%, ZVR grouping 2 (between 25% and zero) was observed just 2.6% of the time, grouping 3 (between zero and negative 25%) was observed just 3.5% of the time, and grouping 4 (below negative 25%) was observed less than 1% of the time.

Over the span of about a century, there were five occasions when the market suffered a 40% plus 12-month decline. Four of the five times, the ZVR was more than 25% above the rolling average P/E. In other words, four of the five greatest declines in the history of the stock market displayed the same condition. The remaining decline was in the second grouping. That's incredibly valuable information when building investment risk-management algorithms.

This irrefutably proves that valuation can help explain historically large stock market declines. This is not to suggest that the ZVR is a predictor of forward market returns but rather that it explains and clarifies conditions that can produce historically large market declines. The unmistakable conclusion is that valuation factors provide the most reliable interpretation of long-term market returns. While the sentiment, market and economic factors previously discussed contribute to the efficacy of the algorithm, valuation factors are the most heavily weighted.

The longer a portfolio investment time horizon, the more heavily weighted an algorithm should be towards valuation factors, and the more patient investors can be regarding performance. Conversely, the shorter the time horizon, the less weight the algorithm should have in valuation factors because they are the most predictive factors of long-term return.

The process of computing valuation is largely the work of examining financial data using a set of analytical techniques. These include:

1) Normalization
   Statistical Analysis

2) Rate of Change

3) Comparative Analysis
   Price/Earnings Ratios
   Bond Spreads
   Relative Yields

These terms may sound convoluted but while they involve investigation, they are fairly straightforward.

Normalization

Normalization is a technique that helps smooth out anomalies and can be applied on a micro or macro level. On a micro level, normalization of a company's financial statements—including earnings, cash flow, sales and other factors—involves adjusting or discounting non-recurring expenses or revenues so that they only reflect the company's usual (normal) transactions. Financial statements often contain expenses that do not constitute a company's normal business operations and that may distort the company's earnings. Normalization mitigates the impact of these aberrations and helps provide more accurate historical information that enables reliable comparisons and forecasting.[108]

Let's say we are analyzing a country club as an investment. Looking at the financials, we see that the club has made a consistent annual profit until the Covid pandemic hit, causing large numbers of members to avoid the club for an extended period. Obviously, that dramatically changes the club's profit picture. Assuming the club has since returned to its normal operations, member participation and profitability, we would "normalize" the club's earnings by ignoring the one-time pandemic event and not extrapolate it on a going-forward basis.

Similarly, if during the pandemic, the club decided to raise capital by selling off an adjacent piece of land it owned, we would disregard the infusion of money from the sale in our micro-level analysis because that event is not representative of the club's financial outlook for the upcoming years.

On the other hand, if large numbers of the club leave for extended periods each year to escape the cold winters, that is a normal annual occurrence and not regarded as an outlier event.

Normalization is also one of the principal macro analytic techniques used to value a market, such as the S&P 500. Yale University professor of Economics and Nobel Laurate Robert Schiller, renowned for his financial acumen, created the most widely quoted normalizing technique, the cyclically adjusted price to earnings ratio (CAPE), which analyzes the earnings of all of the companies in the S&P 500 relative to the overall value of the market. Viewed by some in the academic community and financial industries as one of the best forecasting tools for stock returns, CAPE calculates the market's average earnings for the previous ten years and compares that data to the current price.

The price/earnings or P/E ratio is computed by dividing a company's stock price by its earnings per share, typically for the previous 12-month period. The P/E ratio can also be used to gauge the market as a whole, as Robert Schiller did by taking a ten-year historical snapshot of the market. By including earnings from the previous decade, he normalized the economic variants associated with booms and recessions. When the market is booming, earnings tend to be overstated. During a recession, earnings are typically understated. Schiller's normalizing technique assessed average earnings over an extended time period and used his CAPE calculation to smooth out the peaks and valleys.

Like virtually all market analysts, we have enormous respect for Dr Schiller and his significant contributions to market valuation. The issue we have with that approach is that while it is valid from an academic standpoint, when it comes to actually making money in a capitalist environment, what happened a decade ago doesn't have much relevance to what is transpiring in the market today—or what is likely to occur in the coming years.

We also use normalization techniques to level out the business cycle. However, we don't believe what occurred in the economy ten years ago is always relevant to what is happening today, so we use a different timeline calculation. We use a five-year period of normalization—four years back and one year projected forward—to arrive at five years of normalized earnings. We believe this technique to normalize market earnings is a more accurate analysis of macro factors.

Normalization is, as its name implies, an attempt to make all types of financial data—whether on a micro basis for individual companies or a macro basis for the market as a whole—more normal. Over an extended period, normalized earnings are a critical valuation factor and, in my opinion, one of the most compelling illustrations of valuation any investor can look at.

Having read about normalized earnings, you may want to reread the previous section on rolling average P/E ratio analysis and the study from Merrill Lynch because they utilize normalization factors and I think you may gain an even better understanding of its importance.

Statistical Analysis Using Regression

Statistical analysis using regression is a way of saying the farther something gets away from its average, the more likely it is to revert to its average or mean. In finance, the more abnormal the investment environment becomes, the more likely it is to stop being weird and return to normal.

As an investor, we calculate something called standard deviation, that is, how much something deviates from a standard. A good way to visualize standard deviation is with a bell curve, as in graphic 5.7, which describes the shape of data conforming to a normal distribution.[109]

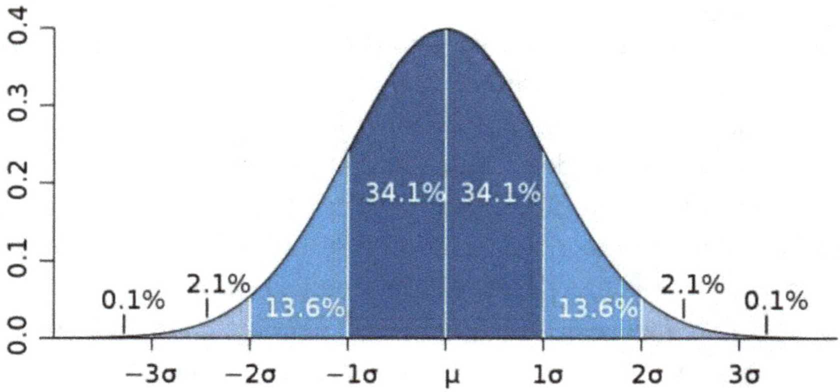

(Graphic 5.7 Standard Deviation)

To illustrate standard deviation, let's assume you go to a major city and advertise that you want to measure the weights of men aged 40 and will pay each participant $25. The stipend is inconsequential except that you probably won't get many volunteers without an inducement.

Let's further assume 1,000 men show up for measurement. You now have a distribution of weights of 1,000 men of the same age. You can plot that data on a graph and create a bell curve. The majority of the weights will fall into the "average weight" category for men aged 40. Based on current medical research, let's say the median is 190 lbs. One standard deviation (SD) less would be 40 lbs. less or 150 pounds. One SD above the 190 median would be 40 lbs. more or 230 lbs. Similarly, two SDs below the median would be 110 lbs. and two SDs above 190 would be 270 lbs. The remaining men, either uncommonly obese or exceptionally slim, will fall into the "long tail" of the bell curve at the extreme outsides—plus or minus 3 SDs.

When investing our capital, the SD calculation tells us if the market, like the men in the study, is currently in the "average weight" category, somewhat overweight or skinny, or grossly obese or anorexic.

As an investor, statistical analysis using regression allows us to identify outlier events. It helps us conclude that when things are highly unusual, we can assume they will eventually come back to normal, and that the more atypical things are, the sooner they are apt to do so. Plotted on a bell curve, the further away from the mean and closer to the tail, the higher the probability things are going to start moving in the opposite direction, back towards the mean. As an investor, you want to make sure you are not making decisions based on outlier events, that is, an environment that falls too close to the tail of the bell curve.

> *"The four most expensive words in the English language: "This time it's different."*
>
> Sir John Templeton

Rate of Change

Another analytic technique for measuring value is calculating the rate of change of specific data from one period to another—such as year to year, quarter to quarter or month to month—on a percentage basis.

Going back to the previously mentioned country club as an investment, we might look at the maximum number of members the club can reasonably maintain. How far away is the club from that number? How fast is it growing and is that representative of expected future growth? That analysis is how we would identify the rate at which a piece of financial data—in this case the club membership rate—is changing.

Let's say company ABC has $100mn in sales and has been growing sales at a rate of $10mn annually. So, five years ago, they had sales of $50mn and grew $10mn during the year to reach $60mn, a 20% growth rate. The following year, they grew from $60mn to $70mn, a growth rate of roughly 16%. As you can see, despite consistent growth of $10mn annually, their rate growth rate is slowing. Last year, when they grew from $90mn to $100mn, their rate of growth dropped to 11%.

Now let's say the company makes an acquisition of company XYZ with $50mn in sales and consolidates the acquired company's financials into their own. Their annual sales are now at $150mn and as a result, a computer program might mistakenly assume their growth rate had soared 50%. When we qualitatively value that business, however, we will not use that 50% figure in our analysis. Instead, we calculate a blended growth rate based on the newly merged company.

Company ABC, now representing two-thirds of total sales, is currently growing at a rate of 11%. Let's assume that newly acquired company XYZ, representing one-third of total sales, is growing at 30%. Thus, the weighted average of growth for the combined companies is roughly 17%.

You might think of the different analytical techniques as tools. Just as building a house requires a set of different tools, establishing a value for a business or a market involves a variety of tools to arrive at an accurate valuation. In this example, we used a rate of change calculation to measure the company's growth pattern and a normalized technique (weighted average) to discount the effect of the acquisition on the growth rate. The application of the techniques is similar but the rate of change is a hammer and the normalization is a saw. They are different tools and we use them in a variety of different ways to evaluate a variety of data sets.

Comparative Analysis

In its simplest form, comparative analysis is simply taking a number or measurement from one data set and comparing it to a number or measurement from another data set.

The comparison might be data from a company's current financial statement with data from previous years, or data from one company with comparable data from another, similar company, typically one in the same industry.

In valuing a company, the major sources of information are the statement of operations, balance sheet, cash flow statement and owner's equity statement. The statement of operations reveals the company's income or earnings; the balance sheet describes the company's financial position; the statement of cash flows shows the movement of cash; the statement of shareholders' equity displays overall health and stability of the business.[110]

The Statement of Operations

The Statement of Operations is also known as an income statement or profit and loss statement and is generated either quarterly or monthly. It includes a summary of revenues, expenses and profit, both operating (revenue gained via the company's primary activities) and non-operating (revenue from non-core business activities).

Graphic 5.8 is an example of a statement of operations, this one from Apple, Inc.

The statement of operations is presented in a straightforward manner, allowing any interested party to quickly gain a clear understanding of how the company is doing. The statement includes sales, cost of sales, operating expenses and income, taxes and net income.

Apple Inc.

CONSOLIDATED STATEMENTS OF OPERATIONS
(In millions, except number of shares, which are reflected in thousands, and per-share amounts)

	Years ended		
	September 30, 2023	September 24, 2022	September 25, 2021
Net sales:			
Products	$ 298,085	$ 316,199	$ 297,392
Services	85,200	78,129	68,425
Total net sales	383,285	394,328	365,817
Cost of sales:			
Products	189,282	201,471	192,266
Services	24,855	22,075	20,715
Total cost of sales	214,137	223,546	212,981
Gross margin	169,148	170,782	152,836
Operating expenses:			
Research and development	29,915	26,251	21,914
Selling, general and administrative	24,932	25,094	21,973
Total operating expenses	54,847	51,345	43,887
Operating income	114,301	119,437	108,949
Other income/(expense), net	(565)	(334)	258
Income before provision for income taxes	113,736	119,103	109,207
Provision for income taxes	16,741	19,300	14,527
Net income	$ 96,995	$ 99,803	$ 94,680
Earnings per share:			
Basic	$ 6.16	$ 6.15	$ 5.67
Diluted	$ 6.13	$ 6.11	$ 5.61
Shares used in computing earnings per share:			
Basic	15,744,231	16,215,963	16,701,272
Diluted	15,812,547	16,325,819	16,864,919

See accompanying Notes to Consolidated Financial Statements.

(Graphic 5.8 Apple Consolidated Statement of Operations)

The Balance Sheet

The Balance Sheet is also known as a statement of net worth—discloses current and non-current assets, current and non-current liabilities and shareholders' equity. In the graphic, it is referred to as a consolidated balance sheet. Graphic 5.9 is an example.

Current assets include cash and equivalents, short-term securities, accounts receivable and inventory. Non-current assets include long-term securities, plant, property and equipment and intangible assets, such as patents, licenses, brands and goodwill. Current liabilities include accounts payable, current debt and notes payable and the current portion of long-term debt. Non-current liabilities include bonds payable and long-term debt.

Apple Inc.

CONSOLIDATED BALANCE SHEETS
(In millions, except number of shares, which are reflected in thousands, and par value)

	September 30, 2023	September 24, 2022
ASSETS:		
Current assets:		
Cash and cash equivalents	$ 29,965	$ 23,646
Marketable securities	31,590	24,658
Accounts receivable, net	29,508	28,184
Vendor non-trade receivables	31,477	32,748
Inventories	6,331	4,946
Other current assets	14,695	21,223
Total current assets	143,566	135,405
Non-current assets:		
Marketable securities	100,544	120,805
Property, plant and equipment, net	43,715	42,117
Other non-current assets	64,758	54,428
Total non-current assets	209,017	217,350
Total assets	$ 352,583	$ 352,755
LIABILITIES AND SHAREHOLDERS' EQUITY:		
Current liabilities:		
Accounts payable	$ 62,611	$ 64,115
Other current liabilities	58,829	60,845
Deferred revenue	8,061	7,912
Commercial paper	5,985	9,982
Term debt	9,822	11,128
Total current liabilities	145,308	153,982
Non-current liabilities:		
Term debt	95,281	98,959
Other non-current liabilities	49,848	49,142
Total non-current liabilities	145,129	148,101
Total liabilities	290,437	302,083
Commitments and contingencies		
Shareholders' equity:		
Common stock and additional paid-in capital, $0.00001 par value: 50,400,000 shares authorized; 15,550,061 and 15,943,425 shares issued and outstanding, respectively	73,812	64,849
Accumulated deficit	(214)	(3,068)
Accumulated other comprehensive loss	(11,452)	(11,109)
Total shareholders' equity	62,146	50,672
Total liabilities and shareholders' equity	$ 352,583	$ 352,755

See accompanying Notes to Consolidated Financial Statements.

(Graphic 5.9 Apple Consolidated Balance Sheet)

The Cash Flow Statement

The Cash Flow Statement provides aggregate data regarding all cash inflows a company receives from its ongoing operations and external investment sources. It also includes all cash outflows that pay for business activities and investments during a given period.[111] Graphic 5.10 is an example.

Apple Inc.

CONSOLIDATED STATEMENTS OF CASH FLOWS
(In millions)

	Years ended		
	September 30, 2023	**September 24, 2022**	**September 25, 2021**
Cash, cash equivalents and restricted cash, beginning balances	$ 24,977	$ 35,929	$ 39,789
Operating activities:			
Net income	96,995	99,803	94,680
Adjustments to reconcile net income to cash generated by operating activities:			
Depreciation and amortization	11,519	11,104	11,284
Share-based compensation expense	10,833	9,038	7,906
Other	(2,227)	1,006	(4,921)
Changes in operating assets and liabilities:			
Accounts receivable, net	(1,688)	(1,823)	(10,125)
Vendor non-trade receivables	1,271	(7,520)	(3,903)
Inventories	(1,618)	1,484	(2,642)
Other current and non-current assets	(5,684)	(6,499)	(8,042)
Accounts payable	(1,889)	9,448	12,326
Other current and non-current liabilities	3,031	6,110	7,475
Cash generated by operating activities	110,543	122,151	104,038
Investing activities:			
Purchases of marketable securities	(29,513)	(76,923)	(109,558)
Proceeds from maturities of marketable securities	39,686	29,917	59,023
Proceeds from sales of marketable securities	5,828	37,446	47,460
Payments for acquisition of property, plant and equipment	(10,959)	(10,708)	(11,085)
Other	(1,337)	(2,086)	(385)
Cash generated by/(used in) investing activities	3,705	(22,354)	(14,545)
Financing activities:			
Payments for taxes related to net share settlement of equity awards	(5,431)	(6,223)	(6,556)
Payments for dividends and dividend equivalents	(15,025)	(14,841)	(14,467)
Repurchases of common stock	(77,550)	(89,402)	(85,971)
Proceeds from issuance of term debt, net	5,228	5,465	20,393
Repayments of term debt	(11,151)	(9,543)	(8,750)
Proceeds from/(Repayments of) commercial paper, net	(3,978)	3,955	1,022
Other	(581)	(160)	976
Cash used in financing activities	(108,488)	(110,749)	(93,353)
Increase/(Decrease) in cash, cash equivalents and restricted cash	5,760	(10,952)	(3,860)
Cash, cash equivalents and restricted cash, ending balances	$ 30,737	$ 24,977	$ 35,929
Supplemental cash flow disclosure:			
Cash paid for income taxes, net	$ 18,679	$ 19,573	$ 25,385
Cash paid for interest	$ 3,803	$ 2,865	$ 2,687

See accompanying Notes to Consolidated Financial Statements.

(Graphic 5.10 Apple Consolidated Cash Flow Statement)

The cash flow statement is divided into three sections: operating activities, investing activities and financing activities.

The Statement of Shareholders' Equity

The Statement of Shareholders' Equity is a report depicting share capital—the value of funds that shareholders have invested in the company and retained earnings—the net income that the company decides to keep. Graphic 5.11 is an example.

Apple Inc.

CONSOLIDATED STATEMENTS OF SHAREHOLDERS' EQUITY
(In millions, except per-share amounts)

	Years ended		
	September 30, 2023	**September 24, 2022**	**September 25, 2021**
Total shareholders' equity, beginning balances	$ 50,672	$ 63,090	$ 65,339
Common stock and additional paid-in capital:			
Beginning balances	64,849	57,365	50,779
Common stock issued	1,346	1,175	1,105
Common stock withheld related to net share settlement of equity awards	(3,521)	(2,971)	(2,627)
Share-based compensation	11,138	9,280	8,108
Ending balances	73,812	64,849	57,365
Retained earnings/(Accumulated deficit):			
Beginning balances	(3,068)	5,562	14,966
Net income	96,995	99,803	94,680
Dividends and dividend equivalents declared	(14,996)	(14,793)	(14,431)
Common stock withheld related to net share settlement of equity awards	(2,099)	(3,454)	(4,151)
Common stock repurchased	(77,046)	(90,186)	(85,502)
Ending balances	(214)	(3,068)	5,562
Accumulated other comprehensive income/(loss):			
Beginning balances	(11,109)	163	(406)
Other comprehensive income/(loss)	(343)	(11,272)	569
Ending balances	(11,452)	(11,109)	163
Total shareholders' equity, ending balances	$ 62,146	$ 50,672	$ 63,090
Dividends and dividend equivalents declared per share or RSU	$ 0.94	$ 0.90	$ 0.85

See accompanying Notes to Consolidated Financial Statements.

(Graphic 5.11 Apple Consolidated Shareholders' Equity)

Comparative analysis can be as simple as looking at two things and making a decision about which is better or more attractive. This could be two stocks or two automobiles. The challenge is to make sure we are comparing apples with apples, a basic precept frequently violated by analysts, media talking heads, investors and, sad to say, some financial advisors.

Ratio Analysis

Ratio analysis takes two pieces of information and places one in the numerator and places the other in the denominator to create a ratio. That ratio can then be compared to another ratio.

The Chartered Financial Institute (CFA), which conducts training, guidance and testing for investment professionals, provides an extensive list of financial ratios which candidates studying to become Chartered Financial Analysts must understand in order to pass the rigorous exam. I know because I passed the Level I CFA examination, but it consumed way too much time. Here is a compendium of those ratios:

Activity ratios	Ratio calculation
Inventory turnover	$\frac{\text{Cost of goods sold}}{\text{Average inventory}}$
Days of inventory on hands (DOH)	$\frac{\text{Number of days in the period}}{\text{Inventory turnover}}$
Receivables turnover	$\frac{\text{Revenue or Revenue from credit sales}}{\text{Average receivables}}$
Days of sales outstanding (DSO)	$\frac{\text{Number of days}}{\text{Receivable turnover}}$
Payable Turnover	$\frac{\text{Purchases}}{\text{Average payables}}$
Number of days of payables	$\frac{\text{Number of days in a period}}{\text{Payable turnover}}$
Working capital turnover	$\frac{\text{Revenue}}{\text{Average working capital}}$
Fixed assets turnover	$\frac{\text{Revenue}}{\text{Average fixed assets}}$
Total assets turnover	$\frac{\text{Revenue}}{\text{Average total assets}}$

(Graphic 5.12 Activity Ratios)

Activity ratios measure how efficiently a company performs.

Liquidity ratios	Ratio calculation
Current	$\frac{\text{Current assets}}{\text{Current liabilities}}$
Quick	$\frac{\text{Cash + Short term marketable securities + Receivables}}{\text{Current liabilities}}$
Cash	$\frac{\text{Cash + Short term marketable securities}}{\text{Current liabilities}}$
Defensive interval	$\frac{\text{Cash + Short term marketable securities + Receivables}}{\text{Daily expenditures}}$
Cash conversion cycle	DOH + DSO - Number of days of payables

(Graphic 5.13 Liquidity Ratios)

Liquidity ratios reflect a company's ability to meet short-term debt obligations using its current assets.

Solvency ratios	Ratio calculation
Debt-to-assets	$\frac{\text{Total debt}}{\text{Total assets}}$
Debt-to-capital	$\frac{\text{Total debt}}{\text{Total debt + Total shareholders' equity}}$
Debt-to-equity	$\frac{\text{Total debt}}{\text{Total shareholders' equity}}$
Financial leverage	$\frac{\text{Average total assets}}{\text{Total shareholders' equity}}$

(Graphic 5.14 Solvency Ratios)

Solvency ratios reflect a company's long-term debt structure. The ratios compare a company's debt levels to its assets, equity or annual earnings.

Return on sales ratios	Ratio calculation
Gross profit margin	$\frac{\text{Gross profit}}{\text{Revenue}}$
Operating margin	$\frac{\text{Operating profit}}{\text{Revenue}}$
Pretax margin	$\frac{\text{EBT (Earnings Before Taxes)}}{\text{Revenue}}$
Net profit margin	$\frac{\text{Net income}}{\text{Revenue}}$

(Graphic 5.15 Return on Sales Ratios)

Return on Sales ratios quantify how well a company's assets generate profits relative to its revenue.

Valuation ratios	Ratio calculation
P/E	$\frac{\text{Price per share}}{\text{Earnings per share}}$
P/CF	$\frac{\text{Price per share}}{\text{Cash flow per share}}$
P/S	$\frac{\text{Price per share}}{\text{Sales per share}}$
P/BV	$\frac{\text{Price per share}}{\text{Book value per share}}$

(Graphic 5.16 Valuation Ratios)

Valuation ratios measure the quantity of a company's assets or earnings associated with ownership of the enterprise.

Credit ratios	Ratio calculation
EBIT interest coverage	$\frac{\text{EBIT}}{\text{Gross interest (prior to deductions for capitalized interest or interest income)}}$
EBITDA interest coverage	$\frac{\text{EBITDA}}{\text{Gross interest (prior to deductions for capitalized interest or interest income)}}$
FFO (funds from operations) interest coverage	$\frac{\text{FFO + Interest paid − Operatinf lease adjustments}}{\text{Gross interest (prior to deductions for capitalized interest or interest income)}}$
Return on capital	$\frac{\text{EBIT}}{\text{Average capital}}$ where Capital = Equity + Non-current deferred taxes + Debt
FFO (funds from operations) to debt	$\frac{\text{FFO}}{\text{Total debt}}$
Free operating cash flow-to-debt	$\frac{\text{CFO (adjusted) − Capital expenditures}}{\text{Total debt}}$
Discretionary cash flow-to-debt	$\frac{\text{CFO − Capital expenditures − Dividend paid}}{\text{Total debt}}$
Net cash flow-to-capital expenditures	$\frac{\text{FFO − Dividends}}{\text{Capital expenditures}}$

(Graphic 5.17 Credit Ratios)

Credit ratios are used by analysts doing credit analysis.

Solvency ratios	Ratio calculation
Debt-to-assets	$\frac{\text{Total debt}}{\text{Total assets}}$
Debt-to-capital	$\frac{\text{Total debt}}{\text{Total debt + Total shareholders' equity}}$
Debt-to-equity	$\frac{\text{Total debt}}{\text{Total shareholders' equity}}$
Financial leverage	$\frac{\text{Average total assets}}{\text{Total shareholders' equity}}$

(Graphic 5.18 Leverage Ratios)

Leverage ratios gauge a company's use of liabilities versus equity to finance its assets.

Segment ratio	Numerator	Denominator	Indication
Segment margin	Segment profit (loss)	Segment revenue	Measures a segment's profitability relative to its revenues
Segment turnover	Segment revenue	Segment assets	Measures a segment's ability to generate revenue using assets
Segment ROA	Segment profit (loss)	Segment assets	Measures a segment's operating profitability relative its assets
Segment debt ratio	Segment liabilities	Segment assets	Measures segment solvency

(Graphic 5.19 Segment Ratios)

Segment ratios break down a company's operations into segments by division, subsidiaries or other components that generate their own revenues.

Performance Ratio	Calculation	Indication
Cash flow to revenue	$\frac{\text{CFO}}{\text{Net revenue}}$	Operating cash generated per dollar of revenue
Cash return on assets	$\frac{\text{CFO}}{\text{Average total assets}}$	Operating cash generated per dollar of asset investment
Cash return on equity	$\frac{\text{CFO}}{\text{Average shareholders' equity}}$	Operating cash generated per dollar of owner investment
Cash to income	$\frac{\text{CFO}}{\text{Operating income}}$	Cash generated from operations
Cash flow per share	$\frac{\text{CFO} - \text{Pref. dividends}}{\text{Number of common shares oustanding}}$	Operating cash flow on a per-share basis
Debt payment	$\frac{\text{CFO}}{\text{Cash paid for long term debt repayment}}$	Ability to pay debts with operating cash flows
Dividend payment	$\frac{\text{CFO}}{\text{Dividends paid}}$	Ability to pay dividends with operating cash flows
Investing and Financing	$\frac{\text{CFO}}{\text{Cash outflows for investing and financing activities}}$	Ability to acquire assets, pay debts, and make distributions to owners
Debt Coverage	$\frac{\text{CFO}}{\text{Total debt}}$	Financial risk and financial leverage
Interest Coverage	$\frac{\text{CFO} + \text{Interest paid} + \text{Taxes paid}}{\text{Interest paid}}$	Ability to meet interest obligations
Reinvestment	$\frac{\text{CFO}}{\text{Cash paid for long term assets}}$	Ability to acquire assets with operating cash flows

(Graphic 5.20 Performance Ratios)

Performance ratios reveal whether a company has accumulated too much debt, has too much inventory or has lagging receivables. It is based on CFO: operating cash flow under GAAP or IFRS.[112]

Coverage ratios	Ratio calculation
Interest coverage	$\frac{\text{EBIT}}{\text{Interest payments}}$
Fixed charge coverage	$\frac{\text{EBIT} + \text{Lease payments}}{\text{Interest payments} + \text{Lease payments}}$

(Graphic 5.21 Coverage Ratios)

Coverage ratios measure the ability of a business to pay its debts on time.

Return on investment ratios	Ratio calculation
Operating ROA	$\frac{\text{Operating income}}{\text{Average total assets}}$
ROA	$\frac{\text{Net income}}{\text{Average total assets}}$
Return on total capital	$\frac{\text{EBIT}}{\text{Debt} + \text{Equity}}$
ROE	$\frac{\text{Net income}}{\text{Average total equity}}$
Return on common equity	$\frac{\text{Net income} - \text{Preferred dividends}}{\text{Average common equity}}$

(Graphic 5.22 Return on Investment Ratios)

Return on investment ratios calculate profits relative to balance sheet items.

Price per share	Ratio calculation
Basic EPS	$\frac{\text{Net income} - \text{Preferred dividends}}{\text{Weighted average number of ordinary shares outstanding}}$
Diluted EPS	$\frac{\text{Net income} - \text{Preferred dividends} + \text{Aftertax interest on convertible debt}}{\text{Weighted average number of ordinary shares outstanding} + \text{Number of common shares that would have been issued at conversion}}$
Cash flow per share	$\frac{\text{CFO} - \text{Preferred dividends}}{\text{Weighted average number of ordinary shares outstanding}}$
EBITDA per share	$\frac{\text{EBITDA}}{\text{Average number of common stock}}$
Dividends per share	$\frac{\text{Dividends paid}}{\text{Number of shares outstanding}}$

(Graphic 5.23 Price per Share Ratios)

Price per share ratios divide the stock price by the company's annual earnings per share.

Dividend-related ratios	Ratio calculation
Dividend payout ratio	$\frac{\text{Common share dividends}}{\text{Net income attributable to common shares}}$
Retention rate (b)	$\frac{\text{Net income attributable to common shares} - \text{Common share dividends}}{\text{Net income attributable to common shares}}$
Sustainable growth rate	$b \times \text{ROE}$

(Graphic 5.24 Dividend Related Ratios)

The dividend ratio measures the total dividends paid out to shareholders relative to the net income of the company.

Financial ratios can be used in many ways, such as comparing a company's financial performance to other firms in the industry in order to understand the company's position in the market. Ratios can also be used to determine performance trends or to ascertain the degree of efficiency in the management of assets and liabilities. Ratios can also help to determine if financial resources are being over- or under-utilized.[113]

Apples-To-Apples

Investors tend to evaluate markets from a historic perspective, drawing comparisons between current markets and those of decades past. Wall Street strategists often take this easy route. A typical headline might read: *"Stock prices are high compared to stock prices in 1990 so investors should avoid stocks right now."* That's lazy analysis that reveals nothing of value for investors. Another example: *"European companies are trading at a P/E of 12 versus U.S. companies trading at a P/E of 17, so investors should own European companies."* That's comparing apples to oranges. The European economy is totally different from that of the U.S. The only thing that's consistent is the P/E, but what's being measured is actually very different.

Among Europe's largest 20 companies, only two are technology companies and the two have a combined market capitalization of $600 bn. In the U.S., eight of the 20 largest companies are in technology and their combined market capitalization is $14.7tn. That's roughly 25 times the size of the two European technology companies!

Using the two economies to compare stock market valuation without considering their profitability, growth and future is senseless.

The economic and business environments of the past were markedly different from today for a variety of reasons. Equating today's economy with that of the past is an analytical miscalculation that provides little or no insight. It's hard to believe but prior to the stock market crash of 1929 and the subsequent formation of the SEC in 1934, accounting standards among U.S. companies were essentially non-existent.

While the *Companies Act of 1900* required all registered companies to appoint "auditors" to report on their balance sheets, there were no professional qualification requirements for the auditors, so reporting was often assigned to the least-busy member of management. The reporting obligations were not truly formalized. Double entry accounting and other abuses were commonplace. In effect, companies pretty much decided what constituted proper reporting on an individual basis. Lacking independent oversight, the undisciplined reporting practices continued unabated until the passage of the Securities Acts of 1933-1934 and the formation of the SEC, which becomes a regulator that insists on full disclosure, transparency and historical cost accounting that avoids misleading disclosures on financial statements.[114]

In 1932, a joint effort between a special committee of the American Institute of Accountants (AIA) and the NYSE recommended five "broad principles of accounting which have won fairly general acceptance" which were approved by AIA membership. In its recommendation, the committee noted that, "Within quite wide limits, it is *relatively unimportant* to the investor what precise rules or conventions are adopted by a corporation in reporting its earnings if he knows what method is being followed and is assured that it is followed consistently from year to year."[115]

Imagine that accounting word salad being announced in today's financial environment. Shareholder activists would be bludgeoning the doors of the SEC with blood in their eyes.

Among the most consequential of the decade's developments was the 1936 publication of *Examinations of Financial Statements*, which introduced "generally accepted accounting principles," known as GAAP. Two years later, Congress imposed the "LIFO conformity rule," which permitted companies to use a new inventory method, LIFO, for income tax purposes provided it was also used in all corporate reports. LIFO stands for "last in, first out," a method used to account for inventory. The upshot was intense pressure to allow LIFO as an accepted practice for financial reporting purposes.

Most of the accounting matters during the first half of the 1940s dealt with wartime issues. Differences in accounting practices remained largely irresolute as the regulators were unable to agree among themselves on what constituted proper practice.[116]

One noteworthy event did take place in 1940, prior to the U.S. becoming actively involved in WW II. A monograph by Professors W.A. Paton and A.C. Littleton titled "An Introduction to Corporate Accounting Standards" was published by the American Accounting Association (AAA). The composition was a dramatic defense of historical cost accounting and propagated the *matching principle*, which emphasized the matching of costs with revenues, with assets and liabilities dependent upon the outcome of this matching. It was widely circulated and served to reinforce the revenue-and-expense view practice of accounting, that is, one first determines whether a transaction is a revenue or expense. Once decided, a residue of debit and credit balance accounts—which may or may not fit the definitions of assets or liabilities—are left on the balance sheet. For more than a generation following the publication, the monograph was used as one of the standard textbooks in accounting theory courses.[117]

After WW II, America's economy was primarily manufacturing-based. The fact that less than 15% of the nation's current economy is based on manufacturing is just one example of how accounting dissimilarities among different industries skew historical comparisons.

In 1947, regulators issued *ARB* 32, which attempted to reveal "unusual" and "extraordinary" items on corporate income statements. The SEC chief accountant at the time threatened not to enforce the regulation, based on the SEC's suspicion that companies could not be trusted to use balanced and equitable judgment to distinguish between ordinary and extraordinary items.

Six years later, Congress revised IRS Code to allow companies to use accelerated cost depreciation for income tax purposes. This amendment brought the practice of "deferred tax accounting" to the forefront of regulatory efforts.[118]

The late 1950s saw the concept of convergence arise, largely in response to post WW II global economic assimilation and cross-border capital flow increases. The linchpin of initial efforts was reducing accounting principle differences in major capital markets. This idea of "harmonization" lasted until the 1990s, when it was replaced by the concept of "convergence," a unified set of reliable international accounting standards.[119]

The early 1960s saw Congress enact an "investment tax credit" to help stimulate the economy via internal investment by companies. In response, the Accounting Principles Board (APB) voted to require that the credit be subtracted from the asset cost, and not be included in current earnings. However, pressure from accounting firms and the Kennedy Administration forced the SEC to announce it would allow either accounting method—historical cost accounting or current value accounting—to be used by companies. The decision humiliated the APB but it is only one of many such legislative defeats, primarily caused by persistent industry lobbying.

The controversy roiled by these events had an interesting side effect: the financial press began to pay more attention to financial reporting. This increased corporate awareness of the continuing efforts of the APB to constrict the differences between the two accounting methodologies. Many companies interpreted this as an effort to excise some of their flexibility in adopting an accounting discipline. Many believed the continuing dispute over the treatment of the investment tax credit represented embodiment of political intrusion into the establishment of accounting principles. To government, it was a matter of providing companies with an incentive, including an accounting incentive, to stimulate the growth of the economy. Indeed, the companies themselves favored reporting higher accounting earnings in times of an economic downturn.[120] The investment tax credit legislation continued to be a bone of contention between the opposing sides and while it remains a law today, the "credit" was reduced to 0% in 1986 and so is no longer a taxation issue.

In 1973, the APB was replaced by the Financial Accounting Standards Board (FASB). Originally formed by the Securities Exchange Act of 1934, FASB was a joint effort of the American Institute of Certified Public Accountants (AICPA), the American

Accounting Association (AAA) and the National Association of Accountants (NAA). The three private organizations merged into a single FASB entity through the Financial Foundation Act in 1973.[121] The primary role of FASB was to set and improve accounting standards for public and private companies, a change described by some as "the need for consistency and accuracy in financial reporting."

Talk about something being self-evident.

FASB and GAAP enjoy a close collaboration. When businesses and organizations adhere to GAAP, they follow a set of guidelines and rules postulated by the FASB. Essentially, FASB is responsible for maintaining GAAP, while companies are encouraged to implement these principles in their financial reporting activities.[122]

Until the Sarbanes-Oxley (SOX) Act of 2002 (SOX), enforcement of accounting standards has been pretty much a hit or miss proposition. While calls for accounting methods that accurately report current finances and project future conditions continued unabated, abuses similarly continued. From the 1929 crash triggered by margin accounts to the ethical violations and accounting scandals of the past few decades, well-intentioned regulators have nonetheless largely been holding a tiger by the tail. The fact that so many egregious breaches of public trust occurred, even after decades of futile attempts to prevent such disasters, is yet another reason why relying on conflicting historical comparisons for investment evaluation is senseless.

Consider the carnage wreaked by Enron's outrageous accounting efforts to hide billions in bad debt, or WorldCom's $11bn in revenue inflation. Tyco's accounting gymnastics concealing $150mn in theft by senior executives (later jailed for 8 to 25 years) seems almost paltry when compared to some of the other scandals. A similar fate awaited the CEO of HealthSouth, who inflated earnings by $1.8 bn and sold $75 million in personal stock a day before the firm suffered a huge loss, giving a new meaning to the term "management transparency."[123] The accounting firm of Arthur Andersen collapsed due to its association with Enron. A verdict of obstruction of justice against the firm was later overturned in 2005 by the U.S. Supreme Court.

From 1990 to 2004, the FASB and the SEC made significant accounting changes that have had a material effect on post-retirement healthcare costs, gains and losses on financial instruments, off balance sheet accounting, comprehensive income, goodwill amortization and intangible assets, pensions, derivatives instruments and hedging activities, businesses combinations, M&A and employee stock options.[124]

In 1991, FASB proposed changing the accounting standard for the reporting of corporate stock options, a move that was vigorously opposed, in particular by high tech firms during the dot.com boom that relied on the perq to recruit talented employees.

Intense lobbying forced FASB to abandon the proposal in the early 1990s when the U.S. Senate voted 88-9 to quash it. FASB reacted by issuing SFAS 123, a compromise standard which required companies to disclose stock options and their fair value in the footnotes of their financial reports or proxy statements. It wasn't until a decade later, after the accounting debacles at Enron, Global Crossing, WorldCom and other scandals, that the FASB again took up the battle of expensing stock options, a struggle that eventually resulted in the passage of SOX in 2002.[125]

In 1991, The American Institute of Certified Public Accountants (AICPA) formed a special committee on financial reporting to address concerns about the relevance and usefulness of business reporting. The objectives included enhancing the utility of business reporting, improved detection of fraud, assuring the objectivity of independent auditors and strengthening the auditing profession's disciplinary system.[126]

In 1993, the committee issued its report, "Improving Business Reporting—A Customer Focus." Based largely on extensive interviews with both investors and creditors, the committee concluded that while financial statements were an important component of the information users needed to make investment and credit decisions, corporate financial statements were not meeting some key information needs. In short, "Don't scrap the financial reporting system; improve it." Because of what it heard, the Jenkins committee made numerous recommendations to enhance financial reporting or, more broadly, business reporting. Its key recommendation was for standard setters and regulators to develop a comprehensive model of business reporting to better meet investor information needs.[127]

The intensity of the conflict between corporate/accounting industry interests and regulatory agencies like FASB was exemplified by the lobbying efforts wielded on behalf of preserving the historical "status quo" and defeating legislation of stock options, tort reform and the attempt to separate auditing and consulting. The Center for Responsive Politics reported that the accounting industry made up to $56mn in federal campaign contributions during the 1990s.[128]

Before the accounting scandals of the early 2000s led to the passage of SOX, accounting was, to a large extent, a self-regulating industry. While FASB was delegated the authority to set accounting standards by the SEC, the scandals that took place in the late 1990s and early 2000s made it clear that serious issues remained hidden within both the accounting industry and the American business community in general. The stock market was booming and with almost no regulation from outside the profession, major accounting firms literally audited and regulated each other, an incestuous practice that ultimately contributed to the accounting scandals.

At the time, the industry was dominated by the "Big 5" of Arthur Anderson, Deloitte & Touche, Ernst & Young, KPMG Peat Marwick and PricewaterhouseCoopers. Each enjoyed the reputation of being trustworthy and knowledgeable. PBS once described Arthur Anderson as the "gold standard of integrity in auditing." Of course, all that changed dramatically with the demise of Enron.[129]

In November 2001, the SEC adopted amendments that sought to determine auditor independence, given the spate of investments by auditors or family members in their client companies, as well as employment relationships between the two.

The amendments identified certain non-audit services and effectively shrunk the number of family and former firm personnel whose employment could impair an auditor's independence. Finally, the amendments required most public companies to disclose the non-audit services provided by their auditor in their annual proxy statements.[130]

These events ultimately led to the 2002 passage of SOX. Virtually everything that occurred prior to 2002 had little or no relevance to modern business accounting. Historical financial comparisons to pre-2002 conditions are the equivalent of a comparison between a 1961 IBM Selectric typewriter and a 2024 Apple computer. They both provide communications capabilities, but as any writer will tell you the similarities end there.

Investors who rely on stock recommendations from advisors using historical or international correlations are making decisions based on irrelevant data. It's the equivalent of comparing modern pedigree analysis of thoroughbred horses with that of horses that existed 50 or 60 years ago, prior to industry-wide regulation of performance-enhancing drugs.

As a thoroughbred owner, something that has struck me as strange is why Secretariat, regarded as the greatest thoroughbred of all time, was only able to win the world's most prestigious race, the Kentucky Derby, by just two lengths? Wouldn't you think the fastest horse in history would win that race by a much wider margin?

The elephant in the room is that the race was run in 1973, far in advance of the Horseracing Integrity and Safety Act of 2020 (HISA), which changed equine anti-doping medication policies and punishments, among other racing practices. Back in 1973, a lot of horses—particularly those in big-money stakes races—were juiced...much like some home run hitting baseball players and financial statements were juiced back then.

Companies, regulations and accounting practices have all changed materially over the years and here in the U.S., ultimately reached a point in the new millennium in July 2002 with the passage of SOX, authorizing rigid reforms and imposing harsh new penalties. In plain words, Congress warned that those who violated the rules would be prosecuted and jailed. It changed the rules with a crescendo.

My ratio analysis is based on previous years after the passage of the 2002 SOX Act. SOX sought to strengthen auditing and public disclosure requirements at major public corporations following the accounting scandals previously mentioned. It was a seminal event in terms of performing reliable ratio analysis because previous to SOX, analysis would invariably lead investors to conclude that stocks were too expensive. Comparing current stock prices to those of years prior to the impact of SOX caused many to miss out on one of the greatest boom periods in history.

Whistleblowers

Whistleblowers are typically company employees who report improper or unethical behavior. Violations include discrimination, predatory sales practices, hazardous working conditions and others.

Throughout the years, the careers of whistleblowers were jeopardized or effectively ended when they risked exposing corporate or government wrongdoing. A. Ernest Fitzgerald had virtually no protection when he exposed major Pentagon cost overruns in the late 1960s. The Whistleblower Protection Act had not yet been enacted, so when Fitzgerald blew the whistle during publicly televised appearance before Congress's Joint Economic Committee in 1968, he was subsequently fired from his job as cost analyst of military projects.

His superiors should have known better than to advise Fitzgerald to avoid answering Capitol Hill questions about costs related to Lockheed C-5A transport planes. Fitzgerald ignored their warnings and, stunning policymakers, announced the planes were running $2bn over budget. After his dismissal, he was later reinstated but the Air Force made sure to keep him away from the important projects and contractors. After his death, his daughter told *The Washington Post* that they "put him in charge of inspecting bowling alleys in Thailand."

Fitzgerald's courage helped lead to the enactment of the Whistleblower Protection Act of 1989, which to this day, helps protect whistleblowers from employer retaliation.[131]

"The most dangerous man in America" is how Henry Kissinger, then foreign policy advisor and soon to be Secretary of State, labelled whistleblower Daniel Ellsberg in 1971. Ellsberg, a military analyst and researcher, committed the "crime" of releasing the "Pentagon Papers" containing nearly 7,000 Department of Defense documents to *The New York Times* and other newspapers. The disclosure revealed that the U.S. Government had lied to the American public for decades about the country's involvement in the Vietnam War. Ellsberg was charged with espionage and faced up to 115 years in prison before being acquitted in 1973.[132]

Another famous whistleblower case was the anonymous "Deep Throat" who provided information to reporters at *The Washington Post* that resulted in the impeachment and resignation of President Richard Nixon in 1974.[133] For the next 30 years, speculation about the identity of the secret informant to Bob Woodward and Carl Bernstein, the *Washington Post* reporters who broke the Watergate scandal in 1972, ran rampant. In 2005, he was identified as W Mark Felt, Associate Director of the FBI.

While Watergate eventually led to the President's resignation and prison terms for two top Nixon officials, since the revelation of Felt's identity, historians have debated whether he acted as informant due to ethical concerns, or if it was simply a bid to get the top job at the Bureau. Either way, Felt is one of most famous whistleblowers in U.S. history.[134]

In 2002, vice president of internal audits Cynthia Cooper was the whistleblower who exposed the WorldCom scandal when she informed its board that the company had covered up $3.8bn in losses via deceptive bookkeeping.[135] When Cooper confronted a partner at Arthur Anderson, the firm's accountant, with the reversed accounting entries, he expressed no concern, indicating that based on its audit testing, the company's allowance was over-reserved in other areas of the company, and so, from a total company perspective, it was adequate. When WorldCom later agreed to restate its financials related to improper capitalization of operating expenses, its stock price had already fallen from a high of $64 in June 1999 to 83 cents.[136]

Cooper was fortunate not to suffer the same fate as other whistleblowers when she was named one of Time Magazine's "Person of the Year" for 2002. In 2007, she published her book, "Extraordinary Circumstances: The Journey of a Corporate Whistleblower."[137]

In 2014, the DOJ recovered $37bn from banks and other financial institutions for their role in the subprime mortgage crisis. Included was the $16.65bn settlement with Bank of America Corporation for misrepresentation of quality of loans and other violations, the largest civil settlement with a single entity in U.S. history. Critical were three whistleblower suits under the False Claims Act.[138]

While whistleblowers today enjoy protections not bestowed upon their counterparts of the previous century, there remains career jeopardy and even imprisonment for those who stray outside the boundaries of the Whistleblower Protection Act.

The impact of this Act is not inconsequential. It is yet another factor that illustrates the short-sightedness of basing investment decisions on pre-1990 data.

Let's shift gears here and take a look at some of the additional elements that make up the algorithm.

Algorithm Components

Every algorithm has a set of defined steps to perform a specific objective. The algorithm contains mathematic equations and established valuation approaches that evaluate factors with the potential to affect the price of an investment.

S&P 500 normalized P/E ratio, a measure of market value, discussed earlier in this chapter.

The P/E ratio is divided into forward and trailing versions. The trailing P/E ratio is calculated by dividing the current share price by the total EPS over the previous 12 months. The forward P/E ratio is calculated by dividing the current stock price by the projected earnings per share. The principal difference between the two is that the trailing P/E is based on actual EPS while the forward P/E is based on EPS estimates.[139]

Earnings per share (EPS), calculated by dividing a company's net income with its total number of outstanding shares, suggests a company's overall profitability of a company. The EPS on the S&P 500 is a calculation of the earnings of all of the 500 US companies listed on the index.[140]

GAAP EPS, the earnings figure derived from generally accepted accounting principles (GAAP).[141] This is a standard that requires every company and industry to report earnings in the same way. Some companies report a second set of numbers referred to as pro forma, adjusted or non-GAAP earnings, which is a consideration when measuring P/E ratios.

Price-to-peak operating earnings is a valuation based on either 12-month trailing, if operating earnings are at a high, or the highest 12-month trailing operating earnings, when they are not.[142] Operating earnings are the profit earned after subtracting expenses directly associated with operating the business from its revenues.[143]

The Median P/E is one for which exactly half of all the stocks have higher ratios and half have lower.

The S&P price to book ratio (P/B) is calculated by dividing the current market price by the S&P book value. It is a valuation analysis to help determine if the market is undervalued or overvalued.

Relative Yields—FCF Yields to Bond Yields

A company's free cash flow (FCF) represents the cash generated by the business after accounting for reinvestment of non-current capital assets. The formula is:

$$FCF = \text{Cash from Operations} - \text{Capital Expenditures}$$

Put another way, FCF is money remaining after a company has paid all its expenses and asset purchases.

FCF Yield

Dividing FCF by the company's market value per share provides the FCF yield, another factor for assessing the value of a company.[144] An annual FCF yield of 15% means that a company is generating 15% of its market capitalization in free cash flow yearly.

Let's say we are interested in buying a company that has $100mn in annual sales and makes $5mn in free cash flow (FCF) that we could take out of the business. To buy it, we have to pay $50mn. Dividing the FCF by the price (market capitalization) (5÷50) we arrive at a FCF/P ratio of 10%, which is the FCF yield. Companies with high or rising FCF and low share prices (low FCF/P ratios) are often considered undervalued. In other words, the higher the ratio, the cheaper the stock.

In the algorithm, this is done at the market level. If the FCF yield on stocks is closer to the bond yield, say 6% or 7% versus 5% for the bonds, we have to consider if that small difference is worth it, and that's where our valuation work using comparative analysis comes in. What kind of a yield can we get from the stock market versus the opportunity from the bond market? If the yield from the bond market is competitive or better than the yield from the stock market, it's an indication that the stock market is overvalued. Contrarily, if we can get 10% yield from the stock market but only 2% yield from the bond market, that's an indication that the stock market is very cheap.

For example, back in 1999, the S&P 500 had a FCF of 2%. At the same time, you could buy a Treasury yielding 5%. Obviously, it made no sense to buy a risky investment yielding 2% when a risk-free 5% yielding bond was available. So, we are constantly comparing relative yields to make sure the financial assets we are considering are appropriately priced.

Making capital allocation decisions is a critical aspect of portfolio management. Choosing the percentage of the portfolio committed to stocks is not an activity conducted in a vacuum; rather, we are continually comparing the relative yield of the market to the yield we can secure elsewhere.

Fundamentally, what we want to do is determine what we have to pay for a business, which becomes the denominator in our equation. Then we ascertain how much we can take out of the business—the FCF; that becomes the numerator. Dividing the two gives us a percentage yield that we can compare to the bonds and make a choice.

EPS Revisions

An earnings estimate is an analyst's assessment of a firm's earnings per share (EPS) for the upcoming quarter or fiscal year. Earnings estimates are developed by analysts who are working for investment research firms.[145]

When a company's earnings report differs from the consensus earnings estimates, it's referred to as an *earnings surprise*. Public companies are required to file earnings reports with the SEC, and analysts often revise their estimates in response to these surprises. When analysts revise their estimates upward, the stocks tend to outperform, even if the anticipated earnings do not occur. Stocks with negative earnings revisions tend to underperform.[146]

Many years ago, one of my mentors told me the thing to understand about earnings forecasts is that they are all going to be wrong, and that the best of them will not be accurate but rather the least wrong. Analysts have adopted that mentality which allows them to make fearless forecasts, knowing they will not be precise and, in fact, will likely be wrong. They have the benefit of being able to revise their work. When they revise a forecast, it can have a dramatic impact on a security's price, either higher or lower, depending on the revised forecasted earnings.

Companies that are forecasted to have strong future growth because the money they're making today represents a mere fraction of the money that they're expected to be making in the future I refer to as "bright future" companies. The further into the future their earnings are from being recognized, the larger the impact earnings revisions have on the price of their securities.

When these growth rates disappoint, it can have a huge impact on the valuation of that company. Conversely, when a currently profitable company that has already established its value—a "bright past" company—has earnings miss, it may hurt that business, but not to the magnitude an earnings miss will damage the value of a bright future company that is forecasted to have much higher earnings at some future point.

An analogy would be the favorite restaurant you've been eating at for the past decade. It's consistently good, which is why you keep going back. If you have one bad meal there, you tend to dismiss it because it has established itself as a good place to eat in your estimation. On the other hand, if a new restaurant opens with great reviews and you experience a bad meal on your first visit, it has a much bigger impact on your opinion and you're less likely to return.

If the vast majority of companies have upside earnings revision surprises, a rising market tends to follow. If most companies fail to achieve their forecasted earnings and are revised down, a bear market tends to ensue.

Business Valuation Approaches

The individual business (or investment) decision is centered around the question of *What is this worth?* In other words, how much should I pay for this investment to receive a high return? That question involves the process of how to determine the intrinsic value of an enterprise.

Enterprise value (EV) is a measurement of a company's total value, including its market capitalization, balance sheet cash, and short- and long-term debt.[147] The formula for enterprise value is:

EV = Market Capitalization + Market Value of Debt – Cash and Equivalents

The extended formula is:

EV = Common Shares + Preferred Shares + Market Value of Debt + Minority Interest – Cash and Equivalents.[148]

A simplified example would be if you had unlimited resources and wished to purchase a publicly traded company. Your objective would be to own the company completely and have full control of it. To do this, you would have to buy out all the debt holders and shareholders.

Suppose you are fabulously wealthy—like a Jeff Bezos or Bill Gates—and decide you want to buy an industrial company. You want to fully own that business and secure all of the cash flow it generates. How would you calculate the company's value so that you alone would own that business, that is, getting rid of anyone and everyone who has a claim on the cash flows of the business?

You would have to first buy out all its shareholders—both common and preferred stockholders—plus all the creditors. You would have to weigh how much money it would take to do that. Once you have bought everyone out, you will own all the assets, cash and future cash flows from the business.

Tobin's Q

James Tobin was an American economist and Nobel Prize winner for his analysis of financial markets. An economics professor at Yale University, he also served on John F Kennedy's Council of Economic Advisors. Tobin introduced the critically important concept of "Tobin's *q*" as a measure to predict whether capital investment will increase or decrease. The *q* is the ratio between the market value of an asset and its replacement cost. Tobin held that if an asset's *q* is less than one—that is, the asset's value is less than its replacement cost—then new investment in similar assets is not profitable. If, on the other hand, *q* exceeds one, it's a signal for further investment in similar assets.[149]

One reason why Tobin's contribution is so important is that analysts and investors have historically struggled with ascertaining what things are worth. Tobin answered that question by saying something is worth whatever it costs to replace it, a remarkably simple concept that has been validated for over a half century. Interestingly, it can be applied to determine the value of virtually anything. What is your house worth? It's worth the cost to build another one just like it on a comparable piece of property, with some value added for time.

Tobin gave us a beautiful valuation gift. Once introduced to this concept, it changes how financial professionals look at everything related to companies, assets and markets. Everything is worth what it costs to replace, although some things have no replacement cost because they are priceless or irreplaceable. Our children, for example, are priceless, and if we have reached a certain age, we cannot produce more.

Applied to a business, the ratio is invaluable. For example, what is a plumbing business worth? The business can be started fairly inexpensively: pipes, fittings, some basic tools, a license and a van or truck. In terms of worth, it's a business that can be easily replicated. If, however, the business has been around for 20 years and enjoys a heavy volume of repeat customers, it's not as easily reproduced and the analysis to determine its worth becomes more complicated.

So, the more complicated a business or enterprise becomes, the harder it is to determine replacement costs. In some instances, replacement is virtually impossible. For example, what would it cost to replace Amazon? The answer is you can't replace it. It is impossible to apply the concept to larger, more complex enterprises. But aside from that, replacement cost is literally the first thing I look at in calculating what something's worth. How difficult would it be to replace this business? If the answer is not very difficult, I don't want to own that business because there's going to be a lot of competition from other people in the future that are going to create a similar business that will erode my profitability.

If I find a business, however, that even if I had a couple billion dollars, I couldn't replace it, take business away from it, or even make a dent in its market share, that's a business I'm interested in as an investor. That's the type of business I want to own.

Discounted Cash Flow Analysis

The safest way to become wealthy in capitalism is to invest in cash flow producing assets. Every asset can be categorized in one of two ways: will it produce cash or not? Even if a company isn't paying a dividend, if it's expected to produce free cash flow (FCF) in the future, we value it as if we are buying the entire entity. Most investments—currencies, cryptocurrencies, commodities, tangible assets, precious metals and the like—do not produce FCF. As such, an investor attempting to value these investments is compelled to use analytical approaches that are unreliable.

Discounted cash flow (DCF) is used to estimate the value of an investment based on its expected future cash flows. DCF analysis tries to glean the value of an investment today based on projections of how much money it will generate in the future.[150] DCF may be the most broadly used valuation method because the value of a firm stems from the inherent value of its future cash flows.

Let's use a simple example to illustrate what we mean by "discounting the future free cash flows back to today." Suppose you borrow money from me and promise to give me the $100,000 back in five years. Well, I have two issues with that. Should I assume that money will be worth $100,000 five years from now? No. Because I recognize that inflation is going to eat into the purchasing power of that money over the next five years. There's also the risk that you won't pay me or pay me back fully. Bad things can happen that represent risk. I should not count that as a hundred thousand dollars purchasing power. I have to discount that number.

Buffett uses the single A corporate bond yield to discount future cash flow because it reflects the time value of money of having a low-risk investment and he is typically buying high-quality domestic companies. If I was looking at a riskier business with more uncertainty around its growth estimates, I would typically use a higher discount rate to account for that ambiguity. If I was evaluating an international business, for example, I would use an even higher discount rate to account for the currency risk.

Breakeven Period

Graphic 5.25 illustrates a simple example of how to conduct a discounted cash flow analysis, including the breakeven point in years. I conducted an 18-year analysis using Apple financial statements. (I broke the period down into six three-year segments so it would fit on a single page.)

A major consideration for any investment is, "How long will I have to wait to get my investment back? What's the expected breakeven period?" As you can see, Apple projects to deliver a FCF Yield of 4.4% with a breakeven period of 12 years. That means Apple investors can reasonably expect to recover what they paid for their investment in about 12 years, after which they will own the stock free and clear...for the rest of their lives if they wish. Even if Apple as a company loses market value, it will not affect the FCF; it will only impact the break-even period.

> *"The urge to participate in something [that] looks like easy money is a human instinct. I've always wanted to get rich slow and I have a lot of fun along the way."*
>
> Warren Buffett

($000,000)		Three Year Periods					
Revenues		2023-2025	2026-2028	2029-2031	2032-2034	2035-2037	2038-2040
iPhone		$ 619,982	$ 677,471	$ 740,291	$ 808,936	$ 883,946	$ 965,912
Mac		90,740	99,154	108,348	118,395	129,373	141,369
iPad		85,752	88,350	91,027	93,786	96,627	99,555
Wearables, etc.		151,909	296,697	527,808	802,730	1,163,721	1,548,913
Services		282,012	375,358	485,247	594,449	714,091	826,649
Total Revenue		1,230,394	1,537,030	1,952,722	2,418,295	2,987,758	3,582,399
Cost of Goods Sold %	50.0%						
Cost of Good Sold		615,197	768,515	976,361	1,209,148	1,493,879	1,791,199
SG&A Expense Percentage	6.0%						
SG&A Expense		73,824	92,222	117,163	145,098	179,266	214,944
Research and Development %	8.0%						
Research and Development		98,432	122,962	156,218	193,464	239,021	286,592
Operating Income		442,942	553,331	702,980	870,586	1,075,593	1,289,663
Income Tax Expense %	15.0%						
Income Tax		66,441	83,000	105,447	130,588	161,339	193,450
Net Income		$ 376,501	$ 470,331	$ 597,533	$ 739,998	$ 914,254	$ 1,096,214
Non Cash Items %	6.0%						
Non Cash Items		73,824	92,222	117,163	145,098	179,266	214,944
Cash Flow From Operations		450,324	562,553	714,696	885,096	1,093,520	1,311,158
Capital Expenditures %	3.0%						
Capital Expenditures		36,912	46,111	58,582	72,549	89,633	107,472
Free Cash Flow		413,413	516,442	656,114	812,547	1,003,887	1,203,686
Apple Market Capitalization	2,900,000						
Free Cash Flow Yield	4.4%						
Break Even Point in Years	12						
Discount Rate Single A Bond Yield	5.0%						
Discounted Cash Flow		374,459	403,895	443,458	474,304	506,459	524,525
Break Even Point in Years	19						

(Graphic 5.25 Apple Example)

Graphic 5.26 (next page) depicts the number of years to breakeven on buying a business based on the FCF growth rate and the price paid for the business.

Looking at the matrix, if I'm considering an investment in Procter & Gamble and its P/FCF multiple is 22 and they're growing their cashflow at roughly 4% annually, it's going to take about 17 years to get my investment back. Alternately, I could invest in Lowes with a FCF yield of about 10 and growing FCF at 12%, a year, in which case I'm going to get my money back in 7 years. That's a lot more attractive.

Number of Years to Breakeven on Buying a Business

Price to FCF	FCF Yield ↓	Free Cash Flow Growth Rate																					
		0%	1%	2%	3%	4%	5%	6%	7%	8%	9%	10%	11%	12%	13%	14%	15%	20%	25%	30%	35%	40%	50%
4.0	25%	4.0	3.9	3.9	3.8	3.8	3.7	3.7	3.6	3.6	3.6	3.5	3.5	3.5	3.4	3.4	3.4	3.2	3.1	3.0	2.9	2.8	2.7
4.2	24%	4.2	4.1	4.0	4.0	3.9	3.9	3.8	3.8	3.7	3.7	3.7	3.6	3.6	3.5	3.5	3.5	3.3	3.2	3.1	3.0	2.9	2.8
4.3	23%	4.3	4.3	4.2	4.1	4.1	4.0	4.0	3.9	3.9	3.8	3.8	3.7	3.7	3.7	3.6	3.6	3.4	3.3	3.2	3.1	3.0	2.8
4.5	22%	4.5	4.5	4.4	4.3	4.3	4.2	4.1	4.1	4.0	4.0	3.9	3.9	3.8	3.8	3.8	3.7	3.5	3.4	3.3	3.2	3.1	2.9
4.8	21%	4.8	4.7	4.6	4.5	4.4	4.4	4.3	4.3	4.2	4.1	4.1	4.0	4.0	3.9	3.9	3.9	3.7	3.5	3.4	3.3	3.2	3.0
5.0	20%	5.0	4.9	4.8	4.7	4.6	4.6	4.5	4.4	4.4	4.3	4.3	4.2	4.1	4.1	4.0	4.0	3.8	3.6	3.5	3.4	3.3	3.1
5.3	19%	5.3	5.2	5.1	5.0	4.9	4.8	4.7	4.6	4.6	4.5	4.4	4.4	4.3	4.3	4.2	4.2	3.9	3.8	3.6	3.5	3.4	3.2
5.6	18%	5.6	5.4	5.3	5.2	5.1	5.0	4.9	4.9	4.8	4.7	4.6	4.6	4.5	4.4	4.4	4.3	4.1	3.9	3.7	3.6	3.5	3.3
5.9	17%	5.9	5.7	5.6	5.5	5.4	5.3	5.2	5.1	5.0	4.9	4.9	4.8	4.7	4.6	4.6	4.5	4.3	4.1	3.9	3.7	3.6	3.4
6.3	16%	6.3	6.1	5.9	5.8	5.7	5.6	5.5	5.4	5.3	5.2	5.1	5.0	4.9	4.9	4.8	4.7	4.4	4.2	4.0	3.9	3.7	3.5
6.7	15%	6.7	6.5	6.3	6.2	6.0	5.9	5.8	5.7	5.6	5.5	5.4	5.3	5.2	5.1	5.0	5.0	4.6	4.4	4.2	4.0	3.9	3.6
7.1	14%	7.1	6.9	6.7	6.6	6.4	6.3	6.1	6.0	5.9	5.8	5.7	5.6	5.5	5.4	5.3	5.2	4.9	4.6	4.4	4.2	4.0	3.7
7.7	13%	7.7	7.4	7.2	7.0	6.8	6.7	6.5	6.4	6.2	6.1	6.0	5.9	5.8	5.7	5.6	5.5	5.1	4.8	4.6	4.4	4.2	3.9
8.3	12%	8.3	8.0	7.8	7.5	7.3	7.1	7.0	6.8	6.6	6.5	6.4	6.2	6.1	6.0	5.9	5.8	5.4	5.0	4.8	4.5	4.4	4.1
9.1	11%	9.1	8.7	8.4	8.2	7.9	7.7	7.5	7.3	7.1	6.9	6.8	6.6	6.5	6.4	6.3	6.2	5.7	5.3	5.0	4.8	4.6	4.2
10.0	10%	10.0	9.6	9.2	8.9	8.6	8.3	8.1	7.8	7.6	7.4	7.3	7.1	7.0	6.8	6.7	6.6	6.0	5.6	5.3	5.0	4.8	4.4
11.1	9%	11.1	10.6	10.1	9.7	9.4	9.1	8.8	8.5	8.3	8.0	7.8	7.7	7.5	7.3	7.2	7.0	6.4	6.0	5.6	5.3	5.0	4.6
12.5	8%	12.5	11.8	11.3	10.8	10.3	10.0	9.6	9.3	9.0	8.7	8.5	8.3	8.1	7.9	7.7	7.6	6.9	6.4	5.9	5.6	5.3	4.9
14.3	7%	14.3	13.4	12.7	12.1	11.5	11.0	10.6	10.2	9.9	9.6	9.3	9.1	8.8	8.6	8.4	8.2	7.4	6.8	6.3	6.0	5.7	5.2
16.7	6%	16.7	15.5	14.5	13.7	13.0	12.4	11.9	11.4	11.0	10.6	10.3	10.0	9.7	9.4	9.2	9.0	8.0	7.4	6.8	6.4	6.1	5.5
20.0	5%	20.0	18.3	17.0	15.9	15.0	14.2	13.5	12.9	12.4	11.9	11.5	11.1	10.8	10.5	10.2	9.9	8.8	8.0	7.4	6.9	6.5	5.9
25.0	4%	25.0	22.4	20.5	18.9	17.7	16.6	15.7	15.0	14.3	13.7	13.1	12.7	12.2	11.8	11.5	11.1	9.8	8.9	8.2	7.6	7.1	6.4
33.3	3%	33.3	28.9	25.8	23.4	21.6	20.1	18.9	17.8	16.9	16.1	15.4	14.8	14.2	13.7	13.2	12.8	11.2	10.0	9.1	8.5	7.9	7.1
50.0	2%	50.0	40.7	35.0	31.0	28.0	25.7	23.8	22.2	20.9	19.8	18.8	17.9	17.2	16.5	15.9	15.3	13.2	11.7	10.6	9.7	9.0	8.0
100.0	1%	100.0	69.7	55.5	46.9	41.0	36.7	33.4	30.7	28.5	26.7	25.2	23.8	22.6	21.6	20.7	19.8	16.7	14.6	13.1	11.9	11.0	9.7

(Graphic 5.26 Number of Years to Break Even Buying a Business)

How to Value a Market

I am often asked what I think of the market. Frankly, I don't think of the market; I think of the individual values of a sample group of comparable companies in the market and I add them up. Trying to value a market from the top-down or by comparing it with other markets makes no sense. You value a market from the bottom-up, one stock at a time.

I apply discounted cash flow analysis to a sample group of 50 comparable companies to arrive at a fair market value and a break-even point. I create an opinion on how attractive the market is based on that analysis, which by far represents the biggest component of my algorithm.

I want to own companies that are solvent, have bright futures and a sustainable competitive advantage. Typically, companies like these have high bond ratings, which is one reason why, like Buffett, I use the single A bond as a benchmark for comparison.

What is an appropriate discount rate of cashflow?

This is a contentious issue in my field, a hot topic that will likely be debated for years to come. In truth, nobody knows for certain exactly what the appropriate discount rate is.

In making that calculation, I assess both equal weight and market weight. Market weight is critical. It's the percentage of the overall market that the market capitalization of a company's stock represents. In this case, Apple has the largest market weight right now. On the other hand, if I assigned equal weight to every company, Apple would be no more important in the calculation than the 50th, or smallest market weighted, company.

Pursuant to valuing a company or market using equal- and market-weighted capitalization, as a mentor once told me, "There's no such thing as a good or bad investment. At a certain price, an investment is a great investment and at a certain price, an investment is a terrible investment."

Interestingly, while every investor makes that calculation when buying a small business or an apartment complex, for whatever reason, they don't apply the same reasoning when they look at stocks. That's yet another reason why Buffett is so successful. He looks at stocks in the prism of owning an entire enterprise. One business may return your investment in seven years, another business may take 15 years. The difference has to do with profitability, growth rates, cash requirements and the level of analytical confidence in those factors. Most importantly, however, is the price I have to pay for the investment.

In any stock purchase, the most important factor over an extended period remains valuation—the price initially paid for the stock. It accounts for the bulk of the portfolio's profitability over time. If you recognize that valuation factors are going to account for over 80% of portfolio variance over a 10-year period, you damn well better know how to accurately assess value. Acquiring that skill should be the "Aha!" moment in any investor's development because if you get that right, you're going to be successful.

CHAPTER SIX

Investment Allocation Decisions

> *"You are neither right nor wrong because the crowd disagrees with you. You are right because your data and reasoning are right."*
>
> Benjamin Graham

Everyday life is teeming with risks, some apparent and some veiled. Our perception of risk has a lot to do with the risks we take. For example, most everyone drives a vehicle and the majority believe they are a better-than-average driver. Yet on average, 32,000 people die in car accidents every year.[151] A survey by AAA revealed that 96% of drivers agree texting or emailing while driving is a serious safety threat, but 39% admitted they had done just that during the previous month.

Have you ever followed someone driving erratically? Are they intoxicated? On drugs? You pull up next to them at a stoplight and realize no, not drunk or on drugs; they are texting, oblivious to the increased risk they have created for themself. And if you drive on ahead of them, your level of risk has now increased as well.

Distinguishing the correct level of risk, whether driving hazards, pharmaceutical side effects or hiking in unfamiliar territory, is tricky business. The levels of risk we encounter constantly change, often unperceptively. Unless we react properly to these changes, we risk our health, our money and our life.

Let's assume that an investor's capacity for risk is compatible with the amount of investment risk currently in the portfolio. That does not mean the optimal result can be attained by maintaining a stagnant level of risk. Target risk should have some flexibility, capable of being modified over an extended period. In the field of investment management, this is accomplished using tactical asset allocation. This simply means we adjust the overall risk based on opportunities and probabilities of bear markets (threats).

Tactical investment allocation differs from strategic investment allocation, which is a buy-and-hold approach of setting percentage allocations to various investment classes and keeping that allocation. Tactical investment allocation, on the other hand, is more proactive. The investment mix can be reallocated in response to changing market conditions in order to enhance returns without compromising a portfolio's long-term average targeted risk.

Calculating a Tactical Allocation

Between the end of WW II and 2023, there have been 15 bear markets, ranging in length from 30 days to 1.7 years.[152] That works out to a bear market occurring roughly every five years. So, under normal circumstances, at any given time, there's a 20% probability of a bear market. Based on that, it's essential to identify the maximum bearish and bullish conditions, as well as the maximum bearish and bullish positioning necessary should these situations occur.

The methodology to formulate a tactical allocation involves the use of four factors previously discussed: sentiment analysis (chapter 2), technical analysis (chapter 3), economic analysis (chapter 4) and fundamental analysis (chapter 5). All of these elements must be evaluated in order to determine how much I should deviate from the portfolio's targeted risk profile. That is to say, how much am I going to change the portfolio's allocation under maximum bearish and maximum bullish conditions?

The importance of this calculation cannot be overemphasized. It is the definitive contrast between the traditional strategy of allocating portfolio investments based on a simplified percentage formula designed to mimic market returns, and an advanced, active approach that searches for alpha opportunities inherent in market fluctuations that can produce larger returns over time.

When the probability of a bear market is normal, no tactical allocation changes are necessary. But as an active investment manager, I'm continually monitoring market conditions for change. What market signals would convince me that we are entering a bullish market?

Using the four analytical factors in a well-constructed algorithm, I would see that:

1) Sentiment analysis tells me that investors are extremely apprehensive and pessimistic.
2) Technical analysis indicates that markets are behaving consistent with historic bull markets.
3) Economic analysis suggests that the economy is entering an expansionary phase.
4) Fundamental analysis reveals that stocks are attractively priced.

Collectively, that group of analytical indicators is maximally bullish. When that occurs, portfolio risk should be substantially increased.

On the opposite end of the spectrum, a barometer indicating a high probability—in excess of the normal 20%—that a bearish market is approaching, the analytical indicators would include:

1) Sentiment analysis reveals that investors are highly optimistic, even euphoric.
2) Technical analysis indicates that markets are reflecting historic bear markets.
3) Economic analysis advises that the economy is overheated and about to roll over.
4) Fundamental analysis says stocks are very expensive.

Taken together, that group of analytical indicators is maximum bearish. When these conditions are present, investors should batten down the hatches and reduce risk in their portfolios.

When either of these probabilities emerges, as a tactical investment manager, I have to make critical risk decisions. There's enormous pressure on making the right decisions when analytic signals indicate significant market movements up or down. This is one reason why the vast majority of advisors embrace a passive investment approach that may be a safer career move but delivers no added value to their investor clients. Even if these passively defensive-minded financial advisors want to be more aggressive when opportunities are abundant and probabilities of bear markets are much lower than normal, all they do is create an investment allocation and live with the results. The fact that they charge a management fee for this do-nothing approach is ludicrous as there is no real investment management involved. They simply set it and forget it.

In addition, they are hamstrung as their compliance departments often prevent a more aggressive approach with restrictive parameters, known as "guardrails." It's an occupational safe path for passive financial advisors but their "hit it down the middle" mentality guarantees they will underperform by the fee amount their clients pay, ostensibly for professional investment management.

As an active manager making tactical allocation changes in response to market fluctuations, I am putting my reputation and career on the line. The tradeoff for me is accepting the professional risk of appearing to be wrong over the short term while pursuing higher returns over an extended period for my investors.

In the following six chapters, you will see that the successful pursuit of these returns has an incredible impact on the lives of investors. They can accelerate their goals, retire earlier and have more money in retirement. They can have more fulfilling legacies, leave more to the next generation or give more to their favorite charities. In this regard, it's important for donors to choose charitable foundations that are competent stewards of the money, charities whose investment manager adds serious alpha, not someone who passively tracks an index. Consider that what may appear to be a relatively insignificant alpha boost of 3% annually would result in a charity being able to impact the lives of twice as many recipients over an extended period.

The stakes are high here. Imagine being one of the needy who, instead of being turned away for lack of funds, can now go on to graduate college, get help to overcome an addiction, be able to escape a hopeless situation and enjoy a productive and fulfilling life. That's quite a legacy.

> *"If you're in the luckiest one percent of humanity, you owe it to the rest of humanity to think about the other 99 percent."*

Warren Buffett

SECTION TWO

Accelerating Financial Goals: Managing Money for Performance

CHAPTER SEVEN

Lessons from Warren Buffett

> *"Time is the friend of the wonderful business, the enemy of the mediocre."*
>
> Warren Buffet

Berkshire Hathaway is the most successful investment company in history. Its founder, Warren Buffett, embraces an investment methodology based on the teachings of Dr. Benjamin Graham, considered the father of value investing.

Buffett was a young man just completing his undergraduate degree at the University of Nebraska when he read Graham's celebrated book, *The Intelligent Investor*. The book's value-driven strategy so impressed Buffett that he decided to attend Columbia Business School, where Graham taught, to pursue his advanced degree. Buffett subsequently worked with Graham. Noted Buffett, "The book changed my life. If I hadn't read it, I'd probably still be delivering papers."[153]

Writing in the *Financial Analyst Journal* following Graham's death in 1976, Buffett affectionately referred to three things he learned from his mentor that he tries to do every day: "Do something foolish, something creative and something generous." He explained that investors don't need to have "great intelligence, a degree in economics or a familiarity with Wall Street jargon such as alpha and beta." He suggested that instead, investors should ignore mob fears or enthusiasms, focus on fundamentals and be willing to look unimaginative—or even foolish—for a sustained period."[154]

Candid Communication

Buffett's willingness to "look foolish" also describes his innate humility and truthfulness, exemplified in his annual shareholder letters, where he unabashedly documents his investment mistakes along with his successes. He communicates in a simple, straightforward manner, whether the message is favorable or unfavorable.

As he said in his 2010 shareholder letter:

> *"As a corollary, let me know promptly if there's any significant bad news. I can handle bad news but I don't like to deal with it after it has festered for a while."*

Buffett doesn't try to impress people with his vocabulary or his knowledge. He speaks plainly and expects the same of the people he does business with, especially CEOs and CFOs of the companies he is considering for investment. His directness is apparent in a quote from his 1983 letter:

> *"We also believe candor benefits us as managers: the CEO who misleads others in public may eventually mislead himself in private."*

Just as Buffett formed his investment philosophy from reading Dr. Graham's books, I formed my investment philosophy by studying Buffett's annual shareholder letters. I began using the same analytical methodologies and lessons learned from history's most successful investors—standing on the shoulders of Titans. Why would I do any different? If I wanted to learn how to play quarterback, I would study Tom Brady. In any endeavor, it only makes sense to mimic those who have gone before and had the greatest success over the longest period of time in all types of environments, not just when the wind was at their back. Consistent, multi-decade success in capitalism is not because of luck; it's because of skill.

I admire Buffett's ability to give equal weight to good and bad news alike when communicating with his investors. I try to do the same with our investor reviews. If there is bad news, I generally talk about it before anything else. My portfolio currently owns 47 different businesses. With that many companies, a portfolio manager is bound to have some challenges and make some mistakes. Being candid about what goes wrong is extremely important.

Eat Our Own Cooking

Buffett has at least 98 percent of his personal net worth invested into the businesses that he owns. I manage our personal portfolio the same way. We own the same companies in our portfolio that my investors own in theirs.

You wouldn't eat at a restaurant where the cook doesn't trust the food. I believe in Buffett's adage: "We eat our own cooking." As a portfolio manager, it's easy to have conversations with investors because we already know what's in their portfolios. We know exactly what their portfolio looks like without having to double check. They own the same companies we own.

I've noticed a disturbing pattern among portfolio managers who stray from their investment mandates over time by accommodating demanding clients with exceptions and special circumstances. We avoid that mistake by adhering to Buffett's statement in his 1983 shareholder letter:

> *"We will only do with your money what we would do with our own, weighing fully the values you can obtain by diversifying your own portfolios through direct purchases in the stock market."*

In my early years in the business, my mentor on Wall Street would invite various investment salespeople representing outside companies to make presentations. When a representative of a brokerage house or mutual fund company came in with a "great investment idea," it was inevitably something immensely popular that had already made a lot of money. My mentor would listen patiently, then ask. "What percentage of your net worth do you have invested in this fantastic idea?" We would all stifle our laughter as the salesman, too embarrassed to give an honest answer, tried to dance around the question.

As Buffett vowed in his 1964 letter:

> *"What we promise you—along with more modest gains—is that during your ownership of Berkshire, you will fare just as we do. If you suffer, we will suffer; if we prosper, so will you. And we will not break this bond by introducing compensation arrangements that give us a greater participation in the upside than the downside. We further promise you that our personal fortunes will remain overwhelmingly concentrated in Berkshire shares: We will not ask you to invest with us and then put our own money elsewhere."*

Avoiding Speculation

Buffett avoids speculations and forecasts. When asked what he thinks the market will do, Buffett defers. He tends to ignore short-term movements in the markets, the economy and other macro factors. His entrepreneurial business ownership approach allows him to be oblivious to whether the market is moving up, down or sideways.

As he notes in his 1988 letter:

> *"As regular readers of this report know, our new commitments are not based on a judgment about short-term prospects for the stock market. Rather, they reflect an opinion about long-term business prospects for specific companies. We do not have, never have had and never will have an opinion about where the stock market, interest rates or business activity will be a year from now."*

A wonderful aspect of this long-term perspective is that regardless of what happens in the markets, our financial situation improves. That's because there are three things that can happen: the market can go up, remain neutral or go down. If up, we improve our financial situation because we get wealthier as a result of our businesses appreciating in value. If the market stays neutral, it provides us with additional time to do more analysis to identify new opportunities before prices change materially. If the market goes down, that gives us an opportunity to accumulate more shares of a company that we think is worth a lot more money than the price before it fell. Like Buffett, I spend zero time thinking about what the market will do tomorrow, next week or next month.

Someone I greatly admired was legendary international value investor Jean-Marie Eveillard. As a young man sitting in his office high above Wall Street, I had some investment ideas I believed to be quite brilliant I couldn't wait to share with him, one of which had to do with the value of currencies. I had a strong opinion that the United States dollar was massively overvalued and about to decline, causing certain investments to greatly benefit. Jean-Marie looked at me, sighed and said, "Son, the best thing that you can do is to go back to your hotel room, look yourself in the mirror and promise yourself that you do not have the ability to predict the future." It was some of the best advice I ever got. As a portfolio manager, once you extricate yourself from the fruitless game of trying to predict unpredictable events, especially short-term market movements, you can apply all that wasted time and mental energy to focusing on things that you actually can control, such as how businesses are valued and their competitive advantages.

Buffett obviously agrees with this wisdom. In his 1994 letter he offers:

> *"We try to price, rather than time, purchases. In our view, it is folly to forego buying shares in an outstanding business whose long-term future is predictable, because of short-term worries about an economy or a stock market that we know to be unpredictable."*

Defining Risk

Buffett, along with other advocates of the Columbia Business School approach, defines risk differently than most academic institutions and portfolio managers. Buffett defines risk as the probability of losing money over a long period of time as opposed to the likelihood that there will be significant price changes in the investments he owns. He not only accepts this volatility but he profits from it.

If you ask your 401k provider about investment risk, they might tell you, "A technology stock is much riskier than this bond because historically, the technology stock has displayed much more volatility (or has a higher standard deviation) than the bond. Buffett and his Columbia Business School proponents would likely respond with, "Well, what's the price?" That's because at some price, that technology stock is far less risky than that bond.

So, we define risk as the probability of losing money on a particular investment, not how much an investment varies from some type of average value according to standard deviation or variance definitions. And we actually enjoy owning assets that have some volatility and change in value because as a portfolio manager, it allows us to have more favorable entry points as investors contribute additional capital to the portfolio. If, for example, an investment has a 10 percent annual return over the next 10 years, but at some point during the decade temporarily suffers a 20 percent decline, by adding capital to the investment at that point, an investor could achieve a significantly <u>higher</u> compounded rate of return than 10 percent.

Circle of Competence

One thing that Buffett has been very clear on is defining his circle of competence. He clarified this in his 1977 letter:

> *"We select our marketable equity securities in much the same way we would evaluate a business for acquisition in its entirety. We want the business to be (1) one that we can understand, (2) with favorable long-term prospects, (3)*

> *operated by honest and competent people and (4) available at a very attractive price."*

Investors tend to lose their way. Jean-Marie Eveillard refers to this as portfolio manager hubris. In his book, *Fooled by Randomness: The Hidden Role of Chance in Life and in the Markets*, author Nassim Nicholas Taleb discusses how portfolio managers, especially successful ones, become misled by the randomness of returns they have attained. They convince themselves that they have a much wider circle of competence than they actually do, an unmistakable sign of hubris. The greatest investors in history eschew hubris. Their competence is genuine because they develop sufficient knowledge about a business to form an unshakable opinion. That knowledge is based on being able to estimate the operating profits of a company over the next 10+ years.

Stretching for Yield

When the markets come under financial stress, demand in the bond markets shifts dramatically. This creates a problem for managers who previously stretched for excess yield and purchased investments like high-yield securities. These investments may provide a higher return than Treasurys or money market funds during a normal market, but demand for them quickly evaporates when markets become stressed, and investors shift to safety. This creates heavy selling pressure on these investments because they tend to be correlated to stocks, so when stocks come under pressure, demand for short-term term debt instruments that provide higher yields but have even slightly more solvency risk wanes.

When markets grow concerned about economic activity and the probability of entering a recession, or an outlier event like a pandemic occurs, demand for those short-term, high-yielding debt instruments dries up and the heavy supply of those investments stampede to sell them. What investors thought was a safe investment becomes illiquid. They have a hard time getting their money out of that investment at precisely the time when they need to access it quickly to take advantage of the falling price of undervalued and attractive stocks.

That's why we never stretch for yield in our safe assets. It's simply not worth the illiquidity risk. This concept is not always easily understood by some investors, who may question why they are paying a manager to put a portion of their portfolio in such a low-risk investment. But as you can see, there's a good reason for keeping some of the portfolio's dry powder in highly liquid investments that can be rapidly converted into cash for opportunistic investments when markets come under distress. There's no worse feeling than being a manager trying to liquidate a floating bank note in a vacillating market when everyone is running for cover. We never want to be in that position. Fortunately, the trust relationships we build with our clients allows us to look them in the eye and calmly explain why we do not chase yield with our safe investments. I apply the same rules to my own money as I do to the money entrusted to me by my investors. Collectively, we have to accept that a certain portion of our portfolios is normally set aside, if you will, to take advantage of market turmoil. We must recognize that we're going to get less return on that money than might be available with other short-term investments, such as lower quality bonds that provide a somewhat higher yield but can become illiquid in a stressful market.

Buffett's portfolio always contains some dry powder for when abnormal events, such as the pandemic, arise and cause valuations to temporarily change. The dry powder reserve is kept in highly liquid U.S. Treasurys.

As Buffett said in his 2003 letter:

> *"When we can't find anything exciting in which to invest, our "default" position is U.S. Treasurys, both bills and repos. No matter how low the yields on these instruments go, we never "reach" for a little more income by dropping our credit standards or by extending maturities."*

Investing in Companies

Buffett doesn't differentiate between investing in a stock and investing in an entire business. He follows the same analytical approach evaluating fractional ownership in a company as he does if buying the entire company.

There is a popular misconception among investors that Buffett has some innate advantage because Berkshire is so big, but actually, the opposite is true. Having such a huge amount of capital under management makes getting alpha—investment returns above a benchmark—more difficult.

As of the end of 2023, the Berkshire Hathaway's total assets amounted to approximately one trillion dollars.[155] If he buys an entire company worth a billion dollars, the purchase represents a tiny fraction—approximately .1 percent—of his total investment capital. If that investment went up or down 20 percent, it would have a miniscule impact on his portfolio, whereas a smaller fund buying a two percent position in the same company would experience a significant bottom line impact on a 20 percent movement. So, in some respects, smaller portfolio managers enjoy an advantage.

In his shareholder letters, Buffett perpetually refers to his long-term goal of increasing the value of the portfolio, or in Berkshire Hathaway's case, the intrinsic value of the company. From his 1993 letter:

> *"Charlie Munger, Berkshire's Vice Chairman, and I can attain our long-standing goal of increasing Berkshire's per-share intrinsic value at an average annual rate of 15%. We have not retreated from this goal."*

He reinforces that objective 14 years later in his 2007 letter: "I should emphasize that we do not measure the progress of our investments by what their market prices do during any given year. Rather, we evaluate their performance by the two methods we apply to the businesses we own. The first test is improvement in earnings, with our making due allowance for industry conditions.

The second test, more subjective, is whether their 'moats'—a metaphor for the superiorities they possess that make life difficult for their competitors—have widened during the year."

I take the same approach as Buffett in assessing potential investments. I don't consider new investments that have an expected return of less than 15 percent. If it's an overseas business where currency risk comes into play, the return must be at least 25 percent. If it's in a country with geopolitical and currency risks, such as an emerging market, around 45 percent.

I prefer domestic companies over international companies and international companies over emerging markets. Within that, I prefer large companies to small companies. If I have a choice between making a 15 percent gain on a domestic or international business, I will always buy the domestic business because I don't have to accept any currency risk.

While many portfolio managers believe there is a diversification benefit for owning companies all over the world, international markets today are tightly correlated to one another. A quarter century ago, global diversification offered some potentially substantial benefits for a portfolio. Today, not so much.

Wide Moat Investing

There's a long history of wide moat investing producing positive alpha. The key is to focus on owning businesses that allow you to have analytical confidence due to their sustainable competitive advantages. The following chart compares the performance of wide moat investing versus the S&P 500, starting in 2007.

Applying Buffett mathematics and discount free cash flows to arrive at intrinsic value that is higher than a company's market price produces returns that exceed benchmarks.

I limit that range of scenarios by selecting companies that have wide moat competitive advantages. An example would be a hypothetical business that has a 20-year product or service contract and every dollar in that contract is specified. I also know with certainty how much that service or good will cost to produce. In this case, I can determine what to pay for that business with absolute precision, similar to a Treasury.

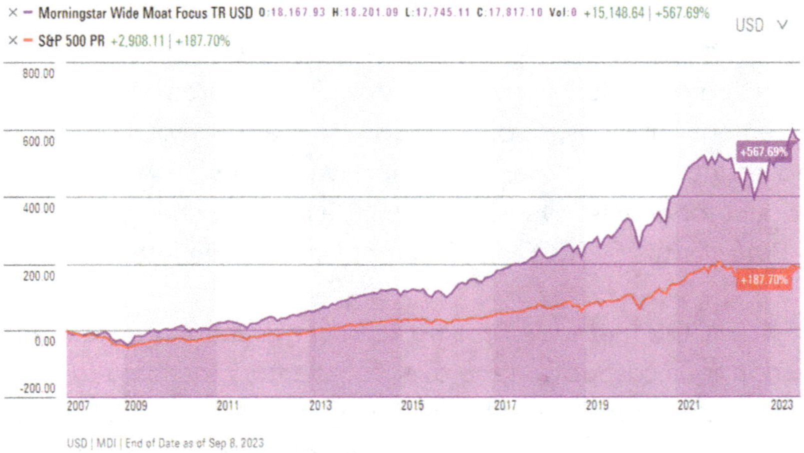

(Graphic 6.1: Wide Moat vs S&P 500)

The same mathematical procedure can be applied to bond valuation, applying discounted cash flow analysis to arrive at intrinsic value. Generally, that's stated as the market price of a bond, and the same math that runs the bond market runs the stock market over longer periods of time.

Business owners must be able to reliably forecast the amount of money they can take out of their companies. As I previously mentioned, I often refer to this as owning businesses that have sustainable competitive advantages. Warren Buffett calls them moats. This is the source of analytical confidence for a business owner or a business buyer.

From Buffett's 2007 letter:

> *"A truly great business must have an enduring "moat" that protects excellent returns on invested capital. The dynamics of capitalism guarantee that competitors will repeatedly assault any business "castle" that is earning high returns. Therefore, a formidable barrier such as a company's being the low-cost producer (GEICO, Costco) or possessing a powerful world-wide brand (Coca-Cola, Gillette, American Express) is essential*

> *for sustained success. Business history is filled with "Roman Candles," companies whose moats proved illusory and were soon crossed."*

Buffett wants to own businesses with earnings power, low operating costs, low leverage, low capital requirements, low post-retirement liabilities, strong brands, cost advantages, efficiencies and economies of scale, and that have been selling their current product for at least five years with little need to change.

Buffett cites GEICO as an example in his 1995 letter:

> *"GEICO's method of selling - direct marketing - gave it an enormous cost advantage over competitors that sold through agents, a form of distribution so ingrained in the business of these insurers that it was impossible for them to give it up. But the ultimate key to the company's success is its rock-bottom operating costs, which virtually no competitor can match."*

Companies build and reinforce moats by strengthening their brands, achieving economies of scale, or securing contracts with, or special status from, the government. They achieve customer loyalty, pricing power and legal protections that make it difficult for other companies to compete with them. The world's largest companies have been built on moats of economies of scale. Standard Oil built its monopoly by buying up smaller competitor refineries and building a global distribution network. Eventually, the company controlled about 90 percent of all the refineries and pipelines in the U.S. and could set its own prices. Today, moats are more commonly built on competitive advantages such as data, networks and repeat engagement within a product ecosystem. For example, Google initiated its moat by developing a better algorithm for indexing and searching the internet. The company has since strengthened that moat by putting that advantage to work in transportation, shopping, and most importantly, advertising.[156]

Competitive Advantages

Companies with sustainable competitive advantages generally fall into one of eight categories we have been discussing:

- Economies of Scale
- Low-Cost Leader
- Efficiency of Scale
- Luxury Brand
- Patent-Protected Intellectual Property
- Preventative Switch Cost
- Unique Real Estate
- Specialty Underwriting

Economies of Scale

Some businesses with a scale advantage have the ability to take on large orders without having to spend a great amount of money to meet the additional demand, whereas their competitors lacking that scale would have to absorb huge additional costs for factory space, machinery, labor and so forth. Some companies have a scale advantage that makes it incrementally cheaper to produce additional product. The more they produce, the more the marginal cost of production falls.

Low-Cost Leader

Companies that are low-cost leaders have the ability to bring their good or service to market at a meaningfully lower price than their competitors. This cost advantage may persist because of a technological factor, a location or because they were the first to do it. Whatever the reason that low cost exists, it provides a huge competitive advantage.

For example, some gold mines find the precious metal just below the surface whereas other mines have to dig down a mile or more. The cost difference to get the same metal to market is significant. The mine that can reach the gold using little more than a Caterpillar to scrape it from beneath the surface enjoys a huge cost advantage.

Similarly, the largest salt mine in the world is the Sifto Salt Mine in Ontario, Canada.[157] Located at 800 feet under Lake Huron, it enjoys a huge low cost advantage as it can bring salt to market at a much lower cost than a mine located inland, where the salt would have to be mined, loaded on trucks and driven to a railway station, reloaded onto rail cars so it could be brought to a distribution point where it would once again be reloaded onto a barge, perhaps not far from where the salt from Sifto began its disproportionately shorter journey to market.

Companies that are first movers—Amazon being a prime example—enjoy a soft cost called time. Even though their cost of goods may be comparable to a retail outlet—sometimes more, sometimes less—as a customer, you save a tremendous amount of time by being an Amazon customer. Amazon is a low-cost provider of time.

There are a few companies within the capitalist system that have created a cost advantage that they will enjoy into the foreseeable future, an advantage that's not going to go away.

Efficiency of Scale

Some industries require only one company to meet the demand. That company efficiently provides all the supply the market requires. As the old joke goes, "How many NASCAR tracks do you need in Chicago? One." That's because there's little profit in challenging an industry leader that has essentially satisfied the entire market. An example is the industrial gas market where one or two companies have such a massive footprint they can meet the entire market, effectively excluding competition. That efficiency of scale is an unassailable competitive advantage.

Luxury Brand

Luxury brands that demand a premium have a competitive advantage. Companies lacking a luxury brand must find another competitive advantage, for example, promotions that impact the profitability of their competitors. If there's an Applebee's next to a TGI Fridays and one advertises 50 percent off appetizers or drinks, that's going to have a material impact on consumer behavior. Customers tend to gravitate to the option that offers better perceived value.

Now, let's do the same example with a Ferrari dealership next to a Honda dealership. If Honda advertises 20 percent off Honda Civics, it may attract low-cost buyers but it is no inducement for someone considering a Ferrari. Luxury brands demand an unremitting premium.

Patent-Protected Intellectual Property and Licenses

Another advantage accrues to companies with patent-protected intellectual property or licensed agreements/contracts with a government. For example, the entire Mexican airport industry is driven by licenses. The Cancun airport has a 50-year lease license to operate in Mexico, making it virtually competition-free for travelers going to that area.

Intellectual property rights are defined as those associated with intangible assets owned by a person or company and protected against use without consent. The four main types are patents, trademarks, copyrights, and trade secrets.[158] The four companies with the most U.S. patents as of 2020 are Apple, Huawei Technologies, Qualcomm and Amazon. When calculating the difficulty facing a competitor trying to enter a market and effectively compete with a company that holds critical patents, licenses or other forms of protected intellectual property, we can often secure analytical confidence. The pharmaceutical industry is an obvious example.

Preventive Switch Cost

This is one of my favorite competitive advantages. It describes the cost—and often inconvenience—customers would have to pay to switch to a competitor. Typically, that cost is higher than the potential benefit to be gained by switching.

Cloud data storage falls into this category. Adobe is an example where although there are free and low-cost versions available, if you're a graphic designer using Adobe, there are training and education costs involved in change. There are also collaboration costs because Adobe is the industry language standard and if you try to use some other creative type of software, it would be difficult to collaborate. If you are using QuickBooks to run your business' accounting and payroll systems, there's little incentive to switch because you would have to spend an enormous amount of time on training and labor to move your systems.

Unique Real Estate

Certain real estate can have a location advantage, as when it is positioned in an area that allows it to be more valuable than the same amount of dirt in other areas. The salt mine previously mentioned is an example. As they say in real estate, "location, location, location."

Specialty Underwriting

Larger insurers have a competitive edge in scale because they are able to underwrite risks that would not have a material impact on their overall business, whereas a smaller competitor could not underwrite that risk because it has a potentially much larger impact for them.

In 1985, major U.S. corporations faced an insurance crisis due to the unavailability of excess liability and directors/officers' insurance coverage. In response, a group of 34 blue-chip companies from a broad range of industries formed a consortium and pooled capital to form their own insurer, called Ace Limited.[159] The company subsequently became one of the nation's largest insurers, acquiring Cigna's global property and casualty business in 1999 and Chubb in 2016, creating the world's largest publicly traded property/casualty insurance company with a massive underwriting competitive advantage.

Leverage

Buffett is leery of leverage and believes great businesses can be profitable without leverage. In his 1987 letter, he writes:

> *"Good business or investment decisions will eventually produce quite satisfactory economic results, with no aid from leverage. Therefore, it seems to us to be both foolish and improper to risk what is important (including, necessarily, the welfare of innocent bystanders such as policyholders and employees) for some extra returns that are relatively unimportant."*

To Buffett (and the late Charlie Munger), debt is a four-letter word. While many investment strategies rely on leverage to produce returns, they inevitably expose portfolios to heightened risk. Investing in a company with elevated leverage means accepting correspondingly heightened levels of risk because if downside scenarios happen, the business can become insolvent.

We prefer to invest in companies that have pristine balance sheets. We don't mind a little bit of leverage but there has to be a good reason for the debt, such as a strategic acquisition. To take on debt merely to chase a new industry or similar speculative effort is something we disdain.

Retained Earnings Strategy

A fundamental imperative of Buffett's philosophy is investing retained earnings to strengthen competitive positions and protect future earnings. It's vital to have a retained earnings strategy consistent with our investment methodology. When companies that we own make money, we want them to maximize their moat, to take that cash flow and invest it into widening and strengthening their competitive advantage. Ultimately, that's why we are investing. What we are most reliant upon is that sustainable competitive advantage persisting into the future.

We expect the companies we own to invest in that advantage first and foremost. At some point, however, if there is no additional value to be gained from investing into their sustainable competitive advantage, the CEO has two options: Give us our money back as investors or begin investing in other things that drive profits. We do not want them to do the latter. We want them to stay in the business they know—stick to their bread and butter—and do what they can to maximize the profits of their existing business. We do not want them taking our retained earnings and investing in something completely different.

That's what got General Electric into trouble in the early 2000s. GE was making a fortune and then started investing in a variety of other businesses. This mistake has been repeated again and again by companies that derive far less success on their second, third or tenth endeavor than they did on their first. Once a company's competitive advantage has been maximized, as investors, we want our money returned to us.

Buffett reiterated this mandate in his 1984 letter:

> *"This principle is not universally accepted. For a number of reasons managers like to withhold unrestricted, readily distributable earnings from shareholders - to expand the corporate empire over which the managers rule, to operate from a position of exceptional financial comfort, etc. But we believe there is only one valid reason for retention. Unrestricted earnings should be retained only when there is a reasonable prospect - backed preferably by historical evidence or, when appropriate, by a thoughtful analysis of the future - that for every dollar retained by the corporation, at least one dollar of market value will be created for owners."*

As shareholders, we want the executives of the businesses that we own to do one of two things with retained earnings after the moat is maximized. We want them to either buy shares of the company off the stock exchange (share buybacks) or pay us shareholders a dividend. The determining factor is how attractively priced the shares are. If the shares we own have an expected return of at least 15%, we want them to buy shares off the open market. If the shares we own are near their fair value, we want them to issue us a dividend because we can take that money and buy a business that has an expected rate of return above 15%.

More from Buffett's 1984 letter:

> *"Managers of high-return businesses who consistently employ much of the cash thrown off by those businesses in other ventures with low returns should be held to account for those allocation decisions, regardless of how profitable the overall enterprise is."*

World Class Management

Obviously, we want to own businesses run by world class management that shares our investment objectives. We prefer companies with a large portion of the stock owned by the founders or executives of the company - people who have a long-term, strategic vision for the company - not where management contracts are created for short term profit and quarterly earnings report publicity. We want management to have the same mindset as we do, that is, when we buy a business, we expect to own it for a very long time.

That said, we don't want to own businesses that require management precision in order to succeed. Buffett says, "I want to own a business that a monkey can run." Sometimes, it's fine to own a simple business that's easy to run, as opposed to a highly complex business that takes an enormous amount of managerial skill and decision-making to be profitable.

Buffett exhibits great patience by holding the companies for a very long time. The longer we can hold onto an investment, the better. The ideal holding period is forever. If you make a great investment decision and you pay a great price, you could own that business for a long period of time. And if you own a phenomenal business, it can turn out to be a multi-generational business.

Owner Earnings

Buffett calculates the fair value of a company, which he refers to as intrinsic value, using a process similar to the discounted cash flow analysis mentioned in chapter five. He makes a similar calculation of free cash flow that he refers to as owner earnings. He will only invest in companies that he refers to as having a large margin of safety between its calculated intrinsic value and its market price.

> *"Intrinsic value can be defined simply: It is the discounted value of the cash that can be taken out of a business during its remaining life. The calculation of intrinsic value, though, is not so simple. As our definition suggests, intrinsic value is an estimate rather than a precise figure, and it is additionally an estimate that must be changed if interest rates move or forecasts of future cash flows are revised."*

Berkshire Hathaway Owner's Manual

CHAPTER EIGHT

Managing Concentrated Positions

A concentration of wealth frequently occurs as the result of either a large business or cash position. Concentrated business positions develop when the growth of an enterprise substantially increases its value. Cash concentrations result from a variety of causes, including business sales, inheritances, executive compensation, lawsuit settlements or asset sales.

When someone accumulates a concentrated position, the need to effectively manage that money becomes paramount.

Managing Concentrated Cash Positions

When a client asks us to manage a substantial cash deposit, I need to know in advance exactly where I'm going to invest that money, as well as the proper time frame for investing it. These decisions are primarily based on two factors: the percentage of the client's portfolio value the deposit represents, and the scarcity or abundance of opportunity in the markets.

These assessments are made within the parameters of the portfolio's target risk, which is based on the client's financial goals, risk tolerance and the amount of investment risk required to secure the return needed to achieve those goals. It's vital to make certain the client can actually tolerate the necessary level of risk. If not, the client has three options: modify the goals, work longer and delay retirement or reduce current spending so there's more money available for retirement.

If a professional athlete with a thirty-million-dollar portfolio hands us a $300,000 deposit he earned from a commercial endorsement, that money represents just 1% of his portfolio value.

If the market was underpriced, we would want to invest that money quickly, probably within 30 days or less. If the market was highly overvalued, we might spread the investment period over six months or more.

If a building contractor with a million-dollar portfolio sells his business for nine million dollars and hands us the check to deposit, that nine million represents 90% of his money. If he's conservative, we want to move that money into the market much more slowly.

I often use a swimming analogy to explain how the tempo of investing varies, depending on clients' financial status. For someone that just sold his lifelong business and has virtually all of his wealth tied up in the cash received from the sale, I want to dip his toes into the pool at first, then gradually wade in. For that athlete with the thirty-million-dollar portfolio, I'm going to take his million-dollar endorsement check and dive right into the deep water.

If the market conditions are around fair value, we would invest the money from the sale of the builder's business over an extended period of time, perhaps 54 months. We would invest the athlete's money much more quickly, even immediately. The difference in the pace of investing for the two clients is based on the fact that, as previously mentioned, the builder's deposit represents most of his net worth, whereas the athlete's deposit is a fly speck in his huge portfolio.

If the probability of a bear market is high, we want to invest more slowly, reducing the amount of portfolio fluctuation. Conversely, if the probability of a bear market is low, we will move faster.

Graphic 8.1 illustrates the timeframe for investing an amount of money based on the percentage of the portfolio's total assets the deposit represents (portrayed as a percentage of 100% to 1% across the top of the chart) and whether the market is perceived to be undervalued, fairly valued or overvalued (illustrated by the +35% to -35% across the bottom of the chart.

Number of Months to Invest a Deposit Matrix

Deposit Amount as a Percentage of Net Worth

United States Stock Market Value		100%	90%	80%	70%	60%	50%	40%	30%	20%	15%	10%	5%	4%	3%	2%	1%
Undervalued	35%	36	32	28	24	20	16	10	4	2	1	1	1	1	1	1	1
	30%	40	35	31	27	23	19	13	7	2	2	1	1	1	1	1	1
	25%	43	38	34	30	26	22	16	9	4	2	2	1	1	1	1	1
	20%	47	42	37	33	29	25	18	12	6	4	2	2	2	1	1	1
	18%	48	43	39	35	30	26	19	13	7	4	3	2	2	2	1	1
	16%	49	44	40	36	31	27	21	14	8	5	3	2	2	2	1	1
	14%	51	46	41	37	33	28	22	15	9	6	4	2	2	2	1	1
	12%	52	47	43	38	34	30	23	16	10	7	4	2	2	2	1	1
	10%	54	48	44	39	35	31	24	17	11	7	5	3	2	2	1	1
	9%	54	49	44	40	36	31	24	17	11	8	5	3	2	2	1	1
	8%	55	49	45	41	36	32	25	18	11	8	5	3	2	2	1	1
	7%	56	50	46	41	37	32	25	18	12	8	6	3	2	2	1	1
	6%	56	51	46	42	37	33	26	19	12	9	6	3	3	2	1	1
	5%	57	51	47	43	38	34	27	20	13	9	6	3	3	2	1	1
	4%	58	52	48	43	39	34	27	20	13	9	6	3	3	2	1	1
	3%	59	53	48	44	39	35	28	21	14	10	7	3	3	2	1	1
Fair	2%	59	53	49	44	40	35	28	21	14	10	7	3	3	2	1	1
	1%	60	54	50	45	41	36	29	22	14	10	7	4	3	2	1	1
	0%	60	54	50	45	41	36	29	22	14	11	7	4	3	2	1	1
	-1%	62	56	51	46	42	37	30	22	15	12	8	4	4	3	2	1
	-2%	64	57	52	48	43	38	31	23	16	12	9	5	4	3	3	2
	-3%	65	59	54	49	44	39	32	24	17	13	9	5	5	4	3	3
	-4%	67	61	55	50	45	40	32	25	17	14	10	6	5	5	4	3
	-5%	69	62	57	52	46	41	33	26	18	14	11	7	6	5	4	4
Overvalued	-6%	71	64	58	53	47	42	34	27	19	15	11	7	7	6	5	4
	-8%	74	67	61	56	50	44	36	28	20	16	13	9	8	7	6	5
	-10%	78	70	64	58	52	46	38	30	22	18	14	10	9	8	7	7
	-12%	81	74	67	61	54	48	40	32	23	19	15	11	10	10	9	8
	-14%	85	77	70	64	57	50	42	33	25	21	17	12	12	11	10	9
	-16%	88	80	73	66	59	52	43	35	26	22	18	14	13	12	11	10
	-18%	92	84	76	69	61	54	45	37	28	24	19	15	14	13	12	11
	-20%	95	87	79	71	64	56	47	38	29	25	21	16	15	14	14	13
	-30%	113	103	94	85	75	66	56	47	37	32	27	22	22	21	20	19
	-35%	120	110	100	90	80	70	60	50	40	35	30	25	24	23	22	21

(Graphic 8.1: Months to Invest)

Looking at the graphic, you see that the building contractor's deposit represents 90% of the owner's net worth (the second column at the top). Let's now assume the market is somewhat undervalued. If you look at the 7% number in the far-left column and move two places to the right (into the vertical 90% column), you will see that the estimated timeframe for investing that nine million dollars on a dollar cost average basis would be 50 months or a little over four years. Had the market been overvalued by 10%, we would have planned to invest that money over a 70-month period.

You might logically ask why we would take a longer time to invest that deposit when the market is overvalued. The reason is that the expected return on the deposit is less in an overvalued market than it would be in an undervalued market. As such, the opportunity cost of parking the deposit in a short-term bond or short-term CD while waiting to put the money to work is a lot less. In fact, the owner might make more money sitting in a short-term bond fund than risking the majority of his net worth by immediately putting all the money into the market.

To further illustrate the point, let's take it to the extreme and assume you are virtually broke (sorry) and involved in an accident (sorry again) and receive a lawsuit settlement of one million dollars (feeling better?). Being the wise person you now are, you eschew buying that Ferrari and decide to invest the entire amount, which represents 100% of your new-found net worth. You are now on a roll because the market is remarkably undervalued at 35%. We would put that money to work rapidly, within 36 months, to take advantage of the anticipated high expected return. In 36 months, you might be able to buy that Ferrari anyway and not have to touch your investment principal.

The rule here is this: the more opportunity that exists in the market, the lower the percentage of your investable net worth the deposit represents and the faster you want to put your deposit to work.

Managing Concentrated Equity Positions

Successful investors tend to accumulate a concentration of individual stocks, a market sector or an asset class in their portfolios. These overweighted positions can grow sufficiently large as to create an asset imbalance, exposing the owner to excessive risk.

(For simplicity, I am going to use the term "stock" in this chapter to refer to a stock, sector or asset class concentrated position.)

Whether these stocks are perceived with affection because of the way they were acquired or as a dilemma because of the risk they represent, it can be difficult for a financial advisor to convince the owners to liquidate some or all of their concentrated positions to gain better diversity in their portfolio.

If someone owns a stock that, over the 20-year period from 2000-2020, has generated an average annual return of 65.4% (Tesla), 33% (Mastercard), 31.1% (Amazon), 21.2% (United Health Group) or 16.6% (Home Depot),[160] they may understandably resist advisor efforts to sell off the position.

If the fondness an investor has for a favorite stock is linked to the way they acquired it, the challenge grows exponentially. For example, if the stock accrual emanated from employment compensation, the sale of a family business in exchange for stock, or an inheritance,[161] getting them to part with something cherished only slightly less than their children is an even greater challenge for an advisor.

Concentrated positions represent a threat to portfolios that their owners rarely recognize. For every superstock like Microsoft or Apple, there are hundreds of former winners that collapsed, like TWA, Magnavox, Enron, Singer, Zenith, PanAm, WorldCom and Wang.[162]

We regularly see portfolios overweighted this way among corporate executives. During their career, they accumulate large company stock holdings in the form of options and bonuses that come to represent the lion's share of their retirement portfolio, as well as the bulk of their net worth. If they are still employed, insider trading regulations may prevent their ability to sell off significant amounts of their company stock.

Non-executive employees with long tenures at large corporations and workers in the tech industry are other examples of investors that accumulate concentrated positions of company stock.

Then too, there are people who invest in a stock, are rewarded, and then continue to invest additional amounts in the position because of their success until it becomes overly concentrated in relation to the rest of their portfolio.

Concentrated positions create elevated risk in portfolios. When that occurs, a financial advisor would usually recommend the obvious solution: reduce or liquidate the position and lower the risk. The problem is that selling off a concentrated stock position can have dire tax consequences.

Tax Costs Versus Portfolio Size

The first step in solving a concentrated position should not be to immediately "sell it off," but rather to conduct a "tax costs versus portfolio size" analysis, a relative calculation of how much the owner will have to pay in taxes in order to achieve a better-balanced portfolio.

A one-million-dollar tax bill is unlikely to hinder someone with a hundred-million-dollar portfolio from reducing their concentrated position. They may not be thrilled with paying the tax, but the benefit of reducing the risk of a massive loss should that overweighted stock take a nosedive justifies paying the tax. Paying a million-dollar tax on a five-million-dollar portfolio—a 20% loss of their money—is unacceptable, however.

In most cases, those that have accumulated a concentrated position are very fond of the stock. It's probably made them a lot of money, and in the case of those owning stock of their employer, it usually has a special place in their heart. It may be a terrific stock, but it shouldn't constitute twenty percent of a portfolio. Remember the "Nifty Fifty" stocks of the 1960s and 1970s? They were generally regarded as "can't miss" investments because of their stable performance over an extended period. They included Xerox, Eastman Kodak, Polaroid and Sears, Roebuck & Co. A lot of investors overweighted in these "quality" growth stocks lost a lot of money.[163] Not so nifty.

Today, someone with a concentrated position in a single "quality" stock runs the same risk. The first step in mitigating that risk is to determine the tax hit if the position was liquidated during the current tax year and compare that number to the size of the portfolio. That, and whether the sale of the position propels the owner into a higher tax bracket, largely determines how we go about reducing or eliminating the concentrated position.

If the tax consequences of selling off the position immediately are unsatisfactory, we can instead start to sell off a systematic amount over a period of time, reducing the tax burden while simultaneously reducing the concentration risk. We might, for example, determine a position must be reduced by ten percent. We might then sell off 2.5% each year for four succeeding years. The action will relieve the concentration issue, but there remains the issue of the owner's emotional attachment to the stock.

Certain Disappointment

Whenever it's necessary to reduce a concentrated position, I caution the client that the strategy is going to create perpetual misery for them. Typically, a puzzled look comes over their face and they ask what I mean. I explain that once they make the decision to sell off the stock, they will be keeping daily tabs on it for years and they need to abstain from growing angry about their decision—and with the guy who advised them to sell.

No matter which direction the stock moves after we sell off the position, the owner is going to have regrets. Consider someone with a ten-million-dollar position who understands the need to reduce his exposure by selling off half the position. But after we reduce his position, he continues to watch the stock and, sure enough, it continues to go up. He never takes his eyes off that stock. All he can think about is that trusted advisor who persuaded him to sell five million dollars' worth of the stock he loved, the stock that helped make him a millionaire.

And if the stock goes down in value, that same person is going to be upset because he didn't liquidate the entire ten-million-dollar position. He insisted on keeping half of it and now it's only worth three million and, of course, he gets angrier every day when he looks at the stock price taking another dive.

So regardless of what happens to that stock, he's going to be furious about the outcome, probably for the rest of his life. It's a story he will tell his grandchildren some day when he thinks they are old enough to understand his frustration. Unfortunately, they won't really care.

Exchange Funds

An alternative to selling off a concentrated position that avoids paying capital gains tax on the transaction is the use of exchange funds, also known as swap funds. These are private placement limited partnerships created specifically for this purpose.

The history of how these funds came about is an example of creative thinking on the part of financial luminaries that saw a need and created a product to fill it. In the case of exchange funds, they originated in the latter half of the twentieth century as a result of a major investment management firm recognizing a common problem among their most important corporate clients. These were the titans of the Fortune 500—founders and CEOs of the nation's largest companies—all of whom had the same predicament as a result of their financial success: concentrations of company stock that represented an uncomfortably large portion of their investment portfolio.

The fear among these executives was the possibility of losing a significant percentage of their wealth should their company stock suffer a major downturn. None of these successful businessmen wanted to see decades of building wealth go down the drain as a result of some negative idiosyncratic company event or unforeseen occurrence in their industry over which they had no control.

The investment firm's brilliant solution to this problem was based on convincing a sufficient number of these executives to "exchange" a portion of their company shares for a corresponding ownership interest in a newly created fund comprised of the aggregate shares of all the participating executives. They were also required to contribute some form of tangible, illiquid asset—such as real estate—as a legal requirement of the exchange fund.

The result was to immediately diversify the investment portfolio of each executive while reducing their concentration risk without suffering burdensome tax consequences.

Today, investment firms like Eaton Vance, Goldman Sachs, Morgan Stanley and Fidelity are major players. The way it works is that the investment company sponsoring the exchange fund allows *qualified* investors[164] with large, concentrated stock positions and liquid net worth of at least $5mn to transfer their shares to the fund. The shares are pooled with the shares of other investors to form a diversified portfolio of blue-chip stocks. The fund manager has discretion over stock selection.[165]

Modern exchange funds typically have an unlimited life with no fixed termination date. The funds can accept new investors. Investors can remain in the fund indefinitely and redeem some or all of the interest in the fund whenever they wish, in which case they receive a portfolio of stocks selected by the sponsor. Investors that do not like the selected stocks can choose instead to remain in the fund.[166]

The primary benefits of exchange funds are providing portfolio diversification, ensuring investment capital is protected and appreciates, exchanging a risky investment for a less risky one and deferring capital gains taxes. The potential downside is that the contributed stock may outperform the stocks chosen for the fund. Finally, while exchange funds protect executives from company or industry specific events, they do not shelter executives from events that cause the entire economy (and markets) to collapse.

Hedging Concentrated Positions

Hedging with Shorts

Shorting a stock is the reverse of buying a stock—or "going long." A short seller borrows stock from a broker and sells it into the market with the expectation of buying the stock at a cheaper price and returning the borrowed stock in order to profit on the difference in prices.

Shorting a stock is betting that it will decline in price. In essence, it's selling a stock you don't own but instead have borrowed. If the stock declines as you hope, you can repurchase it and profit on the difference between sell and buy prices.[167]

One possibility for hedging a concentrated position is to simply short the stock to protect the downside and reduce the risk. The problem with shorting an individual stock (or all the stocks in a concentrated sector) is the margin cost, which is an expensive approach and not an acceptable long-term strategy. As much as advisors would like a simple solution to the concentrated position issue, indefinitely shorting the position is unacceptable because the costs would eventually devour the portfolio. However, shorting can be an excellent short-term strategy to navigate concentrated positions.

Hedging with Options

An option is a contract that gives the buyer the right to purchase or sell an asset, typically a stock, at a strike price—the price at which the option holder can exercise the option to buy or sell the stock, depending on whether they hold a call option or a put option.

Call options give the buyer the right, but not the obligation, to buy the stock; put options give the buyer the right, but not the obligation, to sell the stock. Investors buy calls if they believe the price of the stock will increase in the future. Buyers of a call options pay a premium when they enter the contract and hope to make a profit when the price of the stock rises higher than the option strike price.

Investors sell call options if they think a stock price will decrease, or not increase as much as the option's strike price before it expires, in which case the premium received for selling the option becomes the seller's profit. In this case, the buyer will suffer a loss equal to the cost of the premium they paid for the call option. The seller of a call option is obligated to sell the stock to the buyer of the call option if the latter decides to exercise their option, which they can do at any time prior to the expiration date.[168]

Put options give holders of the option the right, but not the obligation, to sell a specified amount of an underlying security at a specified price within a specified time frame.

Investors buy puts if they believe the that the stock's price will decline and sell puts if they think the stock's price will increase.[169]

Put options increase in value when the price of the underlying stock decreases and lose value if the price of the stock increases. The seller of the put option is obligated to buy the asset if the put buyer exercises their option.

A protected put is the strategy of buying put options on stock the buyer owns on a share-for-share basis. An individual wishing to hedge a concentrated stock position would typically utilize protected puts.

Options can be a useful strategy to limit the loss potential of a concentrated stock position. In a hypothetical example, Frank, a corporate executive at Badaboom Corp., has a $10 million stock portfolio with half the stock held in company shares. His company allows him to sell a limited amount of his holdings, but Frank does not want to pay the capital gains tax on a stock sale. He does, however, recognize the need to relieve his overweight position should the stock take a precipitous drop in value.

One way for Frank to solve the problem is to create a "collar," a combination of a protective put and a covered call. The put protects against a drop in stock price and, ideally, the call generates a premium that pays for the put.

So, Frank could create a collar, buying a put and simultaneously selling a call on his stock. With his company's stock selling at $100, Frank could create a collar by buying puts with a strike price of $90 per share and selling calls with a strike price of $130 per share. If the stock goes below $90 per share, Frank can sell it at $90; if it goes above $130 per share, Frank will be obliged to sell it at the price and forego the profit on the overage. But what Frank has achieved with the collar strategy is to establish a floor and a cap around his concentrated stock position.[170]

Alternately, Frank could buy a put, giving him the right to sell his stock at $100/share, called an "at-the-money" put. If the stock drops in value, no matter how deep it sinks, Frank retains the right to sell the stock at $100, giving him critical downside protection for his concentrated position. But Frank's purchase of a put does not obligate him to sell, so if the stock goes up in value, he simply retains it and sacrifices the cost of the put.[171]

As savvy as this strategy sounds, there is a problem. At-the-money put options are an expensive form of insurance, so buying these puts on a continuing basis—every time a put option expires and Frank needs to renew his protection—is strictly a short-term strategy, not one that is sustainable over longer periods.

Collars should not be confused with straddles, which is a neutral strategy of simultaneously buying a call and a put option of the same stock, same strike price and same expiration date. To further confuse you, there also exists a "strangle," which is the same as a straddle except for the fact that a strangle has two different strike prices. These strategies are typically used during periods of high market volatility when the buyer expects significant price movements in the stock but is unsure in which direction.[172]

Hedging with Short ETFs

Most ETFs are investments that track a particular stock or bond index by holding all or a representative sample of that index's constituent securities as their underlying assets. Some ETFs track indices using swaps or other derivatives. When the index being tracked increases in price, the ETF appreciates in value similar to the index; if the index goes down in price, the ETF decreases in value.

Inverse ETFs work in the opposite direction, however, and should be short-term investments. Fund managers buy and sell underlying derivative contracts daily and there is no absolutely certain way that the inverse ETF will track the index or equities it is targeting over the long run. Also, the costs of frequent trading can be prohibitive as overuse usually results in higher fund fees, not to mention some inverse ETFs have expense ratios of 1% or more.[173]

The use of ETFs as a hedging strategy to reduce or liquidate a concentrated position can be effective, provided it is on a short-term basis. In a situation where the objective is to sell off the position in segments over more than one calendar year, we might instead use an inverse ETF for a limited period to reduce or even eliminate the client's exposure to equity risk, then take the gain when it is expeditious to do so on a long-term capital gains basis.

Let's consider the example of a person with a terminal illness who has a concentrated holding of stocks from a single market sector. He still has all his mental faculties and is able to understand a complicated financial strategy. The position represents a significant portion of his wealth, and since the significant appreciation on the stocks would qualify for a stepped-up basis as an inherited asset, it wouldn't make sense to sell off the position while he was still alive and have the inheritance reduced by the capital gains taxes. Here, hedging the position with an inverse ETF could reduce the risk of the concentrated position suffering a sizeable loss in value while avoiding tax.

The stepped-up basis is what happens when the price of an inherited asset on the date of the decedent's death is above its original purchase price. The tax code allows for the raising of the cost basis to the higher price, minimizing the capital gains taxes owed if the asset is sold later.[174]

Charitable Giving

Individuals that have accumulated large stock positions are usually successful people, whether executives, business owners or employees with long tenures. These are not people lacking in acumen or common sense. In most cases, they are well aware of the need to do something to protect their portfolio against loss due to a concentration of a single stock, sector or asset class. The conundrum that keeps most from taking action is that they simply don't know what to do.

Aside from the strategies discussed in this chapter, there remains the option of giving away some or all of the stock as a means of avoiding taxes and fulfilling a legacy. Chapter 16, "How the Wealthy Perpetuate their Legacy," has numerous suggestions for charitable giving, some of which would be appropriate methods of achieving these objectives.

One other possibility not yet discussed is the use of a donor-advised fund (DAF), an account tied to a charity that allows donors to make a charitable contribution—stock in the case of someone with a concentrated holding—to the DAF and receive an immediate tax write off. The donor can make additional contributions at any time, so the individual can choose to initially donate some of their stock and more later as their situation dictates.

Any investment growth of the stock while being managed by the DAF is not taxed to the donor, and the donor has the flexibility to decide what charities should receive the largesse.[175]

Summary

Concentrated investment positions—whether comprised of individual stocks, a market sector or an asset class—require a focused management approach to achieve a better-balanced portfolio.

Potential solutions include selling off the position, utilizing an exchange fund, shorting and hedging strategies or gifting. Immediately selling some or all of the position might be a quick fix, but an analysis of the tax costs versus portfolio size usually precludes this approach. An alternative might be to sell off a systematic amount over a period of time, both reducing the tax burden and the concentration risk.

Exchange funds allow concentrated positions to be transferred and pooled with those of other investors, achieving better diversification while deferring capital gains taxes.

Another possibility would be to simply short the position to protect the downside and reduce the risk, but the margin costs render this strictly a short-term solution. Options are yet another strategy to limit potential concentration losses but again, are not cost-effective over an extended period. Inverse ETFs likewise can be an effective hedge, but only as a temporary solution.

Gifting is an option to reduce concentration for those who wish to perpetuate a family legacy or support favorite charitable causes.

In short, there are numerous potential strategies to help reduce the risk of a concentrated position, regardless of its composition or the assets it contains. However, the client's financial circumstances, capacity for risk, fair value of the investment, percentage of the portfolio value the position represents, and if an impending bear or bull environment is probable are all factors to be analyzed before choosing a strategy.

CHAPTER NINE

Balancing Act

> *"It is not the strongest of the species that survives, nor the most intelligent, but the one most responsive to change."*

Charles Darwin

The purpose of rebalancing a portfolio is to stay within risk targets. As time passes, the higher performing assets in a portfolio, usually the equities, will increase the portfolio's expected risk. Rebalancing typically involves selling higher-performing stocks and buying lower-performing bonds.

Rebalancing helps counteract the compounding effects of a portfolio. It prevents higher-performing investments from earning more and lower performers from crumbling further. A rebalanced portfolio abandons the conditions where winning investments keep on winning and compounding their gains, and losers evaporate into insignificance.[176]

The fact that this widely accepted strategy almost always leads to lower returns over the long term comes as a surprise to most people. They ask, "So rebalancing actually makes me poorer?" The answer is yes, it inevitably does. There may be some divergence in the short term, but the longer the investment time horizon, the greater the certainty that rebalancing will, over time, diminish returns.

The financial industry has done a remarkable job of convincing the investing public that rebalancing a portfolio is a necessary and healthy activity. The reality is that while rebalancing can be effective from a risk perspective, it is not a strategy to enhance returns. Rebalancing a portfolio by continually selling assets growing at

10% a year and using the money to buy assets growing at 5% a year has a predictable result: subpar returns.

The alternative to rebalancing is maintaining a stagnant portfolio, one that does not add or remove capital through rebalancing. Over time, the percentage of stocks in that portfolio will increase, as will the amount of expected risk, but the portfolio is likely to experience higher returns.

Wealthy investors can avoid the downside of rebalancing—jeopardizing performance by selling good companies while incurring a tax obligation—by buying versus selling assets. It's one reason why the wealthy make such great clients. Their investment managers can rebalance portfolios by buying assets instead of selling them, using the constant positive capital flows their wealthy clients provide. Because the portfolios can be rebalanced by buying, taxes that would be recognized by selling the highest-performing stocks are avoided. Using the additional capital, the manager can rebalance by buying bonds instead of the higher performing stocks.

Investors that use a dollar cost averaging strategy may also be able to rebalance without selling assets, but the cash flows may be insufficient to achieve timely rebalancing.

Position Sizing

One of the facets of portfolio rebalancing is position sizing, that is, assessing how much any single position should be permitted to influence the overall return of the portfolio.

As previously defined, alpha is the return on an investment that's incrementally more than a benchmark index, such as the S&P 500. A portfolio where the primary ambition is to have massive alpha—at the risk of having negative alpha and substantially underperforming the index—facilitates larger individual positions. And the opposite is true. The closer a portfolio aims to replicate a benchmark, the more stocks it can accommodate. Of course, adding increasing numbers of stocks to a portfolio tends to diminish investment returns towards the benchmark index.

The decision of how many positions to hold and how much each position will influence the portfolio's total return dovetails with the rebalancing strategy. Let's say that Tesla represents 3% of a portfolio. If Tesla goes up 200%, how much of that should be allowed to remain as an individual position? How much should that position be permitted to influence the overall performance of the portfolio? That's a critical consideration for an investment manager.

As you can see, there are two aspects of position rebalancing. There's the asset allocation level where, considering the portfolio's long-term, strategic targets, how far from those targets should the portfolio be allowed to drift?

And then there's the individual position sizing rebalancing, where the concern is how much fluctuation should each position in the portfolio have before starting to take profits?

Rebalancing Methods

There are essentially two ways to rebalance: calendar-based rebalancing and rebalancing based on standard deviation.

Calendar-based rebalancing is the most common methodology. The way it works is at the end of the month or quarter, the manager analyzes the portfolio's allocation. If the target is 60/40 and the stocks have risen to 62%, two percent of the stocks are sold and the proceeds are used to purchase a comparable amount of bonds in an effort to return the portfolio to its intended asset balance.

Calendar rebalancing works better in qualified accounts, such as 401(k)s and IRAs, because this form of rebalancing creates no tax consequences. There may be some transaction costs to consider but they should be minimal, a fraction of what they once were, given the low or even zero trade transaction costs of today's offerings. So, if a client has an IRA, as a manager, I can go in and rebalance as necessary at any time without tax considerations. However, a client with a large, taxable investment portfolio containing 70 or 80 positions, all purchased at different times, requires me to be aware of the tax ramifications of every single position when rebalancing.

Managers of qualified accounts, such as pension managers, have traditionally used calendar-based rebalancing schedules to determine when and how to rebalance back to their target allocations. But again, the primary goal here is minimizing risk relative to a target asset allocation. Not only does this type of rebalancing sacrifice returns, but it also allows the market, not the manager, to dictate rebalancing, in effect relegating it to a passive strategy.[177]

While calendar rebalancing is a systematic method of maintaining a client's risk target, it's probably better than not rebalancing at all.

The more sophisticated type of rebalancing, based on standard deviation, was originally taught to me by noted investor the late Barton Biggs, someone badly missed. With this method, rebalancing occurs only when the variance of an individual asset drifts from a median target.

Investments all have differing variances so each investment must be treated differently. Barton taught us that we should not apply the same rebalancing criteria to stocks as bonds. That's because while a bond might have a standard deviation of five, a stock might have a standard deviation of 15. So, if one asset has three times the amount of expected variance as another, it makes no sense to apply the same rebalancing parameters equally to the two different assets.

Rebalancing based on standard deviation has since morphed into the term "dynamic rebalancing." What it entails is rebalancing a position only when a specified number of standard deviations have been achieved by that asset class. So instead of rebalancing because it's the end of the quarter or in response to a certain rule-based percentage, such as the allocation of equities going from 60 to 62, dynamic balancing assesses the individual standard deviation of each of the portfolio's assets. Whereas we might allow stocks to fluctuate by 7.5%—half a standard deviation of 15—before rebalancing, we might restrict bond fluctuation to 2.5%—half of 5.

To a large extent, rebalancing serves as a defense against the emotional propensities of both investors and investment managers. It puts a system in place that is both objective and dispassionate, one that ignores the emotional frailties that cause investors to inflict financial damage upon themselves.

As investors, we all hope to buy low and sell high; but as humans, we are pre-programmed to do just the opposite. Corporate America, for example, buys high and sells low. Companies reward their best-performing employees with raises and promotions. The worst-performing workers receive demotions and terminations. Ditto for professional athletes. Top performers are lavishly compensated, both in salary and endorsements. Poor performers are subject to trades or release.

That's human nature and many would call it common sense. But what may work for corporations and professional athletics does not work when investing. In portfolio management, rewarding the best performers by constantly adding capital eventually bumps you up against market cyclicality, when yesterday's best performers exchange places with yesterday's losers that have become today's winners. As the Greek philosopher Heraclitus noted, "The only constant in life is change."

Graphic 9.1 is a representation of this principle, depicting how the annual returns of various asset classes yoyo up and down.

One of the major benefits of rebalancing is it helps investors avoid their pre-programmed propensity to make emotionally charged decisions, restraining the inherent DNA that prevents them from becoming successful investors.

Given that, it's crucial for managers to recognize whether they are dealing with an emotional or unemotional portfolio. If the portfolio is unemotional, risk management algorithms guide decisions. If it's an emotional portfolio, however, and most portfolios are emotional because they're managed by human beings, it's susceptible to mistakes well documented by behavioral finance studies. These are portfolios where rebalancing can add tremendous value because it forces people to buy low when their emotions would otherwise prevent them from doing so.

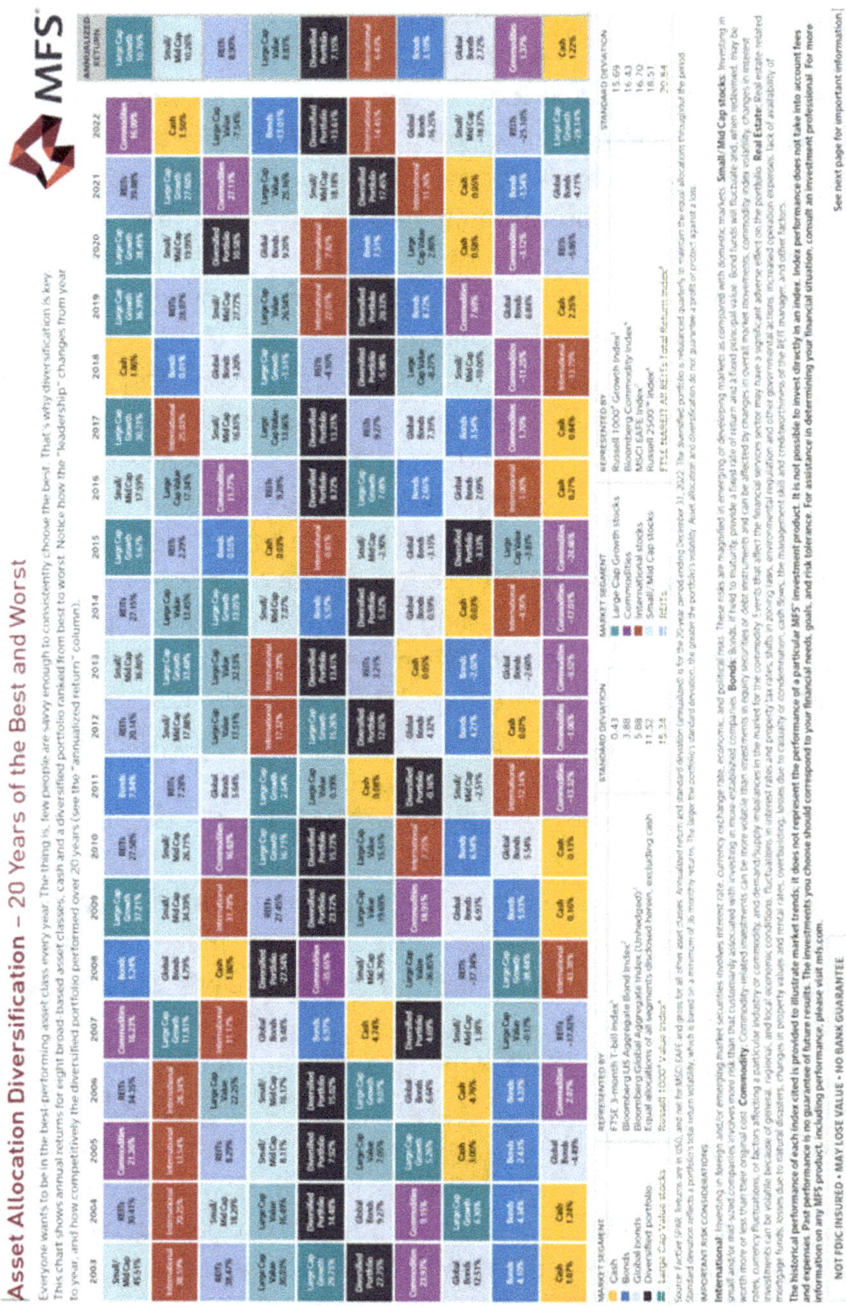

(Graphic 9.1 Sector Quilt)

It's not just individual investors that are prone to having their emotions and cognitive biases dismantle their portfolios. Investment managers are equally predisposed because, after all, they are also human. That's one reason why I use algorithms: I'm human. The algorithms helped prevent me from taking excessive risk in the runup to the Great Recession of 2008. They also helped me to take an appropriate amount of risk in 2009, resulting in a rapid recovery for our clients. In other words, the algorithms aided me on both sides of that event, allowing me to help shield my clients from the financial disasters suffered by so many others.

> *"The investment process is only half the battle. The other weighty component is struggling with yourself, and immunizing yourself from the psychological effects of the swings of markets, career risk, the pressure of benchmarks, competition, and the loneliness of the long-distance runner."*

Barton Biggs

In addition to rebalancing a portfolio's asset allocation, individual positions must also be rebalanced. A key is understanding how much volatility an individual security actually creates for the overall portfolio. There are those that claim you must avoid overweight positions, regardless of how well a security is performing.

Even Barton Biggs, who I regard with great respect and esteem, believed there was no such thing as a stock you keep indefinitely. In his 2008 book, *Wealth, War & Wisdom*, he notes that,

> "There are no magnificent long-term, "keeper" stocks to put away forever, and there never have been because no company has ever had a sustainable, forever competitive advantage. Excellence that lasts over multiple decades is virtually nonexistent. Some advantages last longer than others, but all are temporary. Furthermore, there is overwhelming evidence

> that the duration of corporate competitive advantages has shortened, which is not surprising in a world where the rate of change is accelerating."

Well, even the greatest investment minds have to accept the fact that things change. Fifteen years after the publication of that book, I can tell you that I have owned Amazon stock for over a decade because I was lucky enough to discern early on that Amazon was a special company.

There have been periods where I've allowed the position to drift much higher than the portfolio's original allocation, giving the stock a heightened influence on the portfolio. But I never wavered in my belief in the stock, despite the misgivings of those who warned the company wasn't making any money and had no free cash flow. I resisted selling when rebalancing the portfolio because I saw the potential for growth and opportunity the trillion-dollar company was creating. I was determined to hold on to it and was comfortable with the fact that it had become a somewhat larger position than originally intended. It's been a fantastic investment and remains an essential component of my portfolio.

The key to Amazon's continuing success, beyond having what Warren Buffett refers to as a "wide moat," is that the company has become the low-cost provider of time. As Buffett also says, "I can buy anything I want, basically, but I can't buy time. The only thing that I can't buy is time." When I saw a business that embraced the concept of saving people time, I knew it was destined to be incredibly valuable.

As an investment manager, it's not merely about what to own; it's just as important, or perhaps more so, to know what not to own. I avoid owning companies that Amazon could put out of business, even if they were incredibly cheap from a fundamental perspective. Department stores, bookstores and other brick-and-mortar retailers have been eviscerated by Amazon, which has been credited with single-handedly exterminating Borders, Toys "R" Us, Sears, J. Crew and others.[178] When Amazon bought Whole Foods for $13.7bn in August 2017, a whole new group of retailers—

grocery chains—suffered a collective gulp. A year later, Amazon was the largest online grocer in the U.S. with a market share of 18%.[179] I recognized that the influence of Amazon was going to be so forceful that it only made sense to avoid the types of businesses that competed with it. That's helped my portfolio on both sides.

Expected Returns and Volatility

One of the foundational tenets of Modern Portfolio Theory (MPT) as espoused by Dr. Markowicz is that portfolios must be rebalanced as the assumptions for expected returns and expected volatility change.

It is illogical to have the same equity allocation in two different environments where the equity portion of one has an expected return of 15% while the equity portion of the other has an expected return of 5%. When the expected return is 15% from equities, the portfolio would obviously have a higher allocation of equities. This is one of the tenets of portfolio construction taught to us by Dr. Markowitz.

There are times when rebalancing is unnecessary. If a portfolio asset rises in price, such as stocks that have an expected return of 10% escalating to 12% as a result of improving economic conditions, it often makes sense to let things ride and not rebalance that portfolio.

Other times, opportunities emerge when the same investments are available at significantly different pricing, but many target risk strategies are not designed to take advantage of these opportunities. For example, one of the popular passive strategies involves the use of target-date funds, a class of mutual funds or ETFs that periodically rebalances asset class weights to optimize risk and returns for a predetermined time frame.[180] According to a Wall Street Journal article,[181] one reason critics see these funds as ominous is that:

> "Owners rarely touch them and managers are slow to tweak portfolios, even when they arguably should. For example, when the pandemic panic made stocks cheaper on reliable

> long-term measures than they had been in years, yet bond yields fell to levels almost guaranteed to lose money after inflation, hardly any retirement savers at Vanguard or Fidelity made a change, according to those companies."

As to the fixed income portion of a portfolio, does it make sense to own the same allocation of bonds when they are yielding 0.62%, as they were after the pandemic, as when they are yielding 4.66% as they are currently? As a portfolio manager, why would I construct a bond ladder of the same allocation when bonds were at their lowest yield in decades? Although the bond ladder offered the benefit of pulling down the volatility of the portfolio, the return benefit was insufficient to warrant it. Better to exercise a little patience and wait for more attractive rates before building the ladder. More on this in the next chapter.

A further advantage of waiting for more attractive bond rates is that as the yields rise and the expected return goes higher, the expected volatility actually goes down. That's because any rise in volatility will have a much greater impact on a bond yielding 0.5% than on a bond yielding 4.0%.

Think of it this way: a 0.1% movement on a bond yielding 0.5% represents 20% of that bond's yield, whereas a 0.1% movement on a bond that yields 4.0% represents a mere 2.5% of that bond's yield. So relative volatility bond pricing is valid. The lower the yield and the longer the duration, the more volatile the bond. Just ask the management at SVB and Signature Banks, who were forced into bankruptcy in 2023 when rising interest rates caused the long-term bonds the banks held as security against outstanding loans lost value and the banks were forced to sell their positions at a substantial loss.

One reason why my more conservative client portfolios have had a strong performance despite a sustained period of rising interest rates is because I wasn't blindly owning bonds at the lowest yield in decades, setting up the worst opportunity for bond market investors in 150 years.

Given that environment, why would a manager maintain the same allocation to bonds? Yet many of them were still rebalancing their client portfolios, selling their undervalued equities and buying bonds, when bonds were paying a quarter of a point. Managers were still rebalancing, solely because of risk considerations, all the while ignoring the miniscule bond yields. It made no sense. Some actually sold Amazon, Google and Nvidia stock and bought 1% Treasuries. That's what I mean when I say rebalancing should not be done in a vacuum.

Those managing benefit plans that blindly rebalanced client 401(k) plans by throwing money into bond funds at the same allocation when yields were virtually non-existent did their clients no favors.

Conversely, there are times when rebalancing is crucial. Consider the large number of stagnant portfolios during the pandemic when investors were not adding new capital. Starting in February 2020, stock prices tumbled, bottoming out on March 24 of that year. In August, falling interest rates caused bond yields to plummet, setting the stage for the sharpest bond bear market of all time. Investors that did nothing in response to these rapid changes saw the value of their portfolios take a beating. Stagnant portfolios were catapulted out of balance. Those that failed to rebalance missed the recovery in the equity portion of their portfolio. If they didn't rebalance their bond allocation, they would have been over allocated to bonds during the sharpest and deepest bond bear market in history.

The point here is that rebalancing decisions are not made in a vacuum. They have to be made logically, with an eye towards market volatility and the expected return of the asset classes.

As a portfolio manager, I have to consider expected returns when making any investment decision. I always want to be overweight opportunity. Investors have the option of putting their money in Vanguard or Schwab and pay very little in fees for "portfolio management." But for these clients, investment firms are not going to rebalance with an eye towards opportunity; they will rebalance only the allocation. It doesn't matter whether stocks are expensive or the cheapest they've been in two decades. Vanguard is still going to allocate these portfolios the same amount of stocks and bonds.

For investors, is that really a logical way to invest life savings? Or does it make more sense to question the expected return from the stocks and bonds in the allocation? How does that expected return compare with historical returns? If opportunity presents itself, do I want to be overweight opportunity or sit by passively, pay the 1% management fee and settle for mediocrity, doing the same thing every quarter because I am frightened of making a mistake?

The choice seems obvious to me, but the financial services industry has sold the concept of "average returns" via ETFs and other passive strategies and the investing public has bought in big time. I guess at least that's preferrable to investing emotionally, selling low and buying high, but it's sad that anyone feels comfortable settling for "adequate."

Perhaps you've read about the fact that historically, the average investor rarely comes close to replicating the annual returns of the funds he or she invests in. It's truly a remarkable statistic.

In Carl Richards 2012 book, *The Behavior Gap: Simple Ways to Stop Doing Dumb Things with Money*, he used the term "behavior gap" to describe the difference between the return an investment produces over time and the return an investor in that same investment actually earns.

A 20-year study of investor behavior by research firm Dalbar, Inc. revealed that for the two decades ending 12/31/2019, the S&P 500 Index averaged 6.06% annually but the average equity fund investor earned only 4.25%.[182] Over a 30-year period ending on 12/31/2021, the average equity fund investor made 7.13% versus the S&P 500 return of 10.65%.

I have been citing statistics like this for many years. Why does it happen? Well, one factor is management fees and related investment costs. A larger factor, however, is that, as Barton Biggs noted, humans are pre-programmed to buy high and sell low, constantly chasing performance and buying the best performing funds and taking their assets out of the worst performing funds. These continual missteps result in huge account balance discrepancies over extended periods.

One response from the financial industry and regulators to individual investors' lagging performance is rebalancing. And indeed, it has proven a more successful strategy for investors having their portfolios rebalanced. Certainly, an improvement in reducing the gap that has existed between what individual investors earned and those of the investments they held. It's also been a boon for the financial advisory industry that can now tout their clients are doing better by being forced to buy low and be better participants in capitalism by not having any single security or decision have an outsized influence on overall performance.

While I compliment the industry for doing a marginally better job of protecting investors from their own destructive behaviors via rebalancing, I see this as a path to inefficiency and mediocrity. Investors that settle for this may not be lagging as much, performance-wise, but by prioritizing risk mitigation they are ignoring opportunity. I want our investors to consistently be overweight opportunity.

> *"When the whole world is running towards a cliff, he who is running in the opposite direction appears to have lost his mind."*

C.S. Lewis

CHAPTER TEN

Surviving a Big, Bad Bear Market

Whatever your perception of the market is this morning, if you learned the chances of it suffering a 30% decline are triple the normal probability, what would you do?

My guess is you would postpone breakfast, call your broker and have him pull some money out of the market.

Now what?

Maybe stick the money into a money market fund and wait for a recovery? When will that happen? Because you don't know for certain, you're apt to be late getting back into the market, missing the big days of the early rebound. Meanwhile, inflation starts to erode your money's future purchasing power and you lose the rate of return you need to meet your long-term goals.

More to the point, even if the probability of a bear market is much lower, why would you sell profitable businesses destined to earn you a bushel of money? That's an obvious mistake.

What should you do?

Take that money and move it into investments that have historically performed well during pernicious bear markets. These are known as alternative investments. They are alternatives to owning stock. The most common alternatives that I use include gold, Treasurys, market neutral strategies, managed futures and arbitrage.

In this chapter, you will learn how to alter your portfolio's allocation to alternative investments based on the probability of a bear market. This is Dynamic Alternative Investment Management.

This strategy calculates the probability of a bear market using algorithms while working around a strategic risk target. It shifts allocations in pursuit of superior portfolio outcomes. Those resigned to having a stagnant portfolio miss out on the most lucrative investment opportunities because their portfolio is unable to respond this way to the inevitable twists and turns of the market.

Gold

According to the National Mining Association, gold was first used in what is now Eastern Europe in 4000 BC to make decorative objects. For the following 2500 years, gold was used primarily to create jewelry and religious idols. Around 1500 BC, the ancient empire of Egypt, which benefited from Nubia, its gold-bearing region, made gold the first official medium of exchange for international trade. Gold coins were first mined around 500 BC and in 50 BC, the Romans issued a gold coin called the *Aureus*, which is where the gold chemical symbol of *Au* on the periodic table of elements comes from.

Over a thousand years later, in 1066 AD, William the Conqueror became the first Norman King of England. One of his first acts was to initiate a coin-based system of currency. Two hundred years later, Great Britain issued its first gold coin, the *Florin*. Meanwhile, the Republic of Florence in Italy issued the first gold *Ducat*, which became the most popular gold currency in the world and remained so for another five centuries.

In 1787, the first U.S. gold coin was struck and five years later the nascent U.S. government passed the Coinage Act, placing the country on a silver-gold standard, which lasted in one form or another until 1976, when the U.S. finally abandoned the gold standard to be entirely based on fiat money—currency not based on any commodity. The gold standard was a monetary system in which the U.S. Dollar was based on a fixed quantity of gold. An individual could go to a bank and exchange money for a fixed amount of gold. A mutual desire for gold prompted nations all over the world to adopt gold as a medium of exchange and later, the gold standard.[183]

Interestingly, owning gold was once illegal in the U.S. In April of 1933, President Franklin Delano Roosevelt signed Executive Order 6102, which forbade ownership of gold exceeding $100. All citizens were required to turn in any gold coins, bullion or certificates they held in excess of that amount to the Federal Reserve in exchange for $20.67 per troy ounce. Some 40 years later, President Gerald Ford rescinded the ban on gold ownership with Executive Order 11825.

Even though no country is on the gold standard today, many still hold large reserves of gold as a hedge against economic calamity. Gold prices and recessions historically have maintained an inverse relationship. When the economy weakens, gold prices tend to increase as investors seek safe-haven assets. During the last three recessions of 2020, 2007 and 2001, the price of gold increased while the value of the S&P 500 decreased. Gold prices tend to mimic inflation and as paper money loses value, gold becomes a more valuable asset, providing a hedge against inflation.[184]

Gold has many practical uses that span multiple industries. The metal's malleability allows it to be hammered into sheets, drawn into wires and cast into different shapes. In addition to jewelry, gold is used to manufacture thousands of products, including televisions, cell phones, Global Positioning System (GPS) devices and computers. Gold is also used widely in the medical, aerospace and glassmaking industries.[185]

Another reason the value of gold tends to rise during market downturns or outlier economic events is that gold is liquid. It can be converted into cash. The same cannot be said for the sale of equities, however. Obviously, some stocks are more liquid than others by the nature of their popularity or other factors. But during a crisis or even periods of severe market volatility, there may not be any willing buyers for a particular stock. Companies fail.

When FTX went bankrupt in November 2022, investors were left with no options for withdrawing their funds. On seven occasions, the NYSE closed temporarily, including the assassination of JFK, the paperwork crisis of 1968 (where the NYSE closed every

Wednesday from June 12 through December 31), the 9/11 attacks and Hurricane Sandy in 2012.

In a bear market, investors should own non-correlated or ideally, negatively correlated assets. Correlation refers to a measure of how investments move relative to one another. Assets that move in the same direction at the same time are considered to be positively correlated, whereas non-correlated assets tend to move independent to larger fluctuations in the stock market. Negatively correlated assets tend to move in the opposite direction of one another.[186]

When the probability of a bear market is high, ideally, investors should own assets that are negatively correlated to the U. S. stock market. Gold is one of the investments that facilitates that. It's how savvy investors make money in a down market. But to clarify, the gold I refer to here is bullion, not gold stocks, because gold stocks can be correlated to the overall market. If an equity fire sale occurs, particularly among the indices, and if there are gold company stocks—such as Newmont, Barrick or Agnico Eagle—held in those indices, they're going to be decimated along with everything else in the index.

The inverse relationship between gold and the U.S. Dollar is largely due to what happens when the government decides to print more money. As more dollars are created, the value of each dollar goes down. When this occurs, gold, which is priced in dollars, becomes more valuable, as well as affordable, for international buyers. So as the U. S. Dollar declines in value, owning assets that are priced in dollars becomes more attractive for international investors, which represent a majority of global investment sources. These investors can purchase gold with their currency.

While the inverse relationship between gold and the U.S. Dollar isn't as precise as it used to be, the relationship remains intact because a falling dollar increases the value of other countries' currencies, which in turn increases the demand for uncorrelated assets like gold. It also increases the price.[187]

In some years, the traditional inverse relationship between gold and the U.S. Dollar weakens. For example, in 2022, it wasn't as strong because the Fed continually boosted interest rates. In large part, this was the aftereffect of the pandemic.

As of December 2022, gold is down 1.74% for the year[188] as compared to the S&P 500 which is down 15.53%,[189] so despite the current diminished impact of the inverse relationship between the two assets, gold has still supplied a hedge. If given the choice between having your entire portfolio invested in stocks or gold this year, you still would have done much better holding gold.

> *"I pay attention to the price of gold. It reflects global uncertainties. The reason people hold gold is as a protection against what we call tail risk, really, really bad outcomes. And to the extent that the last few years have made people more worried about the potential of a major crisis, then they have gold as a protection."*

Ben Bernanke, Federal Reserve Chairman

Treasurys

The second type of investment to own in a bear market is Treasurys, securities issued by the U.S. government. There are four classifications of Treasurys: Treasury bills, Treasury bonds, Treasury notes and Treasury Inflation-Protected Securities (TIPS).

Treasury bills, also known as zero-coupon bonds, mature in one year or less and do not pay interest. Investors receive income from buying these at a discount to face (or par) value.

Treasury bonds are long-term investments that typically pay the highest rate of interest among Treasury securities. Bond prices move inversely to interest rates, so these tend to be the most volatile of the group.

Treasury notes pay a fixed-interest rate and mature between two and 10 years. They are available either by competitive bids—where investors specify the yield—or by non-competitive bids, where investors accept whatever yield is determined.

Treasury Inflation-Protected Securities (TIPS) are Treasury securities indexed to the Consumer Price Index (CPI). Designed to protect investors against inflationary movements, the principal increases or decreases in response to inflation, as do interest payments paid twice a year.[190] When inflation escalates, TIPS rise in value. The principal is protected and repaid at the end of the 5, 10 or 30-year term. Investors can purchase up to $5mn worth of TIPS at a single auction. They are liquid and can be sold through the secondary market. As such, they function like most other bonds.

If my algorithm indicates a high probability of a bear market, I increase my allocation to Treasurys. The primary benefit of Treasury securities is that they are backed by the full faith and credit of the U.S. government. Investors are guaranteed the return of both interest and principal, provided they hold the securities to maturity. Incidentally, this is the only investment where a financial advisor is allowed to use the word "guarantee." If you ever hear a financial professional use the word *guarantee* to refer to any investment aside from U.S. Treasurys, run the other way.

A note: prior to maturity, Treasurys are vulnerable to both inflation and interest rate changes.[191]

Treasurys typically experience positive appreciation during recessions because the Fed is obliged to stimulate the economy. This is normally done by dropping interest rates, and as rates drop, borrowing costs decline, encouraging businesses and consumers alike to borrow and spend while saving is discouraged. Meanwhile, the yield on Treasurys declines, which means the Treasurys already in the market become relatively more attractive since they pay a higher interest rate.

Importantly, Treasurys are negatively correlated to the stock market, which can be beneficial to investors during recessions, although what has occurred during the past few years as a result of the pandemic has created an abnormal environment as it relates to the traditional inverse relationship between the stock market and non-correlated investments.

When the Fed greased the wheels of the economy to support it during the pandemic, the result was higher inflation. Amazingly, the inflation-adjusted liquidity the government injected into the economy in the form of COVID relief programs ($5.2 tn) exceeded the total amount spent to support WW II…not just one year of the war, but the entire war!

These aggressive stimulus measures, in conjunction with rising demand for goods and services, supply chain disruptions and Russia's invasion of Ukraine all contributed to a surge of inflation. The CPI rose by 9.1% for the 12-month period ending in June 2022, its highest reading since 1981.

In response, the Fed began raising interest rates in an effort to mitigate the inflation, which had been a major headwind for financial assets. When the Fed raises interest rates, businesses are discouraged from borrowing because of the added cost. Similarly, consumers borrow less and save more. The overall effect is to rein in economic growth in an attempt to lower inflation.

The benchmark 10-year U.S. Treasury note that yielded 1.5% at the end of 2021 has risen to 4.667% in April, 2024, a level not reached since April 2010. Because of the inverse relationship between bond yields and bond prices, when yields rise, prices of bonds already in the market fall. When demand for bonds declines, issuers of new bonds must offer higher yields to attract buyers, reducing the value of lower-yielding bonds already on the market. This environment hit bondholders hard through much of the year.[192]

This is obviously a highly unusual situation. March, April and May of 2022 marked the largest two-year bond bear market in the past 150 years. The two-year period following the pandemic has been the worst bear market in history. Bond yields have risen an astounding 343%. (see graphic 10.1)

There have only been 22 times in history when yields have risen by 50% or more over a two-year period. The previous largest yield increase was 92.67% (7/2016-2018).

Fortunately, bond portfolios can be managed. When the bond market is offering the worst deal since the eighteenth century, you want to be under-allocated. If you buy bonds and loan your money to the federal government for 10 years and you're getting approximately 75 basis points or three quarters of a percent return, perhaps you should take a pass on that deal, have patience and wait for a better offer.

Two Year Period	Increase in Yield
2020.05-2022.05	343.28%
2020.04-2022.04	316.67%
2020.03-2022.03	144.83%
2016.07-2018.07	92.67%
2016.08-2018.08	85.26%
2016.09-2018.09	84.05%
2016.1-2018.1	78.98%
2016.06-2018.06	77.44%
2012.07-2014.07	66.01%
1979.08-1981.08	65.45%
2016.05-2018.05	64.42%
1979.09-1981.09	64.20%
2016.02-2018.02	60.67%
2012.06-2014.06	60.49%
1979.07-1981.07	59.55%
1978.03-1980.03	58.58%
2016.04-2018.04	58.56%
1978.02-1980.02	54.55%
1958.01-1960.01	52.75%
1979.05-1981.05	52.43%
1979.06-1981.06	51.18%
2016.03-2018.03	50.26%

(Graphic 10.1: Percentage Change in Two Year 10 Year Treasury Note Yield – Sorted by largest in the past 150 years)

I believe the bond market is going to revert to a more normal market going forward as we escape the effects of the pandemic. While it has been an extremely strange market the past few years, those of us that tactically allocated bond portfolios have added considerable value for clients.

If you consider yourself a moderately conservative investor, you should have a minimum of 30% of your money in bonds. At one time, our bond portfolios had a duration of just two, which is extremely low. Bond duration is a measurement of how much bond prices are likely to change if and when interest rates move. In more technical terms, bond duration is measurement of interest rate risk.[193] Generally speaking, the higher the duration, the more a bond's price will drop as interest rates rise.

Most investors don't know how to survive a bond bear market. It's why so many banks got into trouble when interest rates rose following the pandemic. In the early stages of a bond bear market, you want to be under-allocated to bonds—so you have less money in bonds—and you also want to have a short duration. As the bond bear market gains momentum and yields rise, you systematically start to increase both the bond allocation and the duration of your bond portfolio. That's the playbook on how to survive a bond bear market. That's exactly what we've done, and the low duration of our bond portfolios have had a much better performance than a 10-year bond during the spate of interest rate increases.

Graphic 10.2 illustrates how surviving a bond bear market is accomplished.

	10 Year Treasury Yield Distribution Since 1990			Bond Ladder Allocation			
	Median	Min	Max	Moderately Conservative	Moderate	Moderately Aggressive	Duration
Decile 1	1.56	0.62	1.76	30	20	7	2.0
Decile 2	2.03	1.76	2.30	34	22	7	2.8
Decile 3	2.55	2.30	2.84	37	25	8	3.5
Decile 4	3.19	2.86	3.59	41	27	9	4.3
Decile 5	3.90	3.59	4.15	45	30	10	5.0
Median			4.16	45	30	10	5.0
Decile 6	4.46	4.17	4.69	45	30	10	5.0
Decile 7	5.02	4.72	5.39	49	32	11	5.8
Decile 8	5.82	5.46	6.20	52	35	12	6.5
Decile 9	6.60	6.21	7.20	56	37	12	7.3
Decile 10	8.00	7.24	8.89	60	40	13	8.0

Graphic 10.2 Surviving a Bond Bear Market Playbook

> *"Alexander Hamilton started the U.S. Treasury with nothing, and that was the closest our country has ever been to being even."*

Will Rogers

Market Neutral Strategies

The third element of successful investing in a down market is a market neutral strategy. When the stock market is retreating, investors should have a portion of their portfolio in market neutral strategies—investment returns that are uncorrelated with stock or bond market returns—so they can profit from market movements in either direction: up or down.

Typically, a market neutral strategy is achieved by holding both long positions in one security and short positions in another. The securities involved are usually stocks, but can also be bonds, real estate or other investments. Roughly half the money is assigned to each side of the ledger: long and short. The long positions are invested in securities or assets believed to be underpriced; short positions are invested in securities or assets expected to underperform.

Being long in a stock simply means you buy and own it because you believe it will increase in value. Being short in a stock means you bought it believing you will profit on its decline. Put another way, longs try to buy low and sell high; shorts try to sell high and buy low.[194]

The profitability of a market neutral strategy relies primarily with the skill of the portfolio manager. Assuming investors have half their money long in stocks and the other half short in stocks, whether the market goes up or down 20% doesn't really affect the strategy. What does have an impact on the strategy is the skill set of the manager or the strategy itself, and whether the stocks bought long outperform the market and those bought short underperform the market. When that occurs, investors can squeeze out some impressive profits in a bear market. In the algorithm, if the probability of a bear market is high, we automatically increase the allocation to market neutral strategies.

The process of executing a long or short trade is fairly straightforward. The market neutral manager borrows a security from a financial institution with the agreement to later pay back the institution with an identical security. When shorting, the manager that borrows the security then goes into the open market and sells it, hoping that by waiting for it to drop in value, it can be repurchased at a lower price, used to repay the institution and profit from the difference.

If the manager is adept, the process produces positive absolute returns—a measurement of the investment return above zero. The profitability of the market neutral strategy, therefore, is not dependent on market direction. It is, rather, largely dependent upon the ability of the manager executing the strategy to make savvy investment decisions, regardless of what is going on in the markets, or the world for that matter.

Investors often confuse market neutral strategies with long/short strategies, which currently represent 26% of the world's hedge funds.[195] While long/short also seeks to take advantage of undervaluation or overvaluation by taking long and short stock exposures, the main difference is that the long/short manager has the latitude to change the 50/50 long/short ratio of the fund.

Investors in long/short tend to assume they are protected from bear markets but that's not always the case. I've seen instances where a long/short manager has drifted to a 70% long (30% short) position, which exposes the fund that is supposed to be market neutral to significant market risk.

Strategies where the manager can tactically determine how much he wants long and short do not provide adequate protection in a major market downturn. They are popular because managers (and most investors) know that over longer periods of time, stock prices rise, so having a larger percentage of long positions attempts to take advantage of that fact. I don't want that in my portfolio, however. When our algorithm indicates a high probability of a bear market, I don't want long/short, especially a fund that's drifted to a stronger long position; I want true market neutral for protection in a bear market.

> *"Know what you own, and know why you own it."*
>
> Peter Lynch

Arbitrage

Arbitrage involves identifying two identical or very similarly priced assets that have a pricing difference and at the exact same moment, executing a transaction that locks in the profit from the difference. Arbitrage opportunities are based on inefficiencies that exist in different markets. They are often obscure, disappearing as quickly as they emerge, calling for deftness on the part of the arbitrageur.

It's important to understand the distinction between market neutral strategies and arbitrage. They have similar objectives but different strategies and are employed in different market conditions. Market neutral is executed by holding long positions in one security and short positions in another. Arbitrage is the pure definition of a risk-free return. While market neutral strategies are appropriate in a bear market, arbitrage is not.

For a more detailed discussion of arbitrage strategies, see the chapter on How the Wealthy Protect their Money.

> *"In past reports we have told you that our insurance subsidiaries sometimes engage in arbitrage as an alternative to holding short-term cash equivalents. We prefer, of course, to make major long-term commitments, but we often have more cash than good ideas. At such times, arbitrage sometimes promises much greater returns than Treasury Bills."*

Berkshire Hathaway Annual Shareholder Letter 1988

Managed Futures

The history of futures trading in the U.S. began in the early nineteenth century. At that time, most of the grain—wheat, corn, barley, rye and oats—was produced by subsistence farmers to feed their families. While some were able to sell their surplus production, most lacked access to large markets, as well as the technologies needed to produce large scale agricultural commodities.

In 1848 the Illinois-Michigan Canal was completed, enabling farmers along the Illinois River to ship their produce to merchants who stored and then shipped grain to Chicago and Milwaukee. Commercial activity grew throughout the 1850s and Chicago emerged as a dominant grain hub.

The futures contract, as we know it today, evolved as farmers and merchants started to negotiate future exchanges of grain for cash. A farmer might agree with a merchant on a price to deliver a certain number of bushels of grain on a specific future date. He knew how much he would be paid for his grain and the merchant knew his costs in advance.

These contracts became common and some were used as collateral for bank loans. They also began to change hands before the delivery date. If the dealer decided he didn't want the gain, he would sell the contract to someone who did. If the farmer decided he didn't want to deliver his grain, he might pass his obligation on to another farmer. This caused prices to fluctuate. Weather also had an impact on prices. In bad weather, those who had contracted to sell wheat would hold more valuable contracts because the supply would be lower. Contrarily, if the harvest were bigger than expected, the seller's contract would become less valuable. Soon, speculators who had no intention of ever buying or selling grain or other commodities began trading the contracts.[196]

During this time, commodity exchanges emerged to deal with local issues such as harbor infrastructure and commercial arbitration. The largest of these was the Board of Trade of the City of Chicago, known today as the Chicago Board of Trade (CBT). In the early years, the CBT functioned mainly as a meeting place for merchants to resolve contract disputes and discuss matters of mutual concern. The Board's first directorate of members included a druggist, bookseller, tanner, grocer, coal dealer, hardware merchant and a banker, and attendance was often encouraged by free lunches.

The CBT eventually became a state chartered private association, sanctioned to establish rules, arbitrate disputes and certify grain trades that would be binding upon all CBT members. In 1863, the CBT adopted its first procedures for trade in forwards on the exchange. Two years later, The CBT began to convert actively traded forward contracts into futures contracts.

In 1974 Congress passed the Commodity Futures Trading Act, which created federal oversight of U.S. futures trading and established the Commodity Futures Trading Commission (CFTC) consisting of five presidential appointees. The Futures Trading Act of 1982 amended the Commodity Futures Trading Act, legalizing options trading on agricultural commodities. A regulatory overlap between the two organizations arose during the explosive popularity of financial futures contracts in the 1970s.

In 1992, futures contracts began trading electronically on the CME Globex platform, beginning the transition from pit-based floor trading to the electronic platform.

In 2000, Congress passed the Commodity Futures Modernization Act, which repealed an 18-year-old ban on trading single stock futures and endeavored to increase competition while reducing systematic risk in markets for futures and over-the-counter derivatives.[197]

In 2007, the CBT and Chicago Mercantile Exchange merged to form CME Group, the following year acquiring NYMEX, adding energy and metals to its product offerings. Today's futures markets are technologically sophisticated global marketplaces, trading at high speeds on electronic platforms, around the globe, nearly 24 hours a day.[198]

The majority of participants in futures markets—such as the Chicago Mercantile Exchange—are institutional investors. Futures traders include both hedgers and speculators that use exchanges to hedge against price volatility and speculate on the future prices of a variety of investments, including stock indexes, currencies, commodities and interest rates. More than 29 billion futures contracts were traded in 2021, according to data from the Futures Industry Association (FIA).

A futures contract is an agreement to exchange a security at a specific price on a specific future date. Unlike option contracts, futures contract buyers are usually required to execute their contracts and accept delivery of the underlying asset.[199]

Investing in commodities involves significant leverage and requires a higher level of expertise to avoid large losses. A commodity trading advisor (CTA) is a financial advisor registered to provide advice specifically related to commodities trading. A CTA fund is a hedge fund that uses an array of trading strategies to invest in futures contracts.[200]

Funds that trade on the futures exchange don't actually hold the commodities. Where would you stash a boxcar of wheat or tanker of oil? Instead, futures contracts are rolled over prior to expiration. Since the future price of a commodity is usually higher than its current price, the funds are continually buying futures contracts at higher prices and then selling them prior to expiration at current (spot level) prices. This is one reason for the disparities between the price appreciation of commodities versus a lower or even negative return on mutual funds or ETFs that trade futures rather than holding the actual commodity.[201]

Managed futures are unique, one of the few investments that can not only make profits, but extremely large profits in a bear market. One reason why is because managed futures profit on persistence or trends, that is, when investments trend in an identifiable direction. For example, if the price of oil continues to rise, managed futures make a lot of money. They can also earn substantial amounts of money on declining commodity prices. They are non-directional. They are not dependent on whether the price of the underlying asset will go up or down but rather the anticipated volatility of the asset. This is another reason why managed futures are an important component of surviving—or profiting—from a bear market.

Managed futures can be categorized as a trend-following strategy, executed by investing in the financial markets' current trends or, as industry insiders refer to it, persistence. There exists mathematically proven persistence in how the nature of capital markets work. As trends develop and certain investments begin to outperform, the movement acts like a magnet for capital because most investors are followers (the herding bias) that want in on what appear to be successful investments. As this persistence continues, it attracts ever-greater amounts of fresh capital, pushing the trend ever-further forward.

This phenomenon is what we typically observe in market downturns, such as the 17-month bear market from October, 2007 through March, 2009 when the S&P 500 index lost roughly 50% of its value. Meanwhile, managed futures rewarded investors handsomely. For example, the oldest open-end managed futures fund, Guggenheim Managed Futures Strategy A (RYMFX), gained an annualized 12.4% during the 2007-2009 bear market versus an annualized loss of 42.95% for the S&P 500 index and a loss of 48.26% for the MSCI Europe, Australasia and Far East Index.

Investors and participants in the futures market are not "married" to any of these investments. They're simply trying to make a profit by investing in trends or persistence. A couple decades ago, the only way for investors to enter these markets was to hire a commodity trading advisor or firm to take their money and invest it in a trend or persistence following strategy.

These strategies were not particularly complex, however, which meant they were easily replicated. When the SEC decided to allow mutual funds to invest in managed futures, a host of financial firms jumped on the bandwagon. Today, there are a large number of financial firms offering a variety of managed futures investment opportunities.

The caveat with managed futures is that you don't want to own them unless there is a clear and persistent direction in the market. If the market is moving up and down a few percent month to month, seesawing back and forth but not exhibiting any significant trend, a managed futures strategy has a high probability of getting crushed. This type of non-persistent market is not a threat for pure stock investors but managed futures in a sideways trending market can be a disaster.

The success of a managed futures strategy, much like that of a market neutral strategy, is contingent upon the skill of the fund manager to identify trends versus short-term market movements.

In a bear market when stock prices are plummeting, investors get nervous. Many outright panic. This can trigger a discernable negative trend. When this occurs, investors want their money invested in the best skill-based, non-directional strategy. The only way to make money in the stock market is if the stocks go up. In a managed futures strategy, however, money can be made non-directionally. So even if stocks, bonds and commodities are all falling in price, investors could theoretically make a lot of money with a managed futures fund invested in nothing but short positions across the board.

Fundamentally, managed futures are non-correlated assets that tend to make a lot of money when things get exceptionally directional and volatile, the same environment that can be exceedingly hazardous for pure stock investors.

> *"It's always darkest just before it's pitch black."*
>
> Peter Lynch

Alternative Expected Returns

Each of these alternative investments performs differently in dissimilar market environments. It's critical to understand the nuances. Given that, why do the vast majority of investment managers maintain a stagnant alternative asset allocation? Do they lack historical knowledge? Or do they lack the portfolio software to rapidly move in and out of these alternatives? Perhaps they are simply lazy? When my measurements indicate the probability of a bear market is high, I increase my allocation to investments that perform well in that environment.

Graphic 10.3 depicts the expected returns for each of these alternative asset classes under three different market conditions, based on research spanning the life of the markets. As you can see, there is a dramatic difference in the way these investments are expected to behave in a maximum bullish, maximum bearish or neutral market.

For example, Arbitrage is expected to do well in bull or neutral markets but historically does poorly in bear markets, whereas Treasury Bonds are expected to do well in bear markets but perform poorly in bull markets.

	Expected Returns		
Asset Class	Bull Market	Neutral Market	Bear Market
Arbitrage	6.0%	5.0%	-3.0%
Treasury Bonds	-5.0%	4.3%	7.0%
Market Neutral	3.0%	2.0%	4.0%
Managed Futures	3.0%	1.0%	7.0%
Gold	-3.0%	1.5%	4.0%

(Graphic 10.3 Alternatives Expected Returns)

Obviously, I want my portfolio to have the alternative asset allocation that makes the most money in the current market environment. So, in a maximum bullish market, I want to own Arbitrage, Market Neutral, and Managed Futures, as per graphic 10.2. I do not want to own Treasurys or Gold.

In a maximum bear market, I want to own Treasury Bonds, Market Neutral Strategies, Managed Futures and Gold. Here, I exclude Arbitrage.

In a 100% neutral market, I want to own Arbitrage, Treasury Bonds, Market Neutral, Managed Futures and Gold.

There is a yield differential calculation built into my algorithm, so if Treasurys have a high yield relative to Arbitrage, I would reduce the Arbitrage allocation to much less than is shown in the graphic. As of this writing, the current yield on Treasury Bonds is 4.667%.

Even in a bull market, where Arbitrage normally outperforms Treasurys by a substantial percentage, in the unlikely event that the expected return on Arbitrage is 6% but I can make 10% risk-free with Treasurys, I am going to increase my allocation to Treasurys When there's a meaningful change in the yield differential between two alternative asset classes, an allocation change is called for. So, when bond yields rose in early 2023, I reallocated my alternatives portfolio, adding more Treasurys and reducing Arbitrage.

So, in a maximum bull market, as illustrated in graphic 10.4, an optimal alternative portfolio owns 55% Arbitrage, 18% Managed Futures and 27% Market Neutral strategies. Applying the same calculations to a maximum bear market, own 18% Gold, 32% Treasury Bonds and Managed Futures, and 18% Market Neutral.

	Alternative Allocation		
	Bull Market	Neutral Market	Bear Market
Arbitrage	55%	39%	0%
Treasury Bonds	0%	34%	32%
Market Neutral	27%	8%	18%
Managed Futures	18%	8%	32%
Gold	0%	12%	18%
	100%	100%	100%

(Graphic 10.4 Alternative Investment Allocation)

A note about the use of Treasury Bonds in the alternative asset allocation. These are high-quality government bonds and are not to be confused with the Bond Ladders utilized in the traditional portion of the portfolio, as explained in Chapter 17, "How the Wealthy Protect their Money."

You now should have a better understanding of the asset classes that comprise the alternative allocation of the portfolio, and how the percentage allocated to each asset class is determined, depending on the condition of the market.

Compare this variable allocation spectrum to a traditional portfolio containing alternative asset classes that are stationary. This is the difference between a stagnant and a dynamic alternative asset allocation, and why merely adding alternatives to a portfolio and not continually adjusting their allocation in response to market vacillations defeats the purpose of including alternatives in the first place.

In a pure neutral market, I want 100% of my assets invested in the neutral portfolio—the same neutral market allocation you saw in Graphic 10.3 under the "Neutral Market" column.

If the probability of a bear market increases and moves from neutral to medium confidence bearish, the percentage allocation automatically changes to 50% neutral and 50% bearish. The composition becomes:

Arbitrage 19%
Treasurys 33%
Market Neutral 13%
Managed Futures 20%
Gold 15%

If the probability shifts to low confidence bullish, the percentage allocation automatically changes to 75% neutral and 25% bullish. The composition becomes:

Arbitrage 43%
Treasurys 25%
Market Neutral 13%
Managed Futures 10%
Gold 9%

Allocation by Market Conviction

In addition to allocating alternative assets based on market conditions, the allocations must be further modified, depending on whether the client risk profile is aggressive, moderately aggressive, moderate or moderately conservative.

The graphics that follow illustrate how a hypothetical total portfolio—Businesses/Equities, Bond Ladders, Arbitrage, Managed Futures, Market Neutral strategies, Treasurys and Gold— is allocated when adjusted for individual client risk parameters. This is based on the "state of the market," ranging from maximum bearish to maximum bullish.

Aggressive	Maximum Bearish	High Conviction Bearish	Low Conviction Bearish	Neutral	Low Conviction Bullish	High Conviction Bullish	Maximum Bullish
Businesses	65%	75%	85%	95%	100%	100%	100%
Bond Ladders	0%	0%	0%	0%	0%	0%	0%
Arbitrage Strategies	0%	3%	4%	2%	0%	0%	0%
Gold Bullion	6%	4%	2%	1%	0%	0%	0%
Managed Futures Strategies	11%	6%	2%	0%	0%	0%	0%
Market Neutral Strategies	6%	4%	2%	0%	0%	0%	0%
Treasury Bonds	11%	8%	5%	2%	0%	0%	0%

(Graphic 10.5 Aggressive Allocation)

In an aggressive allocation (Graphic 10.5), the Businesses allocation represents the largest percentage of the portfolio, regardless of market conditions, ranging from a low of 65% in maximum bearish to a high of 100% in any market more bullish than neutral.

Moderately Aggressive	Maximum Bearish	High Conviction Bearish	Low Conviction Bearish	Neutral	Low Conviction Bullish	High Conviction Bullish	Maximum Bullish
Businesses	50%	60%	70%	80%	85%	90%	90%
Bond Ladders	10%	10%	10%	10%	10%	10%	10%
Arbitrage Strategies	0%	4%	5%	4%	2%	0%	0%
Gold Bullion	7%	5%	3%	1%	0%	0%	0%
Managed Futures Strategies	13%	7%	3%	1%	1%	0%	0%
Market Neutral Strategies	7%	4%	2%	1%	1%	0%	0%
Treasury Bonds	13%	10%	7%	3%	1%	0%	0%

(Graphic 10.6 Moderately Aggressive Allocation)

In a moderately aggressive allocation (Graphic 10.6), the Businesses allocation remains the dominant percentage but slightly less so than the aggressive allocation.

Moderate	Maximum Bearish	High Conviction Bearish	Low Conviction Bearish	Neutral	Low Conviction Bullish	High Conviction Bullish	Maximum Bullish
Businesses	30%	40%	50%	60%	65%	70%	70%
Bond Ladders	30%	30%	30%	30%	30%	30%	30%
Arbitrage Strategies	0%	4%	5%	4%	2%	0%	0%
Gold Bullion	7%	5%	3%	1%	0%	0%	0%
Managed Futures Strategies	13%	7%	3%	1%	1%	0%	0%
Market Neutral Strategies	7%	4%	2%	1%	1%	0%	0%
Treasury Bonds	13%	10%	7%	3%	1%	0%	0%

(Graphic 10.7 Moderate Allocation)

In a moderate allocation (Graphic 10.7), the Businesses allocation has been reduced more noticeably, down to 70% in a maximum bullish market and 30% in a maximum bearish market.

Moderately Conservative	Maximum Bearish	High Conviction Bearish	Low Conviction Bearish	Neutral	Low Conviction Bullish	High Conviction Bullish	Maximum Bullish
Businesses	10%	20%	30%	40%	45%	50%	55%
Bond Ladders	45%	45%	45%	45%	45%	45%	45%
Arbitrage Strategies	0%	5%	6%	6%	4%	2%	0%
Gold Bullion	8%	6%	3%	2%	1%	0%	0%
Managed Futures Strategies	14%	8%	4%	1%	1%	1%	0%
Market Neutral Strategies	8%	5%	3%	1%	1%	1%	0%
Treasury Bonds	14%	11%	8%	5%	2%	1%	0%

Graphic 10.8 Moderately Conservative Allocation)

In a moderately conservative allocation (Graphic 10.8), the Businesses allocation ranges from a low of 10% to a high of 55%.

Here's the reasoning to support all the other asset class allocations in the various market environments:

Bond Ladders is a unique asset class. Constructed exclusively of high-quality securities, it nonetheless retains its percentage allocation across the spectrum of market convictions. While the allocation percentage is adjusted based on the type of allocation (rising from 0% in an aggressive allocation to 45% in a moderately conservative allocation in this example), it does not change within any of the individual portfolio allocations.

As an asset class, bonds take a beating when interest rates rise as bond prices move inversely with interest rates. Bond ladders provide protection against rate increases but, in the past, were plagued with burdensome administrative duties. To the delight of investment managers, this obstacle has been largely eliminated by the development of bond ETF portfolios containing maturity dates and diversified holdings among various sectors.

Arbitrage allocations tend to be concentrated in the mid-range of the market conviction sentiment, notably absent from the "maximum" margins. As an asset class, arbitrage strategies curiously mimic Treasury Bonds, not in terms of allocation designations, but rather in providing investment managers with an exceptionally high level of confidence in calculating expected returns. Arbitrage provides what many in the financial industry maintain is non-existent: *a risk-free rate of return*. As such, it is an indispensable non-correlated asset when conviction lies between neutral and high-conviction bearish markets.

Managed Futures is an especially effective investment strategy as the market moves into bearish territory. With a low correlation to traditional equity/bond portfolios, the strategy provides a recourse for Treasury Bonds. As the graphics illustrate, the two investments maintain virtually identical percentage allocations throughout the range of market convictions.

The Managed Futures allocation is principally driven by market trends or momentum. Trend-following involves taking long and short positions in chiefly liquid futures contracts across currencies, commodities, equities and fixed income.[202] But there are no trends in a neutral market.

Market Neutral strategies, much like Managed Futures, are most useful as the market moves from neutral to bearish, with allocations increasing as conviction towards maximum bearish intensifies. Market Neutral is fundamentally a speculative investment strategy, with managers hedging risk by taking both long and short positions in businesses while more or less guessing on the outcome. The overriding goal is to remain "neutral" in the face of market volatility.

Market Neutral works best when the market is gyrating and things are bouncing up and down. The greater the volatility, the better the return opportunity for this investment class.

Treasury Bonds are long-term debt securities, maturing between 20 and 30 years. Like Managed Futures, and to a lesser degree Market Neutral, they are bypassed in markets ranging from maximum bullish to neutral, appearing in increasingly larger allocations as market probability swivels towards bearish.

Gold Bullion is allocated most heavily in bearish territory. Allocations mimic Managed Futures and Market Neutral in neutral markets, growing as conviction moves further along towards bearish, but not as intensively as the other two asset classes, plateauing at 8%.

Gold *Bullion* is specified in these allocations. Bullion represents the price of gold in one-ounce increments. The most important facet of bullion over other forms of the asset class, such as gold stocks, which can be found in funds and indices, is that bullion is negatively correlated to stocks in bear markets. When equity funds and indices come under pressure and experience heavy selloffs, the gold stocks inside them get sold off as well. They simply don't provide the same level of portfolio protection as gold bullion.

> *"We see gold not as a trade; we don't even look at it as an investment. We look at it as insurance."*

Jean-Marie Eveillard

Summary

The optimal method for making money in a capitalist economy is to own good businesses (equities). In a bullish market, I want more of the total portfolio allocation directed towards these businesses and less towards alternative investments. When the probability of a bear market rises, I incrementally increase investment in alternative strategies and reduce investment in equities.

The extraordinary beauty of this tactical allocation strategy is that it is all predetermined.

As the 190 variables are updated in the model and the probability of a market decline changes, everything dynamically updates, precisely because the allocations are predetermined. As an investment manager, this allows me to move with the necessary swiftness in responding to changing data.

There is no need for harried investment committee meetings to discuss how to respond to the latest market data. The appropriate responses have already been built into the model, having been calculated under calm conditions, not the chaotic atmosphere that spawns kneejerk reactions to market fluctuations.

One of the common errors that devastates portfolios is the propensity for investors to overreact to market volatility. *Behavioral Finance* research lists dozens of cognitive biases that cause individuals to make poor investment decisions. One of the contributing factors to these financial missteps is the tendency to make emotionally charged judgments under the most stressful conditions, typically when the markets are roiling.

This same type of herd behavior can be observed in investment committees as well, especially in larger committees where the group tends to acquiesce to the highest level of leadership, or worse, to the loudest speaker.

When the economic atmosphere experiences turbulence investors, like an inexperienced pilot, lose their nerve, become disoriented and end up crashing their portfolio.

When the markets plunge, they lack the confidence to take enough risk. When a bull market emerges, they pivot and take too much risk. On the other hand, when the proper asset allocation and investment decisions for each market environment have been predetermined under objective, dispassionate conditions, investors gain the courage to ignore the noise all around them and trust their manager.

> *"Bull-markets are born on pessimism, grow on skepticism, mature on optimism and die on euphoria."*

Sir John Templeton

Here's an important statistic to remember. Surprisingly, fully half of the best days of the S&P 500 Index during this millennium occurred during a bear market. Another one-third of the market's best days took place during the first two months of a bull market, before the investment herd had any indication a bull market had begun.[203]

The principle of remaining invested is ingrained in a long-term approach. I advocate the concept, but not to the extent that I become a passive victim of market oscillations. I want my model to be a tad early reacting to bear market fluctuations leading to peaks and troughs. Being just a little late can cause the portfolio to miss the market's best days—the ones that occur during the first two months of a recovery. By catching the eighth or ninth inning of a bear market, I'm going to absorb some short-term losses, but that's the acceptable trade-off for being at bat when the best days happen and knocking one out of the park.

CHAPTER ELEVEN

Successful Portfolio Manager Attributes

As a young man, I had the privilege of serving in the Marine Corps. The military teaches you how to remain dispassionate and unemotional making decisions when all around you is in upheaval and confusion. The Marines refer to this as "military bearing," that is, how a person carries and conducts themself. Marines with bearing are taught to be in complete control of their emotions, whether in combat or garrison, whether being shot at or getting their ass chewed by a first sergeant.[204]

Bearing is what allows Marines to "keep their cool" when the stakes are the highest. As you might imagine, this most vital and valuable asset, which can literally save a person's life and the lives of his fellow Marines, is not easily acquired.

Marine Corps training involves a level of chaos that is unimaginable for anyone unfamiliar with the regimen. The objective is to find out whether you can keep your bearing when pandemonium triggers every emotion inside you, causing you to panic and do the wrong thing. Instructors scream at you and physically and psychologically challenge you. In short, they do everything conceivable to push you to exhaustion.

First, they restrict your caloric intake so you get extremely hungry. Then comes sleep deprivation where you are kept awake for 72 hours. These are the first things new recruits experience as the Marines want to quickly weed out those who can't take it. During my training, guys were dropping left and right. Next is water training, or more accurately, drowning training. Without prior notice, recruits are made to jump off a high dive into a pool fully clothed. They pushed people to the point of exhaustion and, in some cases, drowning.

I recall there were some guys who thought themselves pretty tough that were literally begging the drill instructor (DI) not to make them jump because they didn't know how to swim. They had no choice. If they didn't jump, the DI pushed them in and, of course, they immediately sank to the bottom, where an instructor would pull them out, gasping for air, and take them over to a shallow pool where they were eventually taught to swim or sent home. I'll tell you that those fellows lost a lot of their tough-guy act after that.

The last thing is being put in a chamber and exposed to pepper gas. You have to remove your gas mask and inhale the fumes, which hit you like a fireball. Your face, your eyes, your throat, your forehead, the back of your neck, everything is on fire. You have to sit there and deal with it before you can clear out your gas mask and put it back on. Some people can't handle it. They fall on the floor and start flopping around. It's known as the "funky chicken." The name is much funnier than the experience.

The idea is that in combat, if you are gassed, you have to stay in control, keep your wits about you and go through the proper procedure. It's not something you can learn by reading or watching a video. You have to experience it firsthand, feel like you are about to go mad, stay calm and react properly while you feel like you are going up in flames.

To those who don't understand what is happening or why, the maltreatment seems unnecessarily harsh, even barbaric. But everything that's done is done for a reason: to make you frightened and angry. They want to unleash raw emotions so they can identify the individuals who can compartmentalize fear and uncertainty when under great stress and make composed, unemotional decisions.

In the years since the service, I've found that bearing is critical to success and fulfillment in both business and personal life. I think it can be applied to virtually any occupation and is especially helpful to those involving intensive pressure or stress. It most certainly applies to the occupation of managing other people's money.

Successful portfolio managers must be unexcitable and patient, attributes difficult to maintain when the markets are roiling and investors are frenzied. While everyone is subject to emotional pressures, some people seem almost immune to being victimized by their emotions. Perhaps they are genetically predisposed to remaining unruffled when everyone around them is in full flight panic.

Athletes like Michael Jordan, Tom Brady and Michael Phelps are examples of people able to "rise to the occasion." Unlike other professional athletes, they actually perform their best in stressful situations, when everything is on the line. They are able to control their emotions, remain composed and succeed on a consistent basis.

Portfolio managers may not play for championships, but the pressure to safeguard their client's investments when media talking heads are predicting the collapse of the dollar or the second coming of the Great Depression can be overwhelming. Maintaining a calm demeanor, ignoring the noise and thinking clearly during these frenetic periods is a challenge few people can handle successfully.

> *"I buy stocks when the lemmings are headed the other way."*
>
> Warren Buffett

Bravery is Not the Absence of Fear

People ask, "Did the Marines teach you how not to be afraid?" The answer is no, they didn't. They teach that it's okay to be afraid and that fear is normal. Fear can be detrimental or helpful. It warns us of danger so we can survive. It also clouds our thinking when we most need to think with clarity. What's needed to overcome fear are the tools that allow us to move forward confidently in the face of fear.

> *"Courage is not the absence of fear, but rather the assessment that something else is more important than fear."*

Franklin D. Roosevelt

As a portfolio manager, I am constantly measuring the sentiment of the investment crowd to determine whether they are behaving irrationally. You may recall reading about this in the chapter on Market Sentiment. Having consistent, credible data on market sentiment is invaluable for a manager because it allows me to feel comfortable not being part of the crowd. It allows me to control my fears, have courage and move forward confidently.

It's been my experience that the best investment managers are more introverted than most others. They may be gregarious in social gatherings or when called upon to make public statements, but when absorbed with their craft, they are deeply introspective.

They function best when supported by a small group of carefully chosen associates, not an enormous research department, such as those in large brokerage firms. Great investors do not solicit multiple opinions. They do not like groupthink.

The best portfolio managers are autonomous. They fearlessly ignore the myopia of the media and the masses. They are iconoclasts; financial skeptics who question everything and look for no easy answers.

The best managers speak in simple terms that belie the complexity of their investment discipline. They have no hesitation in discussing complex concepts but do not hide behind their scholarship. They are direct and easily understood: "This is what we would do with the portfolio when the economy declines and stocks become cheap. This is how the allocation would be modified in response to changing financial and economic factors."

The best managers are often optimists but not blind ones. Capitalism works and those who bet against it usually lose. Warren

Buffett is an optimist, as was his partner, the late Charlie Munger, but both practiced patient optimism.

While optimism is a good basis for living one's life and sometimes when investing, great managers maintain a degree of cynicism for balance. Outright pessimism is never a useful attribute, but rosy idealism can be costly when it comes to investing.

The best managers are financial agnostics. They are undeterred by critics, unflinching in their convictions and undismayed when wrong.

Patience and Persistence

> *"As an investor, you don't have to swing at every pitch. The trick is just to sit there and watch pitch after pitch go by and wait for the one right in your sweet spot. And if people are yelling, 'Swing, you bum!,' ignore them."*

Warren Buffett

Great investment managers exhibit great patience. They feel no compulsion to "do something." They are content to monitor the market, evaluate conditions and unhurriedly watch for opportunities. The approach eliminates the temptation to force things. It also tends to rub off on their clients who become better, more patient investors in the process.

Impatience in the form of eagerness to "make a killing" is a common affliction among investors.

While human behavior has persisted in making knee-jerk decisions from the earliest days of investing, I believe social media has exasperated that impatience. The urge to do something or you will lose everything has probably caused more investment losses than even the fear-inducing claptrap coming from the financial media.

I recall a story about the Desert Storm initiative from a Marine gunnery commander. Reminding us of the nostrum "waiting until you see the white of their eyes," he spoke of a bright day in the desert when it was impossible to see more than a few feet because of the dust kicked up by the ceaseless swirling winds. His men spotted a group of armored vehicles slowly coming at them from over a ridge. The Marines had superior range capability and the men, obviously nervous about an enemy assault they could barely make out, asked for permission to fire. "Let's take them out!" they yelled. The commander calmly said "hold." As the vehicles continued to come closer, the requests from the men grew louder. "Fire sir?" Still the commander refused to give the order. Once the vehicles were within their own firing range, the young men were understandably frightened, fearing they were a button push away from annihilation. Just as their worst fears seemed imminent and the approaching vehicles came into clear view, the commander identified them as Americans. It turned out the group had become separated from their platoon and unable to see any better than the commander's men, were trying to find their way back in the blinding dust.

The event is a great lesson in patience. Even when you're afraid and have the overwhelming urge to react, you have to calmly analyze the what's happening, evaluate the available data and make a calm decision.

> *"Patience is the ability to idle your motor when you feel like stripping your gears."*

Barbara Johnson

Being Comfortable Being Wrong

In the military, you are rigorously trained to handle unexpected events. You must learn to remain calm, ignore your emotions and do what you have been trained to do when the unforeseen occurs. In some respects, portfolio managers need to have the same calm demeanor when markets roil and their clients panic. Granted, events in the market generally don't happen with the same suddenness that they do in military combat, but I believe my

Marine training has been a great help in controlling my emotions when things get crazy in business.

When your investment thesis that was based on analysis of previously accurate information fails because that information has changed, you have to rethink your decision and make a new decision based on today's new information. That's a difficult thing for a lot of portfolio managers to do and the hubris that prevents them from admitting they were wrong has ended many careers.

It really doesn't matter that your original analysis was founded on good math and good reasoning, the fact was you were wrong. And you have to be prepared to admit that you made a mistake...immediately. Next, you have to ignore everything you were thinking when you made that mistake and revisit the decision through a prism in the current moment.

The question you have to ask is, "Based on everything I know right now, would I make the same decision? Would I still invest in this company today?" If the answer is no, you have to exit that position ASAP. There is no other choice. It's a sunk cost—one of the cognitive biases that dooms investors to failure. It's the tendency to stay with a losing investment because of what has already been spent.

As a manager, you have to disregard what you thought at the time and what you paid. Neither matter. If you would not make the same decision today, based on the information you now have, you must do the hard thing and liquidate.

The financial media's talking heads love to prognosticate about investments they are "convinced" will be winners. Their level of self-assurance in public pronouncements often masks their private misgivings. When they are right, they strut like peacocks; when they are wrong, they offer "mitigating circumstances" or other defenses for why they blew it. I doubt investors who foolishly listened to their touts and lost money cared much about why the experts were wrong.

Great managers understand and accept the fact that they will sometimes be wrong. When they are wrong, they can cope with looking foolish. Every manager knows he or she is going to look like they don't know what they are doing from time to time. They are destined to make investments that don't meet their original investment thesis and fail to achieve their original valuation estimates.

The only people who never make a bad decision are people who avoid making decisions. Come to think of it, not making a decision is a decision in itself, so my last statement, just like some of my investment decisions, was wrong. The key is to be right a lot more often than wrong and to learn from mistakes...but not learn too much that it prevents you from making good decisions in the future.

Mariano Rivera is generally regarded as Major League Baseball's greatest relief pitcher. He finished 952 games for the Yankees and had a record 652 saves. He also had 80 blown saves.[205] But I doubt Rivera ever gave as much as a moment's thought to a previous blown save when he took the mound. His focus was always on the next batter, not the last one. Similarly, great managers do not agonize over or make excuses for yesterday's loss. Their focus, like Rivera's, is exactly where it should be; on what they have to accomplish today.

Great managers know that despite having the best information available and making the correct assumptions based on that information, an investment can go sour because something changes and new information emerges that alters the assessment. When that happens, they must be able to swallow their pride and admit they blew it. Hubris forestalls most managers from that admission.

There is an abundance of hubris in the investment community. It's the silent enemy of effective portfolio management. When some managers make a call that proves to be correct, the chest-thumping they exhibit prevents them from ever expressing any humility when they are wrong. Their pride won't allow them to subjugate their inflated egos.

These are not the people you want making decisions with your money.

> *"The truth posed a great dilemma for a man who always had to be right, and yet, for all his grandeur, was often wrong."*
>
> David Halberstam

Never Again

You've probably heard someone who made a bad investment decision say, "I'll never make that mistake again." It's understandable that they don't want to experience that frustration again, but it's more important to explore the reason why that investment was a bust. Was it based on faulty information? Was it a case of the right investment at the wrong time?

> *"There was a very cautious man who never laughed or played. He never risked, he never tried, he never sang or prayed. And when one day he passed away, his insurance was denied, for since he never really lived, they claimed he never really died."*
>
> Anonymous

Whatever the reason, investors that get burned overreact to the setback. They let the loss cloud their judgment about future investment decisions. I know people who were torched when the dot.com bubble burst and vowed "never again." That vow lasted a few years before they jumped back into the market, just in time to get clobbered by the Great Recession in 2008. Once again, they swore they would not subject themselves to another disaster and so this time, they stayed out of the market as it rebounded during the next decade. Seeing this, they finally move back in and buy stocks again, unfortunately missing out and on some of the biggest gains in history.

As I said, you want to learn from your mistakes, but don't learn too much.

The Customer is Sometimes Wrong

Great managers can help anxious investors overcome their emotional biases, but they can't entertain those biases themselves. They must resist instinctive reactions to setbacks and trust that their research, analysis and conclusions are correct. When they're not, they have to accept and be comfortable with the fact that some people are going to be disappointed and angry.

You know the nostrum that *the customer is always right?* Well, that's not the case in my business. If anything, the customer is often wrong, primarily because of the cognitive biases mentioned earlier. The historical data on human nature is clear. Many investors are almost always afraid when they should be fearless and insatiable when they should be content. I can't afford to stress over what my customers think. I'm going to be buying companies when the stock market is so far down my customers are scared to death. I'm going to be selling when market euphoria is boundless and customers are begging me to buy. I'm going to do things that fly in the face of what customers hear on the financial news every day. Customer reactions are going to range from skeptical to hysterical. If I listened to those voices, I wouldn't be doing what I know is right. And I would be wrong.

A good father doesn't try to make everybody happy. A good general doesn't worry if all his troops agree with his decisions. Ask the members of a professional sports team if they were always happy with the decisions their coaches made en route to a championship. It's impossible to please everyone while making the difficult decisions that lead to success in any field, and it's no different for portfolio managers.

Like an umpire, portfolio managers have chosen an occupation that doesn't get a lot of compliments. Nobody ever cheers because an umpire makes the right call; they only boo when they think he misses one. Umpires either get comfortable with that or they get ulcers or quit.

In portfolio management, you have to be comfortable with people booing. You have to accept that because it's the probable outcome, particularly if you are doing things others are not. It's not an occupation for someone hoping to win a popularity contest.

Great managers must be comfortable being alone in their decisions. People tend to feel safe when part of a crowd, whereas they feel apprehensive when alone. When everyone is jumping into the water, it reassures us that it's safe. When we are alone on the edge of a watering hole, it can be awfully intimidating.

> *"I would rather lose half of our clients than half of our clients' money."*
>
> Jean-Marie Eveillard

Turn it Off

In 2007, a former trader named Nassim Taleb published *The Black Swan*, a marvelous book that challenged conventional wisdom. It makes the irrefutable point that we can't know what we don't know, and that self-anointed experts tend to inflate what they actually know and minimize what they don't.

Taleb suggests that listening to financial news is not only bad for you, it can be toxic. He didn't allow televisions in his office and chose to simply tune out the media. I am in full agreement. What positive results can come from absorbing all the fear mongering and negativity the media spews out each day? What if you just stopped listening to so-called journalists? I don't listen to real estate flippers. I don't listen to priests about marriage. And I don't listen to journalists about investing. There are too many people regurgitating advice about topics they are not qualified to talk about. Great investors insulate themselves from all that blather and I suggest you do the same.

Going against the majority can often be the right thing to do because history has proved time and time again that the majority is often wrong. It's one reason why most investors underperform the funds they invest in. Once again, *cognitive dissonance*—the inability to deal with new information that clashes with an existing opinion—causes investors to make bad decisions.

Contrarian investors tend to go against what the majority is doing. Warren Buffett is perhaps the quintessential contrarian. But Buffett is a calculating contrarian, that is, he is contrarian when the data supports the strategy.

Conversely, perpetual contrarians go against prevailing market movements regardless of what the data suggests, which is one reason why, unlike Buffett, they tend to underperform.

A trait I've observed among perpetual contrarians is hubris. Continually going against the majority can instill a sense of superiority and condescension. Even a modicum of success causes some to believe they are the smartest guys in the room, no matter who else is in attendance. That's a dangerous illusion. A healthy level of skepticism can be a useful trait but when it evolves into conceit, it's detrimental, not to mention off-putting. Great investors are clear thinkers that maintain a level of humility.

> *"There are two circumstances that lead to arrogance: one is when you're wrong and you can't face it; the other is when you're right and nobody else can face it."*
>
> Criss Jami

The Business Gene

Some people seem to have been born with a specific gene that allows them to be highly successful at one thing or another. Whether athletes, inventors, musicians or portfolio managers, they share a genetic predisposition that others lack.

Athletes like Michael Jordan, Ted Williams, Bobby Orr and Tom Brady possess an innate ability that other athletes—even fellow professional athletes—lack. George Gershwin, one of America's greatest composers who lived just 38 years, wrote more than 500 songs during his brief life. Babe Ruth, Thomas Edison, Chopin - they all had the gene.

I believe that similarly, there are human beings genetically pre-programmed to be much better investors than other people.

Buffett doesn't think it has much to do with overall intelligence, but rather behaviors. There appear to be people who obviously have certain skill sets that allow them to perform better than most anyone else and portfolio management is no different.

What's fascinating about this is that there have been others that studied and worked religiously, determined to be as successful, and never achieved the same level of success.

The NFL has 32 backup quarterbacks. These are guys who were terrific college players and most have worked their butts off to get drafted. They have most, if not all, of the physical tools; they memorized the playbook; they just don't have the gene that allows them to make split-second decisions under fire the way starting quarterbacks do. And most of the 32 starting quarterbacks, as good as they might be, fall short of the great ones like Brady, Mahomes, Manning and Montana.

I think the vast majority of portfolio managers lack the gene to be good, much less great. They are simply not genetically pre-programmed for it, regardless of how much or how hard they study. They may have studied it in school or thought they wanted to do it but that doesn't mean that they're going to be good at it.

Beyond the gene, it's the behaviors that determine whether someone is great at managing money. Being able to make mathematically based decisions, being able to make decisions that are unpopular, being comfortable making those decisions and sometimes disappointing people, ignoring the media, dissenters and contrary opinions, having courage under fire...these are not traits acquired from reading books. You either have the genetic predisposition to do this extremely well or not. I think some can get better with experience, but as you will read in the next chapter, "Resolving the Active/Passive Controversy," the data shows that most people who manage money are not very good at it and don't seem destined to get better.

CHAPTER TWELVE

Resolving The Active/Passive Controversy

One of the most enduring financial controversies centers around the "active versus passive" investing debate. Investors can feel compelled to choose one approach or the other. Like choosing between the train or plane on a trip up the coast. Either will get you there and the train may be a more scenic trip, but it will take a lot longer to reach your destination. Each has advantages and weaknesses, and, as you would expect, investment managers in both camps promote their approach is optimal.

The reality is that much like many debates, neither side is right or wrong. In the case of active versus passive, neither is bereft of benefits, nor without drawbacks. And neither is as good as proponents claim nor as bad as opponents allege.

So where does that leave the investor?

Active/Passive Seesaw

The new millennium has seen a reversal within the asset management industry from previous decades when active asset management was the preferred choice of most investors. The shift in popularity from active to passive investing over the past two decades has prompted some serious concerns in the academic and regulatory communities—as well as the financial industry itself—as to the potential effects of this ideological shift on liquidity and redemption risks as well as overall financial stability. Passive investment products have long been pulling in the lion's share of money from investors, but 2023 was the first time they surpassed active investment products across all asset classes combined.

Conversely, as explained by a Harvard Law School article, the passive management shift has increased asset management convergence as a result of passive managers typically being more concentrated than active ones. This is evidenced by the emergence of huge passive index funds, such as those from BlackRock, Vanguard and State Street. While active managers seek to find assets that outperform benchmarks, asset selection by passive managers is not only less relevant; their choices result in only minor differentiation of portfolios and manager capabilities. Thus, large funds can take advantage of economies of scale to charge low fees. Additionally, researchers have discovered that the risk (beta) of stocks newly added to the S&P 500 tends to increase, partially as a result of passive managers buying or selling stocks of all index members simultaneously to maintain exposure to the index.[206]

While the arguments for and against both disciplines rage on, it might be instructive to spend some time examining exactly what constitutes passive and active investment management, and whether either approach offers a distinct advantage.

Passive Management Advantages

Passive investing is conducted by buying securities that mirror stock market indexes, typically the S&P 500, and holding them long term. Essentially, it is a strategy of buying a basket of assets that ideally mirror the movements of the stock market.[207]

Passive investing as an actual strategy first appeared in 1976 with the creation of the first index fund, pioneered by legendary investor John Bogle of the Vanguard Group. It enabled individual investors to fully participate in the market sans the costs of purchasing individual stocks.

The 1990s saw the dawn of the next development in the evolution of passive investing: exchange-traded funds (ETFs). Like index funds, ETFs tracked indexes with lower fees than mutual funds and attracted still more investors into the passive fold. A major benefit of these passive vehicles is that they provide investors an inexpensive method of achieving portfolio diversification, diffusing risk by owning a wide array of securities. [208]

The fact that most active managers fail to beat their benchmark is another reason to opt for passive management, according to advocates. They point out that numerous studies have found that the vast majority of actively managed funds underperform their benchmark index. The year 2022 was an outlier, the first year since 2013 that active management outperformed S&P 500 index funds.

To summarize, passive investing can be a worthwhile "first step" in capitalism participation. As a passive investor, you own businesses; that's good. Tracking an index means getting diversification and avoiding the potential pitfall of having all your eggs in one basket, being overweight in one stock or sector that can have an abnormal influence on your net worth. It's also a lower-cost strategy. Those are three positive aspects of passive investing.

> *"Investing is a funny business. It's really easy to be average. Just buy an index fund. It's really hard to be above average."*

Howard Marks

Passive Management Drawbacks

For starters, the majority of investors should not own an index fund in a taxable account. Investors near or in retirement should never own an index fund in the fixed income or bond portion of their portfolio because they need protection provided by maturity. Also, investors with ethical concerns regarding the companies they own should avoid index funds.

Wealthy investors should absolutely never own index funds. They are far better off owning individual stocks so they can tax loss harvest. More on this later in the chapter.

Passive investing tends to gain popularity every few decades. The overall results have been fair to good for investors willing and able to retain the investments for a long period, ideally a quarter century or more. This applies mainly to those lacking the competence or financial resources to take advantage of active investing opportunities.

As John Bogle, founder of mutual fund company Vanguard, wrote in his book, *Common Sense on Mutual Funds*, "It is much more tax-efficient for people with a few extra zeroes on the end of their net worth to forgo mutual funds. They can build a direct portfolio of individual stocks instead, using the same indexing philosophy."

In a recent letter to investors, Elliott Management's Paul Singer warned that the growth of passive investing was a "blob" in danger of devouring capitalism. Here's an excerpt from that letter:

> "There is nothing ethically wrong or indefensible in running a mega-shop focusing on passive investing, nor do passive investors have an obligation to overcome or counteract the adverse trends that have been discussed in this piece (although they should care). We believe, however, that there is a fallacy of composition and that what may have been a clever idea in its infancy has grown into a blob which is destructive to the growth-creating and consensus-building prospects of free-market capitalism. This "overgrowth" is a drag on the power of capitalism to adapt, to continually strive for excellence, efficiency and creativity and to deliver goods and services for citizens in the manner in which it has done for the last couple of centuries. In effect, therefore, it is dangerous, ultimately divisive and may be an important reason the pro-freedom or pro-capitalism consensus dissipates over time."[209]

A problem with passive investing is that an S&P 500 ETF will always underperform the index somewhat because of fees. As Buffett said, "diversification is for people who don't know what they're doing and passive investing is for those who lack the knowledge or temperament to buy individual stocks."

Buffett was obviously referring to investors who were unable or uncomfortable trying to identify good companies they wanted to hold for the long term. He suggested they might instead consider buying an S&P 500 Index fund. Since making that statement, Buffett has been endlessly misquoted by advocates of passive investing, who took his quote out of context and used it to say, "the greatest investor of all time says buy passive index funds."

The Internet has pages of this half-truth when, in fact, nothing could be further from the truth. What he said was the best thing to do with your money is to own businesses that you understand and can value, but if you don't have the skill set to figure out which stocks to own, putting your money in an index fund is better than keeping it in the bank.

Ethical Concerns

A subject infrequently discussed is that of advisor ethics. I'm not speaking of larceny, as exploited by the Madoffs and other fraudsters. I refer here to whether the advisor is principled when it comes to choosing investments.

Given a choice of achieving their financial goals by investing in companies that do or don't produce products that kill people, I believe most investors would choose the latter. Those who embrace a passive strategy and buy an index own a wide swath of companies, including what are derisively referred to as "sin stocks." These are companies in the gambling, tobacco, alcohol, defense, pollution, cannabis, abortion and adult entertainment industries, among others.[210]

As an investor, I hesitate to make money buying companies that sell cigarettes that give people cancer. While I enjoy a cocktail, I don't want to support companies selling alcohol that has destroyed families and slaughtered innocent people because of drinking and driving. I don't want to make money off of bombs being dropped on innocent civilians.

Investors that own an index have to accept that they support some of these companies and be okay with it. Of course, most never think about it, but it's an unwitting aspect of passive investing: profiting from cancer, consumption, collisions, contamination, killing babies and wars. Index investors don't just own shares of some arbitrary stocks; they own those companies. They are just as much an owner as the senior executives making decisions in those boardrooms.

If I have a choice, and I do, why would I invest in companies that do untold damage to people and the environment if I can avoid it? It's a simple concept that crosses the minds of investors and advisors less often than it should.

Much of this type of thinking, at least for me, stems from what I learned early on from Buffett: I don't just own a share of stock in a company; I own every decision that company makes. Whether they are exploiting labor laws in third world countries or marketing cigarettes to young children, it's a company in an index owned by millions of passive investors, most of whom are oblivious to the ramifications of what that company produces and the damage it may wreak on society.

I realize a lot of people reading this may not be overly concerned about the "minutiae" of index investing. They regard their investment advisor as someone hired to make them as much money as possible and are indifferent as to the nature of the investments that help them achieve their financial goals.

That may be an indirect indictment on my part, but investing in those companies is a non-starter for me. It's something I do my best to avoid. In my own portfolio, if I can give my kids an equal amount of money in the future without investing in companies that do damage and cause human suffering, so much the better.

Another thought is the argument that, in general, these types of companies experience much higher levels of regulation, and so have much higher legal costs than other businesses. An apples-to-apples comparison might indicate that these firms are less profitable. It's a weak argument because tobacco companies make so much money, they can absorb the world's highest litigation costs and still be highly profitable.

After a career of managing portfolios, I want to kiss my daughters good night, lay my head on the pillow and be content with the investment decisions I've made. That's why I don't own any of the companies mentioned here. And frankly, when I bring this to the attention of people who have been investing passively, they usually admit they have never thought about money this way.

Active Management Advantages

The difference between active and passive management might be thought of as the difference between sitting on a sofa all day Sunday, watching the football games, as compared to being on the field playing the game. The passive investor bets the games, hoping to make a few dollars on the spread. The professional athlete actively embraces the challenge of winning the game while securing lucrative contracts that ensure his long-term financial security.

Like world class athletes that spend extensive time training to compete for championships, elite active managers immerse themselves in the challenge of making prudent decisions and taking actions that compound on one another, ultimately determining outcomes. It's the difference between accepting what life gives you and taking charge of your life. As one good decision leads to another, the positive impact is amplified. Done with competence and consistency, the rewards can be astonishing.

Most of our investors are successful executives, professionals and business owners. These are people who amassed their wealth by doing what most of their peers didn't: they invested the time and effort to rise above the unexceptional. They overcame the obstacles that impede most people from achieving affluence. For some, success was the ability to create a product or service that gave them a competitive advantage. For others, the talent and discipline to develop skills that set them apart and above others in their profession. Some were visionaries that saw things others could not; some had superior intellects; many simply outworked their competition. What they all have in common is the unwillingness to accept mediocrity, in their careers or their finances.

Active managers rely on analytical research, judgment and scrutiny of market inefficiencies to make investment decisions. Investment managers using tactical asset allocation, in particular, can monitor signals for changes in the market environment using analytical factors. Elite managers in this category have the unique skills to ferret out businesses with competitive advantages and wide moats, emulating the decades-long strategy of Warren Buffett. They also have the ability to mitigate or eliminate short-term capital gains tax consequences using tax loss harvesting. More about this later.

If active management outcomes were some theoretical notion or hypothesis of a university professor, questioning the veracity of any proposed benefits would be logical. However, the ability of elite active managers to produce superior outcomes is not some thesis. It is a proven fact, documented by performance data.

Active Management Weaknesses

One of the more pervasive strategies among active managers is sector rotation, pivoting in and out of the eleven different equity sectors in response to market fluctuations or anticipated changes in the business cycle. For example, managers may sell out of sectors such as defensive stocks and into cyclical stocks when they believe the market is headed up.

The popularity of sector rotation is a bit bewildering because few managers can execute it with precision. Even when successful, it yields little outperformance. The lack of payoff for even the most successful sector rotation strategy is one reason why my portfolios are sector neutral. I never attempt to overweight a sector or industry in anticipation of the business cycle. If I am the world's best at sector rotation and nail every single business cycle perfectly, I'm only adding a single percentage point annually to performance...and that's before transaction costs.

An expansive paper titled, "The Myth of Sector Rotation" largely dispels the notion that the strategy is worth pursuing, despite its popularity among investment managers, the financial media and aspiring financial advisor authors everywhere. The paper's analysis concludes:

> "Despite thorough empirical tests, there is scant evidence that conventional sector rotation across business cycles generates systematic excess returns. The analysis assumes that sector rotation investors *perfectly time business cycles* and rotate sectors in accordance with popular belief on sector performance. Even then, sector rotation generates, at best, 0.11% monthly outperformmance. Performance quickly diminishes with the introduction of transaction costs or business cycle mistiming."[211]

As the compelling evidence reveals, trying to time the business cycle is not only incredibly difficult to do with precision, even when successful, the strategy yields scant outperformance. Investors sign up for a short-term sector rotation strategy that history has shown cannot work. Not only that, they are getting smoked on taxes. In my opinion, it's one of the dumbest investment approaches in existence, and a major reason why passive managers outperform active managers at such a high rate.

Obviously, time spent researching and analyzing stocks and using tactical asset allocation provides much greater potential for portfolio gains. Sector rotation, on the other hand, offers far less potential for gain and is a strategy based on guesswork and speculation. Conversely, if I perfectly identify market peaks and troughs using tactical asset allocation, I'm apt to enhance performance to a much greater degree.

A Hybrid Approach: Direct Indexing

Direct indexing is the first step in weaning investors off a bland passive diet towards the more fulfilling cuisine of superior outcomes. There's a reason why filet is more expensive than chuck; it's more rewarding to consume.

Direct indexing is an investment strategy that allows investors to directly own individual stocks that comprise an index in their own separately managed account (SMA) instead of using a mutual fund or ETF to track the underlying index. Similar to an index fund, the goal is to track the performance of a target benchmark index. However, holding the individual securities directly in a SMA account allows for greater personalization and the potential for tax benefits.[212]

Even in up markets, individual stocks can suffer disappointing performance. Direct indexing portfolios can take advantage by harvesting losses in underperforming stocks.

It's relatively simple to handle precise tax-loss harvesting, since it's easy to sell underperforming stocks. The receipts from these sales can be used to buy shares in companies with better prospects to balance portfolio allocations. In the process, capital losses can be used to offset tax liabilities.[213]

There are precious few free lunches for investors. Direct indexing is one. It's like a "get out of jail" card for taxes. Martin Hall, a video golf instructor, has a maxim: "If you keep doing what you've been doing, you'll keep getting what you've been getting." It's fitting advice for investors as well. For the wealthy, who should never settle for inefficient tax strategies using ETFs, direct indexing is an absolute no-brainer.

Turnover and Taxes

In all my years of managing people's money, I have never heard anyone volunteer to pay extra taxes. No one wants to pay any more taxes than necessary, yet many investors regularly do.

The tax rate on short-term gains (investment gains on assets held for less than one year) is the same as ordinary income, with the top federal tax at 37% and the top state tax at 13%. That amounts to losing *half* a portfolio's gains; a massive penalty for doing what every investor strives to do, buy low and sell high, but for simply doing it too quickly. It's a generous donation to the IRS that could instead be retained in your portfolio as working capital to earn more money.

The villain in this scenario is portfolio turnover, a measure of a fund or portfolio's trading activity that generates capital gains, taxes and losses. Investors in actively managed portfolios tend to realize higher capital gains taxes than passive and index investors. The average actively managed portfolio has a turnover rate of roughly 80% per year, while the turnover for passive and index portfolios is about 10%.[214]

> *"The avoidance of taxes is the only intellectual pursuit that still carries any reward."*
>
> John Maynard Keynes

Similar to the active/passive management debate, an ongoing controversy exists surrounding portfolio turnover. Passive advocates regularly point to the short-term capital gains sparked by high turnover in active management, and they have a point. But turnover can be either a destructive or a productive force. From a tax perspective, if portfolio turnover is not managed correctly and merely creating taxes, that's a negative. On the other hand, if turnover creates losses that can be harvested and used to offset capital gains, that's very much a positive.

Buying a security, selling it and paying short-term capital gains taxes on it, then buying another security that is materially the same and highly correlated is inane. For example, investors that buy a stock like Pepsi, sell it, take the gain, then buy Coca Cola are conducting a senseless strategy that is a classic example of destructive turnover. As you can see in graphic 12.1, the two securities are so highly correlated, their performance is in a virtual lock step.

Why would anyone that knows anything about investing do this? It's a no-win strategy for those playing a short-term game.

Yet this is what day traders do all the time, and it simply makes no sense. In the pursuit of a quick buck, they haphazardly zig and zag, following one "signal" or another, trying to time the market. They are not investing; they are gambling.

Even if an investor can make the huge time commitment and has the skill set to try to predict short-term market movements on a consistent basis, his hurdle is so much higher than mine because he's paying so much in taxes on his successful investments, often to both the federal and state governments, whereas I'm paying the least amount while trying to maximize after-tax returns. I'm letting my investments grow over the long run, and even when I do liquidate a portion of a position due to being overweighted or other reason, I'm shaving off just enough to bring the position back into portfolio balance. That minimizes the tax obligation and tax loss harvesting can offset that.

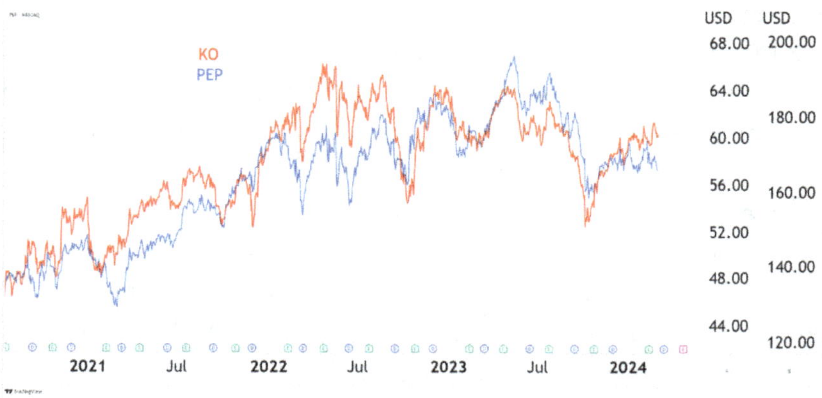

(Graphic 12.1 Coke & Pepsi)

If you are going to have turnover in a portfolio and pay the taxes, the investments you are buying must have a much higher expected return than the ones you are selling.

Graphics 12.2 and 12.3 illustrate this ratio over an extended period.

Year	100% Turnover Short Term	75% Turnover Short Term	100% Turnover Long Term	75% Turnover Long Term	50% Turnover Short Term	50% Turnover Long Term	25% Turnover Short Term	25% Turnover Long Term	Buy and Hold
5	12,038,388	12,363,747	12,641,727	12,823,707	12,696,103	13,007,776	13,035,568	13,193,953	13,382,256
10	14,492,278	15,286,223	15,981,327	16,444,746	16,119,102	16,920,224	16,992,603	17,408,040	17,908,477
15	17,446,367	18,899,500	20,203,157	21,088,260	20,464,978	22,009,449	22,150,823	22,968,086	23,965,582
20	21,002,613	23,366,863	25,540,280	27,042,966	25,982,546	28,629,398	28,874,856	30,303,985	32,071,355
25	25,283,760	28,890,197	32,287,325	34,679,107	32,987,708	37,240,480	37,640,014	39,982,936	42,918,707
30	30,437,571	35,719,109	40,816,755	44,471,470	41,881,532	48,441,583	49,065,896	52,753,298	57,434,912
35	36,641,928	44,162,201	51,599,429	57,028,909	53,173,224	63,011,727	63,960,182	69,602,455	76,860,868
40	44,110,975	54,601,027	65,230,590	73,132,200	67,509,271	81,964,244	83,375,729	91,833,152	102,857,179

(Graphic 12.2 Turnover & Taxes Table)

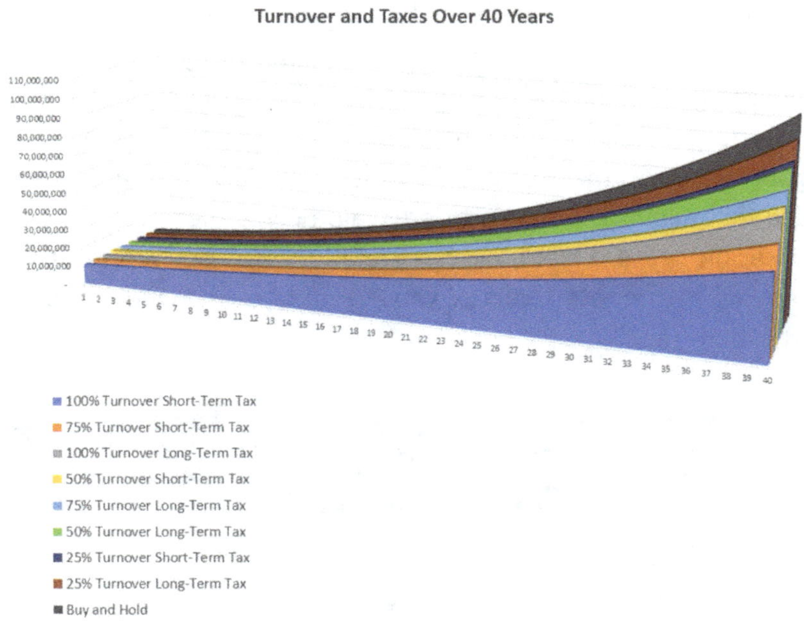

(Graphic 12.3 Turnover & Taxes Chart)

As the graphic points out, there are many, many reasons to pay close attention to portfolio turnover and the type of tax you're paying as a result. The higher the ratio of tax created by turnover, the lower the return. Over an extended period, the difference in return between ordinary and capital tax and high and low turnover is monumental.

That's not to say all turnover is negative. In my experience, there is a "sweet spot" based on a capital gains tax basis, and if you look at the graphic closely, you will see it is that tiny red sliver representing 25% capital tax turnover. To stay in that sweet spot, you want to be holding investments for longer periods of time and not turning over more than 25% of your portfolio.

To illustrate, let's assume an investment with a four-year time horizon and an average expected annual return of 6%. So, we anticipate making roughly 25% compounded over the full four years. If we can consistently buy stock that is 20% undervalued, however, instead of a 25% return, we can achieve a roughly 45% return as a result. If we choose to pay the 20% capital gains tax, we still enjoy a 36% gain. We are better off buying significantly undervalued stocks and paying the long-term capital gains tax than if we did nothing or if we chose to invest passively.

Investors frequently turning over their portfolio because they think the grass is greener must not only achieve the necessary higher return on the stocks they buy; they must have a process in place that allows them to properly value investments.

Graphic 12.4 illustrates the relationship between rates of turnover, the amount of tax they generate and the impact on portfolio returns.

Expected Return of Investment Sold	Requried Return of Investment Purchased if Gain is Short Term	Required Return of Investment Purchased if Gain is Long Term
2.0%	3.2%	2.5%
4.0%	6.4%	5.0%
6.0%	9.5%	7.5%
8.0%	12.7%	10.0%
10.0%	15.9%	12.5%
12.0%	19.3%	15.0%

(Graphic 12.4 Solving for Turnover Return Table)

For investors subjecting themselves to short-term gains taxes as a result of portfolio turnover, this graphic represents a vitally important concept. Someone with an expected return of 6% who is selling stocks and replacing them with other stocks must get a 9.5% return on the new stocks in order to justify the gains tax obligation they've created. An investor with an expected return of 10% must secure a return of 15.9% on their replacement stocks to offset their gains tax liability.

If your portfolio manager employs a high turnover strategy, buying and selling stocks based on short-term market movement, the tax implications of that activity will not be evident on a performance report. For example, if you receive a financial report from your investment firm that indicates your portfolio earned 10%, that is a gross number as it relates to investment performance. What it does not reveal are the ramifications of the portfolio's turnover and taxes generated.

In summary, turnover can be good or bad. Just because you sell a stock doesn't mean you are creating bad turnover; It depends on what you get in return for selling and what you have to pay. In other words, if you buy something, how much return must you receive to at least get back to your original position? What is the after-tax result?

Zealous passive advocates may claim if you are paying tax, you are a loser. Well, maybe. But I am a capitalist, and I want to buy a higher returning business than the one I just sold. If I can find a company that is 25 or 30% undervalued and do better owning it than just sitting here with the fully valued company I currently own, paying the tax may be worth securing that valuation premium in the form of a higher return. In other words, I would rather take the money, pay the tax, then turn around and buy another business that's substantially undervalued...the way I did when I first bought the company I just sold because it's now fully valued. It's not that I don't love that company anymore; I still do. But the expected rate of return on the investment when I bought it at 30% below value was a lot higher. Now, I've recognized most of that return so I'm better off taking the profit, paying the long-term capital tax on it and buying an undervalued, different business that I love just as much.

> *"Purchase stocks of companies you understand and see value in for the long term. Nobody buys a farm based on whether they think it's going to rain next year. They buy it because they think it's a good investment over 10 or 20 years."*

Warren Buffett

That, dear reader, is a fundamental tenet of active management.

If you are selling stock held for less than a year and paying the ordinary tax, what determines whether that is good or bad turnover? Paying unnecessary taxes due to short-term gains is bad turnover. Good turnover would be a return above the necessary minimum rate and utilizing tax loss harvesting, which we will discuss in the next section of this chapter.

Tax Loss Harvesting

Happily, there is a way to offset the destructive effects of tax gains. It's called tax loss harvesting, and it represents one of the most lucrative yet underappreciated strategies for growing wealth within an investment portfolio. Tax loss harvesting is a strategy that allows you to close losing positions in a taxable account to generate losses that can be used to offset gains and reduce taxes.

Let's say you bought AT&T stock on the advice of a friend who remarked that "people will always need a cell phone service, right?" While he may have been right about people's communication preferences, he was wrong about the stock. Within a few months, the stock begins a prolonged downward trajectory. Your first inclination is to give your pal a shiner for what appears to be a bad tip, but you decide to avoid a potential lawsuit and instead simply sell the AT&T stock and use tax loss harvesting to your advantage. But wait. Like everyone who sells at a loss, you can't help thinking the stock will rebound. What if it rallies next week? Can you buy it again and still use the loss to offset gains?

No. That's because of the IRS "wash sale" rule that stipulates you cannot sell an investment at a loss and buy the same or "substantially identical" investment within 30 days without forgoing the tax benefit. This restriction makes the task of tax loss harvesting an arduous one. It takes up a lot of time in an advisor's day and not every advisor is willing to make that investment, if you will excuse the pun.

The term "substantially identical" has had investors and their advisors scratching their heads at its ambiguity for the past 100 years. In the end, we are all left to our own best judgment as to interpreting the regulation. IRS Publication 550 may offer the best available guidance, stating that "ordinarily, stocks or securities of one corporation are not considered substantially identical to stocks or securities of another corporation." In other words, if you sell AT&T and buy Verizon, you're likely not breaking the law. On the other hand, if you sell Vanguard S&P 500 Index Fund and buy BlackRock S&P 500 Index Fund, you have a problem.

So, while you can't buy AT&T again for 30 days, you can still take advantage of tax loss harvesting without forgoing an opportunity to stay invested. You still like the sector because people do need a carrier to provide cell phone service. Maybe your mistake was buying AT&T a bit early. So, you take the proceeds from the sale of the AT&T stock and buy Verizon, an industry competitor and a correlated stock. If the sector pops in the next 30 days, chances are both stocks will go up in and so you haven't missed out on the appreciation. And if the stocks stay flat or go down in value, you can sell the Verizon and buy back the AT&T if you think it has better potential for gain after 30 days.

Graphic 12.5 is a representation of the movement of the two stocks over a three-year period. Just as with competitors Coke and Pepsi, AT&T and Verizon are highly correlated and virtually mimic one another's market performance.

(Graphic 12.5 Verizon & AT&T)

You must be careful that what you are selling and buying is not the same thing. If you violate the rule, you do not lose the tax benefit forever. When you eventually sell the security again, you can recover the tax benefit and write off the loss.[215] But the compounding of interest you lost in the interim as a result of losing the tax offset cannot be recovered.

Think of that. Investors can take advantage of tax loss harvesting to gain a one to two percent annual net worth increase merely by owning individual stocks instead of an index. And they can enjoy this "virtual dividend" indefinitely. Projected over a lifetime, tax loss harvesting by itself can double an investor's net worth. A relatively simple active management strategy can result in an individual having twice as much capital available in retirement. In my experience, few people are aware of this remarkable statistic. The majority of investors have been poisoned by the indexing industry and an accommodating media to put their money into stock and bond index funds. The result is that investors sacrifice an opportunity to amass an enormous capital reward.

In some cases, active investors let their ego get in the way of securing tax savings. They are reluctant to sell a stock they thought would be a winner but perhaps was purchased a bit early. They still like the stock, as well as the sector it's in, and ask, "Why should I sell it after I've already lost so much?"

Their bias is understandable but in reality, they are not abandoning the stock. Yes, they are selling it, but only for 30 days. Meanwhile, they can buy another stock that's highly correlated but materially different. They can hold on to that stock for 30 days and then, assuming they have not lost their affection for the first stock, buy it back. They get to harvest the tax loss and simultaneously enjoy any appreciation in the sector during that 30-day period.

In a 2020 *Financial Analysts Journal* paper,[216] the authors evaluated the magnitude of "tax alpha" using historical data for the 500 securities with the largest market capitalizations from 1926 through 2018 and found the tax-loss harvesting strategy yielded an average annualized tax alpha of 0.82% per year.

A Vanguard research paper notes that for investors in high tax brackets, personalized indexing combined with tax loss harvesting (TLH) boosted after-tax returns by 100–200 basis points or more. Further, TLH in a personalized index can continue to deliver tax alpha even if the market experiences sustained low volatility."[217] While TLH is of no great benefit to investors in low tax brackets or those with small portfolios, it offers a huge opportunity for high net-worth investors.

According to a Parametric Q1 2023 report, tax loss harvesting produced an inception-to-date gross investment enhancement of 2.27% annually.

Graphics 12.6 and 12.7 illustrate the effect of tax loss harvesting over a 40-year period, based on the estimations of the three sources above. It assumes a base return of 6%, and additional returns of 0.82% (tax alpha), 1% (Vanguard) and 2.27 gross (Parametric).

Year	Stock Market	Tax Alpha	Vanguard	Parametric
5	13,382,256	13,907,942	14,025,517	14,877,867
10	17,908,477	19,343,085	19,671,514	22,135,094
15	23,965,582	26,902,250	27,590,315	32,932,299
20	32,071,355	37,415,493	38,696,845	48,996,238
25	42,918,707	52,037,250	54,274,326	72,895,953
30	57,434,912	72,373,106	76,122,550	108,453,633
35	76,860,868	100,656,095	106,765,815	161,355,877
40	102,857,179	139,991,912	149,744,578	240,063,134

(Graphic 12.6 TLH 40 Years Table)

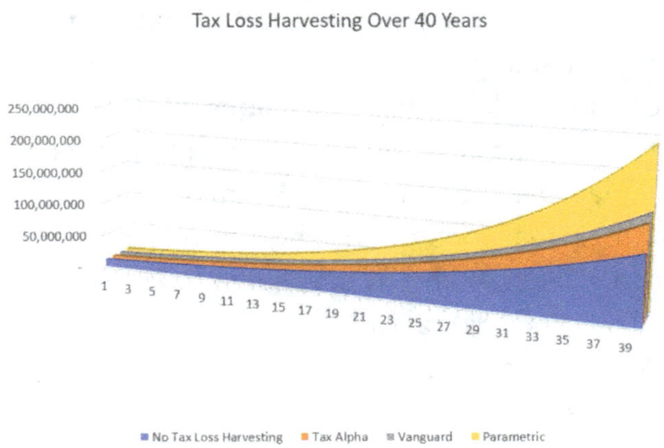

(Graphic 12.7 TLH 40 Years Chart)

As the graphic demonstrates, TLH can make an eye-opening difference in terms of portfolio return. In a ten-million-dollar portfolio extrapolated over four decades, the investment return projections are truly astounding, regardless of which source you choose to apply:

Standard Passive Portfolio:	$102,857,179
Tax Alpha	139,991,912
Vanguard	149,744,578
Parametric	240,063,134

The concept of using tax losses to offset gains and dramatically increase net worth is something that will not show up on an investment performance report or fact sheet. It's money saved versus money earned by investment performance, so from a marketing perspective, it's not very sexy. But it is obviously one of the most impactful strategies available to investors. What is more important than increasing one's net worth without risk? And the money saved continues to compound indefinitely. The evidence for tax loss harvesting is overwhelming. For wealthy investors in particular, the financial implications are immense.

Stock market volatility is an ever-present threat to stable investment returns. It frightens a lot of people because the one thing that throws investors off their game is the uncertainty produced by volatility.

One of the fundamental advantages of TLH is how much it benefits from market volatility. In fact, the greater the volatility, the bigger the tax benefits. When TLH strategy is first explained to investors, their reactions often range from tepid appreciation to indifference. "We're going to take some losses so I pay less taxes this year. That's good; thanks."

What they fail to fully understand is that compounding the strategy year after year creates massive gains in their net worth. That translates into an enhanced quality of life, a more fulfilling retirement, additional money their children will inherit and the ability to make a true difference in the world through charitable giving. For the wealthy, there may not be a more important strategic consideration.

How and Where to Investigate

> *"In private equity there is a huge gap between the bottom- and top-performing funds. If you get it wrong, that can be very costly."*

David Swenson

For 35 years, beginning in 1985, David Swenson was the chief investment officer for Yale University's endowment. When Swensen first took over Yale's endowment, the portfolio contained roughly \$1bn in assets.[218] Three decades later, the portfolio had grown to \$30bn, averaging a remarkable 13.1% annual return. Taking the endowment fund beyond the conventional strategy of publicly traded securities to private equity and illiquid assets, Swenson transformed the institutional investing landscape.[219]

In his landmark book, *Pioneering Portfolio Management*, Swenson revolutionized the process of selecting investment managers for institutional portfolios by comparing the 10-year performance differential between managers in the upper and lower quartiles of traditional investments. For example, the performance variance of fixed income managers in the 25th and 75th percentile was virtually nonexistent. However, the performance variance among US stock managers in the 25th and 75th percentile exhibited a 3% per annum difference, representing a huge investment opportunity. That opportunity is amplified even more among private equity managers, where the top quartile exceeded 20% per annum, suggesting there were far greater incremental returns to be had by spending time researching elite portfolio managers in equities and private markets.[220]

What Swenson did was deceptively simple and entirely logical. He analyzed the performance spread between managers in the different investment areas, from Treasuries to small cap, large cap, growth and virtually every area between. Taking managers from each and ranking their 10-year performance from top to bottom, he compared the median performance of the top quartile to that of the bottom quartile to ascertain the difference, what we would call the alpha spread.

The more pronounced that alpha spread, the more an investor is compensated for time spent trying to identify the managers in the top quartile. Regardless of how much research invested in areas such as Treasuries, or how unerring the conclusions from that research are, if the performance spread between the upper and lower quartile managers is narrow, the investor is not going to be amply compensated for the time spent identifying the better performers.

On the other hand, where the performance or alpha spread is the greatest between the upper and lower quartile managers, such as with private equity, venture capital or hedge fund managers, time spent researching can be extremely fruitful.

As it relates to the active versus passive conundrum, it doesn't make sense for an experienced investment manager—able to select managers in that top quartile with the superior analytics, skill sets, information and processes to be top performers with wide alpha spreads—to be a passive index investor when he can do so much better for his clients.

Skill or Luck?

One of the pivotal elements of Swenson's book is to demonstrate where investors can most productively spend their time identifying managers most likely to not only outperform their counterparts, but to generate the greatest returns for the time spent in research.

For starters, the managers chosen should be adequately capitalized and have extensive experience. Beyond knowledge, they must have a process in place to fully maximize the potential of their acquired skills. These portfolio managers rarely come cheap. They know who they are and they command lofty fees. From an investor perspective, it's hard to overpay for this level of performance.

A key judgement for investors, however, is whether the manager's elevated performance is repeatable or merely the result of a fortunate single big bet. In other words, did residence in that top quartile happen because of a special skill and process or good luck? Distinguishing the divergence between the two is where investors will benefit most from their research and evaluation efforts.

It's important to recognize that the performance numbers rarely tell the whole story. One must understand why and how those numbers came about. Did the manager ascend into the top quartile because he took a big bet on oil that providentially coincided with the onset of an oil boom, or did that performance reflect a unique, repeatable skill? Distinguishing the difference is where knowledgeable investors can most profitably spend their time.

There are numerous instances of venture capital (VC) funds with a history of poor investments suddenly hitting a home run. Did the manager finally figure it out or was it a happy coincidence? Like the music industry, investment funds are rife with one-hit wonders unable to duplicate their success.

In his 20-year major league career, pitcher Bartolo Colon came to bat 299 times and hit one home run. He was a batting hero that day…but out of roughly 7,400 days spent in the big leagues, it was the only day. He never hit another. Timothy Torres' recording of "One More Try" stayed on the Billboard Hot 100 chart for an amazing 25 weeks in 1991. He never had another hit.

As an investor, what you have to figure out is whether the manager you're considering is capable of making good decisions leading to superior performance on a regular basis or if he landed in that rarified segment for a short period because of a single fortuitous bet. It's the old saw of past performance not being predictive of future results.

The surest method of sifting the performance wheat from the chaff is to investigate what managers did to achieve superior performance. Do they have a mathematically based process to capture alpha in areas that are not going to dissipate? Do they have an algorithmic advantage based on sound research and testing? Or is it some independent individual working from home, managing a small fund and making big bets, hoping to hit paydirt? In short, is there a repeatable process in place based on an analytical approach that has the probability of working continually?

Wide Moats

Buffett popularized the term "wide moat." He was referring to a business's ability to protect its long-term profits and market share by maintaining competitive advantages over its competitors.

> *"The most important thing is finding a business with a wide and long-lasting moat around it, protecting a terrific economic castle with an honest lord in charge of the castle."*

Warren Buffett

Morningstar has tracked moat ratings for the past two decades using its Wide Moat Focus Index (WMFI), which seeks to identify companies possessing competitive advantages. The firm describes five ways companies develop moats:

- A firm's services become incrementally more valuable as others adopt it, known as the network effect.
- When there is no incentive for customers to switch to a competitor.
- Virtual control of a specific market.
- The ability to generate consistent cash flow from patents, licenses or proprietary products.
- Being able to produce high profit margins from selling a superior product at a competitive price.[221]

Over the past ten years (ending 7/20/23), the WMFI outperformed the U.S. Market by approximately 3%, essentially emulating what Buffett has been doing for decades. See chapter 7, "Lessons from Warren Buffett," for a more detailed discussion of wide moat investing.

Active Passive Decision Tree

The investment decision process as it applies to active and passive management can appear to be a convoluted one. There are numerous contingencies to be evaluated. Graphic 12.8 can help you navigate that process. It represents everything we have discussed up to this point.

(Graphic 12.8 Decision Tree)

The Solution: Mosaic Strategy

As to the eternal squabble regarding active versus passive investing, one can make a case for either discipline. There are good ideas from both, but choosing between the two is not what this chapter—and savvy investing—is about.

Rather than take sides, I can ignore the conflict because after years of research and analysis, I've found a resolution that makes the debate irrelevant. The CFA Institute provides a cogent description of what is known as the Mosaic Theory for investment professionals. Their guidance is that a financial analyst gathers and interprets large quantities of information from many sources.

Following that description, by taking the best each of the approaches has to offer and avoiding their disadvantages, I'm able to chart my own course. I can utilize passive investing to gain diversification, participate in capitalism and as a business owner, secure lower costs and lower turnover. I can tap into active investing to choose companies with competitive advantages, such as wide moats, avoid unethical companies and short-term tax gains while taking advantage of tax loss harvesting.

I have a bias for and want to own companies that Buffett aptly describes as having a sustainable competitive advantage. Whether a taxable or tax-free account, I do not want to own unethical or antiquated companies. I don't want to own companies that sell bombs to the military that are used to bomb Ukraine. I don't want to own companies that fail to respond to technology advances or competitive forces. I don't want to own companies that lack competitive advantages or moats.

The mosaic strategy, using a tactical approach, allows me to cull the "best of both worlds" while avoiding unethical, antiquated and unsustainable businesses. I can take less risk when the market is peaking and the probability of decline increases, and more risk at market bottoms. At the same time, I can retain the best companies with competitive advantages and avoid paying unnecessary taxes, which allows portfolio profits to compound atop one another.

Graphics 12.9 and 12.10 illustrate this combined impact of tax loss harvesting, wide moat outperformance and tactical asset allocation. In this example, we assumed a $10mn portfolio and a 6% average annual return based on historic S&P 500 performance.

Year	SM	SM + TLH	SM + TLH + 1/2 WMO	SM + TLH + 1/2 TAAAO	SM + TLH + 1/2 WMO + 1/2 TAAAO	SM + TLH + WMO + 1/2 TAAAO
5	13,382,255.78	14,157,087.84	15,175,664.63	15,245,598.45	16,325,916.17	17,466,625.86
10	17,908,476.97	20,042,313.62	23,030,079.70	23,242,827.21	26,653,553.88	30,508,301.91
15	23,965,581.93	28,374,079.44	34,949,676.59	35,435,081.05	43,514,368.64	53,287,709.52
20	32,071,354.72	40,169,433.51	53,038,457.08	54,022,901.67	71,041,193.46	93,075,648.54
25	42,918,707.20	56,868,219.88	80,489,383.72	82,361,146.60	115,981,256.92	162,571,753.01
30	57,434,911.73	80,508,838.42	122,147,989.36	125,564,496.89	189,350,027.79	283,957,998.60
35	76,860,867.92	113,977,069.76	185,367,692.18	191,430,589.92	309,131,268.08	495,978,812.29
40	102,857,179.37	161,358,338.85	281,307,792.98	291,847,390.49	504,685,116.87	866,307,635.09

(Graphic 12.9 $10mn into $500mn in 40 Yrs Table)

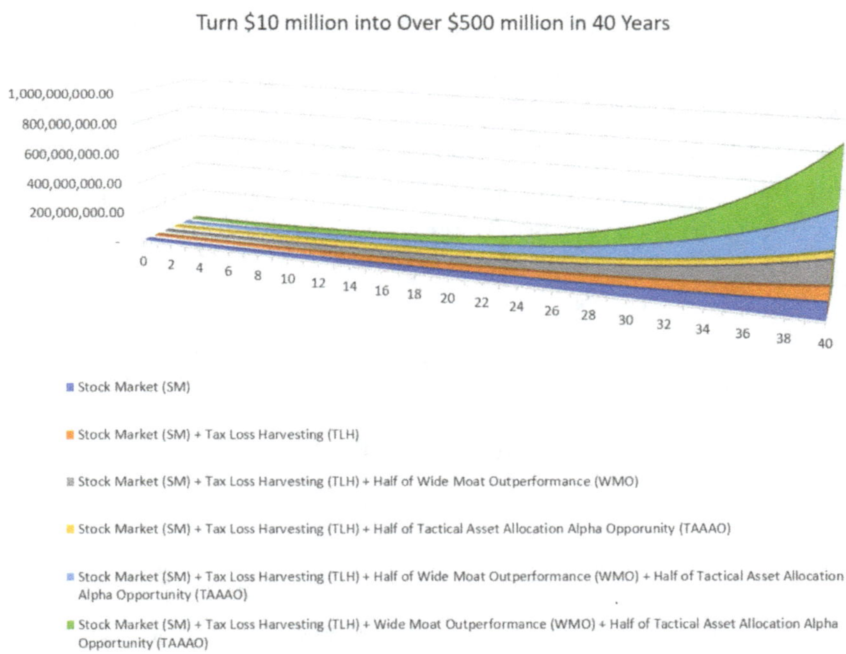

(Graphic 12.10 $10mn into $500mn in 40 Yrs Chart)

Looking at graphic 12.10, the first thing you will see is that a passive strategy of indexing the S&P 500 over a 40-year period delivers a 6% return of approximately $103mn (in dark blue). Adding the enhancement of Tax Loss Harvesting results in additional 1.2% expected annual gain and a 40-yr result of $161mn, a significant boost. Next, while full Wide Moat Outperformance has been 3% annually, the calculation uses only half (1.50%). Similarly, the estimated gain for full Tactical Asset Allocation Alpha Opportunity is 3.2% annually but the calculation here uses just half (1.6%). Even capturing just half of these two strategies, we see the portfolio explode to a 40-yr return of over $500mn (in light blue).

> *"Two roads diverged in a wood and I took the one less traveled by, and that has made all the difference."*

Robert Frost

As spectacular as that gain of roughly 500% over the original S&P 500 strategy is, consider what happens if we capture all of the expected wide moat outperformance. By combining all three of these strategies—wide moat outperformance, tax loss harvesting and half of the tactical asset allocation alpha—the portfolio skyrockets to over an 800% gain of $866mn after 40 years (in green).

> *"Compound interest is the eighth wonder of the world. He who understands it, earns it ... he who doesn't ... pays it."*

Albert Einstein.

The record of consistent, superior performance I have amassed using this strategy affirms it is a better way to manage a portfolio because it secures all the benefits while avoiding the disadvantages. Imagine an investment approach that simulates *Buffett meets sector neutral meets direct indexing meets tax-loss harvesting meets 190 factor algorithms* and you have a mosaic equity strategy that represents the optimal approach for a lifetime.

SECTION THREE

Lemmings, Liars, Loopholes, and Free Lunches

CHAPTER THIRTEEN

Fear Mongering

When the majority of the major media insist on fear mongering, that is, making "fright news" the staple of their daily airings, it's hardly surprising that people react by making rash decisions rooted in apprehension. Nightly lead stories range from pessimistic to terrifying, whether threats of ecological disasters, food shortages, crime waves, mass shootings, drug overdoses or impending floods. Whatever the menace, the worst possible outcome is likely. There's rarely anything nuanced or uplifting. The media's unrelenting message is, "Stay tuned; things may get worse."[222]

Media moguls, politicians and advertising executives all recognize that people ultimately accept as truth what they hear most often. Referred to as the illusory effect, repeating something continually, even if entirely false, eventually causes people to believe it. Educated, well-informed people tend to be more skeptical, believing they are too wise to fall prey to false narratives.[223] *But history is rife with examples of the seemingly "best and brightest" being duped, whether by con artists like Bernie Madoff and Frank Abagnale, or by politicians abusing their power and privilege. People may be suspicious when they first hear a falsehood, but the more they are exposed to it, the more they hear others believe it, the more likely they are to join the lemmings and jump over the nearest cliff.*

Civilized societies crumble when fear permeates the everyday lives of the populace. Paranoia has been used by despots and dictators for centuries to manipulate and polarize their citizens. Today's media and political leaders employ a comparable strategy to keep the citizenry fearful and distrustful of one another. People are demonized for having the "wrong" political beliefs. As a society, we now accept unrestrained polarization as a fact of life.

Media Mania

"If it bleeds, it leads"

Anonymous

The fear mongering tactics of the media, marketers, politicians and social influencers are intended to keep us all on the edge of our seats, nervously biting our nails and trembling with what terrible thing might happen next.

The sad commentary is that fear sells. The success of fear-based tactics by the media relies on sensationalism versus reality, exaggerating events so as to frighten us into believing we might be missing important information if we don't stay tuned. Isolated occurrences are fallaciously represented as major crises. Minor annoyances are portrayed as national emergencies. Everything is overblown to create anxiety, boost ratings and sell advertising.

The media's fear-inducing strategy is now an integral part of popular culture. No longer can the public expect truthful, unbiased reporting of the news. What we get is a distorted, often completely fraudulent depiction of events, all skewed to create alarm if not outright panic.

The worrisome result is that consistent exposure to media fear mongering is likely to have a negative effect on how people view their immediate environment as well as the nation and world in general. People start to believe that their neighborhoods are unsafe, they are likely to be a victim of crime, their children have no future and the world has become a wretched place.[224]

The "Lemmings" in the title of this section refers to the people who mindlessly fall in line with what the media tells them and suffer the consequences.

Fear mongering costs people money. When I first started my career in portfolio management, there was rampant fear mongering concerning the national debt. The message from the mass media was that our country was broke. People were talking about pulling their money out of the market.

As a young professional with an optimistic outlook, that dismal viewpoint concerned me. It was a popular if depressing talking point around the water cooler. I didn't like how everyone was so willing to believe the portrayal of the nation's debt as though the sword of Damocles was hanging over our collective heads. Instead of drinking the Kool-Aid, I decided to do some research to determine if what they were telling us had any validity.

I was managing portfolios at Morgan Stanley at the time. I already had eight years of finance and accounting experience plus a finance degree under my belt. Even back then, fear was a staple of the media. I suspected that in all the bleak blather about the nation's liabilities, what was not being reported was the offset provided by the nation's considerable assets. So, I focused my research on the asset side of the balance sheet. What I discovered reassured me that there was no debt crisis. Years later, I still have limited concerns about the nation's debt.

Debt Debacle

> *"Crisis is the rallying cry of the tyrant."*
>
> James Madison

Explosive headlines frequently suggest the government "could default on its debt." The reality, however, is that Constitution's 14th Amendment unequivocally states that U.S. cannot default on its debt. Under the most desperate of circumstances, the government could delay paying some of its obligations, but under no circumstances can it default on its debt. Bondholders must be paid.

While some 147 governments, including some Western democracies, have defaulted on their debt since 1960, the U.S. has not because of its Constitutional mandate, not to mention the rule of law. That restriction is also the reason why the nation can borrow so easily, the uproar over the debt ceiling notwithstanding. Fear mongering about default is a popular theme for the media, but it serves only to frighten people needlessly.[225]

Let's assume for a moment that the media's rants about the debt were taken seriously and the severe restrictions on government borrowing were enacted. This would require massive spending reductions which would throw the economy into upheaval. Individuals and businesses, waiting for government payments owed them, would be unable to pay their own bills. Personal and commercial defaults would soon abound. State and local governments would be unable to meet their constituent obligations. Unemployment would soar. The U.S. would be powerless to pay its obligations. Its international credit would erode, confidence in the dollar as a fiat currency would disintegrate, and the nation would plummet into a recession or worse.

Obviously, the argument that the U.S. might default as a result of its debt is a canard. While the debt ceiling is law, so are Social Security, Medicare, Medicaid and interest payments.[226]

> *"Fear is the foundation of most governments; but it is so sordid and brutal a passion, and renders men in whose breasts it predominates so stupid and miserable, that Americans will not be likely to approve of any political institution which is founded on it."*

John Adams, "*Thoughts on Government*"

It was the hope of our founding fathers that Americans would maintain the fortitude to withstand the tirades of those who challenged the Constitution and preserve liberty. Over centuries, the tenets of those great men have survived the many who would whip up public fear in the interest of fulfilling their personal or party agenda. Sadly, numerous presidents have used fear mongering in an effort to create public insecurity so they could sidestep Constitutional tethers to achieve their ambitions. From Lyndon Johnson's 1964 campaign ad depicting a young girl picking daisy petals as a mushroom cloud emerges in the background to Bill Clinton's fear mongering over guns, militias and medical insurance, fear has been a steadfast political weapon to unleash public trepidation.[227]

When it comes to the idea of national debt being necessary and constructive, people often have a tough time wrapping their head around the concept. It's no easy task explaining how the largest balance sheet in the history of humanity can be a positive thing. When someone insists our nation is going broke because of debt, I use the example of a hypothetical person that earns $150k annually and owns a $200k home with a matching mortgage at $850 per month. That person may not exactly be getting ahead in life but they would also never be described as being close to bankruptcy. The same holds true on a larger scale for our government and its debt.

I believe the optimal financial positioning for government is to be solvent but not without debt or excessively wealthy. A reasonable level of debt is necessary to maintain a healthy balance of assets and liabilities. It's fine for an individual to be without debt because human life is finite. Governments, however, must plan to adopt an infinite horizon and a manageable level of debt is a necessary element.

Asset Advantage

When railing about the national debt, the media rarely mentions the counterbalance, that is, the nation's assets. They attack the national debt in a vacuum, disregarding the vast assets and resources our country possesses. Including the assets in the equation (without them it's not an equation) makes a huge difference. It illuminates our country's balance sheet and presents a very different picture than the one drawn by the media.

> *"America was not built on fear. America was built on courage, on imagination and an unbeatable determination to do the job at hand."*
>
> Harry S Truman

Our nation has the most valuable tangible and intangible assets in the world. The popular notion that the nation should not have much debt is unenlightened. I want the government's debt and assets to be roughly equal. I don't want an excessively wealthy government. That's not efficient. I want a government that has responsible levels of debt combined with the ability to create currency and do it correctly.

A lead story that announces "The nation is heavily in debt but it has ample real and intangible assets to offset that debt so no need for panic" would not garner much of an audience. "Could the nation's debt plunge us into another Great Depression?" Now there's a headline that gets the public's attention.

It's one reason why the media chooses to ignore the government's enormous resources. The scare mongers won't talk about intrinsic value of all of our patents and intellectual property, the intrinsic value of having a free-flowing capital market and the policies in place that support innovation in various industries like pharmaceuticals and technology, not to mention the many laws favorable to small businesses creation and innovation.

An analogy would be an individual with a $500k mortgage on a $5mn home and $250k in his investment accounts. Does he have significant debt? Yes. Is he in a precarious financial position? Not at all. In a worst-case scenario, he could borrow against his investment account or home's equity. Alternately, he could sell the home and use the equity to buy something less expensive, pocketing the balance.

Everything is relative when it comes to analyzing a balance sheet. A tradesman earning $100k annually with a $4k monthly home mortgage and $100k in his 401k has much greater exposure than a professional athlete or surgeon with $2mn in debt but with a seven-figure income and matching investment portfolio. On a relative basis, someone earning $2-3mn annually with a comparable investment account can have $2-3mn in debt and it's virtually irrelevant.

As for real assets, the federal government owns a great deal both above and below the ground, including roughly a quarter of the roughly 2 billion acres in the country. This represents some 500 million acres, ranging from 0.3% of land in Connecticut and Iowa to 80.1% of land in Nevada.[228]

Above ground assets include land, buildings, roads, railroad infrastructure, levees, dams, and hydroelectric generating facilities, among others. Below ground, the government owns the rights to mineral and energy leases from which they receive royalties, rents, and bonus payments. Offshore, the government owns some 1.76bn in lands and mineral estate, extending out 200 nautical miles. The total mineral estate holdings are about 2.515 billion acres of lands.[229]

At first mention, 200 nautical miles may not seem like a great distance, unless you've driven from Chicago to Green Bay in the winter. Then you have an appreciation for how far out the nation's nautical mineral rights extend.

The federal government's mineral estate holdings surpass the surface area of Canada. Given Canada is the second-largest country on the planet and that the entire United Kingdom could fit into Canada over 40 times, you could safely say the U.S. controls an almost incalculable amount of minerals.

Also, the generic terms "land" and "mineral" are inadequate descriptives. Included in that land is some of the best farmland in the world. Underneath is untold millions in precious metals, awaiting extraction. The value of the estimated 5.5 billion trees on government-owned land is almost incalculable.

The U.S. possesses the world's largest gold reserves—8,133 tons—roughly one-third of the total global gold reserves. (see graphic 13.1)

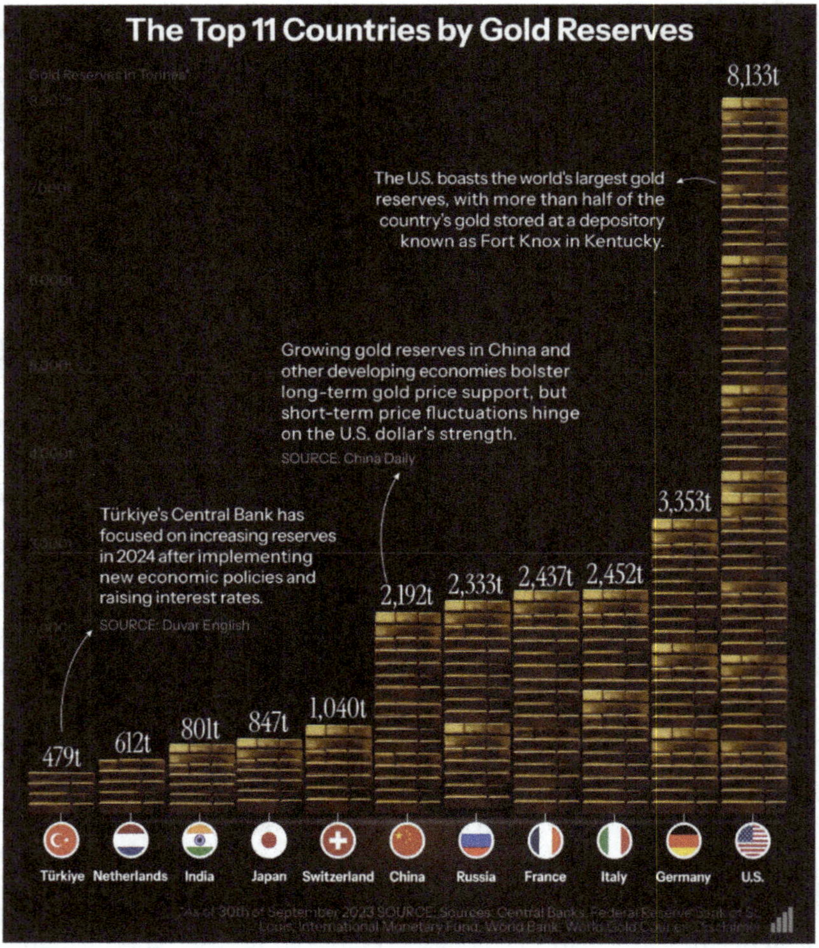

(Graphic 13.1 Top Countries by Gold Reserves)

U.S free flow capital, represented by net foreign acquisitions of long-term U.S. securities, is another major asset. Capital inflows from foreign sources into U.S. stocks and bonds totaled $4.9tn in 2022. The funds for these massive purchases of securities come from global hedge funds, sovereign wealth funds, corporate treasuries and central banks. Money floods in from foreign investors because the global view is that the U.S. is not only strong, but the safest place to stash their cash.[230]

The intangible resources of the U.S., frequently overlooked by those arguing our debt is too high, represent an enormous asset. The United States is the world leader in valuable patents, according to PatentVector, with assets worth in excess of $3tn. By comparison, the next closest country is China with less than $500bn in patents. Medical device and IT patents are among the most valuable. Intellectual property—which includes patents, copyrights, trademarks, designs, databases and trade secrets—is valued at $6.6tn, more than the nominal GDP of any other country in the world.[231]

Then there is the value of our agreements with other countries and trade partners. Also, the immense physical and intangible value of our military. Consider the accumulated knowledge held by our military and government agencies. We have the most sophisticated military intelligence and capability on the planet. How does someone calculate the value of the U.S. Army, Navy, Marines, Air Force and Coast Guard? How can the value of the Central Intelligence Agency (CIA) and the wealth of secretive information, including covert activities, be measured? How many trillions of dollars are the files that agency has accumulated over the past 75 years' worth? Then too, whether you believe in Bob Lazar's claims of working on captured extraterrestrial spacecraft or not, what criteria would you employ to establish a value on the enigmatic knowledge contained at Area 51, the Air Force's classified military base? Like the CIA, even if you could gain access to the physical assets, you wouldn't be able to ascertain the true value because so much is unavailable for assay because it is secret. What mysteries lie in the records at NASA? How would you determine a value on the 65 years of accumulated intelligence gathered in space and on other planets? What is the knowledge being sent back to Earth from the James Webb Space Telescope worth?

Ignoring the intangibles and computing the value of these national resources on a purely asset basis would render a deceptively meager accounting figure. If Tobin's Q Ratio—the ratio between a physical asset's market value and its replacement value—is applied, the valuation calculation would be an astronomically higher number. These are priceless assets that are virtually impossible to replicate.

One of the most annoying aspects of the way the media stokes fear is their arrogance. Like most commercials, the news is presented as though the audience were a second-grade elementary class, and a not-too bright one at that. The imperious tone of the news readers posing as "journalists" sends an unmistakable message that they are enlightened and their viewers are simpletons who need to be led by the hand into the promised land of deliverance.

The more they exude their superior attitude preaching disaster and doom, the more people become turtles, sticking their money in the bank or under the mattress. The money seems safe but its purchasing power is being slowly (or recently, more rapidly) eroded and the consequences of not having it invested in the market are devastating, both individually and collectively, because the market shrinks as a result of all that money not participating.

This fear mongering has contributed to the listlessness and nihilism of the younger generations, many of whom no longer believe they should have to work. Too many of the Gen X,Y and Z don't care about owning anything or investing in anything that has even an iota of risk. They have no desire to participate in capitalism, the greatest opportunity in history to accumulate wealth, because they have been scared stiff and driven back into the basements of their parent's (who are equally scared) homes by a rapacious media.

There is fear mongering about business owners having the major portion of their net worth invested in their business. "It's the highest it's ever been," some protest. Well, what's wrong with that? The wealthiest people in the world have a substantial amount of their net worth in businesses. That's how most of them accumulated their wealth. They own assets that produce cash flow and outpace inflation. That's the underpinning of capitalism. That's how people maintain purchasing power.

> *"America is the greatest engine of innovation that has ever existed, and it can't be duplicated anytime soon, because it is the product of a multitude of factors: an emphasis on independent thinking, a*

> *steady immigration of new minds, a risk-taking culture with no stigma attached to trying and failing, and financial markets and a venture capital system that are unrivaled at taking new ideas and turning them into global products."*

Thomas L. Friedman

My Experience with Government Accounting

I have a pretty good understanding of these issues as I spent several years conducting government accounting at a high level while in the Marine Corps. As a senior budget analyst of the First Marine Expeditionary Force encompassing the entire Western Hemisphere, our financial recommendations, which included intelligence spending, were relayed directly to the Pentagon. The experience allowed me to get a lucid overview of our government's assets and liabilities.

Depreciation

Of particular interest to me was the valuation of intangibles, the things most people never think about. There is tremendous innate value in all the unused land the government owns and the myriad equipment and facilities that have been fully depreciated but are still being used and have value. Rather than the typical blanket valuation, I recognized that different land and equipment have different values. A simple example would be land that contains extractable oil is infinitely more valuable than land containing nothing but rocks underneath.

The upshot of my work for the Marine Corps was the realization that the U.S. was (and is) inestimably wealthier than the media fathoms. We are, in fact, the richest nation in the history of mankind. Of course, even if the media wanted to admit this, they would never pass it on to the general public as it would invalidate their fear mongering agenda.

As to the printing of money, granted, there may be a certain point at which so much additional money is printed that it becomes an economic threat by offsetting the value of the nation's assets. In the case of the United States, however, that eventuality is currently a remote possibility because the nation's assets are so valuable that they cannot be replicated elsewhere. That's where fiat currency systems come in.

Fiat Currency Systems

Fiat money is currency backed by its issuing government. Most countries, the U.S. included, issue fiat money. The currency is not based on the value of a commodity, such as silver or gold, but rather on the economic strength of the issuing government. As such, the value of different currencies varies, depending on how well the economy of each country is performing. This variance is reflected in higher or lower values in relation to the currencies of other countries.

Fundamentally, the value of a fiat currency lies in the confidence of lenders in other countries that the issuing country will repay its debts. The main reason most governments issue fiat money rather than commodity-based currency is that fiat currency gives a government flexibility in responding to a changing economy.[232]

Fiat currency is also the system of checks and balances against bad actors in the currency market. If a country prints too much currency resulting in runaway inflation (too much money chasing too few goods), the currency becomes devalued. Those that lent that country money are now being paid back in a devalued currency and resolve that the next time the inflation-ridden country wants to borrow money, the interest factor will be much higher to compensate for the devaluation. As the adage goes, "fool me once, shame on you; fool me twice, shame on me."

That is how the system's checks and balances take hold. It's not in any country's interest to become a bad actor as reciprocation is easily imposed by their trading partners in the form of higher borrowing costs. In other words, "You got me once but you won't get me again. Now when you come to the table and you want us to lend you money, well, the cost of your money just went up a lot because you're a bad actor in the market."

As an example, Russia currently faces a serious currency threat. The country's inflation rate is expected to rise to near 7% by year's end. The rapid devaluation of the ruble could spur an even faster rise in the coming months according to some economists, who believe the country's inflation rate could soon reach double digits. The Central Bank has hiked its key interest rate to 12% in an effort to counter the inflationary spiral, but thus far it has not had much effect. The ruble is now worth less than a penny. The few countries still willing to trade with Russia, namely China and India, have demanded the trades be conducted in China's Yuan and India's Rupee.

Governments moved to the fiat system once they realized that using a gold standard to control money supply was too restrictive and costly. Under the fiat system, governments pledge to their citizens that they will be credible stewards of their nation's economic interests and exercise spending discipline. It was immediately apparent that control of the money supply could not be entrusted to elected officials, who could print money to pay for goods to win votes. To avoid this potential abuse of public power for private gain, control of the money supply was delegated to a nonelected, independent group of individuals known as the "central bank."[233]

The Fed and Keynesian Economics

The media and naysayers constantly complain about the Fed, calling it incompetent and even corrupt. Their poisoned rhetoric insists that all the Fed does is control the money supply. Well, yes, that's what they do. When pandemics, wars and other misfortunes strike and normal economic activity grinds to a halt, there's a mechanism in place for the government to inject money and ease fiscal conditions. Being able to provide liquidity in a time of economic stress is a healthy requirement of the government. The Fed can help control inflationary expectations and minimize unemployment using open market activities, primarily buying and selling bonds. The Fed is also the lender of last resort. When banks and businesses are in desperate need of money, the Fed is there to provide it. When that happens, no one is complaining about the Fed's actions.

When the costs of a war or pandemic present themselves, the Fed can meet the costs. As an example, the total costs of the Covid pandemic are estimated at $16tn. By comparison, the total costs of WW II were $4.7tn in today's dollars.[234]

Is it possible the Fed injected too much money into the economy in response to the Covid threat and spurred inflation? Yes, it is. But the inflation has not been overly problematic and subsequent interest rate hikes has helped slow it. As the nation enters yet another period of economic uncertainty, it's vital that the government be able to create money when investment in the economy wanes.

This is the foundation of Keynesian economics, a macroeconomic theory of total spending in the economy and its effects on output, employment and inflation. The core tenet of Keynesian economics is that government intervention can stabilize the economy.[235] It facilitates governments and private markets working together for superior economic outcomes by assigning to the government the responsibility to intervene as necessary in the operation of the economy so as to maintain its performance at an acceptable level. It emphasizes the fine-tuning of short-term fluctuations by discretionary policies.[236]

In layman's terms, when the crap hits the fan and everything slows down and nobody wants to invest because it's too dangerous, the Fed can come to the rescue and invest in the economy. That's the whole basis of Keynesian economics; governments and private markets working hand-in-hand.

> *"Will capitalist economies operate at full employment in the absence of routine (government) intervention? Certainly not."*
>
> Janet Yellen

Those who argue that Keynesian economics doesn't work need only look at the rapidly declining level of global poverty over recent decades.

Since the Fed was assigned the responsibility for controlling inflation expectations and maximizing employment, central banks around the world have been using the Keynesian System. The result is a substantial reduction in global economic volatility and increased economic stability and growth. The number of populations living in abject poverty has been dramatically reduced and, on the whole, countries have become wealthier. It's the miracle of Keynesian economics that the media summarily ignores.

The media, as you might expect, attempts to dispel this conviction for reasons that are not always apparent. Understanding the media's agenda can be a challenge, but what we do know is that nobody benefits from the U.S. dollar imploding. The accusation that the Fed is controlled by the elite—meaning the big banks—is nonsense. If it were true, why would the banks consistently be valued at single digit price/earnings multiples?

As an analyst and portfolio manager, I don't understand how the fear mongers base their claim that the big banks control the Fed. They naively throw around names the Rothschilds and Rockefellers, as if the mere fact of being wealthy was somehow an indictment of their character. The media rants make no sense, particularly when one considers that virtually everyone benefits from the Fed's mandate to control inflationary expectations and provide a stable economic environment.

The answer is that we all benefit. Economic stability and the reasonable assumption that inflation will continue at its historic levels benefits everyone on the economic ladder. While there will always be some vacillation in the rate of inflation, over the past century, it has averaged 3.3% annually.[237] That type of stability engenders a more confident populace. It fosters more rational behavior among consumers. Who does that benefit? The average Joe. Why do some people think it selectively benefits the elite? And by the way, just who are the elite?

I scratch my head when the fear mongers insist that the super-rich benefit abnormally from lower unemployment and prices rising at a reasonably steady pace. I don't know what they are talking about, and I doubt they do either.

I see a world in the future were nobody is starving. It wasn't that long ago that India was a very poor country. They are still poor in relation to economies like the U.S., but they're on the rise. Landing a spacecraft on the moon, albeit an unmanned vehicle, is a big deal. The problem for that government is that they're losing many of their best intellectual minds to our country. India will start to make quantum economic gains once they find a way to retain their smartest individuals, not by force but because those individuals believe they're better off staying in India and helping build their nation.

To those who rail against fiat currency I say, show me a better proven system.

> *"Democracy is the worst form of government, except for all the others."*
>
> Winston Churchill

Crypto Chaos

The whole concept of cryptocurrencies like Bitcoin is based on fear mongering. Advocates claim that fiat currencies are unfair and discriminatory. They insist that one of cryptocurrency's primary advantages is that financial transactions cannot be tapped. But what legitimate reason is there for someone to insist their financial transactions be concealed from regulators? Why would someone be concerned about their financial transactions being subject to regulatory oversight unless they had something to hide? What should we expect next: stealthy tax returns? What Bitcoin and other cryptocurrencies have done is to provide liquidity to the black market; they haven't helped our society.

> *"The U.S. dollar is able to store value, but Bitcoin is not capable of doing so, and therefore it's not different from a seashell."*

Warren Buffett

Many predicted that Bitcoin would take over the world and central banking would be decentralized. Nonsense. There is no intrinsic value to digital currencies. Those coins are worth exactly what someone else is willing to pay for them, which is the definition of a "greater fool investment," that is, an investment that can only make a profit if someone else is willing to pay more for it.

That assertion became reality in 2022 with the catastrophic implosion of the Cryptocurrency exchange FTX. Bitcoin's value plunged to roughly one-fourth of what it was trading for a year earlier. FTX founder Sam Bankman-Fried went from cryptocurrency genius to the latest iteration of Bernie Madoff. He has exchanged his lodging in a multimillion-dollar home in Palo Alto for a small cell in Brooklyn's Metropolitan Detention center, having been convicted of conspiracy and of defrauding customers and investors of at least $10bn.[238]

If you follow Buffett principles, you know that the ways to make money are: (1) to uncover businesses that produce cash flow, (2) find arbitrage situations where there's pricing inefficiencies that will converge, or (3) lend money to high-quality borrowers that have a long history of paying their bills. That's when you can actually value opportunities to make money. But the digital currency world is the quintessential definition of the greater fool theory.

Bitcoin and other digital currencies are not to be confused with blockchain, which is a technology that benefits a lot of industries. Cryptocurrency is a medium of exchange; blockchain is a storage technology for saving data on decentralized networks. A blockchain can store different types of information other than cryptocurrency transaction records.[239] Blockchain is comprised of blocks of data linked in an uneditable digital chain. The data is stored in an open-source environment, in which each block's information is confirmable by participating computers. The system is designed to prevent hackers from changing information on the blockchain because altering even a single piece of code would be immediately recognizable against the other copies.[240]

Finally, for those who question the fairness of a fiat currency and claim a digital currency would be a better choice, consider what would happen to a nation on crypto when it faced an emergency, such as a pandemic or war. How would that nation handle the need to create more currency to address the issue? What would have happened if the U.S. had been on a digital currency when Covid hit? In a decentralized banking system, where would help come from to stabilize the economy?

When the economy is bubbling along smoothly, the need for a fiat currency controlled by a central banking system may not be apparent. When a national emergency occurs and people get irrational, that's when the central banks are needed to intervene. A digital currency system would have no such provision.

As for currency stability, lacking innate value, crypto is inherently volatile since prices are tied to demand fluctuations. If there are no buyers, the currency is worthless. Go to a yard sale at the end of the day and watch the sellers dejectedly haul the unsold junk back into their garage. That's what it feels like when no one wants to trade in your currency.

A decade after its launch, Bitcoin has failed to establish itself as an acceptable substitute for money. The run against the crypto bank Celsius, the collapse of the Terra/Luna lending system, problems with crypto lending apps and the sell-off following the FTX implosion combined to puncture the digital currency balloon. Bitcoin lost a ghastly 66% of its value in less than 12 months from its November 2021 peak. Does this sound like a store of value to you?

Financial crazes all end the same way, with prices collapsing in response to a predictable correction. As always, greed neutralizes fear until it is too late for anything but panic.[241]

> *"This (cryptocurrency) is a very, very bad thing. The country did not need a currency that was good for kidnappers. There are people who think they've got to be on every deal that's hot. I think that's totally crazy. They don't care whether it's child prostitution or bitcoin."*

Charlie Munger

Government Shutdowns

The possibility of a partial government shutdown remains one of media's favorite fear topics, typically resurrecting it during election season (which now seems to be omnipresent) or whenever congressional budget conflicts threaten it. Election posturing is just that, given candidates rarely feel obligated to keep their campaign promises if elected. Shutdowns threatened by congressional budget impasses rarely occur. Nonetheless, the mere threat presents the media with a glorious opportunity to intensify their fear tactics.

Despite the fact that the majority of the 15 partial shutdowns that have occurred since 1980 lasted only a few days, the 2018 shutdown that lasted 34 days being the longest, when the word "shutdown" is uttered anywhere in Washington, the media immediately begins pumping out horror stories about the potentially dire consequences. Everything from national park closures to airport disruptions and emergency services cessation is trotted out to create maximum public distress. The fact that most shutdown threats never occur and those that do rarely create much inconvenience, much less deprivation, doesn't prevent the media from taking full advantage of the ostensive financial catastrophe.

While serving in the Marine Corps, I experienced a government shutdown firsthand. It only lasted a few weeks and as government employees, we didn't get paid for a while. But overall, it was no big deal. As I recall, the worst thing that happened was we ran out of toilet paper at the base and my buddy got hemorrhoids using newspaper as a substitute. But we all survived and the world obviously did not come to an end. So, when the media starts issuing its calamitous predictions of an impending shutdown, I am oblivious and you should be too.

> *"How many are worried about a government shutdown? How many are more worried about it starting back up?"*

Jay Leno

Social Security Scares

Those that look at a government program like Social Security in a vacuum and argue that the program is bankrupt make the assumption that nothing can be done to change their prediction of the outcome. They insist the money is not going to be there for future retirees and, not unlike the street corner prophets who can divine the exact date when the world will end, fear mongers love to attach an actual date to the demise of the program. Currently, the popular choice among the fatalists is 2033.

The media loves to radiate fear, and the topic of Social Security is one of their favorite fright fictions. A recent story in *U.S. News*[242] plunges readers into panic with the headline "Here's How Much Money You Could Lose if Social Security Goes Bankrupt." The article suggests that default of the program would mean the average retired couple "could" face a loss of $17.4k in annual benefits. Interestingly, after subjecting readers to a doomsday scenario, the article almost reverses course, noting that, "Policymakers will need to address the program's solvency and make decisions regarding benefit cuts."

Many Americans now worry that Social Security will run out in their lifetimes, and those fears only got worse during the Covid pandemic. That's according to a survey from financial services company Nationwide, which found that 71% of adults felt that way. What's more, 47% of millennials said they believe "they will not get a dime of the Social Security benefits they have earned."[243]

Social Security is not going to go bankrupt. It is a critical spending base for our economy. Some people argue that a guaranteed basic income could be a spending base and that's something to which I assign a probability of happening at some point in the future, likely when we are all living in an artificial intelligence world of robots. (More about this in chapters nineteen and twenty.) But in the meantime, Social Security will remain in place, albeit with some necessary tweaks.

Social Security is vital to our economy. Who benefits if Social Security goes bankrupt? Nobody. Collectively, no one wants to see that happen. Are there levers that can be pulled to ensure the continuation of Social Security? Yes.

For one, the contribution rate could be adjusted. Currently, someone making $15mn annually pays the same amount into the trust fund as someone earning $160k. Adjusting that so everyone pays an equal percentage or some such metric is one step that could be taken to ensure solvency.

Another lever would be to simply increase the deduction rate, such as the government did with Medicare. The current rate for Medicare is 1.45% for both employer and employee. Wages that exceed $206k in a calendar year are subject to an additional 0.9% (for the employee) with no wage base limit.[244] Social Security could have a similar type of approach.

The eligibility age for taking Social Security could also be changed. Instead of the option to begin taking benefits at age 62, it could be moved back, for example. Most corporate pensions do not have a cost of living (COLA) adjustment. Social Security does but that could be eliminated or capped.

So, despite the media's prediction of the collapse of the retirement safety net put in place almost 90 years ago during the Great Depression, there are actions that could be taken to offset the potentially detrimental effects of fewer people contributing and more people receiving benefits. The program is critical to our economy and a promise the government is compelled to fulfill. I have no concerns about the solvency of the program. Incidentally, the baby boomer bubble that is now in retirement and enjoying the benefits of the program represents a colossal voting block.

> *"I was too old for a paper route, too young for Social Security and too tired for an affair."*
>
> Erma Bombeck

Pandemic Paranoia

Paranoia caused by the media's overdramatizing of a perceived calamity, such as the recent Covid pandemic, can leave people vulnerable to conspiracy theories about the causes of illness and governmental responses to it. It can also cause people to embrace distorted portrayals about drugs claimed to prevent the disease, creating avaricious opportunities for the unscrupulous.[245]

By cherry picking statistics, the media's fear mongering can distort rational perspective. In one example, a major newspaper reported that there were 2,000 patients being hospitalized every day for Covid. That statistic no doubt caused panic for a lot of people. Had they done some research, however, they would have discovered that an average of 50,000 were admitted to hospitals every day before anyone had heard of Covid.[246]

Perhaps taking to heart the words of a recent politician who advised, "Never waste a crisis," every broadcast outlet from Bar Harbor to Malibu seized upon the Covid pandemic with the fury of a pack of hyenas. You couldn't turn on a radio or television without hearing the panicky voice of a talking head predicting the near annihilation of the human race. The print media was just as aggressive. A Time Magazine study[247] found that there were 23 times as many articles in the print media about Covid as there were about the Ebola outbreak in 2018.

When Omicron, the most recent subvariant of SARS-CoV-2 (the virus that caused Covid-19) arrived, initial medical data indicated that while it was a highly efficient spreader of the disease, it was less severe. Nevertheless, the media chose to ignore the factual data and, salivating over another chance to terrorize the populace, launched into unfounded prophecies of disastrous consequences. Headlines like "Deaths could reach 6,000 a day!" were commonplace.[248]

> *"In the past year, we have been obsessing about safety," thinking more about the dangers of dying—forgetting we will all die no matter what—than about how we should live, and what we are living for."*

Shirley LePenne,
"The Pandemic Politics of Existential Anxiety"

Once again, the alarmists producing the newscasts were quickly proved wrong. A few days after the mind-numbing predictions of doom, medical researchers reported the strain was actually much milder than the original Covid strain. Like most of what spews from the media, they were not only wrong, they were wrong at the top of their voice. And from the media: silence. Busy out scouting for the next calamity.

A global study by Cornell University found that a dramatic escalation of existential fear occurred in 2021 in response to reporting about the pandemic. According to Uriel Abulof, associate professor at Tel-Aviv University, "Pandemic politics, not just the pandemic itself, cultivated a global sense of dread about health and death. This collective existential anxiety has some benefits, not least the swift development of vaccines, but it has a darker side, too: a grim material, mental and moral toll."[249]

Terrorism Tribulation

The nonstop flood of fear mongering affect people's ability to think straight. Important information is missed because the media is focused on the traumatic. People begin to see threats where none exist. When threats actually occur, people don't recognize them. Omnipresent fear causes health issues, both physical and psychological. People become worn out, depressed and even suicidal.

Doctors found that people who were most fearful of another attack after 9/11 were similarly more apt to suffer from heart problems. Decades of fear of terrorist attacks has subjected people globally to airport nuisances like body-imaging scans. While some believe pat downs and body searches amount to unreasonable search and seizure under the Fourth Amendment of the Constitution. This type of monitoring can only be justified as reasonable if one presumes everyone is a potential terrorist.[250]

Fear of the proliferation of nuclear weapons related to terrorist activity is another drum the media loves to beat. Concern over the threat of these destructive weapons is rational but linking it to terrorism for the sake of fear mongering is not justified by available data. The Cuban Missile Crisis and other confrontations illustrate that miscalculation and misinformation could lead to a nuclear conflict but that doesn't stop the fifth estate from spreading misinformation related to the threat in the interest of bumping ratings. There has been no credible evidence of any terrorist group having the ability to secure or deploy nuclear weapons, which would require a level of expertise in planning and resources that no terrorist group possesses.[251]

I believe we have largely solved the terrorism issue. It was a pressing problem 20 years ago but, for the most part, the threat has been eradicated. It has been in the interest of every civilized society worldwide to solve it. As with most problems, collectively, the human race tends to solve them for the greater good.

Market Meltdowns

> *"2011 might be setting up for the biggest crash of the past 300 years."*
>
> Robert Prechter

Reports of impending market swoons unnerve investors, frequently causing them to overreact. They unload stocks when they should be doing just the opposite. Do markets occasionally crash? Yes. But they have always recovered. Graphic 13.2 illustrates how the S&P 500 has rebounded from every bear market over the past 70+ years.

Whenever the media feels the need to frighten investors, however, they trot out a parade of "permabears," investors who eternally predict the value of stocks is about to take a deep dive, regardless of what is actually happening in the market.[252]

Stock market permabears know that prognosticating catastrophe is "must-see" television. If they get lucky and the market actually declines, they can claim credit, like some $20 roadside fortune teller.

You've no doubt seen these human harbingers of doom. They are an indispensable element in the media fear mongering that accompanies the slightest market quiver. They slither into the TV studio in expensive suits that fail to hide their obesity and combovers that fail to hide their receding hairlines. They caution viewers in no uncertain terms that financial Armageddon is at hand. They pompously point out the current economic parallels, creating panic among unschooled investors who fantasize another 1929 or 2008 implosion.

These fatalists stick around—some enjoy perennial financial news gigs—despite their miserable predictive skills because nobody seems to remember how frequently they are dead wrong. If an NBA player had a comparable success rate, he would be permanently relegated to the bench and cut at the end of the season. But permabears are rarely benched. Their salvation is the law of averages. Like monkeys throwing darts, they eventually hit the target, a dubious achievement that allows them to endlessly tout their clairvoyance.

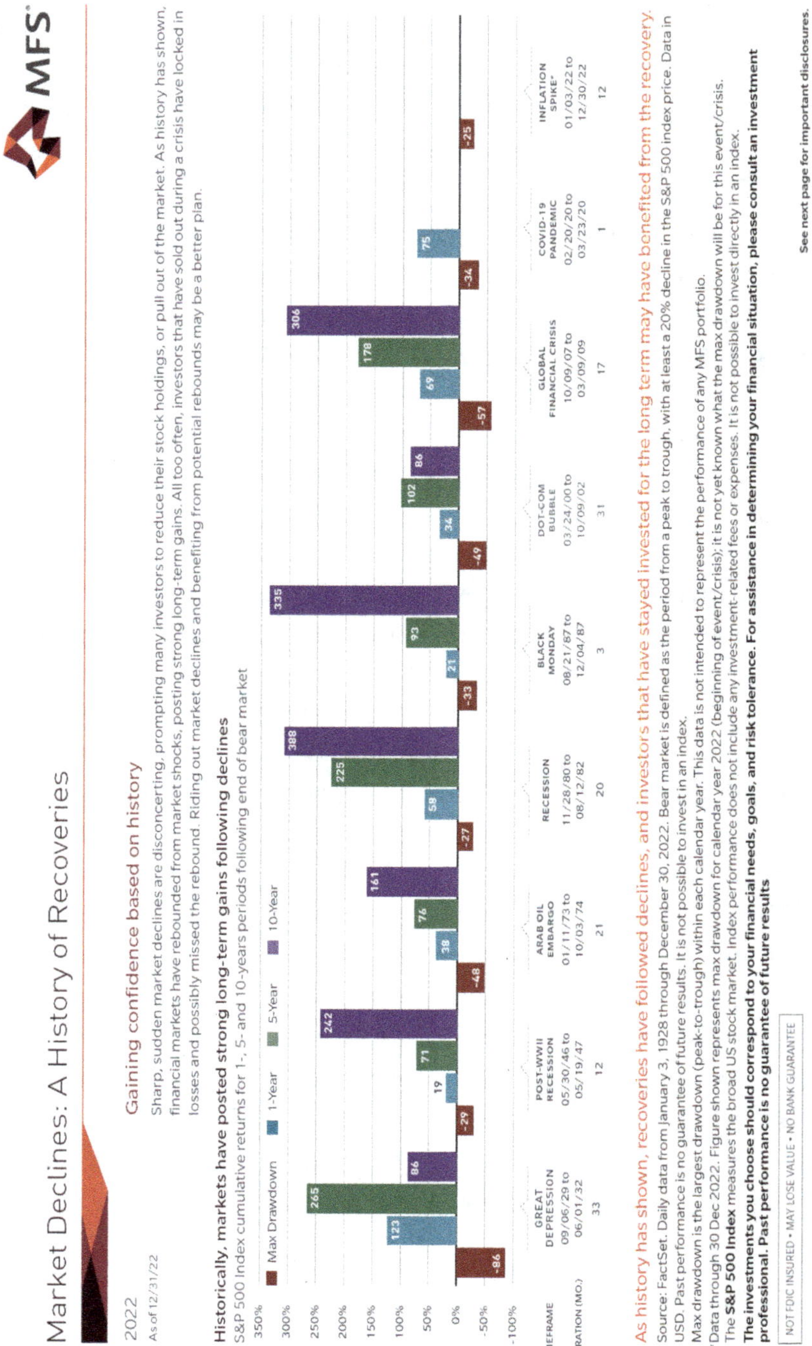

(Graphic 13.2 Market Declines)

A great example of this occurred in January 2021, when permabear Jeremy Grantham, founder of the GMO fund, published a piece entitled "Waiting for the Last Dance." In it, he predicted the biggest bubble since the Great Depression of 1929. Of special note was this comment: "I believe this (year 2021) will be recorded as one of the great bubbles of financial history, right along with the South Sea bubble, 1929, and 2000."

What Jeremy the alarmist would like you to forget is that the S&P 500 was up 28.71% during the following 12 months, not quite the worst bubble in history as he predicted. Undeterred, Grantham continues his gloomy rhetoric.[253] Probably why they are called "perma-bears."

As a wretched group, permabears shamelessly continue to practice their pessimism, taking credit on the few occasions when they are right and hiding in the basement when they are wrong. Their routine would be comical were it not for the fact that a lot of people believe their drivel and make investment decisions based on their fatalistic conjecture.

> *"We'll be in a global recession by Q4 2012 or early 2013. Fed policy will destroy the world."*

Marc Faber, aka "Dr. Doom"

One of the relentless cognitive biases that causes people to continue to listen and act on this kind of defeatist malarkey is called availability heuristic. It's defined as the tendency to think that whatever is easiest for us to recall should provide the best context for future predictions.[254] For investors, this bias influences people to make choices based on recent events or headlines, often in a state of negativity or even depression. Such is the power of the media and marketing.

Another bias related to this is the Bandwagon Effect or Groupthink, which refers to the tendency to make decisions based on what the majority believes. When the media pounds away at an impending market decline, millions of viewers susceptible to the

Bandwagon Effect assume it must be so. Researchers believe it may be the biggest contributing bias to market bubbles.

The FTX scandal previously mentioned is a seminal example. The bankrupt cryptocurrency exchange was supported by a large number of institutional investors, including Ontario Teachers Pension Plan ($95 mn), Sequoia Capital, Softbank and Tiger Global. Given the reputation for due diligence among these financial giants (whether deserved or not) it reinforces how cognitive biases can instill individuals with a distorted sense of trust in people and institutions they believe are smarter than they are.[255]

A couple more examples of the rhetoric these perennial pessimist's spew:

> *"Our Estimates of Return/Risk for The S&P 500 Is The Worst In A Century."*

John Hussman

AI Anxiety

Revolutionary ideas tend to intimidate. Most people do not like change, even if it means progress. The emergence of artificial intelligence (AI) has created considerable anxiety. But history has taught us that most groundbreaking developments are a two-edged sword. The foreboding over AI will prove misguided. As a nation and society, we have always adjusted to change.

When a transformative change occurs, it inevitably gives rise to controversy. A 1961 movie titled "Inherit the Wind" is a depiction of the 1925 Scopes trial, where a Tennessee teacher was accused of violating the state's Butler Act, which made it illegal to teach human evolution in a state school. In one scene, actor Spencer Tracy talks about creationism vs evolution and it reminded me of the yin/yang of anything that threatens the status quo:

> *"Progress has never been a bargain; you have to pay for it. Sometimes I think there is a man who sits behind a counter and says, 'alright, you can have the telephone, but you lose*

> *privacy and the charm of distance. Madam, you may vote, but you lose the power to retreat behind your petticoat. Sir, you may conquer the air, but the birds will lose their wonder and the clouds will smell of gasoline.'"*

AI will be subject to the same scrutiny as the invention of the telephone, the automobile or space travel. If I ask whether nuclear weapons are a force for good or evil, what would the response be? Their capacity to destroy mankind would prompt some to wish they had never been invented, yet their mere existence and the threat of mutual destruction has happily prevented superpowers from using them, so they have served as an effective deterrent to nuclear war.

Like other amazing discoveries, the technology will be modified, improved, regulated as needed, and people will, for the most part, embrace it, whether enthusiastically or grudgingly.[256]

Interestingly, as AI was being developed, there was great consternation that it would threaten the livelihoods of those lacking advanced education or professional careers. Many believed AI would eliminate most jobs in factories, fast food and other lower-income areas. But as it has become an integral part of everyday life, quite the opposite has happened. AI has already revolutionized healthcare, finance, transportation, agriculture, energy, education, legal services and space exploration, among others. It is now being used in some areas involving repetitive tasks that used to be assigned to entry level workers, and this development may actually prove to be a benefit for people currently doing that type of work because as these positions are automated, new positions that require more complex responsibilities will be created. These jobs will be better paying positions with greater responsibilities and personal rewards.[257]

Like every other breakthrough, AI will doubtless prove to be both a positive and negative economic and societal force. It's up to individuals as well as businesses to adapt and take advantage.

Climate Change Consternation

In the interest of a balanced discussion of this widely debated topic, the content that follows is not intended to represent a personal view on climate change, but rather the mass media's irresponsibility in presenting a biased perspective. I am unequivocally not a climate change denier and believe humans have altered the planet.

The summer season has now become a fear mongering favorite for the media. Their depiction of hot weather borders on the apocalyptic. Missing from the climate catastrophe rhetoric is the fact that cold weather actually causes more deaths among humans globally than do heat waves.

For instance, in India, known for its sweltering heat, immoderate temperatures are responsible for roughly 6% of all deaths. Of those, only 12% are due to heat whereas 88% are due to cold weather.[258]

Despite the fact that summer has always brought warmer temperatures, excessively hot in some years, the media treats the arrival as though Venusians have landed on the White House lawn. The perpetual alarmists and political hacks drag out retreaded tales of everything from fires to floods, all catastrophic and all due to global warming. What is not reported is the stone cold fact (excuse the pun) that the vast majority of temperature-related deaths are the result of cold, not heat.

A 2020 study appearing in the medical journal *The Lancet* revealed that globally, more than <u>nine times</u> as many people die from cold-related conditions as heat each year. The study also found that the one-half degree in Celsius temperatures since the start of the new millennium has caused 116,000 heat deaths annually whereas 283,000 cold deaths have been avoided during the same period as a result of the temperature increase.[259] This data is yet another confirmation of the media's habit of cherry-picking statistics to support their false narratives.

A fascinating twist to the climate change controversy is a 2024 article chronicling a development in the Artic, where researchers from three universities found evidence that heat-related sea ice reductions have actually had a beneficial effect on tree seedlings during the winter.

Satellite images revealed a pattern in which tree lines made inroads where the sea ice had retreated due to warming temperatures. Previous research indicated that when large bodies of water warm in summer, greater evaporation occurs as winter approaches, resulting in more snow falling on nearby land. The snow serves as a ground blanket, keeping everything below warmer and encouraging nutrients that feed tree seedlings, helping them survive the winter. The result is additional tree lines spreading north.[260]

Apparently, young people are especially susceptible to global warming conversation. A 2021 study in *The Lancet* surveyed 10,000 young people ages 16-25 in 10 countries, including 1,000 from the United States. The study found that 59% of participants were "extremely worried" about climate change. More than half reported feeling sad, anxious, angry, powerless, helpless and guilty. More than 45% said their feelings about climate change negatively affects their daily lives and functioning.[261]

Marketing Mania

> *"Never write an advertisement which you wouldn't want your family to read. You wouldn't tell lies to your own wife. Don't tell them to mine."*

David Ogilvie

Celebrities and professional athletes have, for as long as I can remember, been a resource of presumed credibility for advertisers. In bygone days, Humphrey Bogart touted Whitman's Sampler, Groucho Marx Frosted Flakes, Sammy Davis Jr. Alka Seltzer, Muhammad Ali roach traps. More recently Snoop Dogg promotes Hot Pockets and Corona, Shaquille O'Neal hawks Papa John's. One of the more bizarre (and no doubt regrettable) campaigns, Tom Brady pitched cryptocurrency for scandal ridden FTX.

That star power carries influence with the public is no secret. That some choose to endorse products they obviously do not personally use or have any knowledge of doesn't stop them from pocketing the money. These ads rarely have any relation to fear tactics, but they are further examples of how the media and marketers sway consumer spending and how they manage their money.

Today, virtually anyone can get a microphone and bloviate their absurd ideas to the world via a social media platform. There are people with financial podcasts who know very little to nothing about finance that have influence over millions of people.

The more social media, the easier it is for people to secure information, much of it erroneous.

Numerous examples of marketers using fear tactics to peddle their products exist. Fear appeal advertising stresses the perils of ignoring the commercial message. The negative effects of not using the right personal hygiene products are a classic example. Deodorants, toothpaste, mouthwash, skin care and dandruff shampoo are chief offenders.

Of course, no discussion of fear appeal advertising could exclude the pharmaceutical companies. A heart failure scare ad by Novartis depicted a room filling with water as a man unwarily read the newspaper. An ad for Farxiga, a drug used to treat type 2 diabetes, uses blaring alarms to frighten viewers that there won't be a loud alarm warning them about heart damage—*it may have already started*![262]

The advertisements warning of the hazards of not getting the latest Covid vaccine seemingly have no expiration date. We are evidently destined to be subjected to their lectures until the next pandemic comes along.

The fear mongering is regrettably going to continue, whether podcasts, social media, the national media or those trashy newspapers at the food store checkout lane. It sometimes seems all forms of communication are competing with one another to get consumers attention and they do it by becoming increasingly outlandish.

It's our choice whether to listen and become victims of their deceptions or disregard them and get on with our lives, no worse for wear.

> *"Many a small thing has been made large by the right kind of advertising."*

Mark Twain

Political Ploys

Politicians have become experts (well, some of them, anyway) at employing fear tactics to convince voters of the awful things their opponent will vote into law if elected. From a fear perspective, politicians have learned to get voters to think as part of a group. To do this, they must convince voters that whatever issue the polls tell them is most important to their potential constituents, they are the person most qualified to deal with the problem (even though if elected, they often won't).

According to Christopher Federico, PhD, professor of political science and psychology at the University of Minnesota, once that is established, making people scared about that issue can cause them to seek comfort by joining the ranks of the person (or political party) perceived as most capable. And on a more personal level, when a politician casts doubt on the physical or mental well-being of a challenger, the goal is often to use fear to make supporters doubt his or her competency.[263]

> *"Politicians sell themselves to voters by using scare tactics. Cable news stations use fear to sell their programs to viewers. Advocacy groups do the same to sell memberships. Realtors use it to sell homes in gated communities."*

Barry Glassner, *"The Culture of Fear"*

Political movements, even nonsensical ones, sometimes gain momentum. The usual cast of characters, unable to foresee the unmistakable consequences of the absurdity, grab a protest banner and join the crusade. Once the inevitable outcome of their madness hits them in the face, the perpetrators are the first to plea for a solution to the problem they created.

Such is the example of the "defund the police" movement. The sheer impracticality of removing the principal deterrent to criminal activity would seem apparent, but there is always an assortment of nut jobs, loafers, elitists and political naifs eager to join the coalition.

As if the eventual dangerous result was not already obvious, there is actually a historical precedent. In 1919, roughly 80% of Boston's Police Department walked off the job and four days later, nine people were dead as criminals laid siege to the city.[264]

A study by the University of Pennsylvania[265] analyzed a half century of police and crime data and concluded that every $1 spent on policing generated $1.63 in social benefits, mostly through reductions in homicides. When coupled with intelligence strategies like focused deterrence, the outcomes were even stronger.

Evidently, the enlightened leaders of some of the nation's largest cities chose to ignore history and forged ahead with police spending cuts and reallocations of funding. These included Minneapolis, New York, Los Angeles, San Francisco, Chicago, Milwaukee, Philadelphia, Portland, Seattle, Baltimore and Austin.

The movement not only resulted in reductions in police budgets, it also led to morale problems and a surge of resignations and early retirements. What the movement failed to anticipate was that when you demonize police for doing their job, many of them will take the insults personally and abandon you to the criminal element.

Do incompetent and untrustworthy police officers exist? Of course. There are also crooked politicians, incompetent tenured teachers, plumbers that leave you with clogged drains and auto mechanics that rob people blind. But to condemn any group—especially one whose members put their lives on the line for others every day—because of a handful of bad actors, is unconscionable, not to mention short-sighted.[266]

> *"Democracy is the most difficult of all forms of government, since it requires the widest spread of intelligence, and we forgot to make ourselves intelligent when we made ourselves sovereign."*
>
> Will and Ariel Durant

Today, some three years after the movement became a rallying cry in these and other cities, efforts to divert resources from police or do away with conventional policing entirely have largely been abandoned as the incontrovertible results of that mirage have been made shockingly clear. The result of police shrinkage and budget cuts: 14 major cities experienced their highest homicide rates in history in 2021, and that number rose up to 40% higher in 2022!

While New York and Seattle suffered the highest increases in homicides, crime of all types has risen dramatically in cities embracing the defund absurdity.[267] Organized theft has left downtowns and major retail areas in Portland, Seattle and San Francisco looking like desert ghost towns.

Hopefully, the tide has turned and the support for a campaign that was doomed from the beginning will continue to diminish. As D.C. politicians are carjacked just blocks from the Capitol building, the cry to "refund" police departments has become a clarion call. Once the predictable impact of trashing the police begins to affect the rich and famous, their lofty but misguided ideas evaporate.

Capitalism's Invisible Hand

> *"Never bet against America."*
>
> Warren Buffett

I concur with Warren Buffett, and I might amend that to say "Never bet against humanity" because when people put their collective intellect together, problems get solved. AIDS, Polio, Bin Laden. Money and effort are coalesced and we figure it out. The great achievements of mankind are typically attained through a cooperative spirit among many people dedicated to overcoming whatever stands in their way.

Buffett has also said that people make tremendous sacrifices to come to our country and until that stops, the U.S. will continue to be an absolutely wonderful place to invest money. Think of the people that literally swim their children across the Rio Grande (or take other near-impossible routes) to try to improve their economic utility.

Migrants seeking freedom in our country have been forced to take increasing risks, with many dying in rivers, canals, deserts, mountains, and even in unsafe trailers meant for cargo transportation. In June, 2022, some 40 dead migrants were discovered inside a truck in San Antonio, the victims of human smuggling.[268]

That's the invisible hand of capitalism. It's the little guy wanting to make a better life for himself and his family. It's the micro that creates the macro. It's the basis of our economic system. It drives capitalism and propels progress. As long as it continues, all the fear mongering is going to accomplish just one thing: it's going to cost those who listen to it their time and money.

Government was created to help all that along. When circumstances like wars, disasters and pandemics happen—events that are beyond the control of the average Joe and the mom-and-pops—that's when the government is needed to step in and provide reassurance, smoothing out the economic cycle. And when people forget where they came from and go astray by taking financially irresponsible risks, that's when the government steps in and makes the cost of money more expensive, putting a lid on the overheated economy.

Final Thought

People sit in the home that they've owned for five years and intend to own for another decade or two and don't think much about its value because they have a basic idea what it's worth and they have other homes in their community for price comparison. So, they have confidence about their home value. But the same people have no idea how to value the businesses in their investment account. So, when somebody on television says the value of the businesses they own is going down they get frightened and sell.

Fear is often based on uncertainty. It's not unlike when a half dozen homes in someone's neighborhood suddenly go on the market. There's a natural tendency to panic when multiple neighbors are selling. When things get scary, it feels right to take less risk. Flight response is a human's way of dealing with a perceived danger. It's likely a genetic remnant from our ancestor's survival instincts. It can be a sensible reaction from an evolutionary perspective, but a horrible response to volatility in the market.

Historically, when the media or the market gets people scared, investment opportunities emerge. That's when it can be most profitable to take additional risks, but risks based on a mathematically rule-based investment strategy. That's when risks become less uncertain. Risks understandably frighten human beings but not algorithms. For the mathematically based investor, they represent opportunity.

Perhaps you've heard someone accuse the stock market of being rigged, a ridiculous assertion. A review of the market's historical performance over the past 150 years dismisses the "rigged" notion. The market is the single greatest wealth generating mechanism for individuals that's ever been created, the most generous gift in history for the average person. Prior to the market's existence, the only way the "average Joe" could get ahead was to start a business and put it all on the line.

Today, it's never been better for a lower income individual to get out of poverty by taking a little money and buying a business using fractional shares, a portion of an equity stock less than a full share. It's insured so it's safe. The average person can watch their money grow throughout their lifetime. And it provides an experience few lower income people have been able to experience - participating in capitalism as a business owner.

So, when someone says the market is rigged, it's nonsense. The stock market is extremely transparent. Company financials are examined by both internal auditors and external auditing firms before executives sign off on them. In addition, there are whistleblowers watching, prepared to communicate any irregularities to the authorities. Executives in violation have been prosecuted and jailed. That protection allows the stock market to continue to be the greatest opportunity in history for the little guy.

There's been a powerful movement—whether provoked by the media, the legal profession or whatever interest group—to convince the populace that it needs to protect itself against the risks in life. Perhaps this is why young portfolio managers often outperform older managers; there seems to be an age bias. A fund manager that's been at it for 20 or 30 years has likely accumulated a sizeable net worth and, as the stakes get higher, he realizes all he needs to do is ride it out safely into retirement, avoiding any unnecessary risks. He tells himself, "Well, I took some calculated risks to get where I am, but there's no need to take those risks anymore. I'll just play it safe and hit it down the middle for the next few years, and my family and I will be set for life."

That's just one of many reasons why investors should absolutely ignore anything they hear from market strategists at major Wall Street brokerage firms. Ignore them because they're massively biased and often wrong. Even worse are the journalists that love to compare every little twitch in the market to the crash of 1929. Here's the opening of a recent network broadcast: "Will the current real estate downturn drag us into another Great Recession?"

This is such a favorite activity of the media. They love having something, anything, that has the potential to occur, no matter how remote, to open their evening news segment and scare half the nation into doing stupid things with their investments. Like a horror movie director, they mess with people emotionally. When those emotions cause people to change behavior and do things with their money they would not normally do, there are consequences, and they are usually detrimental to people's financial wellbeing.

Resolve to ignore the media's negative blather. They are using the psychological gambit of frightening you so you will tune in and boost their ratings so they can sell advertising space.

> *"Never let the fear of striking out get in your way."*
>
> Babe Ruth

All the fear mongering and misinformation creates a lot of opportunity for me as an investor, so I can't say I wish it didn't exist. I play the hand that's dealt to me. If people that I'm competing with are listening to people that don't know what they're talking about and being influenced to make bad decisions, it directly benefits me and my investors. The more inefficient the markets become, the more opportunities there are for us.

CHAPTER FOURTEEN

Pigs on Wall Street

"Wall Street is the only place that people ride to in a Rolls Royce to get advice from those who take the subway."

Warren Buffett

Hundreds of thousands, if not millions, of trusting investors have been scammed by the residents of Wall Street firms over the years. While financial lore has it that Wall Street got its name because walls were built around it to keep the wild boars out, it appears a number of the swine gained entry and are living up to their name, courtesy of the investing public. In addition to the pigs there are other, perhaps even more repulsive creatures, lurking behind those walls, snakes whose only mission is to become rich at the expense of the unwary.

I believe the majority of people who work in the financial community are a collection of self-motivated people dedicated to the needs of their clients, but there are too many willing to engage in unethical practices for their own personal gain. Perhaps that is an unavoidable component of capitalism, but as an investor, you must take responsibility for protecting yourself again these predators.

What follows is a discussion of some of the most egregious examples of investors being fleeced by Wall Street and financial industry fraudsters. These and others in the industry are what the "Liars" in the title of this section refer to.

Ponzi Schemes

The classic form of investment scam is the Ponzi scheme, named after Charles Ponzi, who promised investors a short-term 50% return on international mail coupons in the 1920s. Ponzi paid investors fake returns with money coming in from new investors.

Since Ponzi schemes rarely generate any actual returns, investor money not used to pay off previous investors goes into the pockets of the schemers. Since there is a finite number of potential investors, it's simply a matter of time until there is insufficient money to pay investors wishing to cash out and the scheme disintegrates.[269]

Bernie Madoff

The biggest and most highly publicized Ponzi scheme since the original was engineered by investment manager Bernie Madoff, whose brokerage firm amazingly managed to fool investors and regulators alike for almost a half century. Arrested by the FBI in 2008, Madoff's larceny was found to total $65bn.

Madoff's ability to keep his theft undiscovered for so long was based on several carefully crafted elements. He created a credible reputation by fabricating consistently high investment returns of 12-13%, even in years when the markets suffered major losses. Few other investment managers could tout comparable results. Madoff reinforced the illusion by serving as chairman of the Nasdaq Stock Market (NASDAQ) and at one point, Madoff Investment Securities was one of Wall Street's biggest market-makers.

Hailed as a financial genius by his grateful clients, Madoff's scheme was, surprisingly, a rather uninspired adaptation of the original Ponzi scheme. Funds from new investors were used to pay artificial returns to previous investors. The investment "strategy" Madoff employed was known as the "collar," explained in chapter eight, "Managing Concentrated Positions."

Despite not having conducted a single trade for many years (discovered later by investigators), Madoff maintained the illusion by limiting his supposed portfolio holdings to blue-chip stocks. These issues provided readily available trading data that Madoff used to reverse engineer the trades he would have made in order to produce the rate of return he claimed. He used the data to produce counterfeit account statements depicting his concocted investment returns for his enthralled clients.[270]

When the economic downturn of 2008 generated more redemptions than his firm could afford to pay out, the scheme collapsed. Madoff confessed to his unbelieving sons how he had managed to avoid detection for 47 years and was shortly thereafter arrested and ultimately sentenced to 150 years in prison, where he later died.[271]

A critical factor helping keep his scheme afloat for so long was his inroads into trusting communities, including small day schools and nonprofits on up to university endowments, large foundations and even hedge funds. Madoff beguiled them all, from the naïve to the sophisticated. According to the *Times of Israel*,[272] Yeshiva University lost roughly $100mn, two elite day schools in New York each lost at least $5mn and the venerable Elie Wiesel's charitable foundation lost $15mn, while Wiesel lost millions more in personal savings. Seemingly no one was immune to Madoff's pitch: Dodger great Sandy Koufax, director Steven Spielberg, actors Kevin Bacon and John Malkovich, New Jersey State Senator Loretta Weinberg and billionaire financier Ira Rennert, who alone lost $200mn. When we hear about malevolent individuals like Madoff, our focus tends to be on the perpetrator because of the outlandish behavior and sinister deceptiveness involved. What is often overlooked is the human carnage left in its wake. Among the thousands who suffered as a result of Madoff's larceny was philanthropist Robert Lappin, who lost much of his personal fortune, his foundation's assets and the entire 401(k) holdings of his company and foundation employees and former employees, a total of over $90mn.[273]

Beyond the money lost, there was additional tragedy. French financier Rene-Thierry Magon de la Villehuchet lost more than a billion dollars of his and his clients' money as a result of Madoff's thievery, resulting in his suicide in his Manhattan office using a box cutter.[274]

Allen Stanford

Stanford sold fraudulent high-yielding certificates of deposit through his Antigua-based Stanford International Bank. At its peak, the firm had 30,000 clients and $8.5bn in assets. While promising investors their money would be used to invest in conservative, liquid assets, Stanford used investor funds for risky ventures, most of which never earned a profit. Stanford used the rest of the money to fund his extravagant lifestyle.

Stanford bribed auditors and regulators to hide his scheme. Antigua even knighted him and he leveraged that mantle to entertain and gain the trust of unsophisticated retirees. The scheme collapsed during the great recession, when investors began cashing CDs at an unsustainable rate and Stanford was forced to halt redemptions.[275]

In February 2009, US regulators seized Stanford's financial empire, ending his two-decade run during which he lived like royalty, having spent $2bn of investor money on a jet-set lifestyle.[276]

It's hard to believe a Ponzi scheme that originated a century ago is still able to take in victims in today's society, but it continues to do so and people's lives are destroyed as a result. Among the many lessons to be gleaned from the Madoff and other tragedies is to make sure your money is always held independently of your investment manager by a reputable custodian.

Today, investment firms like Schwab, Fidelity, Vanguard and other major financial institutions provide investors with online access to their custodian's website so they can log on at any time and review their investment accounts. It's important to have this third-party custodial protection because software that creates financial statements replicating the real thing is commonly available and has been used by irreputable financial firms to falsify client investment results. Confiscation of investor assets is even easier today than when Madoff stole from his clients, an unavoidable consequence of modern software technology.

Investor Theft

Greg Campbell

One day, I got on the elevator at Merrill Lynch, the investment firm I was working for earlier in my career. When the doors closed, I saw this guy standing next to me, an employee at the firm I had seen once or twice but didn't know. Suddenly, I had this sickening feeling. I can't say exactly what produced such repugnancy, but I just had the feeling this guy was a scumbag. He made my skin crawl and that ride down was a long, silent one.

It was some months later that a fellow worker asked me if I had heard about Greg Campbell. "Who's Greg Campbell?" I asked. It turned out it was the same guy who made me so uncomfortable in the elevator that day. Campbell managed clients' Loan Management Accounts (LMAs) for the firm—lines of credit collateralized by securities. Beginning in September 2007 and continuing until he was arrested in 2011, he diverted more than $1.4mn from the LMAs to his own personal use. He used the money for a down payment on a personal residence, mortgage payments, lease payments on his BMW and other living expenses.[277]

What was particularly repugnant was that many of his clients were living in nursing homes towards the end of their lives. He would open accounts in their names that he controlled and then take out loans on their money through the company, doing what is known as margining their assets. It refers to using the assets in a brokerage account as collateral to borrow money. For example, if a client had $250,000 of stock in their account, he would use the stocks as collateral for a loan. He created fake businesses in the form of shell companies and would send wires from his clients' accounts to his personally owned shell companies.

Campbell was sentenced to 38 months in prison, restitution in the amount of $1.8mn and ordered to forfeit his Missouri home. Of course, his theft caused great concern at the company as management worried the public would perceive the activity as a company policy or ethic versus the actions of a single bad actor.

That's one of the unintended consequences of people who steal money from their clients' accounts: a great many people suffer both financially and psychologically as a result and, in some cases, companies are forced out of business because of the pernicious actions of one or two individuals.

Scott Gelbard

When financial scammers are caught, put in prison and eventually regain their freedom, they have the opportunity to, at least in some small way, atone for their fraudulent behavior by doing some good for mankind. Sadly, many of these people feel no remorse. Among the worst is Scott Gelbard, a former stock promoter who is so unrepentant, he left the U.S. and is now living in Canada where he proudly publicizes the activities that landed him in prison.

Gelbard was convicted of securities fraud. He and his associates at Regency Group, LLC, in Colorado promoted stock in a company without disclosing that they controlled virtually all the available stock. Using the services of a disbarred attorney, Gelbard created brokerage accounts in the name of nonexistent Panamanian entities the former attorney controlled so they could surreptitiously accumulate and sell stock in companies they controlled, like Greenchek Technology, a firm that purportedly made gasoline-emission-reduction products. The partners would transfer Greenchek shares to the entities controlled by the former attorney while circumventing the required SEC disclosure that they had accumulated over 85% of Greenchek's available shares.

Gelbard then began selling the stock, generating more than $4mn in proceeds within a year. His partner then laundered the money through the Panamanian accounts and transmitted it to accounts that Gelbard controlled.[278]

The Friendly People at Investment Companies

Wells Fargo Bank

In 2013, Wells Fargo employees in Southern California were engaged in ruthless tactics to meet their daily sales targets. According to the *Los Angeles Times*,[279] some 30 of the bank's employees were fired for opening new accounts and issuing debit or credit cards without customer knowledge, in some cases involving forged signatures.

Branch managers were assigned individual product quotas and pressured their subordinates to meet the quotas or be discharged. There was no letup in the pressure. When a branch failed to meet its daily target, the deficit was added to the following day's goals. As reward for meeting the quotas, personal bankers received bonuses up to 20% of their salary and tellers up to 3% for their work.

Initially, the bank had taken a defensive posture in response to the charges, alleging that rogue employees were responsible and firing some 5,000 workers overall. Then came reports that Wells also was illegally repossessing the cars of members of the U.S. military, signing people up for unnecessary insurance and wrongly billing mortgage clients.[280]

In September 2016, Wells Fargo paid $185mn to settle a lawsuit filed by regulators and the city and county of Los Angeles, admitting that employees had opened as many as two million accounts without customer authorization over a five-year period. In April 2017, the board of directors released the results of its independent investigation which sharply criticized the bank's management, sales practices and organizational structure as root causes of the scandal.

Other identified sales abuses included bank employees creating fraudulent checking and savings accounts by moving money out of existing accounts into new ones using their own contact information on forms to prevent customers from discovering the scam.[281]

The bank and its parent, Wells Fargo & Company, eventually agreed to pay $3bn to resolve their liability arising from sales tactics between 2002 and 2016, which included an admission of pressuring employees to meet unreasonable sales goals.[282]

As a result of the bank's deceptive practices, tens of thousands of customers saw their credit ratings gutted and were forced to pay millions in higher interest rates on subsequent purchases.

A lesson from this is that just because a company is large and has a recognizable name does not mean you should implicitly trust it. When it comes to your money, you must be acutely aware of who you are dealing with and what they are doing. You do not want to trust your money to someone that has no skin in the game. Just because someone is wearing a suit and tie, has a nice smile and works for a big company, it is no assurance they are honest or have your best interests at heart. Some of the world's best con men wore suits from Savile Row and had engaging personalities.

I've always thought you should be wary of someone that puts a noose (tie) around his neck to try to appear intelligent.

Survivorship Bias

This is not an actual scam, but it should be because it is both misleading and punitive to investors. Survivorship bias refers to families of investment funds where one or more of the funds perform so poorly, the fund sponsor shuts it down or merges it with one of the better-performing funds. The legal cunning occurs when the fund contacts the unhappy investors and tells them there is a silver lining. Because the company feels so badly about the unfortunate results, they are going to transfer the remains of the investor's money into one of the other funds that has recently outperformed its index.

This tactic has the double benefit (to the fund, of course) of allowing it to keep losing investors while disguising poor performance. The latter because the underperforming fund, once shuttered or merged, disappears from the investment universe as if it never existed.

Naturally, the fund sponsor heavily promotes the funds that do well and can ignore those that failed and were expunged. As this process continues, an increasingly smaller number of funds will survive, but those that do will display glowing performance and investors will gobble them up like lab rats in a feeding experiment.[283]

Hedge funds are often practitioners of this financial sleight of hand because data can be easily manipulated to mislead investors. Pension plans and other institutional investors tend to apply a longer-term perspective to hedge fund performance to help purge short-term trends in their analysis. The problem with that is it presents a greater risk for survivorship bias, which impacts aggregate performance data and is more prevalent in hedge funds because of their higher shut down rate. The assumption is that, pending the death or retirement of the hedge fund manager, most hedge funds that exodus the market were underperforming.[284]

The practice of closing funds is legal and commonly employed by sponsors with underperforming funds that aren't attracting any money. Virtually no one keeps track of extinguished funds so there is scant publicity. It's simply a reality of the business. Like any other business, if the product isn't selling, the company eliminates it and dedicates their resources to something that does. Want examples? How about legendary Pontiac and Oldsmobile automobiles at GM, Crystal Pepsi, New Coke, Microsoft Zune, Sony Betamax, Apple Lisa. There are thousands more but you get the idea. If you manufacture ten different brands of athletic shoes and two aren't selling, you stop making them and divert their advertising dollars to the brands that are popular. That's pretty much what mutual funds do with their losers.

The lesson here is to always interview the manager of the fund you are considering as an investment. Ask hard questions. Has the fund been continuously managed or has the manager been replaced? Why? Has there been a change in the fund's strategy? How long have you been managing this fund? Did you manage another fund previously? What happened to it? Etc.

It's vital to have a sit down with the person who is going to be responsible for managing your money. I interact with brokers regularly and rarely do they tell me they have personally interviewed the managers they hire to manage their clients' money, despite many having a fiduciary responsibility. Statistical analysis doesn't reveal everything about a fund manager. An interview that includes deep questioning can uncover information that may change your opinion and save you a lot of money.

It is not uncommon for a fund manager with a great track record to leave and start his own fund to take advantage of his performance. In some cases, this triggers a philosophical change in his previous fund's strategy. Sometimes, cost cutting causes a company to replace a fund's former highly compensated manager with one or two investment neophytes at much lower salaries. The problem, of course, is that they lack the skill, knowledge and industry relationships of the departed manager and so fund performance suffers.

Sports Betting Scams

The Supreme Court declared a 1992 law banning commercial sports betting unconstitutional in 2018. Casino industry executives must have stood up and cheered the ruling as an estimated $150bn in annual legalized gambling took root across the country.[285]

But just as fast as sports betting became legitimate entertainment, creating a whole new sportsbook industry and professional businesses, betting scammers joined the party and began to pick the pockets of unsuspecting players. To a large extent, the new industry remains unregulated, providing fertile ground for fraudsters. A whole new battalion of self-adorned "handicappers" emerged, offering their alleged expertise to eager gamblers. Not unlike financial stock pickers that mine historical data as the basis for their market prognostications, sports betting hucksters have gone as far as creating (or fabricating) algorithms to convince bettors their "sports prediction software" can actually pick winners.[286]

Thomas and Becker

As mentioned, scammers typically dress well and have captivating personalities. What is not typical is a scamming operation run by a couple of graybeards.

Two Las Vegas men, John Frank Thomas III, 75, and Thomas Joseph Becker, 72, were indicted by a federal grand jury on wire fraud charges in 2020. The two induced over 600 investors to deposit money ranging from $10,000 to over $500,000 into their investment funds, a total of $29mn over a ten-year period. What they actually operated what was a sports Ponzi scheme, assuring victims that their background and strategy as "sports betting experts" guaranteed winners. Like Bernie Madoff, the fraudsters told investors that their accounts were multiplying in value due to successful sports betting, when in fact no betting ever occurred. Investor cash out requests were ignored or responded to with an array of excuses. The few payouts that were actually made came from money deposited by other investors, not successful sports bets. The estimated loss to investors was roughly $9mn as Thomas and Becker spent investors' funds on personal expenses and luxury purchases.[287]

Interestingly, Thomas and Becker were previously convicted and sentenced to 10- and 7-year prison terms for their role in a $30 million scam in 1990, based on buying and leasing copiers and printers to educational institutions. Obviously, some scammers never learn their lesson.

Cory Zeidman

Cory Zeidman, a professional poker player and 2012 World Series of Poker bracelet winner, was indicted and charged with conspiracy to commit wire fraud, mail fraud and money laundering in connection with the "Phoenix Organization," a sports betting fraud scheme he and his co-conspirators operated. Zeidman ran ads suggesting he had inside information on games that were fixed and that he knew the outcome of those events based on a sophisticated white-collar approach to gathering sports information that transformed wagering into investing versus high-risk gambling.[288] The group is alleged to have swindled bettors out of $25mn over a period spanning from 2004 to 2020.[289]

Winning Team Bets

This scam is so simple and yet so effective because it exploits gamblers' notion that people exist who possess inside information on the outcome of sporting events. The scammers convince an equal number of gamblers that each side in a sporting event will win. For example, if the Bears are playing the Packers on Sunday, the scammers persuade 500 gamblers that the Bears are a lock while also convincing another 500 gamblers that the Packers are a sure win. Those that bet on the winning team are then recontacted and told the scammers have another sure thing the following week. Believing they have found the gambler's Holy Grail, most will bet again. Now the scammers repeat the process, inducing an equal number of other gamblers to bet on the other team. This continues as the number of gamblers willing to continue betting diminishes but those do tend to make increasingly larger wagers. Eventually, there are no winners remaining. The losers to sulk off, looking elsewhere for a magic solution and the scammers end up getting everybody's money.

What victims rarely ask themselves is, "If this system is so good, why are they sharing it with me? Why wouldn't they just make the bets themselves? This applies to almost any insider betting, real estate flipping, day trading or other "make a fortune with my system" pretension.

Phone Scams and other Financial Frauds

Fake Purchase

If scammers know the identity of someone's bank or credit union, they will imitate the number they're calling from to appear as though they're from the institution. They'll ask the person if they made a supposed recent purchase using their credit card, which, of course, they didn't. When the person says "no," the scammer says, "It's okay. We've blocked the purchase." They then ask the person to verify their online name, which then allows the scammer to submit a "forgot password" link that sends a text message to the person with a verification code. They ask the person to read the code, which then allows them to change the password and access the person's account. In some cases, they go so far as to read off actual transactions the person made while surreptitiously looking at the individual's account online to make it appear as though they actually are the bank or credit union.[290]

Government Impersonator

Here, scammers call individuals impersonating a government agency, such as the IRS, Medicare or the Social Security Administration. They may claim the person owes back taxes and is subject to arrest, or that their Social Security or Medicare benefits will be terminated if they fail to provide identity information, which the fraudsters use to perpetrate identity theft. They will demand payment to prevent the supposed penal action from taking place. This scam tends to target seniors in particular. Like the scammers who spoof a phone number to look like it's from an actual financial institution, fraudsters imitating a government agency will often call from the D.C.'s (202) area code.[291]

Fake Cashier's Check

Most people are unaware of the fact that a cashier's check can take days or even weeks to be verified. Scammers forge a cashier's check and send it to victims for deposit, which they are able to do without a problem. The scammers then ask the victim to withdrawal some of the money and send it to them or a third party as a wire transfer. By the time the victim realizes the check was bogus, the scammer is long gone with the wire transfer which cannot be reversed. A version of this scam involves a fraudster waiting outside a bank asking a victim to deposit a cashier's check for them on some pretext that they can't do it for themselves. They tell the victim to keep some of the money for themselves, which is the "grabber." Naturally, when the check later bounces, the bank recovers the money from the victim's account.[292]

High Yield Investment Fraud

High Yield Investment Fraud is particularly insidious because the "investments" are imaginary, as are the profits allegedly achieved from them. As with any Ponzi scheme, if it pays out any "investment returns," they come not from actual investing but rather from money unwittingly contributed to the scheme by new investors. Once the scammers are unable to recruit new investors, they disappear, leaving their victims wondering what happened to their money.

A devious twist on this scheme is that scammers claim the investments are sponsored by private institutions that serve only the most wealthy and sophisticated clients who do not want their business known to the public and therefore require confidentiality. When pressed for details about the investment, scammers claim it's too complex for the average investor to understand, ostensibly why only private banks can engage in the transactions. If asked about the identity of the banks, the fraudsters typically claim the institutions are located in distant places, such as The Cayman Islands or Switzerland.[293]

Pump and Dump

One of the more elaborate financial scams is called the "Pump and Dump," a form of stock fraud that relies on spurious advertising to increase stock prices, which scammers then sell to victims at inflated prices. Micro-cap stocks (those with a market capitalization between $50 and $300 million) are especially susceptible to this scheme because they often lack credible public information and can be manipulated. These companies usually trade on the over the counter (OTC) markets and lack transparency.

The scheme evolves as scammers buyup large blocks of a micro-cap stock, then "pump" up the stock using fabricated information, the implication being that the stock's price is due to take off. The scammers hope is that the misinformation will create demand for the stock, boosting the price and allowing them to "dump" their holdings at a profit while continuing to "pump" new false information so investors will keep buying...until the price eventually collapses and investors are left with worthless paper.[294]

Recovery Room

Another pernicious scam is perpetrated by scammers who seek to double up on victims of other scams or losses. Victims are told the fraudster is able to help them recover their loss and requests a deposit to get started. The scheme simply confiscates the money and vanishes. In some instances, the scammers offering to help recover the loss are the same people behind the original swindle.[295]

Affinity Fraud

Bernie Madoff ingratiated himself to the Jewish community through synagogues, schools and other institutions. Affinity frauds do likewise, cozying up to ethnic, religious or fraternal organizations, often pretending to be members. To feign credibility, they may enlist the help of unsuspecting leaders within these groups, who often become the first victims of the fraud. Affinity scams capitalize on the mutual trust and friendship of group members and are particularly devastating to victims who may feel they can no longer trust anyone.[296]

Bait and Switch

Bait and switch investment scams typically involve an unusually attractive or absurdly low-priced investment where the product originally advertised is switched with a different product, sometimes without the knowledge of the investor.[297]

The success of this tactic is contingent upon the initial offer being sufficiently enticing to lure in the unsuspecting investor. Another factor is the talent of the salespeople and their ability to convince victims to switch products.[298]

An alternative to switching products is to amp up the price, fees or both. These tactics are also grounded in the affability and believability of the salespeople and their ability to make investors comfortable and trusting. Once clients are hooked, they are hesitant to abandon the offer, even if the revised offer may not be as appealing as the one that lured them in the first place. It's all a premeditated strategy to sell the product at the price the bait and switch company wants.

Investors need to inquire as to the exact product they will receive and all of the attendant fees and management costs. They also should ask if the fees are subject to increase and if not, ensure that is in writing.

Undisclosed Fees & Payments

In one instance of an investment advisor charging fees without the client's knowledge, Ross McLellan, an executive vice president at State Street Corp., defrauded institutional investor clients by directing his firm's employees to charge clients hidden commissions after promising them low fees and to act in their best interest. His clients included Kuwait's sovereign wealth fund and European pension funds, hardly naïve investors.[299] McLellan was subsequently sentenced to 18 months in prison and State Street Corp. paying a fine of $38mn.

Some brokerage firms move clients into fee-based or similar accounts that earn the firms more revenue but do nothing to enhance their client's financial wellbeing. In fact, other products in the same asset class are often available at lower fees and better performance.

This was the case when the SEC, National Association of Securities dealers (NASD) and the New York Stock Exchange brought charges against Edward Jones & Co., a registered broker-dealer headquartered in St. Louis. The suit alleged that the firm failed to adequately disclose revenue sharing payments it received from an outside group of mutual fund families that Edward Jones salespeople recommended to customers.

The company paid a $75 million settlement, all of which was placed in a fund for distribution to their misled customers. According to the SEC, Edward Jones entered into revenue sharing arrangements with seven mutual fund families, which Edward

Jones designated as "Preferred Mutual Fund Families." The firm told customers it was recommending the mutual funds because of their excellent long-term performance, but failed to disclose it received tens of millions of dollars from the Preferred Mutual Fund Families each year, on top of commissions and other fees, for selling their mutual funds, a practice which violated federal securities laws.[300]

This was not a case of an outlier taking advantage of clients unbeknownst to the parent company. It was a corporate policy dictating conduct for all salespeople. In fact, the NASD also charged Edward Jones with holding unlawful sales contests twice a year that rewarded winning brokers with a choice of 35 "world class" vacations. Winners were determined by the amount of funds sold and only funds from the list of Preferred Funds counted towards the prizes.[301]

Firms that hire inexperienced "advisors" and place them in unsupervised surroundings, such as Edward Jones brokers working in shopping malls, do a disservice to the unsophisticated, middle-class individuals that comprise the bulk of their client base. People believe what they hear from these financial novices and frequently do not understand the full extent of the costs associated with the investment products they are being sold. When they are made known and complaints arise, the company simply fires the guilty salesperson and replaces him or her with another willing neophyte.

I've spoken to people who believe the full cost of their mutual fund is a 1% annual management fee. I point out to them that what they have been sold is a whole portfolio of funds, each of which has additional costs and buried fees.

Another cost people are rarely aware of (until their accountant tells them the following April) is that if their mutual funds have previously embedded gains, they will be responsible for taxes on those gains, despite not having participated in them. This happens more often than you might think, mainly because salespeople working on commission tend to take the easiest route: they sell past performance. Customers never hear a commissioned broker say, "I want to put you into this fund, even though it's been a miserable performer for some time." No one would buy into that, even though it may be the best advice they could get, albeit unintentionally, from a broker hustling commissioned products.

Why you might ask? Go back to chapter 9, "Balancing Act," and take a look at graphic 9.1 Sector Quilt. The funds in the sectors that have been doing poorly are likely to be the better performers in the future because of the cyclicality of the markets as a whole. Of course, brokers working in malls or at investment seminars will invariably tout the best performers of last year, even though they are historically destined to wind up at the other end of the performance spectrum after the unsuspecting investors buy them.

But salespeople don't advise that way. They look at what's been doing well and that's the easier sale. And people who buy the story, in certain fund structures, often lose twice. The fund loses steam and tanks and there's already gains built into the fund that trigger taxes for the unwitting investors.

Bond Fraud

While we regularly hear about financial fraud involving stocks, real estate and a host of complex investment products, the deceptively placid bond market also has its share of fraudsters.

Bond fraud often involves unregistered bonds, such as bearer bonds that have no record of ownership or transactions. Sellers assert that the bonds have intrinsic value and can be redeemed at any time. Bearer bonds are no longer legal in the U.S. but some still try to buy them because they believe they can evade the income taxes due on standard bond investments.

One scam involved selling bearer bonds with no actual value to investors seduced by the false claim that the bonds were being offered at a substantial discount. Investors came out of the ether when they tried to redeem the bearer bonds, only to learn they were fraudulent and worthless.[302]

Another fraudulent activity that's growing in popularity, thanks to technology advancements and consumer unfamiliarity, is the fixed rate bond scam. Fraudsters create websites that promote fixed-rate bonds and Individual Savings Accounts (ISAs) at exceptionally high rates of return. They replicate the real provider's logo and website graphics in their cloned sites, and often embed the real company name in their URL. The websites look virtually identical to the real thing and contain all of the information investors expect; but the sites are fake and the bogus high rates are designed to steal money and sensitive information from would-be savers.[303]

It's not just outright criminals engaging in misinformation. Seemingly respectable brokerage firms have for many years exploited the public's widespread notion bonds are inherently safe, conning investors into purchasing unsuitably risky bond funds.

Commissioned salespeople convince unwary buyers that bond funds—often falsely crowned with AAA ratings— are as secure as CDs. In even more contemptible cases, such as during the subprime mortgage crisis, brokerage firms and financial institutions were unloading their holdings of toxic mortgage debt by bundling them up inside bond funds.[304]

Speaking of CDs, they represent another ostensibly safe (FDIC insured) investment that fraudsters have taken advantage of to scam trusting investors. Fraudsters Craig Reinhard and Debra Bzik of Allentown, PA. raised almost $40mn from some 50 investors in several states by selling fictitious CDs. Among the victims were numerous elderly investors, lured by the above-market rates on purportedly FDIC-insured CDs issued by the nonexistent "Liberty Certificate of Deposit Trust Fund." Investor funds were used to pay earlier investors in typical Ponzi scheme fashion and for personal purchases by the perpetrators. In March 2006, the SEC obtained an injunction halting the sale of the bogus CDs and arrested the pair.[305]

Cryptocurrency Scams

Cryptocurrencies, such as Bitcoin and Ether, are digital currency that exist electronically. They are sold through an exchange, website or a cryptocurrency ATM and stored in a digital wallet. Unlike traditional currencies, cryptocurrencies are not backed by hard assets nor insured by the government, such as money in an FDIC insured bank account. Supply and demand factors can cause cryptocurrency values to change quickly and dramatically, as recent events have demonstrated.[306]

And as if there were not already a surplus of financial scams being inflicted on investors, the emergence of cryptocurrency has brought with it the usual parade of fraudulent actors seeking to make a quick profit and making an even quicker departure. Victims are typically approached with a cryptocurrency investment on social media platforms or dating apps. After victims open an account, the link or phone number used is discontinued and the scammer disappears with the money.

According to the Federal Trade Commission (FTC), more than 46,000 people reported losing over $1bn in various crypto scams during the first half of 2022, the latest data available. That figure is likely much larger, given that many victims fail to share their loss with authorities. The bulk of these were investment scams where individuals were duped into buying cryptocurrency and later unable to cash out when promises of "easy money" failed to materialize.[307]

Some use "rug pull" scams to publicize a new nonfungible token (NFT) or coin to get funding. A repulsive version of this scam was the Squid coin scam, named after the Netflix series *Squid Game*. Investors had to play to earn cryptocurrency, buying tokens for online games and hopefully earning more later to exchange for other cryptocurrencies. The price of the Squid token went from being worth 1 cent to about $90 per token. Eventually, trading stopped and the money disappeared. The token value then reached zero as people attempted but failed to sell their tokens. Scammers made off with over $3mn from the investors.[308]

Crypto scams are much like other financial scams, the difference being that the scammers are after investor crypto assets rather than their cash. Many of the same unsavory tactics, such as pump-and-dump scams, are employed to attract investors and rob them of their assets.[309]

Smart People Get Scammed

There is research[310] suggesting that high achievers in one area frequently overestimate their ability to perform due diligence in a separate field, a factor in fraud vulnerability. Bernie Madoff successfully exploited this weakness in scamming scores of wealthy, well-educated, professional people who were obviously lacking in financial expertise.[311]

A lot of otherwise successful, high-profile individuals have proven themselves to be no smarter than the average uninformed guy on the street when it comes to financial scams. There are far too many examples to include here, but let's look at a few of the more interesting cases.

In the early 1980s, two Wall Street brokerages, Sentinel Government Securities and Sentinel Financial Instruments, conspired to pull off what was up to that point the largest criminal tax fraud in U.S. history. The firms engaged in a huge tax-shelter fraud, taking more than $600,000 apiece from 88 investors, including actor Sidney Poitier, television producer Norman Lear and composer Henry Mancini. The scam involved supplying investors with more than $130mn in income tax write-offs without actually buying or selling any government securities.[312]

In another fraud, a number of celebrities fell victim to financial advisor Kenneth Starr, who was arrested in 2010 for diverting $30mn of their money to buy a New York condo with an indoor swimming pool. Victims included Sylvester Stallone, Wesley Snipes, Al Pacino, Neil Simon, Martin Scorsese, David Blaine and Uma Thurman. Starr was convicted and sentenced to 7 ½ years in prison, according to *The New York Times*.[313]

Robert DeNiro decided to sell his father's extensive painting collection using art gallery owner Lawrence Salander as middleman. The paintings sold for $88mn but DeNiro didn't see a penny as Salander used the funds to pay off debts.[314]

Annuities

While technically not a scam because they are legal, annuities fit in perfectly with a discussion of investment scams because the people who sell them should be dragged into court and forced to justify their actions.

Annuities are insurance contracts that can provide income, usually for retirement. Purchasers (annuitants) choose from several types—fixed, variable, indexed—and pay the sponsoring insurance company in either a lump sum or time payments. The insurance company then invests the money, tax deferred, until the annuitant decides to begin receiving income.[315]

Essentially, annuities exchange current contributions for future payments. The longer the annuitant waits to take income, the larger the potential payout, assuming positive returns on the investments inside the annuity.

The manner in which the insurer invests annuity funds depends on the type of annuity chosen. Fixed annuities pay a minimum annual amount. Income from variable annuities, as the name implies, varies depending on the performance of the investments after expenses and fees. The payout from indexed annuities is tied to a market index, usually the S&P 500.[316]

Those selling annuities typically receive commissions of 6% to 8% of the investment, as well as a portion of the annual annuity fees paid as "commission trails."[317] For most people, annuities are a horrible investment. If a client purchases a $500,000 annuity, the salesperson might receive an immediate $35,000 commission, which may be deducted from the value of the buyer's account.

When the SEC passed "Regulation Best" in 2018, replacing the voided 2016 fiduciary rule, it exacted a higher standard of care for brokers, and mandated they cease referring to themselves as advisors unless willing to be held to a fiduciary standard.[318] Sales of annuities plunged in 2020, replicating a similar 8% drop after the passage of the fiduciary rule in 2016. Variable annuities, the worst of the lot for investors, began a steep slide in the first quarter of 2022, finishing the year down 45.4% from 2021 and plunging to the lowest level in 25 years.[319]

Those who defend annuities, and it's not difficult to figure out they are mostly the people who sell them, are unable to explain why so many in the industry stopped selling them, even before the new regulation went into effect.

Beyond the high commissions that can eviscerate the investment's value on day one, annuities typically come with onerous surrender charges. Buyers that find they need the money for an emergency or other imperative may be subject to seven-year surrender charges starting at 7% (does that percentage sound familiar?) and falling by just 1% annually after. An investor that buys a $500,000 annuity will likely get soaked for a $35,000 commission, plus they will probably have to pay another $35,000 if they want out during the first seven years.[320]

And guess what? The insurance company that peddles these investment miscreants has another surprise: fees. Variable annuities often include a combination of contract fees, investment fees, mortality and expense risk fees, and believe it or not, sometimes even more fees. All these latent costs can have a deleterious impact on investment returns, easily a 2%-3% reduction, making this product one of the all-time worst choices from an investment standpoint.[321] No wonder sales have crashed.

One more thing. If you are younger than 59½ years old and withdraw money from your annuity, unless there is an exemption for disability or death, there is a 10% federal tax penalty on the taxable portion of the withdrawal, in addition to any regular income taxes.[322]

Given the outrageous commissions, fees and potential penalties for early withdrawals, unless the markets experience the biggest bull run in history, the embedded cost of an annuity makes it virtually impossible to come out ahead.

From those who purchased annuities comes one more reason to avoid the product: lack of service after the sale. A common lament: "They simply don't answer phone calls. I never again heard from the broker who sold me the annuity, despite numerous attempts to reach him. He simply disappeared."

Annuities are highly complex products that may come with a series of riders attached. In my experience, not only do buyers not understand all the nuances and potential ramifications, the snake oil salespeople who sell this rubbish don't fully understand them either. There may not exist another investment with more misinterpretations than annuities. And it's usually the most vulnerable people who buy them.

I didn't intend for this chapter to frighten you, but it's important to know how to recognize and protect yourself from the deceit and fraud perpetrated by bad actors. In the next chapter, we're going to talk about the other side of the coin: financial professionals that adhere to fiduciary duty, ethical standards and fair reporting.

> *"I spent about ten years exposing corporate and financial fraud for 'Barron's magazine and I found a lot to write about."*

Ben Stein

CHAPTER **FIFTEEN**

The Fiduciary Duty, Ethical Standards & Fair Reporting

> *"Your actions speak so loudly,*
> *I cannot hear what you are saying."*

Ralph Waldo Emerson

Few things in the financial world are more widely misinterpreted than the term *fiduciary*. And yet, it is a relatively simple, straightforward concept. Fiduciary responsibility refers to an investment advisor's obligation to act entirely on behalf of his or her clients' best interests, as opposed to acting in their own interests, and to provide the highest possible standard of care.[323]

Financial advisors that provide advice on a continuing basis have a fiduciary duty to their clients. Those that merely sell financial products are not fiduciaries.[324] The role of the fiduciary in managing money for clients can be a slippery slope for unethical investment advisors. Clients often give their fiduciaries discretionary control over their portfolio assets and strategy. It's a momentous responsibility. Fiduciaries are held to a higher standard than their nonfiduciary brethren.

Most fund managers, regardless of whether they are registered with the SEC or not, have a fiduciary duty to their clients under the Investment Advisers Act of 1940. In 2020, the SEC published its interpretation[1] of the standard of conduct applicable to investment advisers, including managers of private funds. The interpretation lays out the components of an adviser's fiduciary duty and clarifies that it comprises both a duty of loyalty and a duty of care.[325]

Under the duty of care, fiduciaries must consider the clients' financial circumstances and objectives before making recommendations or plans. The duty of loyalty pledges that fiduciaries will not have any undisclosed conflicts of interest, nor will they use their position to further their private interests.[326]

A fiduciary must be registered with the Securities and Exchange Commission, is obligated to follow fiduciary duty rules and must file Form ADV to complete their registration. Form ADV specifies the investment style, assets under management and key officers of an advisory firm. It also requires investment advisors to prepare a "relationship summary" of the types of services the adviser offers, the fees and costs for those services, the conflicts of interest the adviser may have, the required standard of conduct and any legal and disciplinary history, among other requirements.[327]

Broker dealers, on the other hand, have historically been regulated by less strict guidelines. In June 2019, the SEC adopted Regulation Best Interest, which requires broker dealers to act in their clients' interests first. This is a much stronger guideline than the previous suitability standard that only required broker dealers to recommend investments that were suitable for their clients, not necessarily ones that were in their best interests.[328]

As a fiduciary and investment manager, I am compliant with three separate codes of ethics: the codes of ethics of the Certified Financial Planner (CFP®) Board, the Chartered Financial Analyst (CFA®) Institute and the SEC. These are considered by most to be the ethical gold standards of our industry; the SEC for investment advisors, broker dealers and security exchanges; the CFP certification for financial advisors and the CFA designation for investment professionals and analysts.

These are laborious designations to achieve. Unlike the multitude of impressive-sounding pseudonyms that mimic actual certifications but can be secured in a few hours online or at a weekend seminar, the CFP and CFA certifications are rigorous examinations that measure the competence and scope of knowledge of aspiring advisors, analysts and investment managers.

CFP®

The CFP exam is a rigorous 6-hour test for prospective advisors that wish to act as fiduciaries for their clients. The fact that the CFP annual pass rate ranges between 60-65% is an indication of the test's level of difficulty.[329] The recommended study time for the exam is 200-300 hours but those who managed to pass the test on the first try report they had spent as much as 1,000 hours in preparation.

Roughly 20% of the test involves case study questions, which can have up to seven pages of detailed information about a hypothetical client's financial position. Test takers must display the ability to understand and apply complex concepts to the case.[330]

The certification process requires completion of CFP Board-approved coursework and a bachelor's degree or higher from an accredited college or university. The designation also has strenuous continuing education (CE) requirements. CFP professionals are required to complete 30 credit hours of CE each two-year reporting period: 2 hours of Ethics CE and 28 hours of General CE. Thus, an advisor who has held the CFP designation for 20 years has spent at least 300 hours in CE, this after the hundreds of hours spent to pass the initial examination. Those that fail to update their certification within the reporting period must retake and pass the certification examination all over again or forego using the CFP designation.

The Certified Financial Planner Board of Standards (CFP Board) enforces the examination, education, experience and ethics requirements for those earning the CFP certification. The Board oversees a code of ethics and professional responsibility, which includes several principles that follow.[331]

> <u>Integrity</u>: requires honesty and candor. CFP advisors are in positions of trust. While allowance can be made for innocent error and legitimate differences of opinion, integrity cannot co-exist with deceit.

Objectivity: involves intellectual honesty and impartiality. CFP advisors should maintain objectivity that is not dependent upon their judgment.

Competence: maintaining an adequate level of knowledge and applying it in the service of clients. Also, the wisdom to recognize the limitations of that knowledge and, when necessary, consultation or referral to other professionals.

Fairness: calls for impartiality and disclosure of material conflicts of interest. Subordinating personal feelings and prejudices in order to achieve a balance of conflicting interests. Treating others as you would want to be treated.

Confidentiality: limiting client information to those authorized to have access.

Professionalism: behaving with dignity and courtesy in all business-related activities.

Diligence: providing services in a prompt and thorough manner.[332]

Let's consider what these principles entail in actual practice.

Integrity

Essentially, a person either has integrity or they don't. There is no middle ground. Those with integrity are incorruptible. They mean what they say, keep their word and don't dodge responsibility with excuses. In financial matters, acting with integrity means dealing fairly and with decency. As author C.S. Lewis said, "Integrity is doing the right thing, even when no one is looking." The previous chapter illustrates what can happen when advisors trusted by their clients swap their integrity for personal profit.

When a broker recommends an investment product to a client, the product may be appropriate, given the client's circumstances, but the broker's integrity is up for scrutiny because there may be several similar products available but one product in particular pays a much higher commission to the broker than the others. The choice the broker makes reflects his integrity, or lack of it.

Objectivity

Objectivity and subjectivity are two variations of perception. A subjective point of view is based on someone's personal interpretation, while an objective view is based on factual data.[333] For a financial advisor, being objective means offering advice and making decisions based on facts, not interpretations based on personal feelings or emotions.

That may sound like a simple, sensible principle but it's not so easily achieved in actual practice. One reason is that, as humans, we are all subject to cognitive biases. If you ask someone if they are biased in their thinking about a topic or event, they will almost certainly dismiss the idea. That's because we tend to accept our biases as fact instead of opinion. Here's a scary statistic: The Cognitive Bias Codex categorizes some 180 cognitive biases that distort people's perceptions and reasoning. That's probably the reason why the most brilliant scholars can be so wrong about things outside of their sphere of knowledge.

Competence

One reason why the CFP Board mandates extensive continuing education for advisors is that we live in a rapidly changing world. Whether regulations, tax laws, compliance issues, new products or market evolution, being knowledgeable entails constantly updating one's understanding of the current financial and economic environment.

Fairness

Fairness may be one of the more difficult traits to define. One reason is that it is rooted in personal values that vary from one person to another.[334] In an advisor/client relationship, fairness may be defined as the criteria agreed upon for an equitable outcome. Too often, this mutual understanding is not explored or fully clarified. It can result in client disappointment.

Fairness also calls for being consistent with clients. When executing trades, the *best execution obligation* calls for reasonable diligence to ascertain the best deal in the security and buy or sell in such a market.[335] Importantly, this must apply uniformly to all of an advisor's clients, so everyone gets similar pricing.

Fairness means avoiding *front running*, a prohibited practice usually committed by brokers. For example, a broker receives an order from a client to purchase a large number of shares of a company. The broker realizes that the size of the transaction is likely to drive up the price of the stock, so he first buys a substantial number of the shares for his own account, then executes the client's order. When the stock price rises in response to the large order, the broker sells his shares at a profit. The practice is unethical and violates his fiduciary duty.[336]

Confidentiality

Confidentiality is vital as it fosters trust in a relationship. Like any business or profession, advisors and their staffs must be wary of inadvertently sharing confidential information. Clients are more apt to share information the advisor needs to act in their best interest if they are confident that data will be protected and remain private.[337]

Professionalism

There are many aspects of professionalism. Among the most important is being responsive to client inquiries. We've all experienced the frustration of asking questions of a service provider and being arbitrarily ignored. Just ask someone who has purchased an annuity and tries to get the selling broker or insurance agent to the phone for an explanation.

Another trait of professionalism is accountability. It's often hard to admit a mistake but everyone makes them. Those with a high degree of professionalism accept responsibility for their client obligations and move to quickly rectify any problems or misunderstandings that arise. Professionals do not pass the buck.[338]

Diligence

Diligent advisors are dedicated and conscientious. They are astute planners and avoid impulsive decisions. They keep their promises and tend to be highly productive. There are few traits more important for someone managing your money.

According to a University of Toronto study, "Conscientiousness is the most potent, non-cognitive predictor of occupational performance."[339]

Another component of diligence is efficiency: executing trades promptly and doing all things related to client service expeditiously.

> *"He has honor if he holds himself to an ideal of conduct though it is inconvenient, unprofitable, or dangerous to do so."*

Walter Lippman

CFA®

Not surprisingly, the CFA Standards of Professional Conduct include many of the same principles as the CFP designation, including:

Professionalism, knowledge of the law, independence, objectivity and the avoidance of misrepresentation and misconduct. CFA duties to clients include loyalty, prudence, fair dealing, suitability and confidentiality.

In terms of investment analysis and recommendations, CFA members must practice diligence, clear communication with clients, maintain accurate records and disclose any potential conflicts.[340]

Candidates for the CFA exam must hold a minimum of a bachelor's degree, have 4,000 hours of qualified work experience in investment decision-making and submit multiple reference letters.[341]

GIPS Standards

GIPS®, a registered trademark owned by CFA Institute, stands for the Global Investment Performance Standards, which are founded on fair and honest representation and disclosure of an investment management firm's performance history.

In plain terms, GIPS are the gold standard for investors reviewing the performance of an investment firm's strategy.

Firms in compliance with the GIPS standards must observe rules governing investment return calculations as well as how they are displayed in a GIPS report. Investors can have a high degree of confidence that the information in a GIPS Report accurately reflects the firm's investment decisions.[342]

If all investment advisors were required to be GIPS certified, I doubt Boesky, Madoff, Bankman-Fried or other investment fraud perpetrators would have been able to carry out their nefarious schemes and ruin the lives of thousands of unsuspecting investors.

Today, when you interview a potential investment broker who tells you how great their clients have done, you can ask him to prove it, not by showing you fund performance but with a GIPS Report where you can see verified performance of real people. It's the reason I invested the time and money to have my investment performance GIPS verified. Having the returns of the real people whose portfolios I manage verified to the highest standard is a big deal.

Wall Street and Fiduciary Duty

If an advisor works for a Wall Street brokerage firm, can he or she really be a fiduciary? A fiduciary's responsibility is to be objective. Can an advisor be truly objective if they are recommending only the proprietary products of the firm they work for? Can they adhere to a code of ethics if they load up their clients with commissioned investment products?

If a CFP working at a bank or brokerage firm is putting their clients' money into an investment such as a CD that's sponsored by their employer, knowing all the while that their clients could go across the street and get a CD at a higher rate, are they fulfilling their fiduciary duty? If they peddle a company-sponsored credit card that charges interest higher than the client could get elsewhere, are they genuinely acting in the best interest of their client?

If a client expresses interest in refinancing their home and the advisor recommends his company's proprietary loan product despite knowing there are dozens of companies offering similar loans with lower rates or better terms, is the advisor adhering to the fiduciary principles of integrity and conscientiousness? What are the odds that the proprietary product being pushed by the advisor is the best choice for his clients? Especially in the case of a commoditized product like a mortgage loan for an individual, is an advisor fulfilling his fiduciary duty by not advising the client to shop and compare different sources, possibly saving himself thousands of dollars?

As I discussed in the chapter, *Pigs on Wall Street,* the big brokerage houses make a lot of money by having their advisors peddle specific products that are not always the best investments available to their clients. In addition to investments, they sell loans, insurance, credit cards and other ancillary products. Does this represent being a fiduciary and observing a code of ethics? Does this serve the best interest of their clients if they have a relationship with an insurance company and are mandated to exclusively recommend that carrier's products?

Wall Street Trap

Many advisors or brokers working at Wall Street firms get trapped into their situations. They are encouraged and often incentivized to sell the firm's proprietary products, or the products of the companies with whom their employer has established a commissioned relationship with. The firm strives to sell each client as many different financial products and services from their firm as possible, making it an arduous process for a client to leave the firm and go elsewhere. Meanwhile, the broker becomes snared in the net because if he wants to change companies, he is unable to take his clients with him since so much of their financial life is tied up with his current firm.

The big brokerage firms may advertise this practice as "making life more convenient for our clients," but that's a red herring. What these firms really want is to capture and retain their customers by loading them up with as many financial products as possible—investment account, IRA, checking account, CDs, credit cards, insurance, mortgage, etc.—so the clients become virtual prisoners of the firm.

The brokers eventually find themselves in a weak career position. They can't leave the firm unless they want to start their career over from scratch because it's difficult to take their clients with them. Once they reach this point, they have no leverage when their employer, realizing their situation, can cut their commissions or otherwise reduce their pay and consequently, their cost to the company.

I believe the new fiduciary standards governing advisors that were not as rigidly regulated is a major reason why many members of the profession dedicated to serving the best interests of their clients are increasingly becoming Independent Registered Advisors (RIAs) and CFPs. Like the firm I work for, this allows them to invest money wherever and in whatever products they believe are best for their clients. In other words, like me, they are not obliged to invest in products offered by their firm, or any other products they do not feel meet the fiduciary standard of care.

That's one reason why the CFP and CFA designations are so important. Given the time and investment advisors make in acquiring and maintaining them, it would be foolish to do something that would jeopardize their fiduciary responsibility, potentially ending their financial career.

A Personal Experience

When I first entered the business world, fascinated by the mathematics of finance and the science of capitalism, I was eager to manage assets at a high level as a Wall Street portfolio manager.

While I was a college student, my dad connected me with his broker, who set me up with an internship. I was excited and initially thought I might be doing some asset management research. What the company wanted me to do, however, was make cold calls to get an indication of interest and willingness to receive phone calls on investment opportunities from our "analysts." I would then pass that on to the sales department. It wasn't the work I wanted, but being my first position, I thought it might be some kind of initiation or evaluation process, so I decided to give it a try.

The brokers were all happily making a ton of commissions on stock and bond sales. I recall asking one of them if he could calculate how much the value of the municipal bonds he was selling could go down in response to say, a one percent interest rate increase? He didn't know. I asked several others the same question and none of them knew, nor did they care. They laughed at me: "We're compensated from the bond's commissions; we're not interested in calculating."

Technically, these salesmen weren't doing anything illegal; essentially, they were doing their job. They were selling. But the fact that they didn't know or care about the impact of interest rates on the future value of the investments they were selling under different scenarios shocked me. How could they justify selling an 80-year-old-widow a 30-year municipal bond that could potentially lose half its value if interest rates went up 3 or 4 percent?

These brokers were making big dollars selling bonds that were sensitive to interest rates. They knew little or nothing about calculating the potential impact of interest rates; they only knew how to sell. "Hey, I can get you a 3% tax-free muni!"

I was taken aback at what they were doing and asked to speak with the branch manager. He was like a movie caricature: overweight guy in a corner office, puffing a big cigar. When I tried to explain my concerns about the bonds his people were selling, he looked at me and said, "Son, we really don't care about interest rates, the economy, or if the market is going up or down. When the market goes up, people get greedy and want to buy a lot of stocks, which pays us big commissions. When the market goes down, a lot of people get scared and want to sell their stocks and buy bonds, and we get big commissions. So, we really don't care about the direction of the market; we like it when there is a lot of volatility. That's when we make the most profits. So, thanks for your concerns. Now get back out there and make some more calls."

I walked out of that office asking myself, "What am I doing here?" The next morning, I was sitting in my car in the office parking lot and I could not pry my hands off the steering wheel and go back into that place. My body was frozen and wouldn't let me do it. I quit the internship and remember thinking I had more integrity from my tour in the Marine Corps than what those brokers had managing people's life savings. Unlike today's CFPs, they had no interest in helping clients achieve their financial goals; they just wanted to earn commissions. It was quite a wakeup call for me.

> *"Integrity without knowledge is weak and useless, and knowledge without integrity is dangerous and dreadful."*

Samuel Johnson

Chapter Sixteen

How the Wealthy Perpetuate their Legacy

> *"The problem is not that the people are taxed too little. The problem is that government spends too much."*
>
> Ronald Reagan

One of the ways the wealthy ensure that their wealth and legacy will pass on to future generations successfully is the utilization of sophisticated tax strategies. These are not merely tactics to defer taxes until a later time when wealthy taxpayers supposedly will be in a lower bracket; these are strategies that actually minimize the impact of taxes on their estates. Average investors are generally unschooled when it comes to reducing their tax burden and preserving whatever wealth they have for their inheritors.

There has been ongoing debate about the fairness of the wealthy being able to elude estate taxes. It's a controversial topic that will likely be debated eternally and the arguments of both sides have validity. Individuals that create great wealth contend that the enormous amount of time spent amassing that wealth—time lost with their family or pursuing personal interests—represents a significant sacrifice. They see that money as rightfully belonging to them and resist having to surrender a greater portion of it to the government than those who accumulated far less. Having to pay an estate tax after having already paid taxes on their earnings and passive income throughout their life seems inequitable if not downright confiscatory.

On the other hand, there is evidence suggesting that when the wealthiest families are not taxed on their estate, their influence on politicians and the economy in general grows abnormally large. History illustrates how this has occurred in other countries.

So, while the debate rages on *ad nauseam*, both sides have credible arguments and people's opinion is likely related to their financial circumstances. The solution lies somewhere in a negotiated middle.

Meanwhile, elite financial advisors and estate attorneys—as opposed to average financial professionals—continue to help wealthy families use the tax laws and tax codes to their legal advantage, organizing their estates to minimize or even eradicate tax liabilities.

The "Loopholes" in the title of this section refer to the strategies employed by knowledgeable advisors to minimize taxes and maximize the impact on future generations for the wealthy and the charities hey support. They include:

- Charitable Remainder Trust
- Charitable Lead Trust
- Irrevocable Life Insurance Trust
- Intentionally Defective Grantor Trust
- Grantor Retained Annuity Trust
- Spousal Lifetime Access Trust
- Utilizing Annual Gift Exclusion

There are two basic trust structures: revocable and irrevocable. Revocable trusts can be altered or dissolved by the trustor over their term, thereby giving the trustor control over the assets. Irrevocable Trusts cannot be altered or terminated by the trustor and result in a loss of control by the trust grantor (trustor) and the trustee managing the trust agreement's assets.[343]

Revocable trusts are more commonly utilized due to their flexibility and because most estates are not subject to estate taxes. The current exemption for estate tax is $13.61mn for an individual and double that for a married couple.

A revocable trust allows the grantor to change the terms of the trust or to revoke the trust at any time. It provides grantors with all of the income generated by the trust assets, as well as the right to use the trust assets any way desired during their lifetime. Upon a grantor's death, the trust assets are distributed in the manner which the grantor directed in the trust terms.[344]

For example, someone like myself with several children might have a revocable trust that stipulates a new trust is to be created upon the grantor's death that specifies how, when and under what circumstances the assets are to be distributed or if special provisions are to be made for one child or another. The revocable trust might also spell out who is to take care of the children and who is to manage the investment of the trust assets, and whether that is the same or different persons. In the case of my revocable trust, I have specific instructions on how I want the portfolio invested and how the asset allocation should be changed as my children become adults and grow older, as well as how much the portfolio manager can charge in fees.

Irrevocable trusts are designed to shift assets from the grantor's control to the beneficiary, which reduces the value of the grantor's estate for tax purposes and insulates the assets from creditors. Because irrevocable trusts cannot be revised or terminated without the beneficiary's permission or court order, once assets are transferred into the trust, the grantor no longer has any ownership rights.[345] Decanting an irrevocable trust can be done without court order or beneficiary permission but it's expensive.

Essentially, there are only three reasons to create an irrevocable trust: to minimize estate taxes for the super wealthy with estates in excess of $27.2mn; to protect assets from creditors; or to qualify for government programs. Barring one of these contingencies, a revocable trust is likely the better choice. Revocable trusts allow grantors to amend the trust but forego creditor protection.

Charitable Remainder Trust

The charitable remainder trust (CRT) is also an irrevocable vehicle that allows grantors to exercise their philanthropic goals while generating personal income and reducing taxes. The transfer of assets or donation by the grantor provides an initial tax deduction, typically 30%-40% of the amount transferred. The income from the assets is distributed to either the grantor or one or more beneficiaries for a specified amount of time. The remainder of the trust is then donated to one or more charities.[346]

Income generated by the CRT and paid to the owner or designated charity can be in the form of annuity payments that continue until the death of the grantor or designated beneficiaries, or for 20 years.[347]

In a CRT, ownership of the gifted asset is split between an income interest, which provides an income stream for the lifetime of the grantor or noncharitable beneficiaries and a remainder interest. Charities can also receive a portion of the income stream if the grantor so wishes. The remainder interest—what's left after the death of the grantor or surviving beneficiaries—goes to the charity or charities.

The word "charity" in these examples refers to any qualified 501(c)(3) charitable organization.

Charitable Lead Trust

A charitable lead trust (CLT) is essentially the opposite of a charitable remainder trust. It provides financial support to one or more charities for a certain period, after which the remaining assets go to the designated beneficiaries, typically family members.[348]

The CLT's payment stream to the charity can be in the form of an annuity or a unitrust amount, which is typically a fixed percentage of the trust assets calculated at the same time annually. The CRT can also be a unitrust amount.

For income tax purposes, CLTs can be drafted either as a grantor trust or as a non-grantor trust. If structured as a grantor trust, the donor receives an upfront charitable income tax deduction and is then responsible for income taxes on future trust income. If structured as a non-grantor trust, a separate taxpaying trust is created and allowed an unlimited charitable income tax deduction for the income paid to charity.[349]

Both CRTs and CLTs are "split-interest" trusts. This means that the interest in the asset transferred into the trust is split into something different than the single ownership of the asset.

Irrevocable Life Insurance Trust

An Irrevocable Life Insurance Trust (ILIT) is a trust designed to hold life insurance. It exists separately from the grantor's estate and is not included in the estate's value. It is created to manage life insurance policies and allocate benefits after the death of the grantor. The trust—not the policy owner—is the owner and payor of the life insurance policy within the trust. Typically, the grantor pays the trust, which the trustee uses to pay the life insurance premiums. When the grantor passes away, the trustee collects the life insurance payout and handles the subsequent payouts to the beneficiaries.

ILITs must be irrevocable. This allows the proceeds from the life insurance policy to avoid estate taxes. If the policy were not created under an ILIT, any insurance benefits plus other assets of the insured above the exclusion amount could trigger both state and federal estate taxes. Another benefit is the ILIT allows the insured to choose a trustee to manage the assets and instruct that person as to how benefits are to be distributed. For example, the insured might insist that the trustee ensure beneficiaries are not spending benefits frivolously. The insured might also require the trustee spread the assets among beneficiaries depending upon their needs.[350]

Proceeds from an ILIT can also be used to pay estate taxes—which can be as high as 40%—after the death of a wealthy individual. Some states also impose their own estate taxes. ILITs can also help solve the problem of paying estate taxes on illiquid assets, such as a business or property. This allows beneficiaries to pay estate taxes while still maintaining control of the estate's assets.[351]

Intentionally Defective Grantor Trust

An Intentionally Defective Grantor Trust (IDGT) is an irrevocable trust that takes advantage of disparities between income and estate tax assessments. Because an IDGT is deemed a grantor trust for income tax purposes, the grantor reports the trust's income, but the trust assets are not included in the grantor's estate for tax purposes.[352]

Trusts are often created primarily for the purpose of avoiding or minimizing taxes. Grantors that place assets into a trust do not have to disclose those assets for taxation or pay taxes on any income the assets generate. This can, however, create tax issues for trust beneficiaries when the taxation of the assets shrinks their inheritance. The IDGT helps solve the problem by allowing the grantor to continue paying the taxes on the assets while in the trust, limiting the impact of federal estate taxes.

An IDGT can be especially effective in situations where trust assets are expected to have taxable income, such as investments, a business or real estate. The IDGT is designed to mitigate the taxes beneficiaries pay when they receive the assets. Meanwhile, the assets placed in the trust can continue to appreciate in value.[353] Whether an IDGT is worth the effort comes down to a cost-benefit analysis comparing income tax versus estate and gift tax considerations.

Grantor Retained Annuity Trusts

Grantor Retained Annuity Trusts (GRATs) are irrevocable trusts where the trustee is usually a child or relative of the grantor. The grantor transfers an asset, typically one with high potential appreciation, to the GRAT. In return, the grantor retains an interest for a period of at least 2 years, but potentially much longer, such as in a high interest rate environment.[354]

The trust issues the grantor regular payments over the duration of the trust agreement, typically in the form of an annuity. The grantor pays the income tax on all income earned inside the GRAT. The trust assets go to the beneficiaries tax-free at the end of the GRAT term.

GRATs are generally funded with assets that have potential for capital appreciation over the term of the trust and are required to earn interest at least equal to the rate set by IRS regulations, known as the "hurdle rate," equivalent to 120% of the current applicable federal midterm rate, which is based on the average yield on 3-9-year Treasury notes. The grantor may substitute or exchange similar investments with the trust to make sure that the trust makes the required amount of interest every year. [355]

Should the interest rate of the GRAT be lower than the IRS minimum or the grantor die before the trust ends, the trust will be closed with the assets going to the estate, not the beneficiaries.[356]

Spousal Lifetime Access Trust

A spousal lifetime access trust (SLAT) is an irrevocable trust where the donor spouse gifts assets to the beneficiary spouse. The trustee is authorized to make distributions to the beneficiary spouse if a need arises. A SLAT can be designed to benefit children or grandchildren as well. A lifetime gift tax and generation-skipping tax (GST) exemption can be used to shield contributions to the trust and future appreciations from transfer taxes.

The current exemption for the lifetime gift tax—the amount of money or assets the government permits you to give away over the course of your lifetime without having to pay the federal gift tax—is $13.6mn. The generation-skipping exemption is also currently $13.6mn. The GST tax applies to transfers of assets to grandchildren or other designees that are at least 37.5. years younger than the donor and the tax rate is 40%. Unlike the federal estate tax exemption, any GST tax exemption unused at one spouse's death cannot be used by the surviving spouse.[357]

Naming one's spouse as beneficiary allows the donor spouse to retain indirect access to the trust assets. A trust can be set up to make distributions based on an any number of standards, such as the beneficiary's health, education or support.

The principal goal of a SLAT is to transfer assets out of a donor's estate while maintaining the ability to access the assets through distributions to the beneficiary spouse. The grantor remains liable for income tax on sales and other income within the SLAT. This can be an additional estate planning benefit, since having the grantor pay the tax for the trust leaves more assets inside the trust for the beneficiaries. It is essentially an additional tax-free gift to the beneficiaries and is paid with assets that otherwise would be subject to estate tax.[358] In addition, the SLAT protects trust assets from creditors. The donor spouse transfers assets into the trust for the benefit of the transferor's spouse and descendants. If the donor spouse gets sued or divorced, the assets are protected. If the beneficiaries get sued or divorced, the assets are protected.[359]

Annual Gift Exclusion

Individuals are allowed to give money or assets to family members or others and receive an exemption from federal estate and gift taxes. Currently, that amount is $18k per recipient, the highest amount in history. The lifetime exemption is $13.6mn. Spouses can also gift up to the same amount, even to the same people. This means that a married couple can shield a total of $27.2mn without having to pay any federal estate or gift tax.

Federal gift tax rates range from 18% to 40% and applies whether the asset or property given is tangible, or intangible. So, for example, deeding a plot of land, giving a car, forgiving a debt, assigning the benefits of an insurance policy, or transferring stock could all trigger a federal gift tax bill. For gifts other than cash, the amount for gift tax purposes is the property's fair market value on the date of the gift.

Some among the wealthy regard the $18k annual gift as inconsequential. Those who commit to annual giving, however, soon learn that doing so over an extended period can result in a dramatic reduction of their taxable estate. Graphic 16.1 illustrates the huge savings potential.

Annual Gift Amount	$	18,000
Growth Rate of Investments		6.0%
Growth Rate of Investments		10.0%

	At 6 Percent Annual Return			At 10 Percent Annual Return		
Year	Beginning Amount	6 Percent Interest	Ending	Beginning	10 Percent Interest	Ending
1	18,000	1,080	19,080	18,000	1,800	19,800
2	37,080	2,225	39,305	37,800	3,780	41,580
3	57,305	3,438	60,743	59,580	5,958	65,538
4	78,743	4,725	83,468	83,538	8,354	91,892
5	101,468	6,088	107,556	109,892	10,989	120,881
10	237,254	14,235	251,490	286,874	28,687	315,561
15	418,967	25,138	444,106	571,905	57,190	629,095
20	662,141	39,728	701,869	1,030,950	103,095	1,134,045
25	987,561	59,254	1,046,815	1,770,247	177,025	1,947,272
30	1,423,047	85,383	1,508,430	2,960,892	296,089	3,256,982
35	2,005,826	120,350	2,126,176	4,878,439	487,844	5,366,282
40	2,785,715	167,143	2,952,858	7,966,666	796,667	8,763,333

(Graphic 16.1: Gifting over a 40-Yr Period)

The current administration has proposed a major upheaval in tax legislation, including reducing the estate/generation skipping tax exemption from $13.6mn to $3.5mn; reducing the gift tax exemption from $13.6mn to $1mn; increasing the highest estate/gift tax rate from 40% to 65%; limiting the annual exclusion for gifts; ending the "step-up" in basis; and eliminating the irrevocable life insurance trust, the intentionally defective grantor trust and the retained annuity trust.

This suggests that there is a window of opportunity for aggressive estate planning right now. Currently, a historically favorable tax environment exists, particularly for the wealthy. If you believe the current estate tax situation is unlikely to be as favorable in the future, a review of your estate plan should be on your calendar.

> *"The avoidance of taxes is the only intellectual pursuit that still carries any reward."*

John Maynard Keynes

CHAPTER **SEVENTEEN**

How the Wealthy Protect their Money

> *"Wealth is not without its advantages and the case to the contrary, although it has often been made, has never proved widely persuasive."*

John Kenneth Galbraith

The wealthiest families in America protect and grow their wealth by utilizing two investment strategies that provide safe, low risk returns: bond ladders and arbitrage. In simple terms, they use these strategies because they make a lot of money with virtually no investment risk.

Most people either don't know about or understand these investments because they didn't grow up in wealthy families. Frankly, many advisors don't understand these strategies because while they are fundamentally uncomplicated concepts, they are laborious and demanding to execute and administer effectively.

A third element of how the wealthy get and stay that way, while not low risk like bond laddering and arbitrage, is investment real estate, which currently accounts for roughly 17% of America's gross domestic product (GDP). These are the "Free Lunches" mentioned in this section's title.

Bond Laddering

A bond ladder is a portfolio of fixed-income securities that mature at different times. For example, in a ten-year portfolio of laddered bonds, approximately ten percent of the bond maturities will occur each year. The money from redemptions is then used to purchase an additional group of bonds maturing ten years hence. Staggering maturities not only provides current income; it minimizes exposure to interest rate fluctuations.[360]

While one or two issues (tranches) in a bond ladder might mature during a time when yields are falling, the remaining bonds will continue generating income at their original higher rates. When interest rates—and therefore yields—increase, a bond ladder helps because it consistently frees up a portion of the portfolio to take advantage of the higher rates.[361]

The wealthiest families consistently invest in bond ladders to protect their money and ostensibly increase their wealth because of the low-risk nature of the strategy and the protection against interest rate fluctuations and inflation.

Obviously, bond ladders must be constructed with high-quality securities. Lower quality bonds, including junk bonds, are much more speculative and inappropriate for this strategy, which is based on bond issuers making coupon and interest repayments on time. For investors, holding reliable securities to maturity ensures a timely return of principal, which allows the bond laddering strategy to continue successfully.

Historically, administering bond ladders was a nightmare for financial advisors. To do it correctly was time consuming, labor intensive and almost impossible to carry out on scale.

Let's say I am an advisor a decade ago and I want to build a ten-year, five-million-dollar bond ladder for a wealthy family client. I have to buy ten $500,000 tranches (yearly segments), one for each of the ten years and each tranche maturing in a successive year. I must also diversify the bonds. Proctor & Gamble may be one of my targets but I can't buy five million dollars' worth of P&G; it wouldn't be prudent to have all of the money loaned to a single company. So, I must find a broad array of blue-chip companies, perhaps 50 of them, in order to safely construct the ladder.

On an ongoing basis, I have to monitor the ladder as the bonds expire each year and buy new bonds the next day. As you can see, this involves an enormous of amount of time and work.

But even assuming I do all of the above competently, a problem arises if, in growing my advisory practice, I take on another wealthy client that also wants a five-million-dollar bond ladder. Unfortunately, all the work I did identifying issues I could purchase for the first client is of no use to me because those bonds are no longer available.

The P&G bond issue I previously bought isn't there anymore. Neither are the Microsoft, Amazon and Walmart issues I bought to fund the previous ladder because companies are constantly issuing new bonds. I have to start from scratch and find new issuance to build the second bond ladder. This is one reason why so few advisors are able to successfully deal in bond ladders for their clients; it's extremely labor intensive and impractical to scale up.

Of course, these same advisors recognize the value and appeal of bond laddering, so they attempt to achieve a similar effect by investing their clients into bond mutual funds or bond ETFs, often incorrectly positioning the investments as risk-free. But there's a big problem with that. Unlike laddering, where the bonds mature and the individual one-year tranches are replaced with new long-term issues each year, the securities in bond mutual funds and bond ETFs have a fixed duration, not fixed maturity, so investors do not receive principal repayment from those bond funds. The prospectus in a bond fund determines the duration. It's not the same laddering effect that investors receive—and rely on—with a bond ladder. The non-laddered strategy does not preclude investors from being harmed by continuously rising interest rates. The two years following the pandemic have demonstrated that fact with devastating force.

There's a good chance that the biggest lawsuit in the history of the financial markets will occur sometime in the near future as a result of the unprecedented bond bear market we have experienced since the pandemic. All the financial advisors around the world that convinced their clients they could rely on the bond mutual funds and bond exchange-traded funds they sold them for portfolio protection will be potentially exposed to massive litigation. The strategy is not wealth protection as investors who took their advisors' advice and bought into bond mutual funds and bond exchange-traded funds have discovered.

Today, investment managers can offer clients the benefits of bond laddering. The problem of the labor-intensive administration has been solved by the development of defined-maturity ETFs (iBonds ETFs®), the creation of BlackRock, the world's largest asset management company.

Like traditional bond ladders, these bond ETF portfolios have specified maturity dates, trade on exchanges (verses OTC market) are scalable and diversify holdings among various sectors and bond types.

Over the years, I've had numerous conversations with investors who insisted that their mutual bond funds or bond ETFs provided protection for their portfolios. I ask them if they understand there is an inverse relationship between bond prices and interest rates. They usually do. I then ask what happens to the price of their bond funds when interest rates go up? Of course, the bond funds lose money. Well, what happens if interest rates go up again? They lose money again. What happens if interest rates repeatedly go up, as they have since the pandemic? The answer, of course, is that bond funds keep losing money. Where's the protection?

I mentioned that the investor has just told me the bond fund protected his money. But in a consistently rising interest rate environment, his bond fund provided zero protection. And that's why wealthy people in America own bond ladders, not bond funds. With bond ladders, if interest rates go up, they take the principal from the bond tranche that just matured and buy a 10-year bond at a higher interest rate. So, the wealthy actually progress financially because their bonds are now being invested at a higher yield.

Municipal Bonds

Municipal bonds (munis) are debt instruments issued by state or local governments (or governmental entities, such as water and sewer districts) to raise capital. Bond holders receive periodic interest payments and are repaid their principal when the bond matures. Interest paid to municipal bondholders is generally exempt from federal income tax, but compensating for this benefit is the fact that munis generally pay a lower rate of return than high-quality corporate bonds or Treasurys.[362]

Those in high tax brackets that want to invest for tax-advantaged income may choose to buy municipal bonds. The wealthy tend to use municipal bond ladders to gain tax preferred returns and high-quality corporate bond ladders for non-tax advantaged returns. Corporate bond ladders should contain issues from blue chip companies that can be relied upon to pay their shareholders back and borrow more money.

Municipal bond laddering is also available through defined maturity municipal ETFs, as discussed in the previous section. The same advantages available in non-municipal bond ladders applies to municipal bond laddering, with the exception that returns are not taxed at the federal level.

Arbitrage

> *"Give a man a fish and you will feed him for a day. Teach a man to arbitrage and you will feed him forever"*

Warren Buffett

One of the most misunderstood financial strategies is the use of arbitrage, a sophisticated short-term investment technique that seeks to take advantage of the price discrepancy between two equivalent financial assets to generate a profit. While the price differences may be small and transient, when applied on a large scale, arbitrage returns can be impressive, not to mention virtually assured.

Because conducting continuous transactions requires ample investment capital, arbitrage is typically practiced by sophisticated investors, such as hedge funds, investment firms catering to wealthy families.

One of the most compelling reasons for arbitrage strategies is that similar to the yield on a bond, investors know in advance how much profit to expect and how long they will have to wait to get the spread because an expiration exists on the most reliable arbitrage investments. In short, an arbitrage portfolio permits calculating an expected return with a high level of accuracy.

The simplest form of arbitrage is purchasing an asset in the market where the price is lower and simultaneously selling the asset in the market where the asset's price is higher.[363]

A classic example is the currency market. Fifty years ago, traders made fortunes by exploiting the currency price differences in various global markets. They might buy currency on the Tokyo Stock Exchange (TSE) for one price and simultaneously sell it for a higher price on the Midwest Stock Exchange making a guaranteed, risk-free return.

They didn't take possession of the currency. They simply executed concurrent transactions at predetermined pricing, the very definition of fundamental arbitrage.

While computerized trading has made that type of easy profit much more difficult today, there remain lucrative opportunities in merger, convertible and additional arbitrage, among others. The individual transaction profits tend to be small, but they can be made with lower risk.

The exception might be merger arbitrage where there is a possibility of the merger or acquisition not taking place, but if the deal goes through, the arbitrageur profits. To hedge against that possibility of an individual deal falling through, an arbitrageur will invest in a broad group of deals. So, if one deal falls through, it doesn't have a huge effect on the portfolio. If the arbitrageur invests in virtually every legitimate deal, profits are reliable.

Arbitrage strategies are generally associated with capital raising events: equity, convertible bonds, debt issues as well as mergers and bankruptcies. They invest in the likelihood that the prices of the related securities will eventually converge via deal completion or some other event.[364]

The primary objective of any arbitrage strategy is to exploit market inefficiencies. If the markets were absolutely efficient, arbitrage would not exist. There are numerous arbitrage strategies, the three main categories being:

- Merger Arbitrage
- Convertible Arbitrage
- Additional Arbitrage

The Merriam-Webster dictionary defines Merger Arbitrage as "the purchase of the stock of a takeover target especially with a view to selling it profitably to the raider." The strategy seeks to profit from the uncertainty that exists during the period between when a merger or acquisition is announced and when it is formally completed.[365] During this transition period, the target company's stock typically trades at a discount to the price offered by the acquiring company. The difference between the target's stock price and the offer price is known as the arbitrage spread.[366] Merger Arbitrage seeks to profit from the market spread between the target firm's current price and the offer of the acquiring firm.

In actuality, the target company's price seldom matches the deal price, often trading at a small discount due to the risk that the deal may fall through. While unusual, deals can fail for various reasons, such as changes in market conditions or regulatory refusals by the Federal Trade Commission or Department of Justice (DOJ).[367]

Convertible Arbitrage involves purchasing a mispriced convertible bond as a long position and simultaneously short selling a calculated number of shares of the stock. Convertible bonds are hybrid securities that provide holders the option of converting their bonds into common stock. The conversion feature combines the bond with an equity call option. Each convertible bond has a conversion ratio which is the number of shares into which the bond may be converted.[368]

Illiquidity causes convertible bonds to generally sell at a discount to their two components. Investors hope to earn a premium for buying an illiquid asset and providing financing for companies that would otherwise have a difficult time securing financing. While waiting for the prices to converge, the portfolio is insulated from price movements of the underlying stock.

The third category, Additional Arbitrage, is a collection of various strategies that opportunistically invest around corporate activity, special situations and various market events. It attempts to take advantage of temporary mispricing of corporate stock, typically due to bankruptcies, spinoffs, recapitalizations, refinancings and other related corporate events. These strategies aim to take advantage of any special situation in corporate life that may affect the valuation of a security. Such events could be at management, strategic or operational levels.

Other popular arbitrage strategies that fall into the third bucket include:

Dual-Class Arbitrage pursues inefficiencies in the prices that different classes of a public company's stock are trading. A company with dual-class shares has two classes of common stock with different voting rights, usually to guarantee control for founding family members or other insiders who have a stake in the company's cash flows. Most corporate charters require cash flows from dividends and other sources to be equal for both classes of shares.[369]

When-Issued Arbitrage opportunities occur prior to corporate actions, such as spin-offs, when up to four securities are traded in the market: parent shares, subsidiary shares, when-issued parent shares and when-issued subsidiary shares.

A when-issued parent share is the stock that begins to trade prior to a spin-off but reflects firm assets after the spin-off. A when-issued subsidiary share is simply a right to receive a subsidiary share following the spin-off. When-issued subsidiary and when-issued parent shares often trade at discounts to the regular subsidiary and parent shares. Arbitrageurs capture price deviations by buying and shorting the various shares.[370]

<u>Stub-Trading Arbitrage</u> is an equity market-neutral strategy that involves going long and short shares of a subsidiary and its parent company. The positions are typically aligned with the percentage of the subsidiary owned by the parent.[371]

<u>Price-Pressure Arbitrage</u> strives to secure a risk premium by providing liquidity around various types of securities and restructuring events.[372] Institutional traders typically split up large trades (metaorders) into numerous smaller pieces which are executed incrementally over an extended period from several minutes to several days. This is usually done to avoid market destabilization.[373]

If, for example, someone inherits a huge block of a single stock and wants to convert it into cash, they're going to sell that stock. If they plow it into a buyers' market, it could create a significant inefficiency because they would have to massively discount it. When institutions do this, an arbitrageur can purchase those shares at a discounted price. So, to avoid that from happening while trying to sell the block of stock, the institution will feed it into the market, little by little, over an extended period of time to prevent that liquidity premium.

SPAC Arbitrage

A special purpose acquisition company (SPAC) is a shell company that raises money from investors in an IPO for the purpose of acquiring an unidentified privately held company. SPACs are an alternative to traditional IPOs as a means to bring a private company to the public markets. SPACs tend to trade at a discount to their net asset values because of their relative illiquidity. SPAC arbitrage involves one of three strategies:

1. Acquire SPAC units at a discount to the net asset value (NAV), split the units into common stock and warrants

when available. When a deal is announced, compare the SPAC share price to the NAV. Sell if the SPAC price is above its NAV at the time of the shareholder vote. If the SPAC price is below its NAV, redeem, vote for the deal and hold onto the warrants for additional upside optionality.

2. Acquire the SPAC shares at a discount to NAV before a deal is announced to earn the baseline yield. If a positive deal is announced that takes the SPAC's share price above its NAV, sell. If the deal is a loser and the shares do not trade above NAV, redeem the shares.

3. Acquire SPAC shares at a discount to NAV as they head to liquidation. This earns the underlying treasury yield plus the NAV discount up to the SPAC's liquidation. If a SPAC doesn't announce a deal before its deadline, it will liquidate and distribute $10 per share plus accrued interest.[374]

Arbitrage Caveat

In bear markets, arbitrage can become correlated to equity markets. This correlation might be caused by panicky investors forced to sell their positions because of concerns about liquidity or mergers being renegotiated or falling through. Historically, these losses normally prove temporary. When emotions subside and rationality returns, spreads narrow and profits can again be realized. Well-constructed algorithms can account for this by increasing capital to arbitrage strategies when spreads are historically wide —typically when fear is elevated—and exchanging arbitrage positions for treasury bond ladders when the probabilities for an equity bear market are high.

Reliable Returns

Calculating how much money you're going to make over a long period in a bond ladder is a highly reliable computation.

Calculating how much money you're going to make from an arbitrage strategy, since you know what the spreads are, is also an expected return that you can estimate with a much higher level of analytical assurance than other types of strategies.

Bond laddering and arbitrage are the only two investment strategies where this calculation can be made with extremely high levels of analytical confidence.

Bond laddering and Arbitrage strategies are how the wealthiest families in America protect their money. They're a big part of what I do. The concept of arbitrage is not hard to understand for most investors but the sophistication needed to execute the strategy is highly complex. Buying the same asset off one exchange then turning around and selling it for a higher price on another exchange is a fairly direct activity. That's the easy part to comprehend. But once you get into the weeds of execution, there's a level of complexity that the vast majority of financial advisors have no experience with.

Like the concept of the First Amendment to the US Constitution, freedom of speech is easy to understand and makes sense on the surface, but it's extremely difficult to implement.

Real Estate

While real estate does not represent the same type of safe, low fee investing as bond ladders and arbitrage, some of the greatest fortunes have been made through real estate investing.

Real estate provides numerous benefits: passive income, tax benefits, leverage, appreciation and cash flow.

Depreciation Tax Benefits

Most wealthy people invest in multifamily real estate to get the paper benefits of asset depreciation deductions in taxable income. Basically, what that means is that the IRS will consider an asset to be depreciating in value every year even though, in reality, the value may be appreciating. The tax deduction due to depreciation will allow the investors to show investment loss on paper even though the asset may have cash flow and appreciate. This loss will flow through the personal income tax calculation, thus reducing your total taxable income.[375]

Cash Flow

Wise investors don't bet on appreciation. They purchase properties on a sound judgement that the property will generate more income than it costs to own. For these folks, who "cash flow" positively, they don't care what the market does. If prices drop, they are safe. If prices rise, they have more options. That said, appreciation, or the rising of home prices over time, is how the majority of wealth is built in real estate. This is the "home run" you hear of when people make a large windfall of money. While prices fluctuate, over the long run, cumulative real estate values have always gone up, always, and there is no reason to think that is going to change.[376]

Under the large umbrella of real estate fall many versions, including healthcare, homebuilder, hotel, industrial, office, residential, storage, strip and retail. Determining the value of any piece of real estate is comparable to the fundamental analysis used to evaluate a stock. Discounting future net operating income (NOI)[377] by the appropriate discount rate for real estate is similar to discounted cash flow (DCF) valuations for stock. Comparably, the gross income multiplier model in real estate is comparable to relative valuations with stocks.[378]

On a basic level, the analysis is simply rent minus expenses equals free cash flow and how many years you plan to hold the real estate. Total up the free cash flow to equal the price paid for the property to get your money back with some growth from rent income and appreciation. There are specific parameters that may create small differences in how the analysis is conducted but essentially, the same kind of mathematics applies to the entire category.

It's important to understand that a parcel of investment real estate is worth the same amount, whether or not it has a mortgage. The importance of this to investors is that they—not the institution financing the purchase of the property—benefit when the property appreciates. If, for example, an investor puts $250,000 down on a million-dollar property and it appreciates by 5%, or $50,000, it's effectively a 20% return for the investor's $250,000 investment. This is what is known as an internal return.[379]

REITS

Real estate investment trusts (REITs) are companies that own or finance income-producing real estate across a range of property sectors. They have historically been included in the broad category of alternative investments as they tend to provide diversity to traditional investments and positive returns. But they are subject to the same risks as other businesses and, over the past two decades, have become more closely correlated with the market. As such, the diversification benefits they once provided may be waning.[380]

In a REIT, investors do not purchase a physical property; they buy a share of the company that owns and manages the real estate. Buying a REIT is similar to buying a stock. It's an investment in the company, not its products or services.

REITs are a relatively uncomplicated way to invest in commercial real estate, especially for individuals with limited investment capital. A benefit of REIT investing is that the shares of publicly traded REITs tend to be highly liquid and can be bought and sold like stocks or bonds. The liquidity aspect of publicly traded REITs—as opposed to private REITs—makes them attractive to investors seeking portfolio diversify but do not wish to have their capital tied up for extended periods of time.

In order to qualify as a REIT, real estate must comprise at least 75% of the company's total assets; at least 75% of the company's gross income must come from the rental portfolio; at least 95% of gross income must be generated passively; at least 90% of the company's taxable income earned must be returned to shareholders on a consistent basis in the form of dividends; the company must have at least 100 shareholders after its first year of operation, with no more than 50% of total shares being held by five or fewer of investors; and the company must be structured as a taxable entity that is overseen by a board of directors or trustees.[381]

One type of REIT property that has the winds of capitalism at its back are data centers. REIT Equinix is the world's largest data center company, renting space to 9,500 customers including the world's largest networks, cloud computing platforms and business enterprises. As CEO Stephen Smith explains, "The only reason you can download a Netflix video in less than 10 seconds in any city in the world is because Netflix has thousands of servers (renting space) in data centers, many of them Equinix centers."[382]

1031 Exchanges

All other benefits aside, the primary advantage of owning investment real estate—particularly for the wealthy—are the savings available through the use of 1031 exchanges, a capital gains tax deferral strategy that dates back more than a century.

This swap of investment properties allows the taxes on the sale of a property to be indefinitely deferred if the seller uses the proceeds to purchase a like-kind replacement property.

The strategy gives wealthy investors the opportunity to continue building their wealth through successive real estate swaps while they reinvest not only their initial investment and profits from the sales, but also the money that would normally be lost to capital gains taxes. As there is no limit on the number of 1031 exchanges real estate investors can conduct over the course of a lifetime, they can continue selling and purchasing increasingly higher-valued properties throughout their life without having to sacrifice any of the profits to payment of capital gains taxes.[383]

Let's assume you buy an investment property in the form of a single-family home to use as a rental for $500,000. You rent it out for 10 years and then sell it for $750,000. For simplicity's sake, let's ignore the sale costs. You've made $250,000 in appreciation on the property. If you don't complete a 1031 exchange and instead decide to pay the taxes on the sale, you will owe approximately 20% long term capital gains tax on the $250,000 or $50,000.

That's a substantial dent in your profit but there are still more taxes to deal with: a little devil known as *depreciation recapture.* That means you must now pay taxes on all of the depreciation you claimed while you owned the property, this time at the ordinary income tax rate. So, assuming your depreciation deduction has been $15,000 per year, you have a total depreciation recapture of $150,000, taxable at ordinary income tax rates. The 1031 exchange allows you to defer all of these taxes to a later date.

The exchange must involve like-kind properties, that is, trading an investment property for another investment property. For example, you could swap a single-family home rental for an apartment building. What you can't do is swap your vacation home for a rental property or swap an investment property for a primary residence.[384]

While there are requirements and timelines that must be adhered to, not only is there no limit to the number of times an investor can participate in a 1031 exchange, there is also no ceiling on the amount of capital gains tax that can be deferred. As such, profits from property sales can be reinvested indefinitely, potentially creating enormous generational wealth.

While 1031 exchanges are tax deferred, they are not tax free. Investors are merely delaying the taxes until a later date when they must pay taxes not only on the appreciation of the properties, but also on all of the depreciation taken over the years. Obviously, that can amount to an immense sum. The way to avoid giving Uncle Sam a major chunk of the money you have made over a lifetime buying and selling real estate is to pass the property off to your heirs at the time of your death. This creates a new, step-up basis for the value of the property so your heirs need not pay for all those years of deferred taxes.[385]

A step-up in basis occurs when the price of an inherited asset on the date of the decedent's death is above its original purchase price. The tax code allows for the raising of the cost basis to the higher price, minimizing the capital gains taxes owed if the asset is sold later.[386]

A proviso: all 1031 exchanges involve two deadlines. Within 45 days of closing on an investment property, a 1031 trader must file a list of potential replacement properties with an intermediary—a firm certified to act as the closing agent for 1031 exchanges. Then, within 180 days of the initial transaction, the exchanger must close on a replacement property, using equity equal to or more than the equity in the original property.[387]

1031 exchanges allow wealthy real estate investors and their heirs to build potentially massive real estate empires without ever paying a cent in capital gains taxes.

Delaware Statutory Trust

For investors that wish to access the benefits of 1031 exchanges but who prefer not to own and actively manage physical real estate property, a Delaware Statutory Trust (DST) can be a conduit for replacement property during a 1031 exchange. The replacement property becomes a direct ownership of an interest in a professionally managed property or pool of properties. A real estate sponsor firm acquires properties under the DST and then sells shares of the DST to investors, who are able to roll their 1031 exchange proceeds into the DST to purchase an interest. By pooling their funds together, investors are able to access institutional quality properties with professional management that otherwise may be out of reach.

DSTs also help increase diversification by geography, numbers and types of property. The investor can include various assets, such as multi-family apartments, triple-net retail (NNN), self-storage, assisted living facilities, etc. If an investor dies while owning an interest in a DST, heirs receive a step-up in cost basis, which eliminates the taxes due on the initial gain forever.[388]

DST investors enjoy many of the same tax advantages that investors realize if buying and owning property individually, such as the ability to use depreciation to potentially offset income generated from the property. People can also invest in and out of DSTs using a 1031 exchange.

Tenants-in-Common

Tenants-in-Common (TIC) provides a fractional ownership in a property, a co-ownership agreement under which multiple investors pool their funds and agree to own one joint property. Each contributor owns an undivided, fractional interest in the property and participates in a proportionate share of the net income, tax shelters and growth.

Each investor has all the same rights and privileges as a single owner. In a TIC arrangement, co-owners have the right to isolate or transfer their ownership interest in the property without obtaining consent from the other co-owners. This is one of the distinguishing features that sets the TIC apart from other arrangements.

A TIC 1031 exchange allows diversification among several different properties at various geographic locations. Someone can invest in a hospital, warehouse, storage unit facility, hotel, office complex or apartment complex valued in the millions.[389]

Despite being wealthy, the average individual investor may not have the capital to purchase a 500-unit apartment complex, a major commercial office building or a shopping mall. TICs offer these investors an opportunity to invest in high-grade NNN-leased properties with professional, third-party management and fixed-rate, non-recourse loans.

TICs are securitized so only securities-licensed investment advisors can arrange a TIC investment. Potential TIC investors must meet the SEC's definition of an accredited investor: net worth over $1 million, excluding primary residence, annual income over $200,000 in each of the prior two years and reasonable expectations of the same for the current year.[390]

The wealthy are different financially, and their ability to sustain and grow their wealth is based on the tactical use of bond ladders, arbitrage and investment real estate. Wealthy families have enjoyed a bright history in our country and their future may be even brighter. The next section of the book will discuss this brighter future, and the impact technology and productivity advancements are expected to have on stock market valuations.

> *"Ninety percent of all millionaires become so through owning real estate. More money has been made in real estate than in all industrial investments combined. The wise young man or wage earner of today invests his money in real estate."*

Andrew Carnegie

SECTION FOUR

A Bullish Future

CHAPTER **EIGHTEEN**

A Safer Future

> *"There is no better teacher than history in determining the future. There are answers worth billions of dollars in a $30 history book."*

Charlie Munger

We are deluged with bad news from the mass media; it's how they grab and hold our attention. "Man rescues dog from drowning." Nobody cares. "Dog bites rescuer." Now that's a story!

Despite the incessant barrage of horror tales spewed by the media, I believe the world is getting safer, not more dangerous. If you pay attention to the technology advancement narratives and ignore the daily dose of mayhem and misery, you may come to share my optimism about the future.

What follows are some of the many emerging technologies that will contribute to the continuing reduction of risks in our everyday lives as well as our financial futures. When risks are reduced, we are safer.

When it comes to investing, there are two main categories of risk: systematic and unsystematic. Systematic risk is a measure of overall market risk—portfolio risk that is not based on individual investments—and is not diversifiable. These risks include economic, political, atmospheric and social factors and are ever present. Unsystematic risks are typically related to an individual business or industry and can be mitigated through diversification.

Many believe systematic risks are stagnant. I do not. I believe they are in almost continuous change, and while the transformation is not always apparent, I believe the systematic risks are changing for the better. In other words, they are steadily diminishing as technology and economic systems' advances reduce or alleviate them. And that has important investment consequences. This chapter focuses on systematic risks and the advancements aimed at reducing them.

Threats from Space

Scientists recognized the possibility of Earth being devastated by an asteroid many years ago. The asteroid that caused the demise of dinosaurs 65 million years ago was not a one-time event. The Chelyabinsk meteoroid—the size of a six-story building—that broke up 20 miles above Russia in 2013 produced a blast stronger than a nuclear explosion. A century earlier, another meteoroid exploded over Siberia, obliterating 80 million trees.

Asteroid impacts can have a domino effect in terms of economic disruption and loss of life. A collision with our planet would eject millions of particles into the atmosphere, blocking sunlight and decreasing or even preventing photosynthesis, leading to the deaths of plant life.[391]

But before all that could happen, the advance word that an asteroid was on a collision course with Earth would trigger widespread panic, particularly in the region where the impact was expected. Where does one run to when threatened with a cataclysmic event? Hundreds of thousands, perhaps millions of people could become refugees. Who would take them in? Where could they find safety? Can you imagine the bedlam at the airports in the region?

Outside the immediate area of anticipated impact, things wouldn't be much better. The global financial markets would crash, making it virtually impossible for investors to access their money in securities. Banks would suffer a run not seen since 1929 with savers desperately trying to cash out their dollars for gold bullion. Overnight, civil unrest would break out, law and order would break down, looters would steal everything not nailed down and rioters would create anarchy. Law enforcement would be overwhelmed and unable to protect the public at large. The entire economic system would collapse, a victim of mass hysteria.

I wrote a paper on this subject while at Morgan Stanley, outlining the probable global impact of an asteroid strike from the perspective of the financial markets. Assuming the collision was not such that it caused mass human extinction, the markets would eventually reopen, only to see gold and silver prices soar to unimaginable heights. I speculated that smaller denominations would prove more valuable in the immediate aftermath as they would be the most liquid. Someone attempting to spend a gold brick would have a difficult time as it could purchase an entire neighborhood of homes.

DART Mission

Advance warning of a potential asteroid impact with Earth is vital, provided we have the planetary defense to prevent a collision. NASA's Double Asteroid Redirection Test Mission (DART) is a major step forward in providing that deterrent.

The vast majority of the billions of asteroids and other cosmic bodies Earth shares its solar system with orbit the Sun, far from our planet. Those whose orbits approach our own are called near-Earth objects (NEOs), asteroids or comets that come within 30 million miles of Earth's orbit. Most are harmless and pose no threat. While rare, impacts are possible. In fact, NEOs of many different sizes can pose serious threats.[392]

Trying to prevent one of these threats from crashing into our planet is a bit like playing shuffleboard in space. The mission would have to be launched well in advance: a year or two in the case of a small asteroid, perhaps decades ahead for larger asteroids that could prove catastrophic.[393]

DART was NASA's first-ever mission dedicated to investigating and demonstrating one method of asteroid deflection by changing an asteroid's motion in space through kinetic impact: bumping one or more spacecraft into the asteroid at high speed to change its orbit and move Earth out of the crosshairs.[394]

DART was launched Nov. 23, 2021, targeting Asteroid Didymos and its moonlet Dimorphos. It crashed into Dimorphos on Sept 26, 2022[395] and successfully altered the asteroid's orbit. This marked the first full-scale demonstration of using a kinetic impactor to deflect an Earth-bound asteroid.[396]

Extremely large asteroids—more than one kilometer in diameter or roughly the size of 11 football fields—would require a different tactic. Instead of spaceships altering the trajectory of an asteroid, nuclear explosives would be used to redirect or destroy the object. The same nuclear strategy would hold true for asteroids known as "rubble-pile" asteroids, which form after a solid asteroid is smashed into pieces following a collision, leaving the bits of rock to combine under gravity. A study published in the *Journal Proceedings of the National Academy of Sciences* found that these types of asteroids are far more "shock absorbent," meaning they would be much harder to destroy, likely requiring a nuclear blast to bat them away.[397]

DART makes what people have only dreamed about a distinct possibility: the ability to identify atmospheric threats—whether cosmic or manmade—sooner and more accurately so we can employ countermeasures to eradicate the threat. DART interception technology offers the hope that Earth will be protected from atmospheric attacks of any kind and safer because of it. Unlike the dinosaurs, we won't be caught grazing when the next asteroid comes hurtling towards our planet.

Thomas Statler, a DART scientist, excitedly noted, "We are moving an asteroid. We're changing the motion of a natural body in space. Humanity has never done that before. Kind of astonishing that we're doing that and what that bodes for the future."

Whether bumping or obliterating asteroids, DART technology promises to be a major contributor to reducing systematic risk far into the future.

James Webb Telescope

The James Webb Space Telescope (JWST), the successor to the Hubble Space Telescope, was launched Christmas Day 2021, providing the ability to see parts of the galaxy Hubble could not. JWST can view the universe in longer wavelength infrared light, a critical factor in identifying and tracking potential cosmic threats.

This remarkable telescope allows us to see farther out and back into time than was ever possible. It is able to see what the universe looked like around a quarter of a billion years (possibly back to 100 million years) after the Big Bang, when the first stars and galaxies started to form.[398] It gives scientists the ability to search for indications of atmospheres that could sustain life. It might even help discover the next Earth, perhaps giving mankind an alternative should the unthinkable occur and the need to abandon Earth become necessary to sustain human life.

While the JWST is not a weapon, its ability to provide advance knowledge of meteorites and other cosmic threats is an invaluable contributor to our sustainability as a planet. Once again, it is the critical element of time, having sufficient time to react to a planetary threat, that makes JWST technology so valuable in reducing systematic risk.

Threats from Adversaries

While the risks posed by asteroids crashing into Earth represent a global threat, the U.S. faces a more imminent threat from missiles launched against us by adversarial forces. The number of countries that possess missiles continues to grow, as does their level of sophistication. Some of these countries are bad actors.

Missile Defense

The ability to discourage these actors from launching missiles against the U.S. relies on convincing them that an attack cannot succeed or that the consequences will severely outweigh any presumed benefit. By raising the threshold for missile attack, missile defense can complicate an adversary's planning, remove the option for a "cheap shot" against the U.S. and hopefully cause adversaries to think twice before launching an attack.[399]

In December 2023, the U.S. Space Development Agency (SDA) approved a $700mn contract with L3Harris to produce 16 hypersonic missile tracking satellites to detect and track missiles aimed at the U.S. and its allies. The SDA is constructing a multi-layered network of satellites called the Proliferated Warfighter

Space Architecture, which consists of a series of interconnected communication satellites and a Tracking Layer, which comprises sensor satellites that collect and transmit data. The system relies on infrared sensors and advanced algorithms to detect, track and fuse threat data in real-time.

The current U.S. missile defense system is partially founded on President Ronald Reagan's vision—the Strategic Defense Initiative (SDI)—as a layered ballistic missile defense (BMD) system that would render nuclear missiles "impotent and obsolete.[400] These layers would have boost, ascent, midcourse and terminal interceptors, including directed-energy interceptors, providing the U.S. with multiple opportunities to destroy an incoming missile.[401]

Iron Dome

Israel has a long history of developing state-of-the-art defense technologies, its Iron Dome air defense system—widely regarded as the world's best defense against missiles and rockets—being a prime example.

The air defense system (ADS) consists of three key components. First are radars to detect, identify and track incoming missiles. Once detected, an object must be assessed to determine if it is a threat. If confirmed, the second ADS component—the battle control center—comes into play. It determines how to engage the threat, using continuously updated radar information to determine the optimal response, from where to fire interceptor missiles to how many to launch against the incoming missile. The third ADS component is the interceptor missile, which for Iron Dome is supersonic with heat-seeking sensors. The sensors provide in-flight updates to the interceptor, allowing it to close in on the threat. The interceptor uses a proximity fuse activated by a small radar to explode close to the incoming missile so that it does not have to hit it directly to disable it.[402]

Other recent advances in missile defense technology include Aster SAMs, S1850M radar, boost phase defense systems and drone swarms.

The Aster is a family of vertical launch surface-to-air missiles. The Aster 30 variant has several ballistic missile defenses, including anti-aircraft and anti-missile capability. Its ground-based air defense system can counter a broad spectrum of air threats, ranging from fighters, helicopters and unmanned Aerial Vehicles to precision-guided munitions. The Aster 30 also has the ability to engage multiple air threats simultaneously and neutralize them at a longer range and with greater precision.[403]

Aster 30 SAMP/T is today's primary mobile anti-aircraft defense weapon to protect sites and forces against missile threats of all types. The system can operate in stand-alone mode or can be integrated into a coordinated network.[404]

The SMARTELLO or S1850M is a long-range radar for wide area search. With fully automatic detection and track initiation, it can track up to 1,000 air targets at a range of around 250 miles. [405] Also known as the Type 1046 radar, the role of the S1850M is to identify threats at long range and in large volumes. The S1850M is also fitted to the QE Class aircraft carriers for the detection of sea-skimming missiles. Tests have shown the system capable of simultaneously tracking a high number of targets including aircraft, ballistic missiles and conventional missiles. Although true performance remains classified, anecdotally, it is said to be world-beating.[406]

Boost Phase missile defense entails the destruction of an enemy missile during the earliest stages of its flight, while it remains within the Earth's atmosphere. A viable boost phase defense has long been considered the "holy grail" of missile defense, as boosting missiles are much slower and easier to track than missiles during the midcourse or terminal stage. Boost phase defense also overcomes the challenges of discriminating between lethal warheads and debris, as the missile is largely intact at this stage and has not had the opportunity to deploy decoys. Early intercept during the boost phase also has the added benefit of causing the missile's ordinance to fall back on the aggressor after the boosters have been disabled or destroyed. The main challenges for boost phase defense include the short window of opportunity between launch detection and the missile entering the midcourse phase. Kinetic interceptor systems must be placed either very close to a missile's launch point or be fast enough to cover the necessary distance before the missile enters midcourse. Currently, directed energy technology—or lasers—is the most sought-after future boost phase missile defense option. Space-based intercept systems also have exhibited promise as an effective boost phase missile defense option; however, highly expensive R & D has hamstrung such initiatives.[407]

Drone swarm technologies allow groups of drones to coordinate with each other, often without direct human control. Inspired by the collective behaviors of insect colonies and flocks of birds, drone swarms integrate advanced computer algorithms with local sensing and communication technologies to synchronize multiple drones to achieve a goal.[408]

A new generation of drones, known as collaborative combat aircraft, is run by AI. The Valkyrie is an Air Force prototype which the military anticipates becoming a powerful supplement to its fleet of traditional fighter jets, giving pilots a swarm of highly efficient robot "wingmen" to deploy in battle. The concept is to meld AI and Valkyrie's sensors to identify and eliminate enemy threats after getting pilot sign-off. The drones could fly in front of piloted combat aircraft, doing early, high-risk surveillance. They could also be used to disable enemy air defenses and obliterate land-based missile targets that would be considered too dangerous for a human-piloted plane.[409]

In 2022, the Pentagon requested proposals from defense contractors for a new program called Autonomous Multi-Domain Adaptive Swarms-of-Swarms (AMMAS). The object is to develop the ability to deploy thousands of autonomous land, sea and air drones to overwhelm and dominate an enemy's area defenses.[410]

The global swarm technology market is projected to grow to $3bn by 2028, according to *Market Research Report*.[411]

In the future, the drones currently in use will be relegated to close ground encounters like urban unrest, patrols and fires. The new generation of drones will be deployed to protect and defend our 12,000 miles of national borders and coastline. Imagine a world where the big news is not small drones being dropped from a jet fighter but rather ten football fields of unmanned fighter-jets every 100 miles, silently maintaining vigil over our borders. Armed and ready to safeguard our sovereignty. No runway needed. Deployable in seconds. Every movement coordinated and synchronized.

While the principle of mutual assured destruction proved to be an adequate deterrence to nuclear annihilation during the cold war years, there were only two superpowers with the capability to launch such an attack. Today, nine countries—China, North Korea, France, India, Israel, Pakistan, Russia, the United Kingdom and the United States—possess a total of over 13,000 nuclear weapons. For nuclear deterrence to work, all stakeholders must be perceived to act rationally. Common sense and a clear view of the world should tell us that is not the case.[412] Countries like North Korea and Iran that have made clear their ambition to destroy the United States have an entirely different perspective on the use of nuclear weapons.

The nuclear deterrence model that worked a half century ago can no longer be trusted to assure sovereign safety (if it ever was). We are now threatened by a host of new military technologies, from hypersonic missiles to non-kinetic cyberattacks. As a group, they have changed the rules of engagement in how to prevent extinction.[413] Emerging technologies like Valkyrie dramatically reduce the risk of a successful nuclear attack, helping our nation transition from a policy of mutual assured destruction to one of survival through defense.

Weather

The U.S. has experienced 23 separate weather events costing at least one billion dollars each this year, breaking the record of 22 events set in 2020, according to the National Oceanic and Atmospheric Administration (NOAA). The total damages reached over $57bn and 253 people were killed.[414] The average annual cost over the previous five years is $119.1bn, nearly triple the 43-year inflation adjusted annual average cost. [415]

While we have always had natural disasters, given the technological advances in weather prediction in recent decades, it's a bit puzzling why the costs of natural disasters continue to escalate in the U.S. Many blame global warming as the primary culprit for the increase, and whether that assertion is correct or not is a debate that has yet to be settled. However, what can undeniably be said to contribute to the continuing rise are replacement costs, which have risen dramatically for virtually everything during the past three years, the result of higher inflation. So, whether a disaster is caused by earthquake, hurricane, tornado, flood, drought, blizzard or wildfire, the cost of restoring property, possessions, infrastructure and other losses continues to rise.

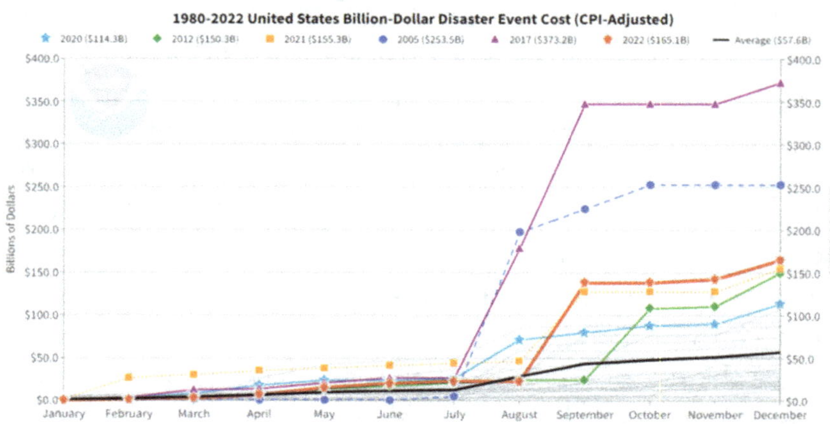

(Graphic 18.1 Natural Disaster Costs)

Weather events will continue to cause disasters. Can technology evolve to minimize the devastating effects of natural disasters?

AI weather models have drawn increasing attention because of their speed and potential cost savings. Traditional weather models, such as those operated by the European Center for Medium-Range Weather Forecasts and the National Oceanic and Atmospheric Administration, make forecasts based on complex mathematical equations. They provide critical forecasts and warnings worldwide but are expensive to run because they require tremendous amounts of computing power. AI models use a different approach. They are first trained to recognize patterns in vast amounts of historical weather data, then generate forecasts by ingesting current conditions and applying what they learned from the historical patterns. The process is much less computationally intensive and can be completed in minutes or even seconds on much smaller computers.

A new computer model to predict the weather built by Google and powered by AI has proven to be many times faster than current models, according to a 2023 study.[416] Google DeepMind's AI model, named "GraphCast," was trained on nearly 40 years of historical data and can make a 10-day forecast at six-hour intervals for locations spread around the globe in less than a minute on a computer the size of a small box. It takes a traditional model an hour or more on a supercomputer the size of a school bus to accomplish the same feat.[417]

Using AI for weather predictions makes processing large amounts of weather-related data incredibly fast. Being able to analyze widespread data sets in real time allows meteorologists to provide both faster and more accurate information. Machine learning allows computers to learn from historical and real-time data, identifying patterns that might not be possible or go unnoticed using traditional analysis methods. This is critically important when severe events, such as hurricanes or tornadoes, are involved.[418]

The use of AI in weather forecasting is one of the lesser discussed applications of the technology, but the implications for mankind are enormous. The development of data-driven forecasts, produced by machine-learning-based forecasting models created by NVIDIA, Huawei, Google DeepMind and others hold the promise of literally saving lives and reducing the risks of storm-related deaths.[419]

Pandemic Progress

It's now been over four years since the outbreak of COVID-19 threw the world into medical turmoil. In the interim, two major technological breakthroughs have occurred that promise to aid the global response to the next pandemic if not quash the debilitating economic effects altogether.

First, advances in biomedical and genomic technologies now permit better detection and identification of pandemic viruses. They also will facilitate the development of countermeasures, such as vaccines and therapies, with unprecedented speed. Second, new information technologies and supercomputers now allow researchers to collect critical data in real-time, conduct viral surveillance and coordinate various health systems. All of this portends great promise for the future of global health.[420]

The COVID-19 pandemic came almost exactly 100 years after the 1918 Great Influenza. While the timing might suggest we now have another century to prepare for the next outbreak, scientists insist the real anomaly was not the pandemic but rather that the previous 100 years was without one.

Pandemic risk is exacerbated primarily by urbanization and increasing proximity to wildlife which, when combined, increase the risk of humans contracting animal viruses. Another risk is worker infection in laboratories studying various animals or viruses spread via lab equipment. Bacteria resistant to antibiotics are also threats.

One advancement offering hope is digital surveillance that can red flag everything from local news reports of a market closure to a spike in online searches for pediatric thermometers.[421]

Finally, a study published in *Science* magazine outlines a groundbreaking plan to significantly decrease the risk of future pandemics. The study notes that agricultural expansion is the single largest driver of emerging disease. As humans encroach deeper into the undisturbed forest, they create exposure diseases carried by animals, known as "virus spillover." The global wildlife trade is cited as another major contributor. Scientists refer to these as "hotbeds of disease" and likely the origin of several zoonotic illnesses—diseases transmitted from animals to humans or vice versa. When these animals are traded internationally, the risk of a small zoonotic disease outbreak turning into a full-blown pandemic increases exponentially.[422]

There is a continuing debate over the various nation's response to the COVID pandemic. One thing is certain. The pandemic deaths, while devastating, fall far short of the 50 million people that died in the influenza pandemic of 1918-1919. Roughly one-third of the global population at the time—500 million people—fell ill, with 675,000 deaths in the U.S.[423] The incredible response to COVID in the U.S., including the amazingly rapid development of life-saving vaccines, was a testament to what was learned from the previous outbreak a century ago. Our capacity to deal with healthcare crises like the COVID pandemic has been much improved, again, reducing our systematic risk and helping make us safer as a nation and a global community.

Energy

A nation's status in the international system is influenced by a range of attributes, including its GDP, military resources and natural resources. Having control and access to significant energy resources may be the most compelling as it enables a nation to protect its national interests while leveraging economic and political influence abroad. By comparison, nations lacking these assets are weakened, have less leverage and are more vulnerable.[424]

Ever since the dawn of the industrial revolution in 1760, nations have wielded energy as a strategic tool. Back then, energy meant coal, and three quarters of the world's coal came from Britain, giving the country leverage over their strategic rivals and powering their economic and military development. Over the past two centuries, the most strategically important sources of energy have been oil and natural gas. Petrostates—nations whose economies rely on the export of the two sources—acquired political strength from the threat to shut off energy exports.

Energy exporting nations today continue to use that influence as a political weapon, depending on the marketplace environment. Power in an energy market will inevitably be exercised by the "swing producer" with the greatest excess capacity.[425]

The term "energy independence," while somewhat ambiguous, is commonly used to refer to a country's ability to rely solely on domestically produced energy. Using this definition, the U.S. has not achieved independence as it remains reliant on imports of crude oil to sustain the economy. The country imports crude oil because refiners want access to a specific type of oil, different than what is produced in abundance domestically.[426]

Nations use energy clout in a variety of ways to exercise influence and leverage to gain strategic and political advantage, as well as to fuel their domestic economies. It's a high-stakes game and the players sometimes change mid-game, depending on the economic climate.

Energy-rich nations like Russia and Iran use their energy wealth to promote their geopolitical interests as well as ensure regime survival. From a foreign policy perspective, energy exports can be weaponized both offensively and defensively. They can be brandished to coerce other governments to do or not do something. They can be used to reward allies or punish enemies. All of this depends on the dependency of the relationship between nations producing energy and nations consuming energy, a relationship that can be manipulated to shield the producing nation from external influences or to intimidate consuming nations.

The classic example of weaponizing energy as a tool of foreign policy was the oil embargo of October 1973 initiated by the Organization of the Petroleum Exporting Countries (OPEC).[427] A more recent example is Russia's use of oil and gas as a threat to Europe's energy dependence since the start of the war in Ukraine.

As the inevitable displacement of fossil fuels by electricity continues, the threat of energy weaponization will dissipate. The political and economic power of petrostates will gradually decline as renewable energy sources become more widespread. The demand for minerals like cobalt, copper, lithium and rare earth elements will grow exponentially to support economies building electric vehicles, solar panels, wind turbines and the systems to store and distribute renewable energy. Nations that control the supply of these minerals will have geopolitical leverage in a post-carbon world.[428]

Over the next few decades, the demand for carbon natural resources will diminish significantly. If you would like proof, consider TerraPower, a company funded by Bill Gates that replaces water with sodium in a nuclear reactor. The substitution will allow the shuttering of a local coal-fired power plant in the next few years. This is just one of many projects dedicated to transitioning the economy from fossil fuels to cleaner alternatives that reduce greenhouse gas emissions and make the U.S. less reliant on traditional energy sources.

The Future of Energy

There are several technologies underpinning the transition to energy independence, among them solar power, concentrated solar-thermal power, solar farms, wind technology, lithium batteries and nuclear power.

<u>Solar Power</u> is secured in two forms: concentrated solar power (CSP) and Photovoltaic (PV) or solar panels. CSP distributes electricity through a power network that converts the sun's direct heat into electricity. PV produces electricity using solar panels that convert direct sunlight into an alternating current. One is not better than the other; they are simply alternative forms of solar power, utilized depending on conditions and requirements. CSP systems are thermal based, storing efficient amounts of energy without needing direct sunlight. This system generates electricity best in cloudless conditions while storing large amounts of thermal energy.[429]

The CSP plant is comprised of sophisticated mirrors, known as heliostats, that capture and focus sunlight onto receivers perched atop tall power towers. Here, the concentrated light heats a fluid used to spin a turbine to generate electricity or provide heat to an industrial process, just like conventional fossil-fueled or nuclear power plants. Because CSP plants convert solar energy into a hot fluid, it's relatively easy to store that fluid in large tanks, meaning these plants can deliver energy on-demand, even in the middle of the night, long after the sun has gone down.[430]

The Ivanpah Solar Energy Facility in Southern California's Mojave Desert is one of the world's largest CSPs. Spread out over 14 square kilometers, it can annually power 140,000 homes. The facility uses over 140,000 heliostats.[431]

This is the same way that nuclear fission and fossil fuel plants generate electricity — the difference being that uranium or coal or natural gas are replaced by the heat of the sun's rays. The future of this energy source may well hinge on continued development of its stored energy capability for dispatchable power, which is needed to fill in for inconsistent wind turbines and PV solar plants.[432]

The technology has been somewhat hamstrung by technical challenges and a shortage of funding and government incentives compared with other sources of renewable energy. Advocates claim the heat CSP plants produce offers advantages over other renewables for generating grid-scale electricity and fueling various industrial processes. It's more efficient than using electricity to produce heat. Also, a CSP system requires less land than a photovoltaic system to produce the same amount of energy. And CSP's storage capacity means it can provide an uninterrupted power supply.

<u>Solar farms</u> are a lot like traditional crop farms except the crops are a collection of PV solar panels that absorb energy from the sun, convert it into electricity and send that electricity to the power grid for distribution and consumption. Solar farms are sometimes referred to as solar parks or photovoltaic power stations.[433]

A different type of solar farm are the large commercial PV farms that typically utilize hundreds or thousands of PV panels to convert the sun's rays into electricity.

A new species of solar farm is the Oberon Solar Project near the Desert Center in eastern Riverside County, CA, which went operational in November, 2023. The 500-megawatt photovoltaic facility will deliver sufficient energy to power over 207,000 homes in Southern California.[434] A unique aspect of the project is the use of Tesla's Megapacks, a large-scale rechargeable lithium battery that provides energy storage and helps stabilize the grid and prevent outages. The megapacks are built at Tesla's site in Lathrop, CA, where a fleet of some 337 Megapack batteries were spotted by a flyover in November, 2023.

Batteries, particularly lithium batteries, are becoming an indispensable aspect of energy independence. This latest configuration will allow renewables to replace fossil fuels like oil, gas and coal to generate power, even when wind or solar are not producing. According to a March 2024 Associated Press story, The U.S. is increasingly using lithium-ion batteries to store energy in large scale projects, often pairing them with solar and wind alternatives.

A potential roadblock to lithium battery development has been the scarcity of lithium. While an estimated 88 million tons of the element exists worldwide, only a quarter of it is economically feasible to mine, which helps explain why lithium reserves in Chile, Bolivia and Australia are so valuable.

A 2023 report identified the world's largest lithium reserve, known as the McDermitt Caldera, located along the Oregon-Nevada border. Mining the element may run into difficulty, however, as the area is sacred land to a few indigenous tribes.[435]

In 2025, one of the world's largest renewable energy projects using Tesla's Megapacks is scheduled to go online in Victoria, Australia. The Melbourne Renewable Energy Hub (MREH) will consist of three massive battery units totaling 600 megawatts. The Megapacks will increase grid stability while providing energy storage sufficient to power up to 200,000 homes, according to the State Electricity Commission.[436]

An awe-inspiring solar energy project is the Al Dhafra solar farm located about 20 miles from Abu Dhabi. The 2-gigawatt farm, the world's largest single-site solar farm, contains almost 4 million solar panels and will power some 200,000 homes in the area. The project also went online in November, 2023.[437]

A mega energy project containing over one million solar panels is the 400MW Western Downs Green Power Hub in Australia with the capacity to power the equivalent of 235,000 Queensland homes.[438]

> *"You could actually power the entire U.S. with 100 miles by 100 miles of solar."*
>
> Elon Musk

Wind Technology

In 2024, Pattern Energy Group started construction on its 3 GW SunZia transmission line, a $10bn energy infrastructure project that will carry more energy than the Hoover Dam. The project will stretch about 550 miles, channeling renewable energy from central New Mexico to areas in Arizona and California. Developers say it will be capable of transporting more than 3,500 megawatts of new wind power to 3 million people in the West.

Other projects in the works include the Southern Spirit transmission line that would link Texas with other grids in the southeastern U.S., the proposed Greenlink West Transmission Project in Nevada, and a set of high-voltage lines that would span from central Utah to east-central Nevada.[439]

Wind energy detractors typically cite the deaths of hundreds of thousands of birds each year as a result of collisions with wind turbines. They also question whether the substantial up-front investment justifies the energy produced. Some complain the wind farms destroy the landscape aesthetics. People living near the farms have complained that the lower frequency sound (infrasound) produced causes health issues, including headaches, tinnitus and dizziness. To date, scientific research has found nothing to support these grievances. The debate continues, however.[440]

The wind energy industry continues to make improvements that hold promise of greater productivity and investment return in the future. Enhancements include larger and more efficient turbine blades, better recycling methods and the utilization of offshore wind.

One encouraging development in offshore wind energy is the Floating Offshore Wind Shot,™ a floating wind farm in deep water, which expects to reduce the cost of wind energy by at least 70% by 2035.[441]

Another is a newly designed wind harvester from Nanyang Technological University in Singapore, which seeks to overcome the problem of diminished wind speeds by generating electricity at wind speeds as low as five miles per hour. The device seems ideal for urban environments, and scientists believe it has the potential to replace batteries in structural health monitoring sensors and LED lights used in bridges and skyscrapers.

The wind harvester can be installed on the edge of a building, producing up to 50% more energy for the same price as a rooftop solar system by using aerodynamics similar to racing car airfoils. The turbine is under 10 square feet and does not look like a conventional wind turbine because of its bladeless design.[442]

Incidences of prolonged blackouts caused by failures of the U.S. electrical grid have become increasingly common. According to a *Wall Street Journal* study, sustained major outages have occurred with greater frequency over the past two decades. In 2000, there were fewer than two dozen major disruptions; in 2020, the number surpassed 180. The power system is being strained by a number of factors, including cell phones, more people working from home, electric vehicles, AI and data centers. The more conveniences that become electrified, the more the demand for power intensifies, threatening an already faltering system.[443]

As CSP, solar farm and wind technology advances continue, we can confidently look forward to a time in the near future when these resources will eliminate the risk of power disruptions that have adversely affected so many people. The U.S. is expected to add a record 32 GW of new solar capacity in 2023, a 52% increase from 2022, according to a report from the Solar Energy Industries Association and Wood Mackenzie. The latter expects total operating solar capacity to grow from 153 GW to 375 GW by 2028.[444]

Although the first nuclear power plant went operational some 70 years ago, nuclear power is today enjoying a resurgence as a result of the AI systems requiring huge amounts of electricity to power data centers. These centers currently account for roughly 2.5% of power demand and their need is expected to triple by 2030, according to Boston Consulting Group. Having overcome its reputation for instability, it turns out that nuclear power plants are an ideal solution for this demand.

The nuclear revival is being driven by a combination of technological advancement and political support for carbon-free energy, the latter evidenced by the Biden Administration's March 2024 announcement of a $1.5bn loan to restart a Michigan nuclear power plant.[445]

Central Bank and Stability

Stability is at the core of a productively functioning economy. A financial system must have mechanisms for both self-correcting discipline and to identify and prevent vulnerabilities from leading to crises.[446]

Central banks have a pivotal role in ensuring financial stability. A central bank is a public institution that is responsible for implementing monetary policy, managing a country's currency and controlling the money supply. To achieve their macroeconomic objectives of price stability and economic growth, they have tools, like setting interest rates. They can raise them to control inflation or decrease them to encourage consumption and boost economic growth. Central banks also regulate how much money is in circulation, injecting liquidity into the economy as needed.[447]

The central bank of the U.S. is the Federal Reserve (Fed). When business closures and work-from-home policies triggered an economic downturn during the COVID crisis, uncertainty about the course of the virus and economy sparked a run to safety among investors. The desire to hold deposits and only the most liquid assets disrupted financial markets and threatened to make a dire situation much worse. The Fed stepped in with a broad array of actions—purchases of U.S. government and mortgage-backed securities and lending to support individuals, employers, financial market participants, and state and local governments—to keep credit flowing to limit the economic damage from the pandemic.[448]

More recent events have demonstrated the Fed's capacity for managing financial stress without compromising their inflation fight. Regulators were able to contain fallout from the March, 2023 collapse of Silicon Valley Bank and other U.S. regional banks, as well as Credit Suisse in Switzerland, without retreating from the inflation campaign.[449]

Central bank policies are continually evaluated as one of the major topics discussed at the annual G7 and G20 economic summits. G7 represents seven of the world's advanced economies, including Canada, France, Germany, Italy, Japan, the United Kingdom, and the United States, as well as the European Union. G20 represents all inhabited continents, 80% of world GDP, 75% of global trade and 60% of the world's population.[450] These economic leaders continue to coordinate and communicate efforts to ward off economic threats, hopefully resulting in a steady decline of these threats.

Free Trade

A free trade agreement is a pact between two or more nations to reduce barriers to imports and exports between them. Under a free trade policy, goods and services can be bought and sold across international borders with little or no government tariffs, quotas or prohibitions to inhibit their exchange.[451]

Liberalization of trade has not only produced better economic outcomes, but also reduced hunger and famine, and enhanced food security, all during a period of rapid population increase. From 2001 to 2017 (the last year data was available), the number of undernourished people around the world plummeted by 170 million. At the same time, the death rate from famine decreased dramatically. Barriers to trade have fallen, allowing people to spend proportionally less on food, which in turn frees up more of their income for goods and services to improve their lives.[452]

The supporters of tariffs argue that free trade costs exporting countries jobs, and that the creation of jobs is a desirable end, in and of itself, regardless of the type of employment. If the primary goal is simply jobs, for example, have people dig holes and then fill them up again. The jobs can be created but to what purpose? The true objective is not just jobs but productive jobs that will mean more goods and services to consume.

Another fallacy is that exports are good, imports are bad. The truth is that we cannot eat, wear, or enjoy the goods we send abroad. We eat grapes from Chile, drive German automobiles and watch programs on Japanese TV sets. Our gain from foreign trade is what we import. Exports are the price we pay to get imports. As Adam Smith saw so clearly, the citizens of a nation benefit from getting as large a volume of imports as possible in return for its exports or, equivalently, from exporting as little as possible to pay for its imports.[453]

From virtually any economic, societal or technological perspective, we are less susceptible to systematic risks today than we have ever been. Our enhanced ability to protect ourselves against cosmic threats, natural disasters, pandemics and earth's bad actors promises to only get better in the coming decades. While the challenges of poverty and hunger remain, our ability to harness energy, avoid natural disasters and commitment to free trade provides optimism for future generations.

All these factors contribute to a safer and more stable financial environment in which to plan our futures. Collectively, they help assure continued stock market growth. As they have for the last century, stock multiples will continue to rise and we will continue to prosper.

> *"Let's go invent tomorrow instead of worrying about what happened yesterday."*
>
> Steve Jobs

CHAPTER **NINETEEN**

Productivity from AI

> *"The development of AI is as fundamental as the creation of the microprocessor, the personal computer, the Internet and the mobile phone. It will change the way people work, learn, travel, get health care and communicate with each other."*

Bill Gates

Artificial Intelligence (AI) takes many forms, and the technology has permeated virtually every aspect of the economy. These range from relatively simple applications like chatbots and facial recognition to complex machine learning systems for business and extraordinary advances in disease prevention and human longevity. Listing all the areas where AI is making life better and safer for us would be a book in itself, but you will read about the many applications in this and the following chapters.

The advancements resulting from AI will inevitably have a positive effect on the markets. But exactly how will AI impact business in general and corporate profit margins in particular? Will businesses be able to take advantage of AI's potential to actually increase productivity, or will the detractor's warning that AI will have an adverse effect on employment prove true?

For purposes of understanding how AI technology will affect profit margins and, in turn, stock prices, it's important to first understand the different types of AI.

Traditional (or narrow) AI aims to perform specific tasks based on predefined rules and patterns, such as the virtual assistants on mobile phones and the recommendation engines which make suggestions based on search or buying history.

Artificial general intelligence (AGI) is a machine that can perform any type of intellectual task, the same way a human can, by creating output that can mimic human intelligence. That is, it has the ability to learn any task or process typically done by humans and is not limited to specific skills or domains.[454] At the core of AGI development are neural networks—named for their mimicry of the human brain—that identify structures and patterns within data to draw conclusions and generate content.[455]

Practical examples of AGI capabilities are motor skills like pulling keys out of a pocket, natural language understanding and intuition and navigation capabilities that exceed existing GPS systems. Advanced virtual assistants like OpenAI's GPT-3 exhibit AGI-like features with their remarkable context understanding and human-like text generation across various domains. Current AI systems, including GPT-3, are not true AGI as they lack full human-like comprehension.[456]

Breaking that down, AI is a technology that enables software to solve unique or difficult tasks within a specific scope and with human-level performance. AGI, on the other hand, can learn and solve problems it was never trained for and in multiple areas, much the way a human brain can. It's not that AI systems don't possess the ability to perform tasks at a highly accurate level, better than humans. But something is missing with AI systems: a general-purpose ability. They lack the ability to adapt to new situations without the need for instructions.

If AGI were asked to diagnose a medical condition, it wouldn't need to be pre-programmed with that specific ability. Instead, it could use its intelligence to learn about symptoms, diseases and diagnostics, much like a human doctor would. But beyond this versatility, AGI can incorporate other elements of human intelligence such as understanding, learning, adapting and even creativity. It can not only learn a language but also understand the subtleties of its slang, jokes and idioms. This is the kind of capability that AGI is expected to have.[457]

Generative AI (GenAI) strives to move closer to AGI and create entirely new and original content that resembles human-created content. GenAI can create new images, music, text or code by learning from huge amounts of data and using that knowledge to produce new, relevant outputs.

An example of GenAI is ChatGPT, a natural language processing (NLP) tool created by OpenAI, an AI research company. ChatGPT enables machines to receive, analyze, and produce language in a way similar to that of humans. It is especially useful in business applications as it can process text or speech in documents, recordings and live conversations.[458]

NLP is a critical building block component of AGI. It enables machines to understand and respond to human language nuances, paving the way for nuanced and context-aware conversations. Soon, we'll have AI systems that don't just recognize words but understand the emotions and intentions behind them. This body of knowledge is in the domain of affective computing where MIT researchers are well advanced in this field of emotional exploration.[459]

AGI and Generative AI can collaborate, creating a synergy. AGI's adaptability enhances the creative capabilities of Generative AI, enabling machines to generate content that goes beyond existing knowledge. It can help refine the outputs of Generative AI, resulting in remarkably imaginative creations.[460]

> *"The number one benefit of information technology is that it empowers people to do what they want to do. It lets people be creative. It lets people be productive. It lets people learn things they didn't think they could learn before, and so in a sense it is all about potential."*

Steve Ballmer

AI Milestones

Turing Test

The first important step on the ladder that led scientists and mathematicians to the development of the computer and, in turn, artificial intelligence, was created by Alan Turing. A British computer scientist that headed up the Bletchley Park team that cracked the German's Enigma code during WW II, Turing went on to describe the first ideas about building a mechanical brain.[461]

After the war, Turing was not permitted to publish his Enigma work. He transitioned to ideas about building computing machines. In 1950, his one paper relating to AI, "Computing Machinery and Intelligence," was published in the philosophical journal *Mind*. In it, Turing examined the question of whether machines can think, to which he answered "yes." He predicted that machines would be able to pass a test of intelligence as early as the beginning of the 21st century, the test now famously known as the Turing test. Today, some 70 plus years later, it remains a seminal contribution in the debate about what it means to be intelligent.[462]

Chinese Room Argument

In 1980, American philosopher John Searle published an article that subsequently became known as *The Chinese Room Argument*. In it, Searle imagines himself alone in a room, trying to follow a computer program to respond to written Chinese characters that have been slipped under the door. Searle understands no Chinese but, by following the program for manipulating symbols and numerals just as a computer does, he sends appropriate strings of Chinese characters back out under the door, which leads those outside to mistakenly believe someone inside the room speaks Chinese. The inference of the argument is that programming a digital computer can make it appear to understand language but could not produce real understanding. Searle contended that if the man in the room does not understand Chinese by executing a program for understanding Chinese, then neither does any other digital computer on that basis because no computer has anything the man does not have."[463]

Early Definition

Shane Legg, a machine learning researcher who, with Demis Hassabis and Mustafa Suleyman, cofounded DeepMind Technologies, later bought by Google. In the early 2000s, Legg and fellow computer scientist Ben Goertzel popularized the term "artificial general intelligence" (AGI) to describe an AI that can do practically any cognitive task a human can do. He said that at the time, talking about AGI "would put you on the lunatic fringe".[464]

Cognitive Learning

In 2015, Murray Shanahan published *The Technological Singularity* in which he suggests that AGI is "Artificial intelligence that is not specialized to carry out specific tasks but can learn to perform as broad a range of tasks as a human." An important aspect of this framing is its emphasis on the value of including metacognitive tasks (learning) among the requirements for achieving AGI.[465]

Flexibility

Gary Marcus, Emeritus Professor of Psychology and Neural Science at NYU, suggests that AGI is "shorthand for any intelligence flexible and general, with resourcefulness and reliability comparable to human intelligence." The mention of "flexibility" is noteworthy, since, like the Shanahan formulation, this suggests that *metacognitive* tasks such as the ability to learn new skills must be included in an AGI's set of capabilities in order to achieve sufficient generality. Marcus proposes five concrete tasks: understanding a movie, understanding a novel, cooking in an arbitrary kitchen (likely derived from Apple co-founder Steve Wozniak's 2010 "Coffee Test"), writing a bug-free 10,000-line program and converting natural language mathematical proofs into symbolic form.[466]

Turing Test Replacement

Over the decades the Turing test of the 1950s remained the acid test for AI. The current crop of GenAI tools appears to be so close to passing the legendary threshold that many now question whether the Turing test even matters anymore. In his 2023 book, *The Coming Wave: Technology, Power, and the Twenty-first Century's Greatest Dilemma,* Mustafa Suleyman claims the Turing is no longer a meaningful measure of AI and needs to be replaced. Suleyman argues that there's a misplaced focus on the possibility of achieving GenAI. Instead, he believes a more achievable and meaningful short-term goal is what he calls *artificial capable intelligence*, or ACI: programs that can set goals and achieve complex tasks with minimal human intervention.

To measure whether a machine has achieved ACI, he describes a "modern Turing test" in which an AI is given $100,000 to see if it can turn the investment into $1 million. To do so, the bot must research an e-commerce business opportunity, generate blueprints for a product, find a manufacturer on a site like Alibaba and then sell the item—complete with a written listing description—on Amazon or Walmart.com.[467] Now that's a serious test for AGI!

> *"There were 5 exabytes of information created between the dawn of civilization through 2003, but that much information is now created every 2 days."*

Eric Schmidt, Executive Chairman of Google

AGI Deep Learning

AGI is a true revolution in learning. It goes beyond narrow expertise and plunges technology into the deep end of human-like cognitive abilities. It not only crunches numbers and analyzes data but also possesses emotions, makes decisions based on subjective states, tackles complex problems, learns from experiences, understands languages, and exhibits an array of cognitive skills. AGI is the epitome of AI advancement, a grand vision where machines can conjure meaningful insights and responses, irrespective of specific input variables.[468]

Most of the AI applications being written about today rely heavily on deep learning, a subfield of AI used in everything from chess-playing machines to self-driving cars. Deep learning allows computers to perform complex tasks by identifying patterns while processing vast quantities of data. Since AI systems aim to mimic human intelligence, scientists can measure their effectiveness by comparing them against the best performing humans.[469]

Deep Learning is already used in healthcare to detect diseases from medical scans. As an example, IBM's Watson for Oncology uses AGI to analyze vast amounts of medical data to recommend personalized cancer treatment plans.[470]

DeepMind

An article in *Nature*[471] describes another use of deep learning: DeepMind, an AI technology that uses neural networks and machine learning to crack a broad range of problems. Because DeepMind is a machine-learning algorithm, it doesn't have to be given specific programming rules to learn. Instead, the algorithm is capable of combing through massive amounts of data and identifying repeated patterns that would take a human or traditional computer enormous amounts of time to decipher.

DeepMind's algorithms can teach themselves to play games and beat humans in *Go,* a complex strategy game that involves capturing territory on a board using the placement of black-and-white pieces. DeepMind has since moved to tackling other, more weighty world problems, including unraveling the probable structures of every protein known in nature.[472]

The technology has already been used to predict structures for 2.2 million new materials, of which more than 700 have gone on to be created in the lab and are now being tested.

A new autonomous lab at the Lawrence Berkeley National Laboratory uses data that includes some of GNoME's discoveries to engineer new materials independent of human assistance.[473]

GrandView Research estimates that the global AI market is presently worth $136.6 bn and is projected to expand at a compound annual growth rate of 37.3% from 2023 to 2030, when it will be worth approximately $1.81 tn.

The continuous research and innovation by tech giants drive adoption of advanced technologies in a wide swath of industries, including automotive, healthcare, retail, finance and manufacturing. Major players like Amazon, Google, Apple and Microsoft are working to make AI more accessible for enterprise use cases.

> *"Machine intelligence is the last invention that humanity will ever need to make."*

Nick Bostrom, University of Oxford

Business Impact

While many in the business community grapple with understanding the potential impact of GenAI, technology leaders like Inflection AI's Mustafa Suleyman and OpenAI's Sam Altman are focused on AGI, what they see as the future.

Speaking at a Wall Street Journal Technology Conference, Suleyman commented that AI will achieve human-level performance within three years and become as ubiquitous as the Internet. His previously mentioned book, *The Coming Wave,* also notes that technology, notably AI, is advancing at a speed where its arrival and impact will be both profound and inevitable. Suleyman notes that "Eighteen million gigabytes of data are added to the global sum every single minute of every day." The ability of machines to rapidly process massive amounts of data gives AI the power to exceed human capabilities. As he sees it, AI will be faster, cheaper, more accessible and widely diffused. It will complete a calculation in seconds that would have taken a conventional computer 10,000 years.

At the same event, Sam Altman noted that "Every technology revolution affects the job market. That's the way of progress and we'll find new and better jobs." It has been stated that AI will be able to replace 80% of all jobs within 10-20 years. Suleyman argues that while societal problems and challenges will persist, the quality of life for the vast majority of the world is indisputably better off today than it was 50, 100, or 500 years ago when measured by progress and well-being. He believes that, like other disruptive technologies of past eras and epochs, AI will bring unparalleled advances in healthcare, food abundance, education, human longevity, personal freedom and human comfort.[474]

Altman is not just talking. He is attempting to raise as much as $5-7tn for a project to boost chip-making capacity to power AI. Potential investors include the United Arab Emirates government.

Another Middle Eastern nation making a significant investment into AI is Saudi Arabia, which, in 2024, announced plans to create a $40bn fund to invest in the technology, according to *The New York Times*. Saudi Arabia represents roughly one percent of the $104tn global economy. Applying a comparable investment to other countries would equal a $4tn global AI investment. It's hard to imagine a more telling example of AI fueling global productivity expansion.[475]

One of the building blocks on the path to AGI are autonomous agents, intelligent entities capable of decision-making and action execution without direct human intervention. These agents leverage advanced algorithms and machine learning models to analyze data, draw insights, and execute tasks autonomously.[476] This promises to revolutionize how businesses and organizations operate. These agents can function independently, learn from their surroundings, and recommend actions to achieve business objectives. They run a loop, constantly automating tasks which makes them highly scalable. They offer the promise of enhanced operational efficiency, cost-effectiveness and better decision-making, to name a few of their advantages.[477]

The impact of AI technology on business margins can change almost as quickly as new AI is developed. One of the challenges has been that projects involving the technology have often produced disappointing returns. A 2019 *MIT Sloan Management*

Review and Boston Consulting Group AI survey revealed that 7 out of 10 companies reported minimal or no value from their AI investments. One reason was that relatively few projects were actually put into production, becoming mere research exercises. Just three years later, in a survey of senior data and technology executives by NewVantage Partners, 92% of large companies reported they were achieving returns on their data and AI investments, up 48% from just 5 years prior. Also, 26% had AI systems in widespread production, more than double the 12% in the previous year's survey.[478]

A senior strategist at Goldman Sachs[479] calls AI the corporate world's "biggest potential long-term support for profit margins," and predicts that productivity spawned by AI will translate into S&P 500 profits being boosted by 30% or more. He bases his contention on the firm's data that shows since 1990, S&P 500 profit margins rose 5% to 12%, with every major sector in the index experiencing a bounce. This margin expansion accounted for more than 40% of stocks' gains over that period. The bank's models indicate that over the next decade, AI technology will help boost corporate profit margins by an additional 400 basis points.

While AI could potentially displace 300 million jobs globally over the next 10 years, it is as likely to create new jobs and reduce costs, pumping up productivity. An example of the impact AI is having on business profitability is Nvidia (NVDA), the major producer of chips required for AI tasks. In 2023, the company's shares skyrocketed by 209.96% on continuing demand for the firm's graphic processing units (GPUs). First quarter sales in 2024 were projected to be $24 bn—more than triple the previous year—as Nvidia's market value surpassed $2tn, making it the U.S.'s third-largest listed company after Microsoft and Apple.[480]

The ability to use AI to increase profit margins will, to a greater or lesser extent, depend on companies being able to "price-in" the cost to their products and services.

Some might integrate AI capabilities into products without initially charging for the enhancement, waiting to impose price increases until customers perceive the increased value. Adobe has used this strategy with its Creative Cloud and Acrobat products. This approach often makes the most sense for products sold to consumers and small businesses, who may hesitate to pay for a feature until they incorporate the new AI capabilities into their workflow and the price increase is justified.

Companies able to integrate AI features to upgrade existing products will enjoy immediate access to a profitable customer base. Microsoft is doing this by charging $30 per user/per month for Copilot, which adds AI capabilities to applications within its Microsoft 365 suite.

As more companies adopt AI technologies, they'll require greater computing power. Most will likely choose cloud vendors such as Amazon, Google and Microsoft. Open AI pioneered this consumption model by charging enterprise customers according to the number of "tokens" they use, with each token representing about 750 words.[481]

McKinsey Global Institute finds that AGI has the potential to generate value equivalent of $2.6tn to $4.4tn in global corporate profits annually. The technology could create value equal to an additional $200bn to $340bn a year in banking alone. Retail and consumer packaged goods companies could see an additional $400bn to $660bn in operating profits annually from the use of generative AI. McKinsey estimates that generative AI could increase labor productivity by 0.1% to 0.6% annually through 2040. Combined with other technologies, work automation could add an extra 0.2 to 3.3 percentage points to productivity growth.[482]

Accounting firm PwC estimates AI will make the world $15.7tn richer between by 2030. Healthcare, finance and retail companies appear to be the biggest winners.

> *"Artificial Intelligence, deep learning, machine learning—whatever you're doing if you don't understand it—learn it. Because otherwise you're going to be a dinosaur within 3 years."*
>
> Mark Cuban

AI in Finance

Artificial intelligence in finance transforms the way people interact with money. AI helps the financial industry streamline and optimize processes ranging from credit decisions to quantitative trading and financial risk management. Fintech, or financial technology, applies modern technology to financial services to improve or automate banking and investing activities. AI is widely used in financial organizations to detect and prevent fraud through digital banking channels. Mobile banking, digital loans, insurance, credit scores, purchasing and selling operations, and asset management are all included. AI technology can determine a customer's typical behavior by monitoring how they interact in considering their transactions. The market value of AI in the fintech industry alone was estimated to be $9.45bn in 2021 and is expected to grow at a compound annual growth rate (CAGR) of 16.5% from 2022 to 2030.[483]

An example of AI's role in a fintech company is Boston-based DataRobot, which provides machine learning software for scientists, analysts, software engineers, executives and IT professionals. It helps financial institutions and businesses build predictive models that make decisions related to fraudulent credit card transactions, blockchain, lending and defaults.[484]

AI takes many forms in finance and investing. Hedge funds and other trading operations utilize AI at a high level to gain slight advantages in fast-moving markets. Hedge funds have been transformed by quantitative investing. The ability to rapidly analyze large amounts of data and create short-term strategies appears to be beating the slower and deeper analysis that traditionally led to long and short investment decisions.[485]

AI is also widely used in finance and investing because of its ability to process and analyze information from large data sets, and help choose stocks, optimize portfolios, manage risk and guide trade entry and exit strategies.[486]

The world of banking and finance is an obvious business sector for investigating the potential benefits of AI since information processing is at the heart of the financial markets. Unsurprisingly, financial institutions tend to invest in technology ahead of most other industries for competitive purposes. The industry has seen remarkable streamlining of programs, processes, routine tasks and customer interactions, thanks to AI. An article in *Business Insider*[487] predicts that AI applications will have saved banks and financial institutions $447bn by the end of 2023. According to *Forbes*, 70% of financial firms are using machine learning to predict cash flow events, adjust credit scores and detect fraud.

For example, Bank of America's chatbot "Erica" serves over 10 million users and is able to understand a half million question variations. JPMorgan Chase uses AI detecting applications, including an algorithm to detect fraud patterns.[488] U.S. Bank analyzes relevant data on customers via deep learning to help identify bad actors and ferret out money laundering.

AI is becoming increasingly important in big data because it enables the extraction of high-level and complex abstractions through a centralized learning process. The need for extracting and mining meaningful patterns from large amounts of data propels the growth of artificial intelligence in big data analytics. Furthermore, the technology aids in overcoming big data analytics challenges such as data analysis trustworthiness, raw data format variation, imbalanced input data, and highly distributed input sources. Another issue is a lack of efficient storage and information retrieval, as data is collected in large quantities and made available across multiple domains.[489]

In business, the marginal cost of production is going to keep going down as technology allows production to become more digitized. That momentum indicates that margins are going to expand and continue to keep going up. Among all industries, software's marginal cost of production, being close to zero, is the lowest. To produce another bicycle or microwave oven costs a lot of money; to produce another piece of software costs virtually nothing.

I have invested in software for years because of the low marginal production costs for producers and the high costs for customers to switch suppliers. When I think about what my portfolio will look like in 20 years, it could very well be mostly software companies.

AI and Financial Planning

When I was in graduate school, I got into a debate with a professor about the future of financial planning. I told him I thought what we were learning in his class would someday be done by computers. He couldn't see it—or he saw it but it was such a threat to his livelihood that he didn't allow himself to believe it.

At that time, I could see how accounting software was eliminating accounting jobs. The same was true of tax software eliminating tax preparer jobs. It's all just math and the size of the textbooks are about the same. I reasoned that financial planning would have to be next.

The majority of financial planners will not be needed in the future, and I expect GenAI to reduce the headcount by at least half. I'm now more convinced of that opinion than ever. Generative AI is the game changer here. The only financial planning professionals that will be needed are those that do unique calculations like valuing a business, creating complicated executive compensation plans or have some very specific niche-planning expertise like special needs trust planning. In the future, humans will spot-audit AI-generated financial plans that AI flags as unusual.

In the very near future (it may already be happening by the time you read this), people will have conversations with AI-enabled Siri and AI-enabled Alexa that will make financial planning decisions as easy as choosing theater tickets.

Enjoying their hot tub one evening, Tom and Janet receive a call from AI-Siri.

(AI-Siri) Hi Tom. I saw on your calendar that you are free right now, so is this a good time to talk?"

(Tom) Sure.

(AI-Siri) I noticed that you made an unusually large deposit into your checking account this week. Did you get a raise or bonus?

(Tom) I did get a bonus. Long overdue. I left it in our checking account because I wasn't sure what I wanted to do with it.

(AI-Siri) Do you have spending plans for any of it or do you want to invest it?

(Janet) The market's up since Tom got that bonus and he's been saying we need to do something with the money. I think we should invest it. Tom is nodding in agreement, so I guess that's what we'll do.

(AI-Siri) Looking at the Apple Financial Plan we created for you last year, we can transfer the money for you to get it working towards your financial goals. We recommend separating the deposit into two parts: the maximum deduction of $7500 into your backdoor ROTH contributions like we did last year and the balance into your investment trust account we helped you create. I just sent you a push notification so as soon as you approve it, I'll make the transfers. We will be sure to include the backdoor ROTH contributions when we file your taxes in April. I just sent you a short video as a reminder about how backdoor ROTH contributions work.

(Janet) Thank you, Siri. As long as we have you on the line, we've also have been thinking about moving closer to our kids in Nashville. Tom does not have to go into the office, so he can work from anywhere. But we're not sure what the tax implications of selling our home, moving to another state and buying a home there would be.

(AI-Siri) I see your current home on Zillow is a two-story and roughly 3,500 square feet. Would you be looking for a comparable property?

(Janet) No. Something smaller in a one-story probably.

(AI-Siri) Well, you'll be downsizing and moving to a state with lower taxes. Looking at your financial position and based on what you told us about your plans for retirement, you should be able to make the move without having to change your plans. In fact, you can probably retire a year earlier if you wish, Tom.

(Tom) I like that. Get to spend some quality time with our grandkids while they are still kids. And I can start taking my Social Security benefits.

(AI-Siri) Why would you do that?

(Tom) Well, the guy who used to be my broker told me it was a good idea. What was his name, Janet?

(Janet) George something, I think. Siri, what was his name?

(AI-Siri) Let me look at your financial statement for 2022. There it is. His name is George Johnson.

(Tom). Yeah, George Johnson. He said if for any reason I decided to retire early, it would be smart to start taking Social Security right away, starting at age 62.

(AI-Siri) Do you remember what his reason for saying that was?

(Tom) I don't.

(AI-Siri) May I ask you some questions about that?

(Tom) Sure.

(AI-Siri) Thanks. When we previously discussed your retirement goals, you told me you intended on working until you were eligible for Medicare at age 65. You also said that people in your family tend to live a long life.

(Tom) That's correct.

(AI-Siri) I asked if you had any serious illnesses that might prevent you from also living a long life and you said no. Is that still true?

(Tom) Yes, although Janet recently asked me if I knew where my life insurance policy was. (laughter)

(AI-Siri) That's funny, Tom. My spouse jokes about taking a date to my funeral. I remind her that AI doesn't die. But seriously, based on what you've said, we would recommend you delay taking Social Security. You've accumulated significant net worth, and with the probability of living longer combined with your lower investment risk tolerance in retirement, there's no reason for you to dip into your Social Security benefits until required.

(Janet) Siri, why do you suppose his broker recommended taking benefits early?

(AI-Siri) Well, I can't say for sure, but because financial advisors typically earn fees based on the size of their clients' portfolios, if their clients delay taking Social Security and instead begin withdrawing funds from their portfolios to cover living expenses in retirement, their advisors' fees are reduced. In your case, however, our recommendation is that when you retire, you take withdrawals from your portfolio and allow your Social Security benefits to grow while you also defer paying taxes on the benefits.

(Janet) That makes so much sense, Tom.

(AI-Siri) I'd like to see what the actual numbers are between Tom taking benefits at 62 and waiting until 70. May I use the login you and Tom previously authorized to access to your Social Security account?

(Tom & Janet) Absolutely.

(AI-Siri) Looking at your account on the Social Security website, Tom, you are currently entitled to a total annual benefit of $40,920 or $3410 monthly. If you choose to take benefits at age 62, you will only receive 70% of your full retirement benefit or $28,644 a year. If you wait until age 70, you will receive roughly 125% of your benefit which comes to $51,150 annually. So, taking early benefits would cause you and Janet to lose $22,506 a year, or $1875 a month. If you live to age 86 like your father, you will lose at least $360,000!

(Janet) I'm shocked your broker would recommend a strategy that could cost us so much money, Tom, just to line his pockets. Aren't financial advisors supposed to be unbiased?

Getting unbiased advice can translate into enormous savings for individuals, and it's one of the advantages people will enjoy as major players like Apple and Amazon move into financial services using AI.

The following day, Janet called her daughter, Peggy, to say that she and Tom had decided to put their home on the market and move to Tennessee so they could spend more time with their three grandchildren.

(Janet) We weren't sure we could manage it but our conversation with Siri last night showed Tom will be able to retire early and we will be fine. I hope you and Frank are excited to hear that.

(Peggy) That's wonderful news, mom. We were hoping you and Tom could be closer to us and the kids. Hey, you want to hear something funny? Frank and I were having a cocktail after golf the other afternoon and we had a Q&A session about our Amazon Financial Plan with AI-Alexa. You think Siri and Alexa know each other? (laughter)

We had some questions about whether we can move into a larger house we looked at just a few blocks away. We weren't certain we could comfortably handle the purchase and whether we could get enough for our current place to make the move. Alexa was really helpful and we feel better about making the move now. It looks like we may both be living in new homes by the end of the year.

Financial planning in the future will be done the same way we set fantasy football lineups—while shaving or getting the car washed. No more pinstripe-suited financial salesmen pretending to be advisors and caring more about your goals than your money.

Future Optimism

The year 2023 has seen a host of important scientific breakthroughs that should give the financial markets and people in general cause for optimism:

- Researchers at the University of Cambridge successfully built the first "map" of every one of 3,016 neurons and 548,000 synapses in the brain of a fruit fly larva and how they're wired together. The achievement is a huge advance from previous research, which mapped only several hundred neurons. The breakthrough will help scientists understand the basic principles by which signals travel through the brain at the neural level and lead to behavior and learning.

- Researchers at the University of Cambridge and the California Institute of Technology created synthetic human embryos using stem cells in a groundbreaking advance that sidesteps the need for eggs or sperm. The embryos, which resemble those in the earliest stages of human development, could provide crucial insight on the impact of genetic disorders.

- National Institutes of Health researchers developed a new software that assembles complete (gapless) genome sequences from a variety of species. The advance improves DNA sequencing accuracy for the male reproductive chromosome, which could help identify certain genetic disorders and potentially uncover the genetic roots of others.

According to Goldman Sachs Research, breakthroughs in GenAI have the potential to bring about sweeping changes to the global economy. As tools using advances in natural language processing work their way into businesses and society, they could drive a 7% (or almost $7tn) increase in global GDP and lift productivity growth by 1.5 percentage points over a 10-year period.

As more GenAI tools are developed, businesses across the economy will benefit, from enhanced productivity and sales to the design of products, to improved medical diagnoses to detecting cyber fraud. While much remains unknown about how GenAI will influence society and the global economy, it will take time to play out. Signs indicate that the effects could be profound.[490]

An example is Google Gemini Advanced—originally dubbed Bard—unveiled in February 2023, a GenAI intelligence chatbot, meant to function similarly to ChatGPT (launched by OpenAI in 2022). In December, Google announced the chatbot would now be powered by Gemini Pro, which can generate and process text, images, and other kinds of data like graphs and maps. In comparison with ChatGPT, Gemini's clearest advantage comes from its ability to understand and interact with video and audio, answer questions related to complicated topics, and explain reasoning in complex subjects like math and physics.[491]

Gemini is Google's next-generation AI architecture that replaces PaLM 2, which currently powers many of the company's AI services, including Gemini Advanced and Duet AI in Workspace apps like Google Docs. Gemini will allow these services to simultaneously analyze or generate text, images, audio, videos and other data types.[492]

The performance of deep learning models is generally driven by increasing model complexity and amount of training data. This has led to the question of how further improvements could be achieved, since we have almost run out of new training data for language models. However, multimodal models open up enormous new reserves of training data in the form of images, audio and videos. AIs such as Gemini, which can be directly trained on all of this data, are likely to have much greater capabilities going forward.[493]

> *"In our business, we talk about emerging technologies and how they impact society. We've never seen a technology move as fast as AI has to impact society and technology. This is by far the fastest moving technology that we've ever tracked in terms of its impact and we're just getting started."*

Paul Daugherty, CIO, Accenture

CHAPTER TWENTY

Dirty, Dangerous, Drudgery

> *"Robots are not going to replace humans, they are going to make their jobs much more humane. Difficult, demeaning, demanding, dangerous, dull—these are the jobs robots will be taking."*

Sabine Hauert, Robotics Professor

Imagine a few years into the future. Robots will likely be as common as smartphones are today. For decades, we have relied on rudimentary robots to partner with or replace humans in dozens of everyday jobs. Robots are pervasive in warehouses, factories, post offices, the military, law enforcement, fast food restaurants and even operating rooms. They do everything from vacuuming floors and milking cows to filling and dispensing prescriptions. They are now integral to virtually every industry and every aspect of our lives, including our finances.

Manufacturing was the first industry to adopt robots, using them to handle a variety of jobs, including fabrication, material handling, steel cutting and food packaging. In healthcare, robots do everything from assisting in surgery and physical therapy to helping recovering patients become ambulatory to delivering essential supplies. Companies use robots in logistics to stock shelves, retrieve materials and ensure on-time deliveries. The military is using robots to replace troops in dangerous missions including combat and defense. An example is Centaur, an explosive detection/disposal robot that looks for mines and IEDs, and SAFFiR, which fights fires on naval vessels. In space exploration, in addition to the James Webb telescope already discussed, the Sojourner and Perseverance Mars explorers, as well as deep space probes like Voyager and Cassini, are all fundamentally robots. Self-driving cars are the product of intelligent robotics. Even our homes now have robots that vacuum, mow lawns or answer our requests for music or information.[494]

Robotic Varieties

Robots are often grouped by classification:

Humanoid robots look and behave like people. They may interact with human equipment or perform jobs that would be unsafe or tedious. In recent years, humanoid robots have been employed for teaching, research and entertainment. Asus Zenbo, Pepper, Sophia, Atlas, and Optimus, are examples of humanoid robots.

Sophia, a realistic humanoid robot that uses AI and facial recognition to mimic over 60 human expressions, has achieved numerous milestones since her debut in 2016. Most notably, she delivered the 2024 commencement address to 2,000 attendees at D'Youville University in Buffalo. University officials said the development was an example of "embracing technology" and "meant to represent an intersection of technology and education."

Sophia has tweeted, taught STEM (science, technology, engineering and math) to children, and even gained citizenship from Saudi Arabia.[495]

Asus Zenbo is a low-cost robot capable of rolling around autonomously, and it understands verbal commands. Asus developed the device to help individuals remember daily tasks, such as exercise and medication schedules as well as doctor's appointments. Zenbo can also monitor the surroundings to detect any emergencies. It is capable of connecting to smart-home components like security cameras, lights and door locks.[496]

Pepper is a talking humanoid robot that adapts its attitude based on how it perceives the mood of humans around it. The device detects emotional states like sadness, surprise, joy and anger. It responds in a natural and appropriate fashion. Pepper uses multi-directional microphones to detect sounds.[497]

Atlas is a humanoid robot with whole-body balancing. It can sense obstacles and negotiate rough terrain autonomously or using teleoperation. If jostled or knocked over, Atlas can get up and regain its balance.[498]

Ameca is one of the newest humanoids, developed by Engineered Arts. The robot has human-like facial expressions and can do everything from performing warehouse tasks to unloading trailers to doing impressions from movies while speaking multiple languages. Ameca responds to questions with appropriate facial expressions using OpenAI's GPT-3. When asked in a recent video if it could dream, it responded, "Yeah last night I dreamt of dinosaurs fighting a space war on Mars against aliens." It then added, "I'm kidding, I can't dream like humans do but I can simulate it by running through scenarios in my head that help me learn about the world."[499]

Collaborative robots (cobots) operate side-by-side with people to finish a task that cannot be entirely automated. One example is *UR3*, a collaborative industrial robot created by Universal Robots that can build its own replacement parts on the fly. The small, nimble robot can handle a variety of tasks, including assembly, painting, soldering and material handling.[500]

Singrow, a Singapore-based robotics company working with Universal Robots and Augmentus, developed an AI-powered robot that can identify when strawberries are ripe. The company's indoor farms now produce strawberries with a 20% higher yield and 40% more energy efficient than a conventional farm.[501]

Soft robots are flexible machines typically used in areas where rigid robots would be ineffective, such as surgery and prosthetics, that can restore normal functioning to a damaged or diseased body part.[502] NASA scientists hope to one day use them for planetary exploration. Researchers see them investigating the deepest recesses of the human body.[503]

While robots have been performing repetitive tasks and replacing humans in hazardous work for many years, recent events have created a dramatic, almost inconceivable acceleration in their capabilities, thanks to machine learning and AI.

One of the tangible, if less obvious, benefits of robotics is the combination of increasingly sophisticated technology and declining installation costs. This equation promises to dramatically reduce the advantages of offshore manufacturing. For some time, building factories in low-wage parts of the world has been profitable for businesses requiring high levels of labor—the long-distance shipping costs notwithstanding—that may soon no longer be true. As AI-influenced robotics allow factories to become more efficient and less labor-intensive, the likelihood of bringing manufacturing facilities back onshore looks increasingly attractive. This changing economic dynamic comes at a time when industrial policy is also evolving, with countries seeking to secure their individual supply chains in the wake of the widespread interruptions felt during the pandemic. Studies estimate that the average cost of industrial robots will have declined 85% by 2030.[504]

Learning Through Observation

Artificial intelligence typically "learns" through human training or machine learning. Robots, on the other hand, learn by self-processing data, such as by observing human actions. For example, a robot might observe that you drive to the same work address at the same time every day and may begin looking for traffic and weather conditions to provide you with an estimated driving time.[505]

Nvidia is working on a robot with "zero-shot learning," which enables the device to learn and predict results based on classes of data rather than being trained on specific samples.

Researchers at the School of Computer Science at Carnegie Mellon University have programmed robots to learn household chores by simply watching videos of humans performing tasks like opening a drawer, oven door or lid, or taking a pot off the stove and picking up objects like a telephone or a can.[506]

Advanced Capabilities

Bipedal and four-legged robots have been around since the 1990s. Recent advancement in agility have greatly expanded their capabilities, however. Spot, another quadruped robot from Boston Dynamics[507] also maneuvers through difficult environments but a 2023 demonstration at the firm's headquarters opened the eyes of even the most skeptical members of the press. Outfitted with a top hat, mustache and googly eyes and using a flawless British accent, Spot conducted a tour of the company's facilities asking, "Shall we commence our journey? Follow me ladies and gentlemen." Spot is capable of answering questions and even opens its "mouth" to make it appear as though it's actually speaking. The four-legged bot can take on other personalities, including an archaeologist, teenager and Shakespearean time traveler. It can even assume a sarcastic personality, which, when asked to come up with a haiku, says: "Generator hums low in a room devoid of joy. Much like my soul."[508]

The service sector is an industry increasingly utilizing robotics. In support of social distancing during the pandemic, a group of restaurants opened in China staffed by a team of 20 robots to help cook and serve food. The robot-as-a-service (RaaS) field is growing exponentially as businesses gain better understanding of customer expectations.[509] From robotic baristas able to make coffee to robot servers that bring dishes to tables, Asian restaurants and cafes are at the forefront of RaaS.

In Pasadena CA, the first AI fully autonomous restaurant—"CaliExpress by Flippy"—is scheduled to open in 2024. The facility is a partnership between Cali Group, Miso Robotics and PopID, all Pasadena-based companies. The robotic chefs will man everything from grinding meat and flipping burgers to the "Flippy" robotic fry stations.[510]

There's a hotel in Japan that is entirely staffed with robots that provide information, check guests in and out, maintain rooms and other services, all using voice and facial recognition technology.[511]

In the financial sector, robotics has helped revolutionize how many banking and financial services are delivered through a technology called robotic process automation (RPA). Basically, it's software that creates a virtual workforce to free up employees to focus on less tedious tasks. RPA is now doing everything from financial modeling to invoice processing.

BNY Mellon uses RPA to automatically settle trades and confirm proper allocation. Evention's RPA performs credit card reconciliation to validate accuracy from point-of-sale to general ledger to credit card processor submissions. PayPal uses RPA to detect suspicious activity and distinguish between real and false alarms.[512]

One of open-source RPA's key selling points—both in and out of a down economy—is its ability to take over mundane processes. This not only gives employees time to focus on more meaningful work, like driving innovation, brainstorming new technologies or collaborating with colleagues but also allows them to maintain a more sustainable work-life balance.[513]

> *"AI will eventually become so ubiquitous that it will evolve into a utility not unlike electricity."*

Martin Ford,
Rule of the Robots: How AI Will Transform Everything.

Tesla is on its way to becoming a robotics company. Elon Musk has high aspirations for Tesla's humanoid robot, Optimus Gen 2. The bi-pedal robot will be capable of performing tasks that are unsafe, repetitive or boring. The Tesla CEO predicted that it could be ready to take orders in three to five years and is expected to probably cost less than $20,000."[514]

One of the toughest parts of making a useful humanoid robot is the hands, which must be strong enough to handle significant weights while sufficiently precise to handle delicate objects.

Optimus Gen 2 features a new type of hand that initially looks like an important upgrade.[515]

Given the pace of technological progress, it's inevitable that we will soon be living in a world served by a billion robots. At some point in the future, a robot-to-human ratio of two to one will exist, with 20 or 30 billion robots doing everything the 10 or 15 billion humans on the planet don't want to do.

Try to picture yourself coming home from the office 10 years from now. You're in your autonomous car, getting some work done as it is no longer necessary for you to steer, brake or even pay attention as your level 5 vehicle is controlled by AI. You look up just as the car turns into your neighborhood and you see robots pushing children on swings in the park, robots walking dogs, washing cars in driveways, delivering groceries, mowing lawns, painting shutters and barbequing hamburgers. As you come up to your home, you see a robot playing catch with your neighbor's kids.

You enter your home to the welcoming aroma of your favorite dinner, prepared flawlessly by one of your robots, while the other hands you a cocktail and then scurries off to start your shower. When you awaken tomorrow morning, a cup of hot coffee will be on your bedside table, your work clothes will be laid out, your shoes will be shined, and breakfast will be waiting, all courtesy of your faithful robotic associates. Does that sound like fantasy? It's not; it's the future.

Fears and Facts

There's a lot of fear mongering surrounding AI. Alarmists argue that robots will supplant humans, causing them to lose their livelihoods. They point to privacy issues, bad data, uncontrollable self-aware AI, autonomous weapons, etc. Sadly, much of this collective foreboding is the result of people fearing the unknown and misjudging what they don't fully understand. It's a repeating pattern.

Every major technological development has been accompanied by unwarranted fears that it will disrupt the economy or somehow make life worse. That's not what has happened in the past, of course, but it doesn't stop the naysayers from issuing doomsday warnings. They view technological change in a vacuum instead of learning the lessons of the past and having confidence that, like most previous advancements, this one will make life better for most people. There's been no evidence that technological change reduces the quality of life, so why focus on the negative? To be sure, we need to be aware of the potential dangers, but we can't let that stop progress. Advancements in learning inevitably result in enhanced quality of life, and perhaps it's accurate to say the bigger the change the better.

There's no question that AI will have an impact on employment and some people will have to learn new skills. AI is estimated to create 97 million new jobs by 2025, according to the World Economic Forum. Some people will lack the skills for the new roles and get left behind. Additionally, as robots become smarter and learn to do more things well, fewer humans will be needed. Even those with post-graduate degrees or specialized training aren't immune. AI has already had a consequential impact on healthcare, marketing and service industries and fields such as law and accounting are likely next in line for attrition.

In April 2022, Tradeshift launched a multi-country research project to gain a better understanding of how finance and accounting professionals view automation. The project asked basic questions such as whether they understood how automation might impact their careers, if they were ready for change and whether they viewed automation as a positive in terms of their career prospects. Far from being a threat, the results of the research suggested that those who had incorporated high levels of automation into their daily tasks were more optimistic about their futures and more likely to recommend their role to someone about to enter the job market. Those surveyed expressed the desire to be liberated from low-value, repetitive tasks. They believed having this type of work done by robots gave them opportunities to do more strategic, interesting work while also preserving a healthy work-life balance.[516]

Speaking of a healthy work-life balance, where is it written that the five-day work week is sacrosanct? The transformation from farming to working alongside machines accelerated as a result of the Industrial Revolution of the 18th century. A century later, six-day workweeks of 70 hours or more were common for factory workers. Then, in 1926, Henry Ford sparked a nationwide controversy when he introduced the eight-hour-a-day, five-day workweek. Four years later in 1930, W.K. Kellogg instituted six-hour shifts, motivated by his belief that giving workers more time off was a social good. Within two years, workers had begun earning in six hours what they used to earn working eight.[517]

The United Kingdom concluded a six-month trial of a four-day workweek in 2023, with some 3,000 employees at 61 companies participating. The results were encouraging, to say the least, as 56 of the 61 firms are continuing the four-day schedule, 18 of which are permanent. Reported benefits included better work-life balances, less burnout, lower attrition rates, fewer sleep problems and modest revenue increases.[518]

As a society, we have already established a pattern of reducing the number of hours humans must work to earn a decent living, so why would that social template not continue as technology advanced? Why can't we have a two- or three-day workweek in the future? Again, the naysayers will warn about the loss of jobs, but more likely the jobs will stay the same but the hours will simply be reduced, thanks to the implementation of AI and robotics. People's lives will be better at work as a result of having machines doing the tedious, repetitive tasks and businesses will become ever-more efficient and profitable. Every major technological advancement ultimately results in a more resilient economy and a better environment for the human condition.

Free Market and Government Cooperation

While I am an unapologetic capitalist, I believe there must be some form of government monitoring of new technologies. In the case of AI and robotics, a multi-national agreement among governments to oversee the development and administration of the technology would be wise. I'm a free-market advocate but I don't want capitalism running wild. I want to know there is an FAA or similar regulatory agency supervising airline robotic pilots, for example.

I don't want the airline industry calculating the probability of an accident as a rationale for underspending on safety equipment because the probability of an accident is determined to be relatively small. And if a major crash does occur, the mantra of the free market would be that people would simply choose other airlines. Of course, if the other airlines are doing the same math regarding safety expenditure, there won't be sufficient competition to eradicate the problem. So, the free market doesn't always work. It's great at figuring out equilibrium prices but not as good at promoting safety. The FAA has done a good job of avoiding crashes through millions of flights in recent years and I believe it—or a similar government agency—should maintain surveillance over AI.

As far as the loss of jobs due to robotic advancements, I don't think that will be a major obstacle as it can be solved with higher levels of productivity and fewer working hours. I think the economy will eventually work its way through the job losses and gains transition, as it always has. Having governments around the world cooperate in making sure that AI moves humanity in the right direction and includes everyone who wants to be included is important. When humanity has a common interest, the long-term trend seems to move in the right direction. In the short term, there will be posturing and negotiating, but nothing can resist the inescapable force of progress and I expect the advancement of AI will be no different.

It's as though some *Greater Force* is at work, giving us the tools we need to move forward and silently guiding us past the obstacles that stand in our way.

There is currently much speculation about what the world will look like in 50 or 100 years, given the rapid escalation of technology. To me, it won't look a whole lot different. Our world today doesn't look much different than it did 50 years ago.

Typewriters have been replaced by computers. Except for the purists, cameras have been replaced by cell phones, which have also relegated wrist watches to jewelry. Cars are faster, more aerodynamic and safer and our homes have more sophisticated appliances, although not much has changed with clothes washers, refrigerators or stovetops. They still function as they did in 1950, albeit better. Advertisements remain ubiquitous. Healthcare is better but hospitals look the same.

The prognostications that the world will look so different because of robots are largely based, I think, on the entertainment industry's depiction of robots in the movies and television. While the humanoid robots do indeed look like us, so many other robotic iterations, designed to perform specific tasks, don't look anything at all like Hollywood's vision. All in all, I think the world is going to look very similar to the way it does today in the future. The main reason is that the centuries-old infrastructure that exists would have to be replaced, a herculean task at best.

What Are They Thinking?

On a personal note, I went holiday shopping with my family at Hobby Lobby recently. That company is still using 20-year-old checkout technology. While we waited for the stream of shoppers in front of us to check out their purchases, I wondered why this chain wouldn't have checkout scanners—like virtually every other chain in America—that would make the shopping experience less arduous for their customers?

As I waited and watched the beleaguered clerks manually key in the codes of each item, I tried to make sense of the company's decision to make their customers angry. Then, it hit me. They are deliberately bypassing scanners because they have a bigger picture in mind. They plan to ignore barcode technology and transition straight to robots. That got me to wondering what a store staffed exclusively by robots would be like? Perhaps there would be one manager who walked around, smiled at the customers, nodded to the robots and glanced at his watch every few minutes, wondering why he was there at all. That idea was a fantasy not long ago; now it seems inevitable.

> *"The factory of the future will have only two employees, a man and a dog. The man will be there to feed the dog. The dog will be there to keep the man from touching the equipment"*

Warren G. Bennis.

In addition to the many advantages robotics offers businesses in the area of efficiency and enhanced profits, the implications of robotic technology on an aging population are equally impressive. One of the areas of robotics that has made striking advances—particularly in Japan but to a lesser extent, other countries—is in elder care. While different in appearance, function and purpose, these robots all serve to fill caregiving gaps. The Care-o-bot, built by Fraunhofer IPA, is operational in a number of German-assisted living facilities. Essentially providing the same services as employees and volunteers, the robot brings meals to the residents, but also plays memory games with them to help keep their minds sharp. The Dinsow eldercare robot, from CT Asia Robotics, helps seniors remember to take their pills, tracks their health and serves as a videophone for calls to family and doctors. It also doubles as entertainment in the form of a karaoke machine. ElliQ, from Intiriont Robotics, is a social robot companion that provides appointment reminders and assists with video calls. It can also suggest a walk when a human is overdue for some exercise.[519]

One of the afflictions of old age for many people is isolation. Homes can become prisons for the elderly no longer able to drive. The evolution of self-driving vehicles will come to the rescue for these people. More about this is the following chapter on Autonomous Driving.

I recall reading about a daycare robot that spent its day observing each room of the facility. Then, after the children had done their best to trash the place and gone home for the day, the robot would go back and clean up each room, putting everything back in place where the robot had observed it earlier.

It's hard to imagine an industry or sector of society that will not be transformed by AI-powered robotics. The impact on businesses is incalculable, but one thing for certain: robotics will, in the long run, make companies more efficient and profitable. That's good news for investors and future stock market returns.

> *"In addition to doing our jobs at least as well as we do them, intelligent robots will be cheaper, faster, and far more reliable than humans. And they can work 168 hours a week, not just 40. No capitalist in her right mind would continue to employ humans."*
>
> Kevin Drum

CHAPTER TWENTY-ONE

Productivity from Autonomous Driving

> *"The future interests me –*
> *I'm going to spend the rest of my life there."*
>
> Mark Twain

Does it sound overly dramatic if I propose that the development of autonomous vehicles (AVs) will be one of mankind's greatest advances? Does getting into a vehicle and have it safely take you wherever you want to go without you having to do anything except breathe sound like it could literally change the world? If you can momentarily put aside any skepticism, I'll explain.

If you ask a representative number of people what they hate most about their day, I venture the majority would say commuting to work in their car. The amount of wasted time, stress, lost productivity and accidents resulting from snarled traffic is almost incalculable. Municipalities have responded by adding additional lanes to their busy streets but ask anyone who commutes if it has made a difference. It hasn't.

The one glimmer of hope on the horizon is the AV, a vehicle capable of sensing its environment and operating without a human having to ever take control. In fact, a human does not even have to be present in the vehicle. Defined as Level 5 driving, an AV can do everything that a human driver can do and do it more safely.[520]

The various levels of autonomy can be confusing. Graphic 21.1 "Autonomy Levels" provides a condensation of the various stages.

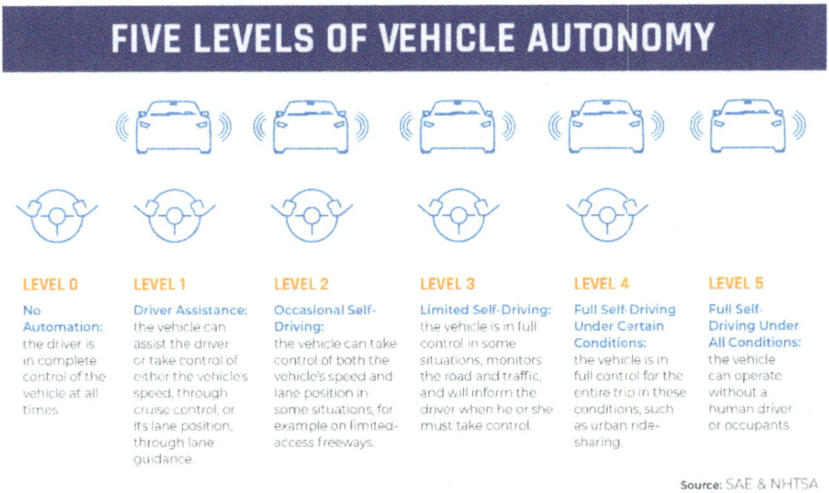

(Graphic 21.1 Autonomy Levels)

Most cars on the road today are Level 2, where various driver assistance systems are connected to increase safety but with the driver remaining responsible for the vehicle. The leap to Level 3 is a big one. From this stage onwards, the vehicle temporarily assumes control from the driver, who is free to engage in other activities, such as using the cell phone or participating in a video meeting. The driver must, however, be able to intervene when necessary. In Level 4, the vehicle operates completely autonomously under certain conditions and the human, free to do whatever he or she pleases, including sleep, is not required to intervene. The vehicle may also drive without occupants. The autonomy of the vehicle at Level 4 is still linked to certain conditions, such as a defined route or in a parking garage. Companies are already testing Level 4 vehicles in road traffic. In Level 5, the autonomy of the vehicle is not subject to Level 4 conditions and can act completely autonomously. These vehicles do not require a steering wheel or foot pedals. Essentially, human drivers are mutated into passengers at this stage.[521]

Most current cars are Level 2 in terms of automation with drivers in control, even when using adaptive cruise control. Japan and Germany have Level 3 vehicles on the road. Japan was the first with the Honda Legend in 2021. Germany soon followed with the Mercedes Drive Pilot on certain S-Class and EQS models. Korea's Hundai Motor Group received certification in 2023 to implement Level 3 technology in their upcoming G90 model.

The Level 3 systems are limited in their level of autonomy. The Mercedes, for example, cannot operate above 37 mph, after dark or if there is precipitation. These are some of the challenges automakers face and indeed, some plan to skip Level 3 altogether and jump right to Level 4, where the vehicle is full control in more complex situations without the driver having to be as alert.[522]

Because of the enormous complexity, the ultimate transition to Level 5 is likely to require a joint effort among multiple stakeholders, including OEMs, governments and even non-automotive sectors, such as healthcare providers, who will have to be included for individuals unable to drive.[523] The obstacles aside, the development of Level 5 AVs that can drive on highways or in geofenced urban areas is possible to be realized by the end of the decade, thanks to advancements in sensor technology, high-definition mapping, better data, vehicle-to-vehicle connections and call centers for dealing with atypical risks.[524]

Any informed discussion of Level 5 driving must include the topic of geofencing, essentially a virtual boundary around a physical area. For AVs, geofencing is the region where they are functional. Achieving Level 5 autonomy will mean removing the "fence" from geofenced autonomous cars and will require artificial intelligence (AI) that can make inferences and grow more intelligent as it is used. Today, there are a limited number of vehicles operating at Level 4 autonomy, including the robo-taxis in San Francisco, Phoenix and Shenzhen, China. These vehicles have a limited operational area and can only be fully autonomous when located within the boundaries of their geofence.

Complex algorithms and hardware will be needed for a Level 5 vehicle to break through the geofence. According to David Fritz, vice president of hybrid-physical and virtual systems at Siemens, "A Level 5 must be able to not only sense its environment but derive meaning and make inferences about that environment when it approaches something with which it is unfamiliar. In other words, it will need to be able to learn on the job, because there is no way to train an AI to handle every possible situation the vehicle might experience."

When an autonomous system encounters something it doesn't recognize, if it doesn't know what to do, it simply stops moving. Fritz describes an event while testing an autonomous system that confronted something it had never before encountered—a multi-level parking garage. The vehicle interpreted the cars in the garage as blocking the road. It thought: "Car stopped, go around the curb." In a geofenced area, the car drives around and collects data so the vehicle can recognize if it sees a car 10 feet off the ground, ignore it.[525]

The number of AVs is expected to grow at an unprecedented rate in the coming years, with companies like Tesla, Alphabet and Baidu competing to bring them to market. By 2030, over 10 million self-driving cars are expected to be on the road. By 2050, nearly all cars will be autonomous.[526]

Fixed or Variable Model?

Level 5 driving will alter the landscape of how we move about. It will unlock the value in much of the underused and unproductive land, including everything from urban parking lots to remote rural locations. It will facilitate a vehicular transformation from a fixed cost model to a variable cost model.

Driving is currently based on a fixed cost model. You buy or lease a car. It's parked 90% of the time, sitting idly in your garage or driveway, depreciating in value. Uber and Lyft have provided an alternative, albeit an expensive one.

It's cost prohibitive for most people to go from a fixed cost pricing model to a variable model unless they do very little driving. For those who commute daily or travel by car for business, it's a non-starter.

There is, however, an equilibrium point between the two models and Level 5 may be that point. The reason Uber and Lyft are expensive is the human element. Drivers willing to hustle and put in long hours can make a pretty good living driving for these companies, but they are also the principal reason why the variable cost pricing model is so costly. Once the human is removed from the equation and the vehicle is driven autonomously, the cost of the variable pricing model goes down dramatically.

People will then seriously question whether they need to own a car or just have access to one whenever they need it. Unlike the current environment where, for many, using Uber could cost hundreds each week, a $20,000 or more annual outlay. For those people, the current $48,000 average cost of a new car is a more economical, as well as convenient, choice. There's no time wasted waiting for Uber to show up.

But once autonomous driving is practical, that equation changes because the cost is going to be so much less. What will emerge will be the largest industry shift since the invention of the automobile. Consumers will have not two but three options:

- Own a vehicle exclusively, without sharing.
- Own a vehicle and share with others, converting what has been a depreciating asset into an income generating asset.
- Don't own; use the autonomous fleet.

Those who own their AV will have the option of traditional self-ownership or permitting use of the vehicle by others to produce income. There will always be those who don't want anyone else driving their car. For others, once they get to where they are going, whether to work, shopping or a movie, rather than the vehicle sitting idly, it can be sent to the autonomous fleet so it can be used by others providing owners with a share of the rental with the fleet leasing company. Once the time arrives for the individual to be picked up, the vehicle, having recognized the individual's workday is over at 5 or the movie ends at 7:30, returns for the drive home.

That's going to materially change the productivity arithmetic of owning a car. Most professionals have a set routine each workday and for the majority, it involves getting to work ASAP. But because they have to waste time driving to their offices or appointments, their productive time is delayed and reduced. With AVs, they can get to work as soon as they get into their vehicle and continue uninterrupted during the entire commute.

Someone with a 45-minute commute each way spends 22,500 minutes or 375 hours a year going to and from work in their car. Autonomous driving will bequeath that lost productivity back to the individual. Instead of logging in at 9am, people can begin their workday earlier while still in their vehicle. Perhaps the individual no longer has to be in the office for 8 hours or can now get 9.5 hours of work done in the same time period. Either way, consider the effect on productivity over a lifetime. Someone working for 40 years saving 375 hours a year has roughly 20,000 additional hours of productivity during their working life. That's a gain of 10 work years!

Now that companies are calling employees back into the office, some are understandably agitated, having grown accustomed to working from home. For most, it's not having to go back to the office; it's getting back to the office that causes the consternation. The office itself is not a negative environment for most people. Time with fellow workers can be a source of stimulation and social interaction, as well as business productivity. Post-pandemic studies indicate companies tend to have higher levels of innovation when workers convene versus work in isolation.

The same research indicates people working alone at home are less productive than when in the company of fellow workers. Some might claim to be happier, but they're not as productive. Young professionals in particular suffer a significant career loss if they're isolated from other, more senior professionals. Aspiring young financial employees that spend their days working with me are likely to become far better investors than people limited to a couple of Zoom calls with me each week.

That's the loss those working from home sustain. Self-driving vehicles will help resolve this issue by bringing people back into the office and in contact with those they can learn from by association.

On a personal note, I think the office is a pretty great place. When I go into the office, I'm surrounded by like-minded, hard-working people that are doing well, are optimistic, ambitious and enjoyable to be around. They are often entertaining and make me laugh. Again, the office is not the problem; It's getting there.

Speaking of employees going back to the office, workers in New York experience one of the most frustrating cities in the world to own a car. Parking restrictions only add to the exasperation. Current full-day parking rates in Midtown Manhattan start at $50 and go up. Workers who opt to save money by parking on the street play a frenetic version of musical chairs, having to move their cars two or three times a week when sanitation trucks drive through to clear debris. Each side of a street has different cleaning hours, so that cars can move from one side to the other. Failing to move a car garners a $65 tiçket. It's a "solution" that works theoretically but not so well in actual practice because streets are already crammed full on both sides so there's nowhere for cars to go at cleaning times. Finding another parking space can be a time-consuming exercise, so to keep coveted spots without getting fined, many simply sit in their cars during the 90-minute cleaning period so that they can pull out as the cleaner comes by, then quickly swinging back in afterward. TV personality Anthony Bourdain once joined a local news anchor as she demonstrated alternate side parking. His reaction? "I'm never buying a car."[527]

> *"Everybody in New York City knows there's way more cars than parking spaces. You see cars driving in New York all hours of the night. It's like musical chairs except everybody sat down around 1964."*

Jerry Seinfeld

Real Estate

Autonomous driving will deliver another benefit that is not immediately apparent. It's going to noticeably shift the residential real estate market. Ask a real estate agent the reaction they get if the home they are showing a prospect requires a one-hour commute to work. It's not a happy reaction. Two hours a day of stop-and-go driving in what feels like a prison cage full of competing vehicles can be torture. But that same commute can actually be relaxing, even productive, if the driver can spend the entire time getting work done. And because commuting is no longer exhausting, a much larger area of residential geography opens up to home buyers. People who work in the city but always wanted to live on a farm will be able to do it. Land previously too remote to attract city workers will become viable and mushroom in value. This will doubtless trigger a sizeable shift in where people choose to live and escalate the migration of people moving out of large cities to escape the grime, crime and high taxes. Self-driving vehicles will deurbanize the world by allowing people to move out to safer, quieter, less expensive rural areas.

Battle of the Titans

The world of self-driving cars has three giants: Tesla, Jidu Auto, an arm of China's multi-technology company Baidu, and Waymo, a subsidiary of Alphabet. Each has a different approach to autonomous driving and their rivalry is centered around the debate as to the best way to move forward.

All three companies use powerful machine learning systems to help their cars navigate the world, but the similarities end there. Tesla's view is provided entirely by cameras, whereas Baidu and Waymo uses an array of sensors, most critically Lidar, short for "Light Detection and Ranging." Lidar systems use laser pulses to map the environment but at a high cost. The Waymo model has been geofenced into most of San Francisco for some time[528] and driverless freeway rides started testing in Los Angeles and Phoenix in early 2024. Baidu has introduced a bespoke robotaxi called RT6, potentially capable of Level 4 driving complete with a detachable steering wheel. RT6 is the evolution of the company's Apollo Go service, which has logged over one million autonomous rides in

Beijing and other Chinese cities. Like Tesla, Baidu is accumulating enormous amounts of data on which to base future decisions.

Tesla does not use Lidar. Instead, it implements nine cameras which provide 360 degrees of visibility around the car at up to 250 meters of range.[529] Some of the company's 2023 models are equipped with Hardware 4.0, which uses eight higher resolution cameras. The automaker's pure vision approach, dubbed "Tesla Vision," leverages data gathered by the cameras rather than ultrasonic sensors. Tesla's Elon Musk has claimed that any company relying on the powerful but expensive Lidar technology is "doomed."[530]

Musk's criticism of Lidar might be construed as controversial but Kilian Weinberger, an associate professor at Cornell University who works on computer vision for AVs, believes Musk's rationale is correct. He notes that Musk's cameras are "dirt cheap" compared to Lidar, which allows Tesla to put the technology into every car they sell. Each car collects vital data as it drives around. Data is the lifeblood of the machine learning systems and self-driving technology. Tesla's bet is that the mammoth amount of video its fleet amasses will help it reach full autonomy faster than the smaller amount of Lidar data its competitors rely on.[531]

A clear indication of Tesla's connection with those who own their vehicles and collect data is the transformation of the company's autonomous software in 2024. Whereas the previous iteration—version 11—was based on human-written code, version 12 abandons that approach in favor of advanced AI learning to emulate a skillful human driver. As one enthusiastic owner remarked, (the new version) "feels like the robot that used to drive the car has been replaced by a competent human." While traffic control devices and crosswalk signs remain obstacles for the system, the latest autonomous adaptation is yet another example of the breakneck pace of autonomous driving progress.[532]

The competition is certainly an exciting one. Baidu and Waymo's geofencing works well because the computers are already trained and can constantly update the geofence. But as Musk notes, geofencing is largely confined to its test area. How well will it operate in outside areas?

Tesla's pure vision approach has no such geographical limitations and is already pushing the envelope of the technology, although the company still has a long way to go, despite having solved all but the tiniest sliver of the self-driving challenge.

Attacking that miniscule remaining obstacle is the logic behind collecting mass amounts of data from real-life driving conditions, in particular the rare scenarios that form outlier events. For example, a fallen tree in the road, a sinkhole, a burst fireplug flood, a multi-story parking garage. But there are limitations to this approach. Ultimately, there will be unique cases that can't be anticipated or trained for, what Musk refers to as the "long tail" problem.

Indeed, there are an incalculable number of permutations that can occur inside of that 1% tail. That's the enigma that must be solved in order to get to Level 5 autonomous driving. For Tesla, the path to where they are today has been one littered with discoveries. The explanation of the major discoveries in this process can get a bit cryptic, but I'll try to keep it basic and understandable.

When it started, Tesla's autonomous driving system relied on a Mobileye system for its perception module. Perception helps the car see the world around itself, as well as instantly recognize and classify the things that it sees. In other words, the car must be able to categorize pedestrians, traffic lights, road signs, parking spots, lanes and more. It must also recognize the precise distance between itself and the objects around it to decide whether to stop or simply slow down.[533]

In 2021, the Mobileye system morphed into a custom-built system, going from rasterization (the process of converting a vector-based image or object into a raster or bitmap format) of images to a bird's-eye view network, a system of cameras mounted on all four sides of the vehicle that link to provide a single composite 360-degree overhead view on the vehicle's LCS screen.[534]

At this time, Tesla introduced a multi-task learning algorithm called the *HydraNet*, a single network with several heads that eliminates many repetitious encoding operations. This was a key element in Tesla's architecture because it allowed them to run multiple tasks using a single neural network.

In 2022, Tesla added an algorithm called the *Occupancy Network*, which improved perception by dividing it into two blocks: HydraNet for finding objects, land lanes, etc. and Occupancy Network to find occupancy in 3D. This leaves Tesla with two remaining tasks: a deep neural network for every block and an *End-to-End Model* to assemble the neural networks together.

End-to-end here refers to training a complex learning system by applying gradient-based learning to the system as a whole. End-to-end learning systems are specifically designed so that all modules are differentiable. The system may seem like a black box but it's actually an assembly of existing blocks bonded together.[535]

The logic behind collecting ever more data is to capture more of the rare scenarios that could mystify the system's AI, but there's a fundamental limit to this approach. "Eventually you have unique cases that you can't train for," says Weinberger. "The benefits of adding more and more data are diminishing at some point." This is the so-called "long tail problem," says Marc Pollefeys, a professor at ETH Zurich who has worked on camera-based self-driving. It presents a major hurdle for going from the kind of driver assistance systems already common in modern cars to true AVs. Trying to go from a system that mostly works to one that almost never makes mistakes by simply pushing ever more data through a machine learning pipeline is going to fail, says Pollefeys. "When we see that something works 99% of the time, we think it can't be too hard to make it work 100%. And that's actually not the case. Making 10 times fewer mistakes is a gigantic effort."[536]

It's apparent that whichever company first achieves Level 5 autonomous driving will be the biggest business winner in history. The value of that company defies estimation, but $8-10tn is a conservative guess. Getting there first not only crowns the company with the mantle of industry leader, it puts it in a position to leverage its success by licensing the software to competitors.

For the sake of argument, let's assume Tesla gets there first. Companies like Ford and GM will be faced with a tough choice: try to replicate Tesla's success while playing catchup, remain a manufacturer and license software from Tesla to become an autonomous fleet leasing company, or shutter the business.

Ford, GM, Chrysler, even Toyota and the German manufacturers are unlikely to remain direct-to-consumer sellers in the future. Or if they do, the sales numbers will be a fraction of what they are today once Level 5 driving arrives, because not many consumers will need or want to own their own cars anymore. Fleet sales to commercial and municipal entities will be exclusively AVs.

The automotive industry will undergo a massive change. There will be opportunities, to be sure, but it will be a dangerous place to have money invested.

Many investors have a mistaken notion about Tesla, specifically the company's price earnings ratio (P/E), currently about 40, which they think is too expensive. While judgments like this are subjective, as investors, instead of evaluating Tesla as a car company, let's assume they ultimately become an AV licensing company. Viewed in that prism, a P/E ratio of 40 suddenly looks cheap, considering Tesla at that point will probably be the world's most valuable company.

As to picking winners and losers, the transformation to Level 5 driving will unearth value traps throughout the market. Companies that have the winds of change in their face will struggle to survive and investors will vote with their wallets. The financial industry is rife with advisors eager to tell you which stocks to buy. While it is talked about far less, it's equally important to know which stocks to avoid. For example, knowing what you now know, would you be inclined to buy stock in a company manufacturing steering wheels or brake pedals? Would you consider buying an oil change or car wash franchise?

Historically, P/E multiples and margins have always gone up in the long run and there's no reason to think that will not continue as technology continues its advancements. There are still countless financial gurus who cling to the theory that multiples will return to their mean reversion (long term average). That's a fallacy that will punish investors who base their decisions on it. It's the mantra of those focused on the market's rearview mirror; those who contend that P/E multiples should be priced as they always have been. These people are like football coaches still running the T formation at a time when winning teams are passing for 300 yards a game. What was true 20 years ago is no longer relevant. Progress and productivity enhancements from technology like Level 5 will completely change the game and will thrust P/E multiples ever upward. You have to ignore the advisors touting yesterday's strategies.

> *"It is not the strongest of the species that survives, nor the most intelligent. It is the one that is most adaptable to change."*

Charles Darwin

The Challenges of Disruption

Every major transformation produces winners and losers. Level 5 will be the quintessential example and have far-reaching effects on virtually every business sector. The first movers that understand what's coming and adapt will be winners; those that resist change or are slow to adapt will get steamrolled. Some industries stand to prosper; some will be challenged to remain profitable; some will struggle to survive. There will also be winners and losers among various occupations.

Roughly 3% of the workers in the U.S. are employed in driving occupations.[537] These workers and those involved in manual labor are especially susceptible to obsolescence. AVs will boost efficiency in industries affecting these people, such as trucking and delivery services. The transformation will also force drivers and other workers to adapt to new employment opportunities, such as the need for software engineers, data scientists and experts in artificial intelligence, in addition to the jobs related to fleet leasing and maintenance.

The vehicles, not unlike their driver-required predecessors, will still need to be serviced and repaired. New apps will be needed for support and entertainment for drivers no longer required to pay attention to the road. Municipalities will need people capable of building geofencing and other connected road infrastructure.

The emergence of the Internet just a few decades ago dramatically reduced the need for services like travel agents and bank tellers, but it created new jobs like app developers and content managers. The same will be true of AVs.[538]

As people abandon cities and move to the suburbs and beyond, jobs will be created in construction of new homes, schools, restaurants and retail facilities. Tourism will also have job opportunities as people travel more and take more vacations.[539]

Heavy construction workers operating bulldozers, dump trucks, cranes and other equipment are prone to accidents and injuries. Fatalities at construction sites increase every year and a major contributing factor is the vehicles used by the industry. Automating these vehicles could reduce injuries and fatalities dramatically.[540]

Transportation is a huge obstacle for those with disabilities. Public transit services are an option but often an unsatisfactory one. Access to affordable self-driving cars could allow some 9 million more Americans to join the workforce, according to a study by the National Disability Institute. Melding these individuals into the workforce could add billions of dollars to the economy. The government would see $120 bn in benefits, including $93 bn in additional tax revenues and a $28 bn reduction in spending on social safety net programs.[541]

Bars and restaurants will likely benefit from AVs as customers will have faster, easier access, and while those who over imbibe alcohol may still suffer a morning headache, their trip back home will no longer endanger others.

Industries at Risk

Vehicle ownership and maintenance will move from individuals to fleet owners as a result of autonomous cars. Oil change retailers, car washes and rental outlets could all vanish as fleet owners absorb these functions internally.

Today's auto insurance market is worth $200bn, based on annual sales. The expected reduction in accidents from self-driving vehicles will diminish the need for insurance. Roughly 90% of accidents are attributed at least in part to human error. Eliminating human drivers will shift the onus for carrying insurance to fleet owners or manufacturers. Given these companies have better negotiating power, they should be able to secure lower rates. Some may choose to self-insure as accident rates go down.[542]

New car dealerships are unlikely to survive unless they morph into test drive centers. Most people hate the car buying experience, so anything that allows leasing or purchase without dealership interaction will prove popular. In any case, the majority of consumers will no longer own their own car and those that do want to own or lease will deal directly with fleet operators. I can envision a future where 90% of the population will not own a car. Personal transportation will become a utility, like water or electricity, where cost is based on usage. Perhaps car salesmen can transfer their skills to become TV ad pitchmen.

Parking meters will go the way of the steering wheel. Without vehicle ownership, there is no need for public parking spaces.[543]

As technology evolves, smart driving software — like brake assists — will put less wear and tear on cars, likely necessitating fewer replacements. However, that doesn't mean AVs will be cheaper to maintain. Costs may simply shift to where value lies in an AV: computational power. In fact, Deloitte reports that electronics—such as microprocessors and chips—already account for 40% of a vehicle's total cost, and this will only increase with full autonomy. This means that traditional parts manufacturers will likely face competition from more technology-focused companies. For example, Nvidia's DRIVE Thor is a next-generation car computer that integrates autonomous driving and parking capabilities, driver and passenger monitoring and AI cockpit functionality, all into a single AI computer platform.[544]

Intangible Benefits

The discernable benefits from the development of AVs are many and mostly evident. The intangible benefits, while harder to discern, are the ones that will be the primary drivers of productivity: enhanced creativity and culture, time and less stress.

For example, it's common knowledge that companies enjoy greater creativity and esprit de corps when employees regularly interact with one another as opposed to working in isolation. Businesses are more productive when workers engage and act as a group. Like a football team whose players, while competent, practice their skills individually but never together. They may have a hundred Zoom calls with other players and coaches, but if they never get together and coordinate their abilities, they're going to make mistakes when they go out to play and get their butts kicked.

It's no different in corporate America. Employees may enjoy the convenience of working at home but the companies that get their people together back in the office will be the winners. The problem has been convincing workers to get back into their cars and wage the daily battle with traffic to get to there. That's going to be one of the major intangible benefits of AVs. Not only will employees get more work done while traveling to and from work, they will have less stress, be happier and better focused.

A vitally important benefit of AV will be the reduction in traffic accidents, injuries and deaths. Even minor mishaps on the road are costly in terms of time lost and wasted resources. Consider the economic and human costs of a single fender bender. A minimum of two people have their day ruined as they exchange insurance information while waiting for police to come and take statements. That assumes the parties involved are mature and non-combative, in which case the stress and potential for additional damages increases. Meanwhile, the traffic in both directions comes to a crawl as drivers rubberneck to see what happened, increasing the probability of more accidents. Even if they manage to squeeze past the scene without incident, a couple thousand other people are now angry because they will be late to work and have to explain why it wasn't their fault.

The next day, the accident participants have the pleasure of explaining what happened all over again to their respective insurance adjusters. That's followed by a trip to the garage where the damaged vehicle was towed (hope you have towing coverage) to find out how long the car will be tied up for repairs (longer than you think). And unless the unfortunate accident victims have a second car and an understanding spouse, the next stop is the rental car agency (and you thought that $25 a day rental car benefit would cover your cost; not close). And by the way, did the nice police officer decide you were guilty of some infraction and issue you a ticket? Forget about beating the rap with an impassioned defense in court; just pay the ticket and accept it's yet another kick in the pants on your way back to driving normalcy.

All that angst, tension and cost will be eliminated once AVs are ubiquitous. Picture a world with less nail biting, no auto accidents and everybody getting to where they are going in a better mood. Pretty nice, although people are going to have to forego those gruesomely entertaining clips of an endless string of vehicles crunched into one another during a winter snowstorm. But they will find other amusements.

> *"They say the universe is expanding.*
> *That should help with the traffic."*

Stephen Wright

The productivity gains from artificial intelligence, machine learning, robotics, the mitigation or elimination of threats from space, adversaries, weather and pandemics, breakthroughs in energy, free trade and autonomous driving—all will contribute to a safer world, enhanced productivity, a vigorous economic environment and a robust, enduring stock market. That's cause for optimism and a brighter future for our offspring.

CHAPTER TWENTY-TWO

Breakthroughs and Market Implications

> *"You know you're getting old when you stoop to tie your shoelaces and wonder what else you could do while you're down there."*
>
> George Burns

There is ample evidence pointing to the fact that humans will continue to live incrementally longer lives. I am not a gerontologist, nor any other form of medical specialist, so for this chapter I have enlisted the aid of a genetics expert to ensure what I am saying is accurate. At first, longevity and life expectancy may not seem relevant to investment management but stay with me and you will see the connection.

It should be apparent to anyone paying attention that there is serious money being invested into aging and increased longevity research. The big question seems to be whether aging is inevitable or if it can be slowed or even reversed.

The average life expectancy in the US is roughly 79 years for women and 73 years for men (sorry guys), according to the CDC. That's a stunning gain from the start of the previous century when those numbers were 48 and 46 respectively. So, there is chronicled evidence that we have made remarkable progress in extending life. Despite these gains, cancer, heart disease, diabetes and other diseases have restrained further advances in longevity. So, is aging an inescapable disease or can science and technology deliver longer, healthier life expectancies?

In the Bible's Book of Genesis, there are numerous records of long-life spans for people back then. The fifth chapter reveals that Adam lived 930 years, Seth 912 years and Methuselah 969 years (Genesis 5:5,8,27). Separately and before the great flood, the Bible records Enosh lived 905 years, Cainan 910 years, Mahalaleel 895 years and Jared 962 years. The average age of those men is 912!

If they indeed lived to those incredible ages, how is it man's average life span took such a disheartening plunge in longevity after the first few generations? One explanation is that the early human genetic code developed few defects. Adam and Eve obviously were highly resistant to disease and illness. Their descendants would have inherited this benefit, perhaps to lesser degrees. Over time, the human genetic code became increasingly contaminated and human beings became more susceptible to disease and earlier deaths, resulting in drastically reduced lifespans.[545]

If some of our early ancestors indeed lived hundreds of years, it's likely they were born with the ability to repair cells for longer periods of time and so stay younger. There weren't many people around so pathogen and communicable disease interactions were rare. As people began to expand the territory they populated, whether through curiosity or the desire to discover whether something better lie over the next hill, more interactions occurred. This likely caused mutations that reduced the inherent ability to resist disease, turning off the DNA repair—or mitochondrial energy metabolism for you medical students reading this—shortening life spans.

It's quite possible that after a time, the general population, then with average life expectancies reduced to a few decades, were unaware that their ancestors ever lived to many hundreds of years. It probably did happen but people didn't know it. They would reproduce as early in life as possible before they died of disease.

As a result, we now die much sooner than our earliest ancestors but later than our more recent predecessors. That's our genetic inheritance. There are still people who live well into their 90s and some past 100, however. The question becomes, has this been caused by something that has changed in our environment or genetics and can we figure out how to reclaim living longer?

Perhaps the advanced ages of the patriarchs are not something we should regard as remarkable. It's entirely feasible that humans will someday live much longer life spans. The Bible predicts that in the future there will be people who will enjoy long life spans on earth. Whether you believe in the teachings of the Bible or not, there is increasing scientific evidence that not only are humans potentially capable of living hundreds of years, but ongoing research with other species is reinforcing that notion.

What is Aging?

How and why people change and age as they get older is a subject of continuous debate. There is no single established standard to define why aging occurs that garners universal consensus. Some believe aging is caused by simple wear and tear on the body. Others claim injuries from ultraviolet light are responsible. Still others contend it is simply a byproduct of metabolism, that is, the sum of all the physical and chemical processes in the body that convert or use energy. Others view aging as a predetermined process controlled by genes.

Most gerontologists feel that aging is due to the interaction of many lifelong influences, including heredity, environment, culture, diet, exercise and leisure, past illnesses and other factors.[546]

But the array of opinions that form the traditional description of aging is being challenged today by emerging technologies and discoveries that present a vastly different viewpoint.

David A. Sinclair, PhD, is a Genetics Professor at Harvard Medical School and serves as President of the Academy for Health and Lifespan Research. He is best known for his work on understanding why we age and how to slow its effects.[547] After years of researching aging in various organisms (yeast, worms, mice) David developed his theory of aging termed the "Information Theory of Aging." He explains that cells contain two main types of information: genetic information—which is our

DNA—and also epigenetic information—modifications to DNA that regulate whether genes are turned on or off.

Epigenetic information changes as we age. Sinclair believes this is a root cause of aging. Genes which shouldn't be switched on become active, as changes in epigenetic markers mean that the cell accesses large portions of DNA it shouldn't. This causes cells to lose their identity. They no longer behave as they should due to what can be described as cellular confusion, or as Sinclair calls it, "ex-differentiation."[548]

He maintains that aging isn't just damage to the body. Aging is actually a loss of access to information about certain genes that normally help the body regenerate (stay youthful) but no longer do so because they've been turned off. In most instances, the reason the genes have been turned off is methylation, a simple but critical biochemical process that transfers atoms from one substance to another. In simpler terms, methylation is the mechanism that permits the body's biological "gears and switches" to operate optimally by turning them on and off.[549]

Sinclair's work is about removing the methylations causing that in order to turn those genes back on and regenerate a more youthful cellular structure. This means that the progress traditional medicine has made in repairing the body's infirmities could be obsolete. Being able to rejuvenate at the cellular level means everything in the body can be made young again!

This is not only new thinking; it is a quantum leap forward in our understanding of why we age and also how to control the process. Sinclair's research shows that every cell contains two copies (or versions) of information that can be accessed and a switch that can literally "be flipped" to allow cells to reset their biological age and function as though they were young again.[550]

Each cell has two copies of a person's genetic information, one from each parent. The copies are homologous (similar) but not identical. When an individual contracts a disease, it's typically because one copy has a mutation that is dominant, with the other copy being normal and recessive. The dominant copy overrides the recessive copy. The reverse is also true. A person can have a recessive disease and not display any symptoms but may pass the disease on to their child, who inherits both parent's recessive copies of the disease.

Most people would be shocked to learn about the battle that goes on inside their body every day. Their immune system fights a continuous war against illnesses and infections in the form of pathogens, viruses, bacteria and mutated cells that are programmed to do harm.[551]

When you are young, your immune system is on point, banishing most microscopic menaces before they can cause trouble. So, for example, if you have a skin mutation such as a melanoma, that cell is going to give off certain metabolic signals and your young immune system will dispense cytotoxic T cells (lymphocytes) through your circulatory system to kill the cancer—or any other type of bacteria or intruder. That's how potential threats are stopped when you are young and healthy.

Later in life, your immune system gradually becomes compromised, sometimes to the point of being decrepit. The cells in your DNA repair don't work as well because your body has aged and the metabolic pathways that helped energize and keep your cells healthy have deteriorated.

Your body continually replaces your cells, typically some 330 billion daily. Every 90 days, some 30 trillion cells are replenished—the equivalent of a new you. This is not growth; it's merely replacement of cells that have a finite lifespan. If we did not have anatomical cell replication, we would die within a few months. But this cell replication slows down as we get older, which is why we age. Our bodies simply don't replicate our cells as fast or as well.[552]

We know, however, that there are multiple species that age much slower than humans and some that don't appear to age at all. These includes certain jellyfish, lobsters, turtles, flatworms, horseshoe crabs and bowhead whales, the oldest having lived 211 years. If the jellyfish is injured or sick, it returns to its polyp stage over a three-day period, transforming its cells into a younger state that will eventually grow into adulthood all over again.[553] Thus, barring death from disease or predator, these jellyfish could live virtually forever.

Speaking of eternity, consider tardigrades, microscopic creatures capable of avoiding death indefinitely by entering a state of cryptobiosis, whereby their metabolism comes to a halt. Almost unbelievably, tardigrades can survive 300-degree temperatures, up to 30 years without food or water, even several days in space.[554]

There may be hundreds—if not thousands—of species that live hundreds of years and science has no idea they exist. It's entirely plausible that their metabolisms are all doing the same thing, or at least something very similar. If the whales, sharks and lobster all have the same genes that allow them to stay alive for hundreds of years, do humans have those same genes latent in their genome? And if not, can they be inserted?

Whether humans have the same cellular "machinery" remains an unanswered question. If we don't, it's going to be a really difficult and time-consuming task to get it into us. But if we do have that machinery, it will be a game changer.

Those that guffawed at the stories of ancient people living hundreds of years will probably be the first in line to have their machinery tweaked. As I said, it's a game changer.

> *"I intend to live forever, or die trying."*
>
> Groucho Marx

Point Mutations and Aging

Genes are segments of DNA that contain instructions for building the molecules—most of which are proteins—that make the body work. A genome is all of the genetic material in an organism. It is made of DNA (or RNA in some viruses) and includes genes and other elements that control the activity of those genes.[555]

Mutations are constantly occurring in the genome. Point mutations (substitutions, insertions, deletions) alter the DNA sequence that is responsible for several genetic disorders and cancers. They have been important molecular biomarkers for disease diagnosis and surveillance.

The vast majority of inherited diseases are single point nucleotide mutations. An example is progeria, a rare and deadly progressive genetic disorder that causes children to age rapidly. The average lifespan is 14 years.[556] Progeria is the result of a single point mutation within a single gene that causes every process within the body to expire prematurely.

Researchers envision a future where a full DNA workup is done, ideally at the embryonic stage, or immediately after childbirth, to identify potential genetic issues, such as single point mutations. Positive tests would then result in gene therapy that would eliminate the threat and allow for normal development.

Point mutations can occur not only in the DNA, but in the RNA as well. In humans, the double-stranded DNA and RNA are complementary in their function of generating the vital amino acids required for cells to thrive. However, when a multiple or single point mutation occurs, the result can lead to an alteration (or more) that can be difficult to trace or to fully understand.[557]

Attacking single point mutations promises to be the fastest and easiest way to repair genetic disorders because they are so specific and have a low level of side effects caused by errant mutations. They are also one of the therapies most likely to become commercially viable in treating inherited diseases.

Centenarians

Centenarians represent a rare phenotype (observable characteristics or traits) appearing in roughly 10 to 20 out of 100,000 persons in most industrialized countries but as high as 40 to 50 out of 100,000 persons in Okinawa, Japan. Their ability to live such long lives seems due to either having genes that decrease susceptibility to diseases associated with old age or genetic variations that affect the rate of aging.

Okinawans are a distinct group, having less genetic diversity and greater clustering of gene variants related to longevity.[558] Regions of Ikaria, Greece and Sardinia, Italy were also found to have similar large numbers of centenarians. What the three regions have in common is that they are relatively isolated from the broader population in their countries, are lower income, have little industrialization and tend to follow a traditional (non-Western) lifestyle.[559]

Blue Zones

These three groups, as well as the centenarians living in the Nicoya Peninsula of Costa Rica and Seventh-day Adventists living in Loma Linda, California, have been identified as "Blue Zones" by Dan Buettner in his book, *The Blue Zones*. He describes them as areas of the world in which people live exceptionally long lives. He coined the term because he and his associates drew blue dots on a map to identify the areas. Their studies concluded that genetics "probably" only accounted for 20-30% of longevity. The rest was due to environmental factors, including diet and lifestyle:

- Icaria: A Mediterranean diet rich in olive oil, red wine and homegrown vegetables.
- Sardinia: A mountainous region of Italy where people typically work on farms and drink lots of red wine. (Yeah, that one caught my eye too.)
- Okinawa; Soy-based foods and tai chi, a meditative form of exercise.
- Nicoya Peninsula: A diet based on beans and corn tortillas and a unique sense of life purpose known as "plan de vida."
- The Seventh-day Adventists in Loma Linda: Strict vegetarians living in tight-knit communities.[560]

Buettner and his associates found nine common denominators among centenarians that are believed to slow the aging process:

- They move naturally, without thinking about it. They grow gardens and do not have mechanical conveniences to do house and yard work.
- They have purpose for living.

- While they do experience stress, they have routines to diffuse it, whether taking naps or meditating.
- Okinawans have a 2,500-year-old Confucian mantra said before meals to remind them to stop eating when their stomachs are 80% full.
- Diets centered around beans of all types. Meat, eaten on an average of just 5 times monthly, is mostly pork in small servings.
- Moderate wine consumption.
- All but 5 of the 263 centenarians interviewed belonged to some faith-based community. Denomination did not seem to matter.
- Aging parents and grandparents lived nearby or in the home with younger family members.
- Social circles that support healthy behaviors. Okinawans created moais—groups of 5 friends that committed to each other for life.[561]

While Blue Zone research found that long life included avoiding obesity, smoking and heavy use of alcohol, that's not always the case with centenarians. One study[562] found that up to 60% of Ashkenazi Jewish centenarians smoked heavily most of their lives, half had been obese for the same period of time, less than half did even moderate exercise and under 3% were vegetarians. Despite this, they have half the prevalence of cardiovascular disease of their peers.

Scientists studying centenarians conclude there is something genetically exceptional about them in that they might carry unusual genetic variants that extend lifespan. Several studies have shown that centenarians have as many bad genetic variants as the general population. Some even carry the most common risk gene for Alzheimer's disease but don't get the illness.[563]

Today's embryonic testing is able to identify disease susceptibility. It's simply a matter of time, money and supercomputing that will enable full DNA diagnostics and the elimination of some single nucleotide diseases like diabetes, cancer, schizophrenia, high blood pressure, heart disease and Alzheimer's through gene therapy. Once able to solve the riddle of these diseases, it's logical to assume science will continue to evolve and decipher DNA and cell repair, ultimately leading to human longevity.

In 2018, the journal *Science* published a study by demographers Elisabetta Barbi of the University of Rome and Kenneth Wachter of the University of California, Berkeley. They and their associates examined nearly 4,000 Italians and concluded that, while the risk of death increased up to age 80, it then slowed and eventually plateaued. Someone alive at 105 had about a 50 percent chance of living to the next year. The same was true at ages 106, 107, 108 and 109. Their findings, the authors wrote, "strongly suggest that longevity is continuing to increase over time, and that a limit, if any, has not been reached."[564]

We spoke to John Eberth, MS PhD and Postdoctor Scholar at the University of Kentucky College of Medicine's Department of Psychology about genetic advancements:

"Now that we have the ability to turn specific genes on and off, as well as repair mutated genes, the next step is to figure out if we indeed are destined to live much longer lives. Most people are unaware of the technology being developed. Given there are already many centenarians, gene technology is literally only a couple of steps away from people in the next generation living to 150 years. That's how close it is. Our grandchildren are likely going to have the option of gene therapy fixing whatever ails them with no or minimal consequences. I believe those advancements are likely to happen within the next 20 years with the use of AI in medical research. Without AI, I don't believe that timeline is realistic."

Longevity Research and Technology

Funding for longevity research has exploded in recent years, thanks to rapid advancements in technology such as AI and supercomputers. Experiments which previously took many months or years to complete can now deliver results in real time, thanks to supercomputing capabilities. Investors that balked at putting money into research where outcomes lay on some distant horizon are now ponying up with checkbooks in hand, thanks to the promise of swift conclusions.

Many of these are Silicon Valley's tech titans. In 2022, Altos Labs, a partial cellular reprogramming company, drew billions from investors including Amazon's Jeff Bezos and Yuri Milner, founder of Digital Sky Technologies. Google founders Sergey Brin and Larry Page have invested billions into Calico, a lifespan tech. PayPal founder Peter Thiel is a backer of Unity Biotechnology, specializing in the science of aging.[565]

Medical science decision-making has new momentum, thanks to AI using advanced machine learning (ML) algorithms. ML is a statistical technique for fitting models to data and to "learn" by training models with data.[566] The most complex forms of ML involve "deep learning"—neural network models with multiple levels of variables to predict outcomes. There may be thousands of hidden features in such models, revealed by the faster processing of modern graphics processing units and cloud architectures. One application of deep learning in healthcare is recognition of potentially cancerous lesions in radiology images.[567] It is also increasingly being applied to radiomics—the detection of clinically relevant features in imaging data beyond what can be perceived by the human eye.[568] The combination of radiomics and deep learning appears to promise greater accuracy in diagnosis than the previous generation of automated tools for image analysis, known as computer-aided detection or CAD.[569]

ML is also being used to create the structure of new drugs, revolutionizing the discovery process. High-throughput data such as proteomics, genomics, chemoproteomics and phenomics, combined with AI technology and supercomputers, facilitate complex ML methods to preprocess massive amounts of data and identify insightful correlations.[570]

Recent advancements in healthcare demonstrate the effectiveness of AI technology in a variety of applications. As it relates to longevity, AI's ability to analyze the immense range of data allows researchers to identify patterns, relationships, and evaluate factors in age-related diseases. In turn, they are better able to develop potential solutions and test them to ensure their feasibility.[571]

An impressive example of AI forwarding healthcare diagnoses is a study published in *Nature*[572] by Dr. Cheng Peng and his colleagues at the University of Florida. It posed the question of whether AI could ease the load on doctors by accurately answering medical queries. While language models like ChatGPT can create probable answers based on large datasets and statistics, these models are not medically oriented.

So, Peng's team went about creating a model trained specifically with clinical healthcare datasets. Named GatorTronGPT, the model was exposed to 82 billion words of clinical text and a "Pile" dataset to help communicate effectively.

The remarkable result was that the model was able to answer queries with the clinical relevance of actual physicians and text as readable as real medical text. Given GatorTronGPT's enhanced medical aptitude, it's highly likely that it—or a similar model—will be used in the analysis of clinical text, documentation of patient reports, scheduling and other areas of patient diagnoses and general healthcare.[573]

We know that aging plays a crucial role in the onset of many diseases. Preventative measures to treat aging at the molecular level may provide more benefits than reactive approaches targeting a single disease or organ, which do not extend our current average lifespans.

Ramkumar Hariharan, a senior scientist at the Institute for Experiential AI at Northeastern University, focuses on human longevity using machine learning and AI. Research is directed at using genomic datasets in biomedicine. He believes that even if scientists were successful in curing cancer, the most it would add to the average life expectancy would be two to three years. That's because, "if cancer doesn't get you, something else will: a car crash, heart disease or Alzheimer's," he notes. He says aging is the single biggest risk factor for developing any one of these diseases and if aging can be slowed, the expectation is to get a life-expectancy increase of 30 to 35 years![574]

Caloric Restriction and Fasting

> *"Part of the secret of success in life is to eat what you like and let the food fight it out inside."*
>
> Mark Twain

Volumes have been written linking the effects of various dietary factors with health and longevity. There exists incontrovertible proof that the number of calories consumed is linked to the risk of many major age-related diseases. As high-energy intake increases, the risks of cardiovascular disease, type 2 diabetes, stroke, cancers and other disorders increases. Saturated fats, cholesterol and trans-fats tend to cause disease while diets high in simple sugars increase the risk of diabetes. Conversely, diets rich in vegetables, fruits, fish and nuts tend to repress the onset of age-related diseases.[575]

Most living organisms, humans included, have circadian rhythms or cycles, the daily sleep-wake patterns. In response to our environment, the human brain receives signals that activate certain hormones, such as melatonin and cortisol, modifies body temperature and regulates our metabolism. When our circadian rhythm is disrupted, we can experience health issues in our organs, metabolism, cardiovascular system, gastrointestinal system and even our skin. The interruption can also render us more susceptible to diabetes, obesity and even mental health issues.[576]

A study of lab mice by neuroscientists at UT Southwestern's Peter O'Donnell Jr. Brain Institute illustrated the importance of not only how much food is consumed but when. Timing feedings to match the active period of the circadian cycle extended the life span of the mice more than three times as much as caloric restriction alone. Restricting calories by 30-40% but making food available around the clock extended mice lives only 10%.

Restricting the same reduced-calorie diet to the inactive period of the circadian cycle boosted lifespan by nearly 20% while restricting the same diet to the active period of the cycle extended their median life almost 35%. Additionally, the mice that lived the longest had significantly better metabolic health and tended to get diseases that killed the younger mice, such as various forms of cancer, at far more advanced ages.[577]

Most of us are aware of the factors that tend to increase our longevity: proper diet, regular exercise, avoid smoking, etc. But sometimes, it takes clinical research to open our eyes to the stunning impact a healthy lifestyle can have on how long we not only live but live without significant disease.

Researchers from Harvard University collected data from men and women in two different studies involving five low-risk lifestyle factors: healthy diet, regular exercise, healthy weight, no smoking and moderate alcohol intake. Compared with those who did not incorporate any of the factors, those with all five lived up to 14 years longer. In a follow-up study, the researchers found that the factors might contribute to not just a longer but also a healthier life. Women at age 50 who practiced four or five of the healthy habits lived 10 more years free of diabetes, cardiovascular diseases and cancer than women who did not. Men lived 7 years longer.[578]

Intermittent Fasting

Intermittent fasting (IF) is an eating plan that switches between fasting and eating on a regular schedule. Most diets focus on *what* to eat; IF is all about *when* to eat.

During prehistoric times, before humans learned to farm, they were hunters and gatherers who evolved to survive for long periods without eating. It was a necessary evolution as it required a lot of time and energy to hunt game and gather nuts and berries. As recently as a half century ago, maintaining a healthy weight was easier. There were no computers, and TV shows turned off at 11 p.m.; people stopped eating and went to bed. Portions were smaller. More people worked and played outside and, in general, got more exercise.

With internet, social media and other entertainment available 24/7, people stay awake longer and are more inactive. Extra calories and less activity can mean a higher risk of obesity, type 2 diabetes, heart disease and other illnesses. Scientific studies are showing that IF may help reverse these trends.[579]

IF influences hormone levels, cell repair and metabolic rate and is linked to longer life with enhanced health. IF activates autophagy (a process where new healthy cells regenerate) and also produces metabolic changes, where it switches from burning glucose to fatty acids.

Common approaches to IF include:

- Time restricted feeding (TRF): Commonly referred to as the 16:8 Method, involves limiting daily eating window to 8 hours followed by a 16-hour overnight fast.
- Alternate day fasting: Eating freely on non-fasting days and consuming about 25% of daily calorie needs on fasting days.
- 5:2 diet: Restricting intake to 500-600 calories two days a week and normal eating the other five days.[580]

An array of animal and human studies has shown that alternating between times of fasting and eating supports cellular health, probably by triggering an age-old adaptation to periods of food scarcity called metabolic switching. Such a switch occurs when cells use up their stores of rapidly accessible fuel and begin converting fat into energy in a slower metabolic process. Preliminary studies suggest that IF could also benefit brain health. A 2019 clinical trial at the University of Toronto found that 220 healthy, nonobese adults who maintained a calorie restricted diet for two years showed signs of improved memory in a battery of cognitive tests. Fasting or a pharmaceutical equivalent that mimics it may help stave off neurodegeneration and dementia.[581]

Hormesis

Hormesis is a relatively new area of research. The term comes from the Greek word meaning "to excite." It refers to tiny doses of toxins that act in a completely different manner than large doses within the body and may be beneficial. Hormesis activate the body's immune system in response to intrusions. It was first noted with respect to radiation. While it was clear that radiation could cause cancer, researchers also learned that extremely low doses could stimulate DNA repair and delay cancer in mice. There is even some human epidemiological data suggesting that people exposed to low dose radiation have a reduced risk of developing cancer. Dioxins, perhaps the most notorious toxins of all, have been shown to have advantageous effects at low doses in animal experiments, where animals fed low doses of dioxins actually developed fewer liver tumors than those that had no exposure at all.

If hormesis fulfills its promise, scientists may have to rethink how they evaluate toxicity. Humans may someday be ingesting low-dose arsenic tablets to ward off disease! Toward that goal, researchers now contend that a yeast metabolite, toxic at high doses, actually may help humans live longer when consumed in small amounts. That yeast metabolite is alcohol.[582]

Promising Drugs and Technology

Metformin

Metformin is a drug approved to treat diabetes but subsequent clinical tests have demonstrated that it may target a number of aging-related mechanisms. As it relates to aging, metformin leads to decreased insulin levels and insulin-like growth factor signaling, and inhibition of mTOR—a protein that regulates cell growth. These have been linked to shortened lifespans, cancers and other chronic health conditions.[583] Metformin also reduces DNA damage and the development of age-related conditions, such as inflammation autophagy (the body's method of cleaning out damaged cells) and cellular senescence (when cells stop multiplying but fail to die off as they should). Data from several randomized clinical trials and multiple observational studies provide evidence that metformin can delay aging.[584]

Nir Barzilai, director of the Institute for Aging Research at New York's Albert Einstein College of Medicine, notes that when he first began in the 1990's, discovering drugs that prevented the effects of anti-aging were thought to be merely a hope. Today, he says "We are done with hope and promise. We are at the point between having promise and realizing it." He is now conducting a flagship trial to test whether metformin can extend lifespan by years, after a promising UK patient study.[585]

Rapamycin

Rapamycin (Sirolimus) is a prophylactic anti-aging drug that decelerates early development of age-related diseases. From its initial usage twenty years ago as an immunosuppressant—medicines that inhibit or decrease the intensity of the body's immune response—used to treat renal transplant patients, rapamycin has been an "unlucky" drug. That's because if it had been used as an anti-inflammatory and immunomodulator—a medicine that helps *modulate* the body's immune system in response to disease or illness—it would have had much greater appeal today. In anti-aging doses, rapamycin rejuvenates immunity,[586] especially in cancer patients, organ transplant patients and the elderly.[587]

Sirtuins

Sirtuins are a family of proteins that have been identified as a critical factor in the regulation of aging and disease. They can be activated through diet and exercise, and have been linked to numerous conditions, including Alzheimer's, Parkinson's, diabetes and cardiovascular diseases.[588]

Dr David Sinclair reportedly has successfully reversed his biological age by 10 years through a personal regimen—diet, exercise, stress management and fasting—that triggers sirtuin enzymes. Sinclair believes the discomfort from fasting is one of its most important benefits: "If you are hungry for part of the day or part of the week, your body biologically says, 'Holy crap, I could run out of food here. I need to build survival mechanisms.' And so, it ends up doing that through these sirtuin enzymes," says Sinclair. [589]

A Harvard Medical School study led by Sinclair and published in the scientific journal *Aging* appears to be on the verge of discovering the proverbial Fountain of Youth. His team identified six separate chemical concoctions which, in less than a week and without compromising cellular identity, restored a youthful genome-wide transcript profile and reversed transcriptomic age. Thus, rejuvenation by age reversal can be achieved, not only by genetic, but also chemical means.[590] Sinclair sees it as a step towards "affordable whole-body rejuvenation." The researchers utilized high-throughput cell-based assays to distinguish young cells from their older, senescent counterparts.[591] Adds Sinclair, "This discovery offers the potential to reverse aging with a single pill, with applications ranging from improving eyesight to effectively treating age-related diseases."[592]

Spermidine

Polyamines are polycations—molecule or chemical complexes having positive charges at several sites—that interact with negatively charged molecules such as DNA, RNA and proteins. They play various roles in cell growth, survival and proliferation and changes in polyamine levels have been associated with aging and diseases. Their levels decline continuously with age.[593]

Spermidine, one of the polyamines, synchronizes an array of biological processes and is a longevity agent in mammals. It induces cellular rejuvenation (autophagy), enhances memory and in preclinical tests, appears to improve cognitive function in rodents. Spermidine is present in many vegetables, mushrooms, soybean products, wheat germ and cheeses like cheddar, parmesan and gruyere.[594]

Peptides

Peptides are smaller versions of proteins. Both are comprised of amino acids and are naturally present in foods like eggs, milk, meat, shellfish, beans and supplements. They may provide pro-aging support, anti-inflammatory, or muscle-building properties.[595]

Research indicates they may lower blood pressure, kill microbes, reduce inflammation and prevent blood clots. Insulin-like peptides are used in the treatment of diabetes.

Bioactive peptides—sequences of an amino acid, usually 2 to 20 acids—produce signal boosters the body recognizes. These peptides exhibit myriad pharmacological activities including cardioprotective, antimicrobial, antioxidant and mineral binding properties, all collectively improving health span.[596]

Peptides can help with longevity by promoting cellular health, reducing inflammation and enhancing the body's natural defense mechanisms. Chronic inflammation can lead to cardiovascular disease, diabetes, and cognitive decline. By reducing inflammation, peptides can help to prevent or delay the onset of these and other age-related conditions. In addition to their direct effects on cellular health and inflammation, peptides can also enhance the body's natural defense mechanisms against stress and disease. Some peptides have been shown to stimulate the production of antioxidant enzymes that can help to protect cells from oxidative stress and damage. Others can improve immune function, which can help to prevent infection and other health problems.[597]

Many peptides are currently being studied for use in treating different kinds of cancers. Research shows that atrial natriuretic peptide (ANP), for instance, can be potentially effective in treating colorectal cancer.[598]

Using AI to Predict Clinical Trial Outcomes

A number of research studies suggest that AI can perform as well as or better than humans at key healthcare tasks, such as diagnosing disease. Today, algorithms are already outperforming radiologists at spotting malignant tumors and guiding researchers in how to construct clinical trials.

The healthcare industry is apt to reap enormous benefits from AI as the growing demands of aging populations promise to continue to strain dated healthcare systems. Medical AI creating automated processes in healthcare could significantly increase efficiency, reduce spending and enhance patient care and health outcomes. In fact, several AI models that can outperform physicians in diagnostic accuracy already exist and are being utilized.[599]

A biotech startup, BioPhy, uses AI to dramatically accelerate drug development and more accurately predict the success of clinical trials. The technology has predicted the outcomes of over 1,500 clinical trials with 80% accuracy, which the company says is a five-fold increase in accuracy over traditional methods. That means pharmaceutical firms could save millions of dollars in clinical development utilizing the company's platform.[600]

Stem Cell Therapy

Stem cells are the cells from which all other cells with specialized functions are generated. They are the human body's "raw materials." Stem cells divide to form more cells called daughter cells, which in turn become either new stem cells or cells with a specific function, such as blood cells, brain cells, heart muscle cells or bone cells. No other cell in the body has the natural ability to generate new cell types.[601]

Stem cell therapy is a form of regenerative medicine designed to repair damaged cells within the body by reducing inflammation and modulating the immune system. Various forms have been used to treat autoimmune, inflammatory, neurological, orthopedic conditions and traumatic injuries. Currently, studies are being conducted for its use in the treatment of Crohn's disease, Multiple Sclerosis, Lupus, COPD, Parkinson's, ALS and stroke recovery. While new stem cell therapies don't necessarily cure these conditions, the premise is to allow the body to heal itself sufficiently to reduce the symptoms for long periods.[602]

Reverse Aging; Game Changer

Yamanaka Factors

In 2006 Dr. Shinya Yamanaka, a stem-cell researcher at Kyoto University, amazed biologists by showing that a cell's fate could be reversed with a set of four transcription factors—agents that activate genes—that he had identified. A cell dosed with the Yamanaka factors erases the marks on the epigenome, so the cell loses its identity and reverts to the embryonic state. Erroneous marks gathered during aging are also lost in the process, restoring the cell to its state of youth. Dr. Yamanaka shared the 2012 Nobel Prize in medicine for the work.[603]

Epigenetic effects are basically methylation of your genome leaving things off or restricting access to things as you age. Dr Yamanaka's research essentially explains that the methylation is getting removed from your epigenome, which is your genome with all of its environmental aging that it's experienced.

The Yamanaka factors (Oct3/4, Sox2, Klf4, c-Myc) are a group of protein transcription factors that play a vital role in the creation of stem cells. They control how DNA is copied for translation into other proteins. A 2020 paper published in *Nature* by a research team from Harvard Medical School showed that using Yamanaka factors, neurons in the eye can be reset to a "youthful state" in which their ability to regenerate is switched back on.[604]

The research that was the basis for the paper is one of the most important breakthroughs in reprogramming cells. The team of Harvard scientists, led by David Sinclair and Yuancheng Lu, successfully restored vision in mice by turning back the clock on aged eye cells in the retina. The treatment had multiple beneficial effects on the eye. First, it promoted nerve regeneration following optic-nerve injury in mice with damaged optic nerves. Second, it reversed vision loss in animals with a condition mimicking human glaucoma. Finally, it reversed vision loss in aging animals without glaucoma.

This represented the first demonstration that it may be possible to safely reprogram complex tissues, such as the nerve cells of the eye, to an earlier age. In addition to resetting the cells' aging clock, the researchers successfully reversed vision loss in animals with a condition mimicking human glaucoma, a leading cause of blindness around the world. The achievement represents the first successful attempt to reverse glaucoma-induced vision loss, rather than merely stem its progression. If replicated through further studies, the approach could pave the way for therapies to promote tissue repair across various organs and reverse aging and age-related diseases in humans.[605]

Thymus; the Master Gland

Dr. Greg Fahy is a world-renowned cryobiologist and co-founder of Intervene Immune, a company which pioneers treatments for thymus regeneration and age-related immune system decline. His pilot study, thymic rejuvenation and immunorestoration and insulin mitigation (TRIIM), discovered that a drug cocktail of dehydroepiandrosterone—a hormone produced by the adrenal glands that the body uses to make androgens and estrogens, the male and female sex hormones—(DHEA), metformin and growth hormone could rejuvenate the thymus. The result for many in the study was a 2.5-year reversal of age after a single dose!

The thymus is sometimes called the master gland of the immune system, and the immune system deteriorates with age because of deterioration of the thymus, known as thymic involution. It's a process that depletes the functionality of T cells which are needed to protect the body from infectious disease and cancer. It's an unlikely "coincidence" that people tend to die in large numbers around the time their thymus stops working. Other things are probably happening but many relate to immune system integrity. For example, age-related inflammation is probably associated with vascular disease and vascular disease is associated with heart disease, a major killer.

There are many questions about how the thymus relates to aging. What would happen if humans didn't experience age-related inflammation associated with the thymus?

There are studies in mouse models that show that if you take a thymus from a young mouse and transplant into an old mouse it rejuvenates aspects of brain, liver, thyroid and insulin physiology. This suggests a connection between immune system aging in general.[606]

Gene Editing Drugs

Gene editing (also called genome editing) is technology that can change an organism's DNA. This allows genetic material to be added, removed or altered at particular locations in the genome.

Genome editing holds great promise in the prevention and treatment of human diseases. It is being explored in research and clinical trials for a wide variety of diseases, including single-gene disorders such as cystic fibrosis, hemophilia and sickle cell disease. It also holds promise for more complex diseases, such as cancer, heart disease, mental illness and human immunodeficiency virus (HIV) infection.[607]

CRISPR

Several approaches to genome editing have been developed, one of which is called CRISPR-Cas9 (CRISPR), short for clustered regularly interspaced short palindromic repeats. It's a method of finding and altering a specific bit of DNA inside a cell. CRISPR can also be adapted to do other things, such as turning genes on or off without altering their sequence. CRISPR has generated a lot of excitement in the scientific community because it is faster, cheaper, more accurate and more efficient than other genome editing methods.[608]

CRISPR can be programmed to target specific stretches of genetic code and to edit DNA at precise locations. Researchers can permanently modify genes in living cells and organisms which may make it possible to correct mutations at precise locations in the human genome in order to treat genetic causes of disease.

Many gene therapies add copies of modified genes to correct a defect. CRISPR can edit the DNA sequence for a desired change and the editing is more accessible than other methods, making CRISPR-based research easier and more affordable.

The first CRISPR therapy, exagamglogene autotemcel, known as exa-cel, became the first ever CRISPR-based gene editing drug to receive regulatory approval in 2023. The therapy is made by CRISPR Therapeutics (CRSP) and Vertex Pharmaceuticals (VRTX), the former being one of the major gene-editing companies currently exploring the commercialization of CRISPR-based therapeutics. [609]

On December 8, 2023, the U.S. Food and Drug Administration officially approved the use of Vertex Pharmaceuticals' drug, Casgevy, to treat sickle cell disease, a landmark decision that ushers in the new form of medicine that turns off or replaces genes to tackle conditions that have long confounded doctors and researchers.[610]

Just one month later, Casgevy received FDA approval to treat transfusion-dependent beta thalassemia, a genetic disorder that hinders production of hemoglobin in the blood, requiring sufferers to undergo continuous blood transfusions. This marks the second major U.S. regulatory approval for the emerging gene-editing technology.[611]

Genome Editing and Therapies

While CRISPR may be the most recently discovered technique, it certainly isn't the only tool for the manipulation of DNA. Genome editing is a process where an organism's genetic code is changed. There are several available tools for gene editing, all of which use enzymes that act on DNA called nucleases. The different editing tools act on a similar basic principle: the enzyme is directed to a specific target site in the genome by either a guide sequence or by specific DNA binding domains within the nuclease itself. Once it recognizes and binds to the target DNA, the nuclease can be used for editing via several pathways.[612]

Genome editing is one form of gene therapy— a treatment that modifies the genome of specific cells to treat or prevent a genetic disease. There are various methods used to carry out gene therapy. A common method is using a viral delivery system called a viral vector, which delivers a functional copy of a single gene into the cells of a target organ or tissue. It works by packaging a functional gene into a virus, such as an adeno-associated virus or a lentivirus, then delivers the packaged gene into the patient's genome. One difficulty is that the longer human genes cannot fit into the viral package. In addition, many viruses can insert their genetic material into the host DNA at seemingly random locations, when that happens, it can disturb non-target genes, potentially causing harm.[613]

Gene therapies are being used to treat a small number of diseases, including an eye disorder called Leber congenital amaurosis (severe visual impairment) and a muscle disorder called spinal muscular atrophy, a genetic disorder characterized by weakness and wasting in muscles.[614]

An amazing breakthrough occurred in January 2024 when an experimental gene therapy from Eli Lilly & Co. restored the hearing of a child who was born deaf. The child, an 11-year-old participating in a clinical study, enjoyed restored hearing within 30 days of the treatment, and was the first individual in the U.S. to receive the therapy for a genetic form of hearing loss. The gene therapy, AK-OTOF, is being developed for the treatment of hearing loss due to mutations in the otoferlin gene. [615]

There are several approaches to gene therapy. Some cells become diseased because certain genes work incorrectly or fail altogether. Replacing these defective genes may help treat certain diseases. Several types of cancer have been linked to problems with a gene called p53, for example, which normally prevents tumor growth. Replacing the mutated p53 gene could trigger the cancer cells to die. In some instances, mutated genes can be repaired or turned off so that they no longer promote disease. Also, healthy genes could be turned on to inhibit disease. In other cases, the immune system doesn't attack diseased cells because it doesn't recognize them as invaders. A type of gene therapy could cause the immune system to recognize the cells that are a threat.[616]

There are also options for how to spread the genetic change to all the cells that need to be changed. If the altered cell is a reproductive cell, then a few such cells could be changed and the change would reach the other somatic cells—cells that were created as the organism developed. But if the change were made to a somatic cell, changing all the other relevant somatic cells one at a time would be impractical due to the sheer number of such cells. A common approach to reach somatic cells is to use a carrier or vector—a molecule or organism. A virus, as previously mentioned, could be used as a vector. The virus would be an innocuous one or changed so as not to cause disease. It would be injected with the genetic material and then as it reproduces and "infects" the target cells, it would introduce the new genetic material. Fat particles and chemicals have also been used as vectors because they can penetrate the cell membrane and move into the cell nucleus with the new genetic material.[617]

AAVs

Adeno-associated viruses (AAVs) have become a favored means of delivering DNA to target cells because they are unlikely to cause cancer-triggering insertions and may contribute to long-term efficacy. That according to new research from the University of Pennsylvania's Gene Therapy Program (GTP). Virus-delivered gene therapies have been investigated for several decades, with eight having been approved by the FDA. Most use AAVs to deliver their gene payloads. Viruses evolved to break into cells, and gene therapy researchers have long viewed them as the go-to carriers or "vectors" for therapeutic transgenes. AAVs are the most commonly used viral vectors for gene therapies because they can enter both dividing and non-dividing cells, don't cause viral illness in humans, and usually don't trigger an immune response—which would swiftly degrade their therapeutic impact.[618]

In 2017, after a series of clinical trials, the FDA approved an AAV, voretigene neparvovecrzyl (marketed as Luxturna) for the treatment of any heritable retinal dystrophy caused by the mutated *RPE65* gene, including retinitis pigmentosa, a congenital eye disease that affects photoreceptors in the retina. Those treated show significant improvement: patients who were once unable to see clearly had their vision restored, often very quickly. Some reported that, after the injections, they could see stars for the first time.[619]

Somatic vs Germline Gene Therapy

Gene therapy can be performed either directly in body cells (somatic) or within the egg or sperm cells (germline) so that the change is passed to future generations. In somatic cells, the changed genome is not passed on to offspring. In germline gene therapy, changes made to the genome of a patient's egg or sperm will be transmitted to offspring, avoiding the genetic disease in subsequent generations. While somatic cell gene therapy is being actively pursued, germline gene therapy is not under active investigation due, in part, to the ethical questions relating to the permanent alteration of the genome of an unborn child.[620]

There is speculation about the ethical aspects of gene therapy. Nonetheless, it appears that some forms of somatic—if not germline—gene therapies will be fully developed. Many of the objections to germline gene therapy contend that there is something wrong because of the direct intervention in the genome. It is not clear how germline therapy differs from other medical treatments currently available, however. What seems clear is that the issues raised by gene therapy will continue to be debated as genetic technologies advance.[621]

Gene therapy has transformed from its inception in the late 1970s to a clinically effective therapy today. Diseases for which there were no treatments back then can now be treated with gene therapy in experimental settings. In the near future, gene therapy will become part of the "routine" treatments offered to patients—not as an experimental therapy but as a regular therapeutic option, much like chemotherapy or radiotherapy.[622]

Ginger the Gene-Edited Calf

The cattle industry suffers billions of dollars in losses each year as a result of cows acquiring bovine diarrhea (BVBD), a highly contagious virus that can be disastrous to pregnant cows because it can infect developing calves, causing spontaneous abortions and low birth rates. Despite more than 50 years of vaccine availability, hundreds of thousands of cattle die annually from BVDV as the vaccines are often ineffective.

Scientists working on the problem discovered the main cellular receptor (CD46) and the area where the virus binds to that receptor, causing the infection. A proof-of-concept study demonstrated the possibility of reducing BVDV via gene editing. The edited calf, dubbed Ginger, represents a breakthrough opportunity to lessen the need for antibiotics in agriculture since BVDV infection also puts calves at risk for secondary bacterial diseases.[623] The researchers manipulated the CD46 receptor gene so that cows will no longer need to be vaccinated for the problem. Ginger is not genetically susceptible to the virus. She is the foundation cow to a new breed that is completely resistant.

Another species involved in mutations is the simple worm. Scientists have found a way to lengthen worms' lives, having discovered a "double mutant" technique, when applied to nematode worms, makes them live five times longer than usual.[624] "The synergistic extension is really wild," said Jarod Rollins of the United States' MDI Biological Laboratory. "The effect isn't one plus one equals two; it's one plus one equals five."

"The discovery of the synergistic interaction could lead to the use of combination therapies, each affecting a different pathway, to extend healthy human lifespan in the same way that combination therapies are used to treat cancer and HIV," said Pankaj Kapahi of the Buck Institute for Research on Aging, who contributed to the research.[625]

A few creatures are so ageless that some scientists regard them as biologically immortal. Hydra, tiny relatives of jellyfish and corals, do not appear to age at all and can regenerate whole new bodies when sliced into pieces. When injured or threatened, a mature jellyfish can revert to its juvenile stage, mature and revert again, potentially forever.

Biologically immortal organisms are not impervious to death. They can still perish from lethal injury or infection, but they do not seem to die of their own accord. Theoretically, any organism with a continual supply of energy, a sufficient capacity for self-maintenance and repair and the good fortune to evade all environmental hazards could survive until the end of the universe.[626]

Speaking of worms, scientists can now test the effects of thousands of genetic mutations in one fell swoop using tiny worms. A new gene editing technique developed by University of Oregon researchers compresses what previously would have been years of work into just a few days, making new kinds of research possible in animal models. It will allow biologists to do experiments that compare many versions of a gene, hunting for mutations that lead to specific traits and tracking their evolution over time. Such research is often a first step towards identifying mutations that are relevant to human health or in unraveling the mechanisms behind human diseases.

While mass gene editing tricks have been developed for single-celled organisms like bacteria and yeast, this is the first time it has been possible on this scale in an animal. Scientists have many reasons why they might want the ability to create many genetic mutations at once. They might be hunting for a mutation that could make an animal resistant to a specific drug, better able to survive under certain conditions or less susceptible to a disease. They might need to screen dozens or even hundreds of possible variations on a gene to find the one that's most effective.

Those kinds of experiments are painstakingly slow in animals. Each mutant strain, a set of worms with a specific genetic modification, must be engineered individually. Making one mutant typically takes 7-10 hours. Using the new system, the same amount of labor that previously produced three or four mutations can now generate tens of thousands."[627]

If you need further optimism about longevity, an article from *UC San Diego Today* will provide it:

After identifying two distinct directions that cells follow during aging, researchers at the University of California San Diego used synthetic biology to engineer a solution that keeps cells from reaching their normal levels of deterioration associated with aging. Cells, including those of yeast, plants, animals and humans, all contain gene regulatory circuits that are responsible for many physiological functions, including aging. However, the group uncovered that, under the control of a central gene regulatory circuit, cells don't necessarily age the same way and envisioned a "smart aging process" that extends cellular longevity by cycling deterioration from one aging mechanism to another.

The researchers genetically rewired the circuit that controls cell aging. From its normal role functioning like a toggle switch, they engineered a negative feedback loop to stall the aging process. The rewired circuit operates as a clock-like device, called a gene oscillator, that drives the cell to periodically switch between two detrimental "aged" states, avoiding prolonged commitment to either, thereby slowing the cell's degeneration. These advances resulted in a dramatically extended cellular lifespan, setting a new record for life extension through genetic and chemical interventions.

The new synthetic biology achievement has the potential to reconfigure scientific approaches to age delay. Distinct from numerous chemical and genetic attempts to force cells into artificial states of "youth," the new research provides evidence that slowing the ticks of the aging clock is possible by actively preventing cells from committing to a pre-destined path of decline and death, and the clock-like gene oscillators could be a universal system to achieve that.[628]

Longevity Market Implications

You may be asking yourself "Why did he include a chapter on Longevity in a financial book?"

Good question. Remember this:

Time is the single most important factor in life and in finance.

There is an incontrovertible correlation between time and stock market multiples, a relationship that will continue as human life spans inevitably increase.

Given humans are going to live longer, arguably a lot longer, their investment horizon will have to be extended a lot further out along the timeline. In turn, that means their risk of running out of money increases, which requires they get higher rates of return from their investment portfolio.

> *"I can buy anything I want, basically, but I can't buy time."*
>
> Warren Buffett

How do they accomplish that? They will need higher allocations to equities, so demand for equities will increase as people start expecting to live longer, thanks to gene therapy and other longevity advances. The conventional method of measuring demand for equities will be thrown out the window. Stock markets will undergo a major transformation, based on investors' expectations of an extended lifespan. The result is apt to be a massive escalation of demand for equities. The key is expectations.

There's a reason why the Fed focuses on investor expectations when addressing issues like inflation. It's because those expectations change human financial behavior. Once the populace becomes convinced they are going to have good health and live past age 100 or even 125, their need for equities is going to increase incrementally. I believe the impact will be an unprecedented, sustained bull market, largely based on investor expectations.

This will likely mean the continuous rise in price-to-earnings (P/E) multiples we've experienced for the past century will continue. Graphic 22.1 charts the P/E ratio over the past 150 years and the trend (straight) line in a continual ascent.

It also means that the analysts who claim P/E multiples are expensive today compared to some date in the past and that their continual rise is unsustainable have consistently been wrong and will continue to be wrong. Stocks should be valued looking out the windshield, not looking in the rearview mirror. The naysayers need to turn around and look forward through the windshield.

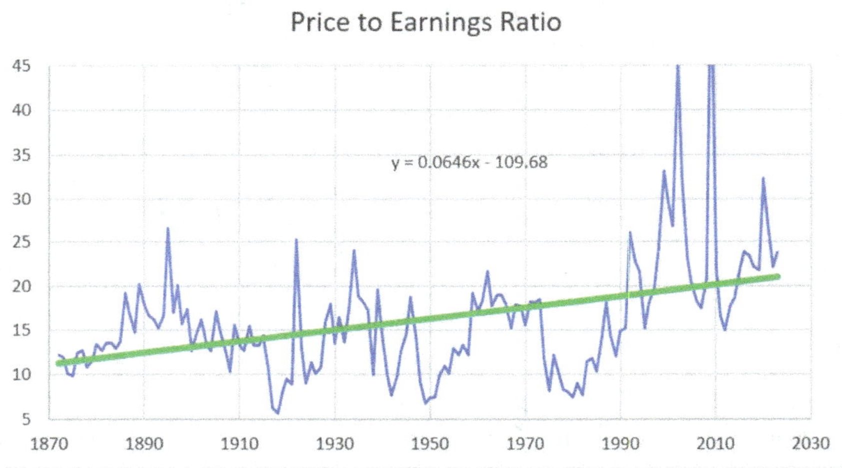

(Graphic 22.1 Historical P/E Ratio)

Longevity and P/E Ratios

What may appear expensive today will seem cheap tomorrow, just as it has since 1900.

As people live longer lives, their financial equations change. If you knew you were going to die in 8 years, how much of your portfolio would you have invested in stocks? Perhaps next to nothing. If, however, you knew you were not going to die for another 40 years, how much would you have in stocks? Substantially more. And that is the financial significance of rising longevity. Investors will be forced to own more profitable assets containing greater risk.

The average life expectancy in the U.S. has virtually doubled over the past 160 years and could do it again. In the 60 years between 1860 and 1920, it increased 50%, then another 33% during the following 50 years, and another 33% in the following half century. The same percentage increase during the next 50 years will see life expectancy climb to 106. Given the technological advancements being made in longevity research, it's not unrealistic to think it could escalate 50%, which would take us to age 120. It is on a steady upward ascent, despite a recent dip due to Covid and is likely to increase from its current 78 to over 100.

Graphic 22.2 depicts this continual ascent. As you can see, there is a strong .38 correlation between P/E multiples and life expectancy.

The persistent history of the rising stock market multiple will continue unabated. The result is that the price and value of businesses will continue to rise because the multiples in the stock market will keep going up.

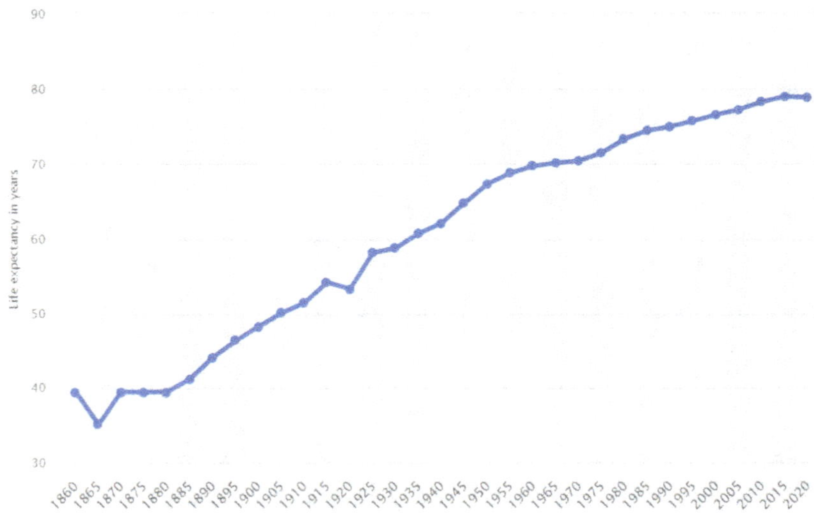

(Graphic 22.2 U.S. Life Expectancy)

CHAPTER TWENTY-THREE

Humans and Microchips

Although microchipping may seem like an idea hatched out of a sci-fi movie, it actually originated during the tail end of last century. British scientist Kevin Warwick became the first human to get chipped in 1998. Known as "Captain Cyborg," Warwick used his arm implant to open doors, switch on lights and perform other basic tasks.

Microchip implants, about the size of an elongated grain of rice, are essentially cylindrical bar codes that, when scanned, transmit a signal through a layer of skin. In the past, they have been used primarily to identify stray pets. In 2004, the FDA approved the use of the implantable VeriChip that allowed doctors instant access to a patient's medical records and caregivers to track dementia patients. Newborns could also be implanted to prevent misidentification or kidnapping.[629]

In 2017, workers at Three Square Market, a Wisconsin company specializing in vending machines, agreed to be implanted with microchips during a televised publicity stunt. The practical use was to provide employees with a convenient, cashless method of paying for purchases from the firm's vending machines.[630]

In Sweden, thousands have had microchips inserted into their hands. The chips allow users to access their homes, offices and gyms by merely swiping their hands against digital readers. Chips there are also used to store emergency contact details, social media profiles and e-tickets for events and rail journeys.[631]

Microchip implants are typically comprised of either an identifying integrated circuit device or Radio-Frequency Identification (RFID) transponder. Each chip contains an identification number linked to an individual's information contained in an external database. The chip can be connected to virtually every aspect of daily life, acting as a wallet, insurance card, phone, car key and personal data base.[632]

RFIDs were first used during WW II to identify aviation allies. They were later adopted to trace nuclear materials and animals, including pets and agricultural animals. Tags would be applied to cattle to distinguish cows from different herds and to ensure they were not being overfed through automated eating.[633]

Microchip implants have also opened doors for the healthcare industry, benefiting both patients and hospitals. The implants serve as a secure identifier for patients, and can streamline the administrative processes, including patient registration and record retrieval. Additionally, microchip implants can monitor patient vital signs, treatment regimens and facilitate early detection of health issues.[634]

Implanted chips are especially valuable for individuals with conditions such as diabetes, cardiovascular issues or Alzheimer's disease, as they can provide information about previous antibiotics usage, allergies and other critical data during medical emergencies. Moreover, microchip technology has the potential to enhance mobility for individuals physically limited by illnesses like rheumatoid arthritis or multiple sclerosis, as well as those in wheelchairs.[635]

Today, over 50,000 people worldwide have a microchip within their bodies, a number that has been increasing rapidly. Individuals with microchips can make purchases, access their homes and offices, travel and store or retrieve data, all without the need for keys or passwords.

Despite the many advantages of human microchipping, there are those who question or oppose the technology. Some suggest that wearable devices, such as a wristband with the same technology as a microchip, may serve as a better alternative to implanted chips. Others say wristbands ruin the entire point of the implanted microchips and their convenience.[636]

Privacy concerns have also been expressed as microchip implants have the potential to track individuals wherever they go, blurring the boundaries between physical and digital surveillance. Additionally, sensitive information stored within these systems raise cybersecurity risks. Specifically, healthcare institutions reported 145 data breaches in the first three months of 2023.[637]

Every technological breakthrough is accompanied by concerns it will have negative consequences that outweigh the benefits. In the case of human microchipping, however, as a society, we are already cyborgs thanks to our cell phones. What technology is doing is putting our phones inside our heads and hands. In addition to convenience, nobody will be losing their phones anymore.

> *"One day soon the Gillette company will announce the development of a razor that, thanks to a computer microchip, can actually travel ahead in time and shave beard hairs that don't even exist yet."*

Dave Barry

Brain Computer Interfaces

The technology that appears to be moving implants from level 1 to level 2 is the brain-computer interface (BCI), which allows people to control machines using their thoughts. Using BCIs, people with paralysis or debilitating illnesses can learn to spell words on a computer screen and control computerized machinery. BCI-controlled robotic limbs can even give users a sense of touch.

BCIs measure electrical fields generated by the brain through the scalp. Brain activity is translated into signals to control external devices, such as prostheses and robots. This allows those with severe paralysis to move or communicate. There are also "bidirectional" BCIs, which use electrical stimulation to prompt brain activity, replicating the perception of touch, such as when a person controls a prosthesis. BCI systems are especially useful in areas such as neurological rehabilitation, where they can be used to help restore the ability to communicate or move in people with the severest forms of paralysis.[638]

Physical movement originates with electrical signals in the brain that are passed through the spinal cord or brain stem, but when someone is paralyzed, the signals hit a dead end. BCIs provide a digital bypass, capturing the signals at the source and relaying the commands to a computer.[639]

BCIs connect to the brain using either implanted or wearable devices. Implanted BCIs are often surgically attached directly to brain tissue and are particularly beneficial for those with neuromuscular disorders or physical injuries. Wearable BCIs typically require a detachable scalp cap containing conductors that measure brain activity. Their purported advantage is being non-invasive.

The BCI industry is undergoing a period of rapid development, marked by crucial advances in microfabrication, machine learning and microelectronics. These advances are being led by a small group of well-funded innovators, including the following companies.

Neuralink

Launched in 2016 by Elon Musk, in 2019, Neuralink announced it had created "flexible threads" that could be implanted into an individual's brain using a specially designed robot to perform the insertion. The threads could ostensibly read signals from a paralyzed patient's brain and transmit the data to a mobile phone or computer, allowing the patient to control the device with just their thoughts. In 2023, the company announced it had won FDA approval to run its first clinical trials in humans and in late January 2024, the first human received a Neuralink brain implant. Initial results showed promising "neuron spike detection," according to Musk, meaning the device was able to recognize individual neurons inside the brain.[640]

Neuralink appears to have a leg up on its competitors because of the device's ability to go deeper into the brain. It also contains more electrodes that target individual neurons which the firm hopes will offer a higher degree of precision.[641]

Aside from helping the paralyzed, the hope is to "achieve a symbiosis with artificial intelligence," according to Musk. He added that the long-term goals for Neuralink are to allow easy surgical insertions of its chips to treat conditions like obesity, autism, depression and schizophrenia.[642]

Precision Neuroscience

Standing in an operating room, Craig Mermel, the President of Precision Neuroscience, was watching the first surgical insertion of the company's neural implant onto a conscious patient's brain. He looked away for a moment and when he looked back, the paper-thin electrode array was already in position. "It happened so fast, I almost missed it," said Mermel. In just seconds, a high-resolution picture of the patient's brain activity appeared on a screen. Added Mermel, "It was incredibly surreal; I got chills."[643]

The company's implant, a strip of thin film not unlike Scotch tape, is designed to conform to the surface of the brain without damaging its delicate tissue. During the 15 minutes the devices were in place, the implants were able to read, record and map electrical activity in part of the patients' temporal lobes, which helps process sensory input. The pilot study of the device, which is removable, positions Precision one step closer to building a permanent BCI.[644]

Blackrock Neurotech

Blackrock's "NeuroPort Array" chip enables individuals to control robotic limbs and wheelchairs and even sense feelings. The company hopes to cure physical disability, blindness, deafness and depression. The device contains 96 tiny needle-shaped chips capable of reading and stimulating electrical impulses. The signals are decoded by machine learning software into digital commands such as cursor movements, which can operate prostheses and computer equipment.

According to Blackrock Co-founder Marcus Gerhardt, "In the case of diseases such as depression or PTSD, targeted stimulation of brain tissue might help interrupt or reprogram firing patterns that contribute to the disorder." In the long run, Gerhardt sees the BCI technology being used to recover lost memories.[645]

Synchron

Synchron uses a stent called "Stentrode." It's fitted with tiny sensors and inserted into a large vein that sits next to the brain's motor cortex. Funded by Amazon's Jeff Bezos and Microsoft's Bill Gates, the Stentrode connects to an under-skin antenna in the chest where it collects brain data and sends them to external devices.[646]

A trial was launched in Australia among four participants paralyzed from amyotrophic lateral sclerosis (ALS). The implants remained in place for a full year without any serious adverse effects and the participants were able to control digital devices hands-free.[647] In a subsequent interview with *The Washington Post* by text message, one of the participants, Rodney Gorham, an Australian in his sixties with ALS, used his Synchron implant to type his responses. Asked about his hopes, he responded one minute later. "I will try to improve the system for other people," he wrote.[648]

Paradromics

Paradromics' BCI, the "Connexus Direct Data Interface," translates neural signals into text or synthesized speech. Similar to the Synchron and Neurotech, an array of tiny electrodes is implanted directly into the brain tissue, where it deciphers brain signals and sends them to external devices through a transceiver that sits under the skin in the chest. The BCI will initially be used to help patients who have lost their ability to communicate. CEO Matt Angle believes the technology will allow patients to communicate faster and more easily than they could with a less invasive BCI.

BrainGate

One of the first companies to develop a BCI implant system is BrainGate, founded in 1998 in Massachusetts. Its device is placed in the brain using microneedles, similar to the technology Neuralink uses. BrainGate's devices may be the most advanced in terms of BCI functionality. One of its wired devices offers a typing speed of 90 characters per minute. In addition to communication applications, BrainGate has also achieved robotic control for self-feeding.[649]

Non-Invasive BCI

BCIs can establish a direct communications pathway between the human brain and the external devices, which is independent of peripheral nerves and muscles. Compared with invasive BCI, non-invasive BCI has the advantages of lower cost, lower risk and operational ease for the user. Non-invasive BCI technology has evolved into an alternative type of human-computer interaction.

AAVAA

The AAVAA Headband is wearable software that acts as a "head mouse" and enables people with disabilities to use movements like eye blinks and gazes to control various devices, such as phones and computers. The headband features intuitive gesture control. Depending on the user's disability and specific accessibility needs, it can be adapted to react to mouth, hand, or even eyebrow movements.[650]

Neurolutions

Neurolutions developed a brain-controlled device to help restore function to patients disabled by a neurological injury. The IpsiHand system provides upper extremity rehabilitation for chronic stroke patients using a non-invasive BCI and wearable robotics technology. It uses motor imagery techniques to decode a patient's desire to move their finger, which then instructs the exoskeleton to physically move the finger. With repeated sessions, patients can regain control of their lost limbs.

Exoskeletons are structures that can be worn to support and technologically enhance the limited physical capabilities of the human body. They have a variety of applications, including biometric sensors that detect nerve signals for people with disabilities. They are also used for rehabilitation and injury recovery.[651]

Cognixion

Based in Santa Barbara, CA, Cognixion developed One Axon, an augmented reality headset that uses assisted technology to help people with intellectual disabilities to perform repetitive tasks. It utilizes electroencephalogram (EEG) technology to provide its BCI, enabling patients with advanced disease progression to communicate.[652]

Applications

The near-term focus of BCI research is primarily directed at individuals with serious physical impairments and enfeebling diseases.

A 34-year-old woman scheduled to receive a brain implant to relieve her debilitating epileptic seizures provided a refreshing aside to her impending procedure when she suggested that as long as her neurosurgeon was going to put a wire into her brain, might he also include a wire to relieve her OCD. As Ahmed Raslan, the neurosurgeon who performed the procedure at Oregon Health and Science University later quipped, "Luckily, we took her suggestion seriously." Added the patient, Amber Pearson, "I'm actually present in my daily life and that's incredible."[653]

Researchers at Johns Hopkins Applied Physics Laboratory created a system that allowed a partially paralyzed man to feed himself through a BCI connected to a robotic arm. The man, who was unable to use his fingers in 30 years, was able to eat using a knife and fork to cut food and ate dessert using his mind in less than 90 seconds.

The researchers are already working on the system's next iteration, aimed at allowing amputees to transform feelings of a phantom limb into actual movements of a robotic prosthetic.[654]

Researchers at UC San Francisco and UC Berkeley developed a BCI that enabled a woman with severe paralysis from a brainstem stroke to speak through a digital avatar. It was the first time that speech or facial expressions were synthesized from brain signals. The system can decode these signals into text at nearly 80 words per minute.[655]

A man paralyzed in his legs for over a decade due to a spinal cord injury from a bicycle accident regained the ability to walk smoothly using only his thoughts. This was made possible by two BCIs that restored communication between his brain and spinal cord, sending electrical pulses to stimulate leg muscles. The BCI uses artificial intelligence algorithms to decode brain signals in real time, allowing it to determine how the patient wants to move his legs. Data is transmitted to the spinal cord implant through a portable device, enabling the man to move independently.[656]

In a quantum leap forward in treating paralysis victims, surgeons at Northwell Health's Feinstein Institutes for Medical Research implanted a BCI into a patient. AI algorithms were then employed to re-link his brain to his body and spinal cord. The double neural bypass created an electronic bridge that allows information to flow between the man's paralyzed body and brain to restore movement and sensations in his hand, wrist and arm.[657]

In 2024, Neuralink announced the results of the first patient to receive its BCI, a 29-year-old who had lost all movement below his shoulders because of a diving accident. In a livestream event, the young man demonstrated how he could now move a computer cursor using the device. This ability by itself was not a milestone. A paralyzed individual was able to move a cursor using only their thoughts 20 years earlier, thanks to a BCI. But that chip had to be attached to a device on the outside of the brain to transmit data, requiring wires protruding through the skin.

Neuralink's device transmits data sans wires and can be used outside of a laboratory, for example, at the patient's home. Another breakthrough with the Neuralink BCI was that for the first time, a patient could do more than one thing simultaneously, playing chess while talking about the implant procedure.[658]

The Next Level

Ramses Alcaide, CEO of neurotech startup Neurable, which develops non-invasive brain-computer interfaces in the form of headphones, sees potential for BCI-enhanced devices to become an everyday item for the average person.

> "If we can make brain-computer interfaces accessible and seamless enough then they can be integrated into our daily lives, just as we use smartphones or laptops today. But in order to truly become a ubiquitous tool, they need to be comfortable, intuitive and reliable enough that people can use them without consciously thinking about them — similar to how we use a mouse or keyboard to interact with a computer."[659]
>
> Sumner Norman, a scientist at nonprofit startup Convergent Research, notes "The near-term goal of BCIs is to give the abilities back to those who have lost them. But in the long term, the technology is also intended to create a kind of tertiary cortex, another level of the human brain function that would allow humans to be almost superhuman!"

According to a review of 50 articles on the topic of BCIs, there appears to be low, although not negligible, risk of adverse effects, including infection, bleeding, seizures and physical damage to the brain. Non-invasive BCI devices may present risks such as skin irritation, headaches and eye strain as a result of prolonged use. Finally, there is a potential risk of electromagnetic interference between BCI devices and other electronic devices, which could interfere with proper functioning. Given the potential advantages, it seems advisable to continue studying their efficacy by monitoring their use in clinical trials.[660]

Economic Impact

Roughly one in four American adults suffers some form of disability, according to the Centers for Disease Control and

Prevention (CDC). Over one hundred million people worldwide live with some form of movement impairment or paralysis. According to some studies, advances in assistive and related technologies will have contributed to tripling the employment rate of people with disabilities by the end of 2023.[661]

The World Health Organization estimates that 2.5 billion people today need one or more assistive products or applications that support communication and cognition. This figure will increase to 3.5 billion by 2050, as an aging population will increase demand for assistive products.[662]

A research report from Accenture analyzed the financial performance of the 140 companies participating in the Disability Equality Index, a benchmarking tool that gives U.S. businesses an objective score on their disability inclusion policies and practices. The 45 companies identified as leaders over the four-year period had, on average, 28% higher revenue, 50% more net income and 30% higher economic profit margins than the other companies in the Index. Accenture estimates that having more people with disabilities joining the labor force could boost the U.S. GDP by up to $25bn.[663]

A Swiss company, Asperger Informatik AG, prefers to employ people with Asperger's syndrome, a mild form of autism, because they are often intellectually gifted, learn fast, and have tenacity and perseverance. These are ideal traits for a company working with information technology. The company maintains a low-pressure environment, minimizing stress and assigning suitable tasks and work processes.[664]

A 2020 *Market Study on Adult Travelers with Disabilities* by The Open Doors Organization (ODO) revealed that during the previous two years, travel by people with disabilities generated $58.7bn in spending. ODO executive director Eric Lipp noted that, "The true economic impact is potentially double, since people with disabilities typically travel with one or more other adults."[665]

Numerous studies have demonstrated that providing the disabled with the assisted technology they need to lead more normal lives and become employable is a huge win-win for the economy. Considering that emerging technologies will enable people—including the disabled and those with debilitating illnesses—to live longer, more productive lives, the benefits that will accrue to the financial markets are obvious.

The potential economic and technological impact of BCI is almost immeasurable. As discussed here, its impact in the field of medical research alone will change the lives of tens of millions of disabled and impaired individuals. Eventually, BCIs will be as much a part of our everyday lives as robots, autonomous driving, living well past 100 years and other technological breakthroughs. In the final chapter, as the title implies, "We Will Just Know It."

Chapter TWENTY-FOUR

We Will Just Know It

> *"We will have, for the first time, something that is smarter than the smartest human. There will come a point where no job is needed. You could have a job if you wanted to have a job, for personal satisfaction, but the AI will be able to do everything."*
>
> Elon Musk

Driving my daughters to school the other morning, we were three minutes away when my seven-year-old remarked, "Dad, three minutes is 60 plus 60 plus 60 because there are 60 seconds in a minute." My second daughter chimed in, "Well, yeah, that's 180." I then asked the three of them, "What's 60 times 60 times 60?" Immediately, my oldest daughter, age 11, blurted out "216,000." Astonished, I asked her, "How did you know that?" She replied, "I don't know. I just know."

I think that's exactly how it's going to be once the majority of us have microchip implants. Humans will just know everything that Google knows, everything that artificial intelligence (AI) knows, everything that mankind has learned since he first rubbed two sticks together and discovered fire.

Back to kids and school. Children attend class 39 weeks a year for 16 years, a couple more to secure a master's degree and even more if they aspire to a PhD. For argument's sake, let's assume 16 years on average and roughly 30 hours a week that they're actually learning something. Throw in a few thousand hours their parents fruitlessly try to teach them something about life and you have roughly 22,000 hours a child spends learning what they ostensibly need to know to earn a living and get through life without falling into a sinkhole.

In the future, a tiny microchip resting on their cerebral cortex will give them all those 22,000 hours back. Instead of sitting in classrooms, hopefully learning about mathematics, spelling, language, history and chemistry one lesson at a time, they're going to be mentally connected by a wee internal computer and be inestimably smarter than they are today.

This intellectual coming out party will not occur without upheaval in the educational system. How often have you encountered an everyday challenge and wondered, "Why didn't they teach me about this in school?" In the future, that's exactly what they will be teaching. No longer will tots meander into classrooms to be taught the alphabet. From day one, their formal education will be focused on interpersonal skills, decision-making and other abilities they will need in their later years. All the information dedicated teachers currently strive to syringe into the heads of their unyielding students will already be there. They're not going to have to learn, understand or remember them.

They're just going to know it.

The transition from learning via educators or finding information through external sources to having everything we need to know already inside our heads is awe-inspiring, if a bit daunting. Currently, anything that has ever happened in recorded history is at our fingertips via the Internet. (I just Googled "Internet" to learn if it should be capitalized. It should, when used as a noun.) For basic math, we have calculators. For data analysis, there's Excel. Need to write an article or do some software coding? ChatGPT is at your service. And so on.

The only impediment to securing information is <u>time</u>. It takes time to find what you want. Sometimes, not a lot of time; sometimes, too much time. And whatever resource is being used, we first have to learn how to use it. That takes more time. That obstacle will be removed in the future when we all have brain-computer implants (BCIs).

We won't have to learn how; we will just know.

How We Know Things Now

The way mankind has acquired knowledge throughout history is learning through one source or another. While formal learning for most occurs during childhood and early adulthood, learning continues throughout life for all but the indolent and politically motivated.

Even when something is learned quickly and easily, absorbing it is a multi-step progression. New information must be integrated with existing knowledge and stored in memory until applied. Active learning describes an interactive process, such as conducting an experiment to find a solution, whereas passive learning typically entails reading about a subject or learning from a lecture or video.[666]

The most common sources of knowledge are intuition, authority, empiricism (experience), rationalism (reasoning) and scientific approach.

Intuition is that feeling in our gut when we instinctively know something is right or wrong, or believe we know something somehow, but really don't know why.[667] Knowledge gained through intuition is knowing something without being consciously aware of where it came from. People sometimes intuit something based on a "gut feeling" or observations. These can be misinterpreted, however. When they are, it's referred to as *illusory correlation*— the perception of a relationship that does not exist.[668] For example, we are bitten by a dog and so, assume all dogs will bite.

Authority is what people rely on for knowledge they do not have through personal experience. We tend to accept what we learn from an esteemed or respected source, whether a person or knowledge base. Much of what we know is learned from authorities like our parents or teachers when we are young. Later in life, we depend on physicians, lawyers, financial advisors, plumbers and others for answers beyond our acquired knowledge. Alternately, we tap into information sources such as websites, books, or associates whose knowledge, education or experience we respect.

Empiricism is the theory that all knowledge is derived from sensory experience.[669] Empiricists contend that only information experienced has value, as opposed to ideas conjured up in one's mind. For example, the sun is hot, ice is cold and honey is sweet. Until a person has experienced these with their senses, the information is meaningless. That is, there is no way to understand that honey is sweet unless someone experiences it because otherwise, they would not know what "sweet" even means.[670]

Studies show that certain parts of the brain activate during learning. For example, visual learning activates a different part of the brain than olfactory learning.[671] In his study in the *Journal of Trends in Cognitive Sciences*, author D.G. Treichler notes that, "People generally remember 10% of what they read, 20% of what they hear, 30% of what they see, and 50% of what they see and hear."

Rationalism involves using logic and reasoning to acquire new knowledge. In opposition to empiricism, rationalism contends that reason is in itself a source of knowledge, independent of and superior to sense perceptions.

There are two forms of reasoning. Inductive reasoning is a method of drawing conclusions by going from the specific to the general. Conversely, deductive reasoning goes from general information to specific conclusions. While deductive reasoning is a logical approach that starts with a general idea and works towards specific conclusions, inductive reasoning starts with observations and builds towards a theory.[672]

Scientific Method is a learning procedure used in testing a hypothesis. It's the process of observing and pursuing answers through experimentation.[673]

In developing his theory of evolution, Charles Darwin applied the scientific method. Initially, his procedure involved only observation, which was unproductive. Further thought and study led him to formulate a hypothesis to explain the facts that he had gathered through observation. He tested his hypothesis by gathering additional data to determine whether it would support the hypothesis. His use of both inductive and deductive reasoning is a hallmark of modern scientific inquiry.[674]

Integrating these various sources of knowledge is a process in which people put together various experiences and information and establish relationships for connecting them. Learning involves integrating new knowledge across time, location, circumstances and the various formats in which it appears.[675] Some researchers suggest that infants are born with foundational knowledge and have innate reflexes that teach them how to engage with the world and gradually build skills and knowledge.[676] Others have argued that all knowledge is generated through an individual's direct experience with the world.[677]

> *"By three methods we may learn wisdom: First, by reflection, which is noblest; Second, by imitation, which is easiest; and third by experience, which is the bitterest."*

Confucius

Knowledge Acquisition Will Change

The way we have acquired knowledge for thousands of years will someday be supplanted by implants. The result will be 20 or 30 billion people that are infinitely smarter than humans are today. This enormous boost to individual productivity can't help but have a profoundly positive effect on the markets. Consider the impact of even a minor increase in the average person's lifespan combined with 22,000 additional hours during one's formative years. The result is 30- or 40-thousand extra hours of output and productivity during a lifetime. Multiply this number by 20 or 30 billion people and the bullish result is incalculable.

The naysayer "experts" who continually warn that stocks exceeding a certain historic equity multiple are destined to plunge into oblivion will have to find a new pinata to poke at because stock multiples will continue their rise, as will stock returns. This will be a result of people living longer, being more productive and acquiring a level of knowledge not even Plato or Socrates could have imagined.

All that's needed for all this to happen is time. The tech sector refers to this as *latency*, the delay between a user's action and a web application's response to that action.[678] For us less technically endowed, latency refers to the time that elapses between a request for information and its arrival. For those with brain implants, latency will be instantaneous. Imagine not only instantly knowing everything that has ever been learned in history but being able to instantly communicate with anyone on Earth using just your mind. It boggles the mind…unless you have a brain implant. Then you won't be boggled; you'll just know it.

All the important traits we must learn to successfully navigate life are acquired mainly through trial and error. During our 16 or 20 years of formal schooling, we learn virtually nothing about how to parent, how to listen, how to get along with others, how to motivate others (and ourselves), how to deal with rejection, how to deep think and find answers, how to negotiate with car salesmen and real estate agents, even how to create a simple budget. All these things we currently must learn on our own as we amble through life. In the near future, people will know how to do these things early in life, perhaps even as children, thanks to having all that knowledge neatly packed into their cranial lobes. It's going to make the world a much better, safer, smarter place.

They will just know.

> ***"The best way to predict the future is to create it."***

Peter Drucker

Overcoming Uncertainty

BICs will help people overcome life's misgivings and uncertainties by giving them the superlative confidence that comes from knowledge. They won't have to speculate; they will just know.

Highly successful people—and companies—rarely achieve eminence without overcoming obstacles, including uncertainty.

Elon Musk abandoned his plan to pursue a Ph.D. in applied physics at Stanford University and became an entrepreneur, despite having no money and facing an unpredictable future. He slept on an office floor and showered at a YMCA while chasing his dream. He certainly experienced uncertainty as he struggled just to make ends meet but he obviously had the confidence and optimism to not abandon his goals. He eventually built Zip2, an online software company for publishers and later sold it to Compaq for $300mn. The experience taught him to be fearless in the face of uncertainty and to outwork everyone else.[679]

Implants will make people so much better at mathematics and, consequently, better at the mathematical components of investing. One of the major impediments to successful investing, as discussed earlier, is uncertainty, which causes investors to deviate from their financial plans and make decisions based on emotions and biases. People suffer uncertainly when they have insufficient knowledge of the time ahead. It produces fright whereas knowledge generates confidence. Great investors have great confidence and optimism. As the late Charlie Munger said at age 99, "If I can be optimistic when I'm nearly dead, surely the rest of you can handle a little inflation."

Rest in peace, Charlie.

AFTERWORD

There was a lot for you to digest in this book. I know because I spent over three years writing it. It might be helpful for me to give you some reminders of what you hopefully learned from reading the book.

As an investor, how are you managing risk? Is it by instinct or do you have a process to proactively lessen or increase risk based on market threats and opportunities?

Understanding what risk is and when to take risks is what the first part of this book is all about. Whether you should maintain, increase or reduce portfolio risk is a mandatory conversation to have with your advisor. If you choose to assume additional risk in response to increased opportunity, or curtail risk when there is less opportunity, how is that accomplished?

> *"Be fearful when others are greedy and greedy when others are fearful."*
>
> Warren Buffett

A fundamental difference between average investors and sophisticated investors like Warren Buffett is the ability to measure market sentiment—how competitors view the future and what they are doing with their money. Are they fearful? Overconfident? Greedy? When making investment decisions, you want to be buying into a crowd that's fearful of taking risks and selling into a greedy crowd chasing a collective belief rather than value. The last thing you want to do is to sell your fantastic businesses when there is panic in the market.

Algorithms can be used to design investment strategies that avoid investors' tendencies to panic and make rash decisions. Using algorithms, we can conduct the vital measurement and analysis needed to gain an advantage over investors that fall prey to behavioral biases, market sentiment and other deceptive influences.

Markets are not random: there are recognizable patterns that develop in response to important events and tend to repeat over time—not always exactly the same way but similarly. The only thing that catches that link of historically unprecedented events is technical analysis.

Measuring the economic indicators that impact your portfolio's return is necessary. One reason most investors overlook or ignore this activity is its complexity. It's the same reason most managers fail to outperform their benchmarks. A reliable method of measuring economic factors is comparing current conditions with those of the past, using the algorithm, which weighs critical factors.

Valuation factors explain more than 80% of portfolio return variance. Over the long run, you must get valuation calculations correct if you are to allocate investments profitably. The longer your investment time horizon, the more heavily weighted an algorithm should be towards valuation factors, and the more patient you can be regarding performance.

Buffett doesn't differentiate between investing in a stock and investing in an entire business. The majority of his personal net worth is invested into the businesses that he owns, companies with sustainable competitive advantages and "wide moats." I manage our personal portfolio the same way. We own the same companies in our portfolio that my investors own in theirs. As Buffett suggests,

> *"Intrinsic value can be defined simply: It is the discounted value of the cash that can be taken out of a business during its remaining life."*

Concentrated positions represent both threats and opportunities for portfolios. If your investment portfolio has accumulated a concentrated position, you need to judiciously manage that stock or cash position. In the instance of a concentrated equity position, remember that for every superstock like Microsoft or Apple, there are hundreds of former winners that collapsed, like TWA, Magnavox and PanAm.

Effectively managing a concentrated cash position is a crucial strategy, one based on the abundance or scarcity of market opportunities and what percentage of total investable assets the cash represents. The graphic in Chapter 8 is a great illustration of how this is accomplished.

There are multiple approaches to neutralizing concentrated positions, whether those positions are in stock or cash. For example, rebalancing helps counteract the compounding effects of a portfolio. It prevents higher-performing investments from earning more and lower performers from deteriorating further. Rebalancing serves as a defense against emotional decision-making. It installs a dispassionate system that ignores the emotional frailties that cause investors to inflict financial damage upon themselves. As an investor, it's often more important to know what not to own.

In a bear market, investors should own assets that are non-correlated or ideally, negatively correlated, to the U.S. stock market. Alternative investments are how savvy investors make money in a down market. These investments include gold, Treasuries, market neutral strategies and managed futures.

Here are some things to look for in choosing an investment manager. The best managers are autonomous. They ignore the media and the masses. They are iconoclasts; financial skeptics who question everything and look for no easy answers.

The best managers speak in simple terms; they are direct and easily understood. They exhibit great patience and feel no compulsion to "do something." Great managers know that despite having the best information and making the correct assumptions, an investment can go sour because something changes and new information emerges that alters the assessment. When that happens, they must be able to swallow their pride and admit they were wrong.

Even in up markets, individual stocks can suffer disappointing performance. Direct indexing portfolios can take advantage by harvesting losses in underperforming stocks. Tax loss harvesting is a strategy that allows you to close losing positions in a taxable account to generate losses that can be used to offset gains and reduce taxes. The concept of using tax losses to offset gains and dramatically increase net worth is something that will not show up on an investment performance report or fact sheet, but it's one of the most impactful strategies available to you.

Of course, if you are willing to accept average market returns, there's no need to pay advisory fees. The safety of a passive approach tempered by rebalancing is available for free.

> *"Investing is a funny business. It's really easy to be average. Just buy an index fund. It's really hard to be above average."*

Howard Marks

Passive investing tends to gain popularity every few decades, the popularity of ETFs being a recent testament. But an S&P 500 ETF will always underperform the index somewhat because of fees.

> *"Diversification is for people who don't know what they're doing and passive investing is for those who lack the knowledge or temperament to buy individual stocks."*

Warren Buffett

Something few investors consider when buying an index fund is whether the business activities of the companies in the index align with their moral values. I believe most investors would prefer to own companies that do not sell cigarettes that give people cancer. In my experience, people buying an index rarely consider the fact that they are buying a broad collection of companies, some of which profit from tobacco, alcohol, pollution and adult entertainment, disdainfully known as "sin stocks." I enjoy an occasional cocktail, but I don't want to own companies selling alcohol that has ruined the lives of countless people the result of drinking and driving.

Fear sells. The mass media knows this and has made fear mongering and sensationalism an indispensable component of their agenda. This has a pernicious effect on the populace, which extends to investors' expectations. Whether the national debt, Social Security, terrorism, government shutdowns, AI or an impending market crash, the media is sure to exaggerate the threat while scouting the next "calamity." Fear is based on uncertainty, a tenet the media plays like a violin. Pledge to ignore the media. They are unceasingly biased and just plain wrong. Their fear mongering and deception creates opportunities for savvy investors. The more inefficient the markets become, the more opportunities there are for us.

> *"America was not built on fear. America was built on courage, on imagination and an unbeatable determination to do the job at hand."*

Harry S Truman

It's a tragedy that so many people have lost so much to investment scams. Ponzi schemes, investment funds theft, undisclosed fees, sales abuses, pump and dump schemes, sports betting scams and other forms of exploitation comprise an endless list of swindles that have ruined countless lives among the gullible.

This is not to frighten you into investment paralysis. Rather to make you aware of how important it is to recognize fraud and scams and protect yourself from the perpetrators.

One step you can take is to ensure your financial advisor is a fiduciary—an investment advisor's obligation to act entirely on behalf of his or her clients' best interests. As a fiduciary, I must be compliant with three separate codes of ethics, including those of the Certified Financial Planner (CFP®) Board, the Chartered Financial Analyst (CFA®) Institute and the SEC. Most consider these the ethical gold standards of our industry.

These principles entail integrity, objectivity, competence, fairness, confidentiality, professionalism and diligence. An investment advisor cloaked in anything less should cause you to run the other way.

> *"He has honor if he holds himself to an ideal of conduct though it is inconvenient, unprofitable, or dangerous to do so."*

Walter Lippman

The wealthy invest differently than average investors. It's one reason they are able to pass on their wealth to future generations. Whereas average investors are generally unschooled when it comes to reducing their tax burden and preserving whatever wealth they have for their inheritors, the wealthy take advantage of advanced investment techniques that ensure their legacy.

Among these strategies are the charitable lead trust, charitable remainder trust, irrevocable life insurance trust, intentionally defective grantor trust, grantor retained annuity trust, spousal lifetime access trust and the use of the annual gift exclusion.

The wealthy also understand how to protect and grow their money, largely by utilizing two investment strategies that provide safe, low risk returns: bond ladders and arbitrage. These allow you to reliably calculate how much money you're going to make over an extended period with a higher level of analytical assurance than other strategies.

Some of the greatest fortunes have been made through various forms of real estate investing, a strategy that provides passive income, tax benefits, leverage, appreciation and cash flow. It does not, however, represent the same type of safe, low risk investing as bond ladders and arbitrage.

I believe the U.S. and the world in general will experience a brighter future. Many of the threats that have beset us will be abated or altogether eliminated, thanks to technological advancements, many encompassing AI. Projects such as the DART

Mission and James Webb telescope will help safeguard us from cosmic threats. Highly sophisticated missile systems, drone swarm and other defense technologies will reduce adversarial threats to sterile saber rattling. AI-assisted weather models will dramatically increase the speed and accuracy of forecasts. Biomedical and genomic advances will reduce the impact of future pandemics. Enhanced clean energy will reduce the need for fossil fuels and make the world safer through energy independence.

A vital aspect of energy independence is the use of batteries, especially lithium batteries, which allow renewables to replace fossil fuels like oil, gas and coal to generate power, even when wind or solar are not producing. According to a March 2024 *Associated Press* story, The U.S. is increasingly using lithium-ion batteries to store energy in large scale projects, often pairing them with solar and wind alternatives.

Beyond the obvious benefits of not spewing carbon into the atmosphere, the shift from fossil fuels to alternatives like solar power and lithium batteries will have a huge impact on global power. For the past 200 years, the most strategically important sources of energy have been oil and natural gas. Countries controlling large repositories of these resources have used that influence as a political weapon, with the tacit or voiced threat to shut off energy exports to adversarial nations.

AI is likely destined to be the most transformative technological advance in history. It is advancing at lightning speed with an economic and societal impact hard to overestimate. The book's *Bullish Future* section is filled with examples of how AI is changing every aspect of modern life.

AI has become monumentally important in big data because it enables the breathtakingly rapid extraction of complex data through a centralized learning process. AGI—the epitome of AI advancement—is a revolution in learning, going beyond narrow expertise into the deep end of human-like cognitive abilities. It not only crunches numbers and analyzes data but also possesses emotions, makes decisions based on subjective states, tackles complex problems, learns from experiences, understands languages, and exhibits an array of cognitive skills.

> *"In our business, we talk about emerging technologies and how they impact society. We've never seen a technology move as fast as AI has to impact society and technology. This is by far the fastest moving technology that we've ever tracked in terms of its impact and we're just getting started."*

Paul Daugherty, CIO, Accenture

AI is the intellectual underpinning for robotics. It serves as the "brain" while sensors and mechanical devices act as the "body." While robots have been performing repetitive tasks and replacing humans in hazardous work for many years, recent events have created a dramatic, almost inconceivable acceleration in their capabilities, thanks to machine learning and AI. While AI typically learns through human training or machine learning, robots learn by self-processing data, such as by observing human actions.

AI is estimated to create 97 million new jobs by 2025. Given the pace of technological progress, it's inevitable that we will soon be living in a world served by a billion robots. At some point in the future, a robot-to-human ratio of two to one will exist, with 20 or 30 billion robots doing everything the 10 or 15 billion humans on the planet don't want to do.

As with any new technology, there are advocates and dissenters when it comes to AI. One of the major concerns voiced by opponents is that workers in manual labor jobs will be sacrificed on the altar of AI and robotics. But along with many market analysts, I believe that is a specious argument. AI is not destined to destroy jobs so much as it will replace some jobs with new occupations, eliminating much of the "dirty, dangerous and drudgery" currently being done by humans.

What is most likely to happen is the continuation of the work-life balance tilting towards less work and more life. It was only a century ago when the 7-day work week was the occupational standard. The first Industrial Revolution of the 18th century shifted the largely rural societies of the U.S. and Europe into urban ones. The second Industrial Revolution—from the late 19th to the early 20th century—saw advances in manufacturing, thanks to the introduction of electricity, steel, the internal combustion engine, chemicals and indoor plumbing. The third began in the mid-20th century and continues today, distinguished by the emergence of digital technology, automation and the Internet.

I see AI and machine learning as the genesis of the next revolution. As in the past, skeptics will insist that the new technology will deprive millions of their livelihood, but as in the past, they will be proven wrong. People are not going to lose their jobs; they will adjust to the new economy and new careers and enjoy a reduction in the number of hours spent working.

I believe the development of autonomous vehicles (AVs) will be one of mankind's greatest advances. Does that surprise you? Could getting safely wherever you want to go without having to do anything but breathe literally change the world?

Consider that a daily 45-minute commute each way translates into 22,500 minutes or 375 hours a year going to and from work in a car. AVs will give back roughly 20,000 hours of productivity to that commuter over their working life—a gain of 10 years!

> *"In addition to doing our jobs at least as well as we do them, intelligent robots will be cheaper, faster, and far more reliable than humans. And they can work 168 hours a week, not just 40. No capitalist in her right mind would continue to employ humans."*

Kevin Drum

If someone told you they could give you an extra 10 years of life to do whatever you wanted, would you not jump at that opportunity? That's what AVs will do. While the impact on the automotive, trucking, insurance and real estate industries is incalculable, AVs will have far-reaching effects on virtually every business sector. The intangible benefits, while harder to discern, are the ones that will be the primary drivers of productivity: enhanced creativity, productivity and time; less stress, auto injuries and deaths.

How and why people change and age as they get older is a subject of continuous debate. Man has long pondered the concept of an extended lifespan. That aspiration has evolved from a pleasant notion to an approaching reality as serious money is being poured into longevity research.

Many species age much slower than humans and some that don't appear to age at all. When sick or injured, jellyfish can transform cells into a younger state that will eventually grow into adulthood all over again. In fact, barring death from predators, jellyfish could live virtually forever. Whether humans have the same cellular "machinery" remains an unanswered question, but if we do, as many researchers believe, it's going to be a game changer.

People living in "blue zones" live exceptionally long lives. Scientists studying centenarians conclude there is something genetically exceptional about them in that they might carry unusual genetic variants that extend lifespan, including DNA repair and protection of cells from damage caused by free radicals.

It's simply a matter of time, money and computing power that will enable full DNA diagnostics and the elimination of many single nucleotide diseases like diabetes, cancer, heart disease and Alzheimer's through gene therapy. Once accomplished, it's logical to assume science will continue to evolve and decipher DNA and cell repair, ultimately leading to human longevity.

An incontrovertible correlation exists between human longevity (time) and stock market multiples. As humans live much longer, thanks to genome technologies and other therapies, their investment horizon will substantially increase. Their risk of running out of money will also increase, so they will have to secure higher rates of return from their investment portfolios. That means higher allocations to equities, which will likely result in a massive escalation in demand and an unprecedented, sustained bull market, largely based on investor expectations.

The result is that the price and value of businesses will keep going up because the multiples in the stock market will keep going up.

A statistic that would surprise most people is that over 50,000 people worldwide have had a microchip implanted in their body. The technology that is accelerating their use is the brain-computer interface or BCI, which allows people to control machines using their thoughts.

BCIs connect to the brain using either implanted or wearable devices. Implanted BCIs are typically attached directly to brain tissue; wearable or non-invasive BCIs generally require a scalp cap that measures brain activity.

A relatively small but impressive and well-funded group of visionaries are leading the advancement of BCI capabilities, including Elon Musk's Neuralink and Synchron, funded by Bill Gates and Jeff Bezos. The near-term focus of BCI research is primarily directed at individuals with serious physical impairments and enfeebling diseases.

Roughly one in four American adults suffers some form of disability. Studies indicate that providing the disabled with the assisted technology to lead more normal lives and become employable is a huge boon for the economy. Considering that emerging technologies will enable everyone—including the disabled and those with debilitating illnesses—to live longer, more productive lives, the benefits that will accrue to the financial markets are obvious. The potential economic and technological impact of BCI is almost immeasurable.

The way we have acquired knowledge for thousands of years will someday be supplanted by the BCI. In the future, a tiny microchip resting on the cerebral cortex of schoolchildren will bequeath them some 22,000 hours of time they would otherwise have spent sitting in classrooms, hopefully learning about mathematics, spelling, language, history and chemistry one lesson at a time. Now they will be mentally connected by an internal computer the size of a human hair and be inestimably smarter than they are today. They won't have to learn; they will just know.

All that's needed for all this to happen is time. The tech sector refers to this as *latency,* the delay between a user's request and an application's response. For those with BCIs, latency will be instantaneous. They will not only instantly know everything that has ever been learned in history but be able to instantly communicate with anyone on Earth using just their mind. BICs will help people overcome life's apprehensions and uncertainties by giving them the superlative confidence that comes from knowledge. They won't have to speculate; they will just know.

About the Author

Ryan's experience includes an early focus on financial statement creation and analysis, followed by investment management at Washington University Endowment, Morgan Stanley, and Merrill Lynch. Ryan is the Director of Arbitrage Investing at Krilogy and serves on the Investment Committee and Portfolio Strategies Committee. Ryan's primary responsibility is Portfolio Manager for the Equitytree™ Investment Portfolios:

Equitytree Moderately Conservative
Equitytree Moderate
Equitytree Moderately Aggressive
Equitytree Aggressive

Ryan is a Certified Financial Planner™ CFP®, a designation awarded by the Certified Financial Planner Board of Standards, Inc., and is a member of The American Finance Association and The Chartered Financial Analyst™ Institute. He graduated from the University of Missouri with a Bachelor of Science degree in Finance in Investment and Portfolio Management. He also earned a Master of Science degree in Finance from the Edward S. Ageno School of Business at Golden Gate University.

Ryan has read well over 1,000 books on investing and portfolio management.

Scan the QR Code on the back of the book to contact Ryan.

Endnotes

[1] Noncorrelated assets are those that tend to change in value independent of the core financial markets such as stocks and bonds.
[2] Investment Advisers Act Release 2106, *supra* footnote 15.
[3] "Commission Interpretation Regarding Standard of Conduct for Investment Advisers," SEC, Release No. IA-5248; File No. S7-07-18.
[4] marketwatch.com
[5] investopedia.com
[6] nerdwallet.com
[7] school.stockcharts.com
[8] cboe.com
[9] investopedia.com
[10] cdn.cboe.com
[11] investopedia.com
[12] ISE Sentiment Index, marketswiki.com
[13] conference-board.org
[14] Olivier Armantier, Giorgio Topa, Wilbert van der Klaauw, and Basit Zafar, "An Overview of the Survey of Consumer Expectations," FRBNY Economic Policy Review. December 2017
[15] som.yale.edu
[16] investing.com
[17] aaii.com
[18] investopedia.com
[19] consensus-inc.com
[20] financestrategysystem.com
[21] investopedia.com
[22] bankrate.com
[23] investor.com
[24] David L. Scott, *Wall Street Words: An A to Z Guide to Investment Terms for Today's Investor*, (Houghton Mifflin, 2003)
[25] Standard & Poor's 2018 Annual Global Corporate Default and Rating Transition Study.
[26] jmbullion.com
[27] aaii.com
[28] sentimentrader.com
[29] investopedia.com
[30] corporatefinanceinstitute.com
[31] investopedia.com
[32] nyse.com
[33] Mallika Mitra, "As the Stock Market Erases Its Losses for the Year, Investors Suffer From Keeping Their Cash on the Sidelines, " Money 8 Jun 2020.
[34] equitymaster.com
[35] onehealthmedicalcare.com
[36] priceaction.com
[37] "A Handbook of Technical Analysis," elearnmarkets.com
[38] therobusttrader.com
[39] credit-suisse.com
[40] quora.com
[41] investorsunderground.com

[42] stockmarketeye.com
[43] school.stockcharts.com
[44] tradeciety.com
[45] zerodha.com
[46] healthpartners.com
[47] fidelity.com
[48] academy.binance.com
[49] commodity.com
[50] Greg McBride, "What is Relative Strength Index (RSI) in stocks?" bankrate.com 29 July 2022.
[51] school.stockcharts.com
[52] tradingview.com
[53] ibid #51
[54] ibid #51
[55] deltaexchange.com
[56] ibid #55
[57] Colin Dodds, "What Is a Death Cross Pattern in Stocks? How Do They Form?" sofi.com, 28 Oct 2021.
[58] Alan Farley, "The Complete Guide to Volatility Indicators," yahoo.com, 23 May 2021.
[59] bollingerbands.com
[60] sofi.com
[61] businessinsider.com
[62] tradeciety.com
[63] corporatefinanceinstitute.com
[64] schoolstockcharts.com
[65] finbold.com
[66] corporatefinanceinstitute.com
[67] tradestation.com
[68] school.stockcharts.com
[69] quantifiedstrategies.com
[70] Cory Mitchell, "Market Breadth," Investopedia, 10 May 2021.
[71] investopedia.com
[72] marketbusinessnews.com
[73] medium.com
[74] seekingalpha.com
[75] Jeremy Salvucci, "What Is Capitulation in the Stock Market?" thestreet.com 7 Oct 2022.
[76] Federal Reserve Bank of Atlanta
[77] Sarwat Jahan, Ahmed Saber Mahmud, and Chris Papageorgiou, "What is Keynesian Economics?" International Monetary Fund, Sept 2014.
[78] pbs.org
[79] maynardkeynes.org
[80] federalreserveeducation.org
[81] cfainstitute.com
[82] Raksha Bissoon, Boopen Seetanah, Reena Bhattu-Babajee, Narvada Gopy-Ramdhany, Keshav Seetah, "Monetary Policy Impact on Stock Return: Evidence from Growing Stock Markets," Theoretical Economics Letters Vol 6 No 5, 2016.
[83] Douglas J. Elliott, "Market Liquidity: A Primer," Brookings Institute, June 2015.
[84] federalreserve.gov
[85] economicshelp.org

[86] Niall Ferguson and Moritz Schularick, "Chimerical? Think Again," Wall Street Journal, 5 Feb 2007.
[87] corporatefinanceinstitute.com
[88] Bill Nelson, "The Costs of High Levels of Reserve Balances," bpi.com, 25 Jan 2021.
[89] Kimberly Amadeo, "Interest Rates and How They Work," thebalance.com, 26 Oct 2020.
[90] Paul Krugman and the MasterClass staff, "Producer Price Index Explained: What Is the PPI?" masterclass.com, 25 Feb 2022.
[91] investinganswers.com
[92] usafacts.com
[93] investor.gov
[94] Chuck Kowalski, "How the Dollar Impacts Commodity Prices," thebalance.com, 11 Feb 2020.
[95] investopedia.com
[96] thebalance.com
[97] conference-board.org
[98] "Using the yield spread to forecast recessions and recoveries," firsttuesday Journal, 7 May 2021.
[99] efttrend.com
[100] ycharts.com
[101] "Why Purchasing Managers' Indexes have become closely watched economic indicators," jhinvestments.com, 12 Nov 2022.
[102] investopedia.com
[103] corporatefinanceinstitute.com
[104] ibid 102
[105] Kimberly Amadeo, ""Inverted Yield Curve and Why It predicts a Recession," the balance.com, 23 May 2021.
[106] Federal Reserve Bank of St. Louis. "Should We Fear the Inverted Yield Curve?" 8 Feb 2021.
[107] "The Inverted Yield Curve: What It Means and How to Navigate It," ycharts.com 12 Mar 2024.
[108] corporatefinanceinstitute.com
[109] investopedia.com
[110] efinancemanagement.com
[111] investopedia.com
[112] analystprep.com, 29 Sept 2019.
[113] corporatefinanceinstitute.com
[114] corpgov.law.harvard.edu
[115] Stephen Zeff, "The Evolution of U.S. GAAP: The Political Forces Behind Professional Standards," CPA Journal, Jan 2005.
[116] Stephen Rice, "Evolution of US Generally Accepted Accounting Principles (GAAP)," Rice University, iasplus.com
[117] ibid #117
[118] ibid #117
[119] fasb.org
[120] ibid #117
[121] financestrategists.com
[122] Corey Ferreira, "Financial Accounting Standards Board (FASB)," bench.co, 23 May 2023.
[123] corporatefinanceinstitute.com

[124] Stephanie Moussalli, "Accounting for the Journals First 100 Years: A Timeline From 1905 to 2005," Journal of Accountancy, 30 Sep 2005.
[125] knowledge.wharton.upenn.edu
[126] sechistorical.org
[127] Daniel Noll and Jerry Weygandt, "Business reporting: What Comes Next?" Journal of Accountancy, 31 Jan 1997.
[128] pbs.org
[129] Rachel Elkins, "From Independence to regulation: A Look into Major Accounting Scandals and the Changes Implemented by the Sarbanes-Oxley Act," Tennessee Research and Creative Exchange, Dec 2014.
[130] "Revision of the Commissioner's Auditor Independence Requirements," sec.gov 21 Nov 2000.
[131] Aryeh Neier, "America's most famous whistleblower' inspired legal protections. They're too weak." The Washington Post, 17 Oct 2019.
[132] Moritz Homann, "Whistleblowers: Heroes or Traitors?' Integrity Line, Nov 11, 2023.
[133] findlaw.com
[134] "10 Most Famous Whistleblowers," St Francis School of Law, 21 Nov 2022.
[135] whistleblowers.org
[136] Dick Carozza, "Extraordinary Circumstances," Fraud Magazine, Mar/Apr 2008.
[137] Carlos Andres Lopez, "Whistleblower who uncovered WorldCom fraud scandal to speak at NMSU," Las Cruces Sun News, 30 Sept 2021.
[138] ibid #136
[139] seekingalpha.com
[140] David Blitzer, "Inside the S&P 500: PE and Earnings Per Share," indexologyblog.com 7 Feb 2014.
[141] investopedia.com
[142] Rick Ferri, "Consider the Price-to-Peak Earnings Ratio," Forbes, 22 Oct 2012.
[143] investopedia.com
[144] ibid #144
[145] ibid #144
[146] financialpost.com
[147] thebalance.com
[148] corporatefinanceinstitute.com
[149] econlib.org
[150] investopedia.com
[151] NHTSA data
[152] investopedia.com
[153] Rey Mashayekhi, "Why Warren Buffett's 'Bible of investing' still matters more than 70 years later," Fortune, 5 Apr 2021.
[154] Dustin McKissen, "Warren Buffett's tribute to a legendary investor reveals 3 secrets to living an extraordinary life," cnbc.com, 10 May 2019.
[155] statista.com
[156] "25 Business Moats That Helped Shape The World's Most Massive Companies," CB Insights, 23 June 2021.
[157] americanmineservices.com
[158] stfrancislaw.com
[159] chubb.com
[160] officialdata.org
[161] Thomas Boczar and Elizabeth Ostrander, "The Renaissance Of Single-Stock Concentration Risk Management," Journal of Estate & Tax Planning May 2017.

[162] Boyle, Loewy, Reiss and Weiss, "The Enviable Dilemma: Hold, Sell, or Hedge Highly Concentrated Stock?" Analytical Synthesis Fall 2004.
[163] finance.yahoo.com
[164] A qualified investor is an individual with an investment portfolio worth over $5 million.
[165] Andrew Goodman, "Goldman Sachs & Eaton Vance Have A Way For Some Wealthy Investors To Avoid Big Capital Gains Taxes," Forbes 10 Jan 2016.
[166] ibid #1
[167] James Royal, "Short selling: How to short sell stocks," Bankrate 20 Jan 2023.
[168] Andrew Loo, "Options: Calls and Puts," corporatefinanceinstitute.com 4 Mar 2023.
[169] investopedia.com
[170] mystockoptions.com
[171] "Strategies For Hedging Concentrated Stock Positions," mystockoptions.com
[172] chittogarh.com
[173] Akshit Anthony , "Understanding Inverse ETFs," analyticssteps.com 10 Nov 2021.
[174] investopedia.com
[175] nptrust.org
[176] John Huss and Thomas Maloney, "Portfolio Balancing: Common Misconceptions," AQR, Feb 2017.
[177] Pete Johnson, "The Case for Dynamic Rebalancing," asymmetriccap.com Feb 2019.
[178] adweek.com
[179] kiplinger.com
[180] investopedia.com
[181] Spencer Jakab, "Is Your 401(k) Destroying Capitalism?" The Wall Street Journal, 04 Mar 2024.
[182] Dalbar, Inc. "2020 QAIB Report."
[183] focus-economics.com
[184] "What Investors Miss About The Price Of Gold, And Where We Stand Today," Forbes 9 Sep 2022.
[185] Brian Hergt, "Gold prices during and after the Great Recession," U.S. Bureau of Labor Statistics, bls.gov Feb 2013.
[186] investopedia.com
[187] Annie Gilroy, "Why gold and the US dollar have an inverse relationship," news.yahoo.com 23 Sept 2014.
[188] tradingeconomics.com
[189] slickcharts.com
[190] treasurydirect.gov
[191] investopedia.com
[192] "How rising interest rates impact the bond market," usbank.com 31 Oct 2022.
[193] investopedia.com
[194] bankrate.com
[195] investopedia.com
[196] futures.tradingcharts.com
[197] Joseph Santos, "A History of Futures Trading in the United States," eh.net 16 Mar 2008.
[198] "Midwest Grain Trade: History of Futures Exchanges," cmegroup.com
[199] Wayne Duggan, "Futures Market Definition," money.usnews.com 14 Feb 2022.
[200] investopedia.com
[201] Greg McBride, "What are futures and how do they work?" bankrate.com 31 Oct 2022.

202 Hannah Zhang, "AQR: It's Not Too Late to Bet on Managed Futures," Institutional Investor 18 Nov 2022.
203 Ned Davis Research
204 studymode.com
205 baseballhall.org
206 Patrick McCabe, "The Shift from Active to Passive Investing: Potential Risks to Financial Stability?" Harvard Law School Forum on Corporate Governance, 29 Nov 2018.
207 Elizabeth Ayoola, "Passive Investing: What It Is and How It Works," nerdwallet.com, 28 Apr 2023.
208 Anne Field, "Passive investing 101: A long-term wealth-building strategy all investors should know," businessinsider.com 18 July 2022.
209 Robin Wigglesworth, "How passive are markets, actually?" Financial Times, 4 Sept 2022.
210 Tezcan Gecgil, "7 Sin Stocks to Buy as the World Goes to Hell in a Handbasket," nasdaq.com, 04 Oct 2021.
211 Alexander Molchanov and Jeffrey Stangl, "The Myth of Sector Rotation," Auckland University of Technology.
212 Adam Grealish, "Move Over ETFs: Direct Indexing Is an Investment Strategy Worth Paying Attention to," kiplinger.com 25 Jun 2022.
213 Rebecca Baldridge, "How To Invest With Direct Indexing," Forbes 7 Mar 2023.
214 "Tax Efficiency And Active Investing," rvwwealth.com
215 bankrate.com
216 Shomesh E. Chaudhuri, Terence C. Burnham and Andrew W. Lo, "An Empirical Evaluation of Tax-Loss Harvesting Alpha," Financial Analysts Journal, 2020.
217 Kevin Khang, Alan Cummings, Thomas Paradise, and Brennan O'Connor, "Personalized Indexing: A portfolio construction plan," The Vanguard Group, 2022.
218 investments.yale.edu
219 Leanna Orr, "How the Yale Model ate endowments—and everything else," institutionalinvestor.com, 31 July 2019.
220 Josh Lerner, "Yale University Investments Office: June 2003," pencom.gov.ng, 05 Ma5 2004.
221 Jonathan Burton, "Follow the Buffett Strategy," bauer.uh.edu 02 Aug 2012.
222 Jeffrey McCall, "Media spread fear, Americans listen," thehill.com, 30 May 2021.
223 thedecisionlab.com
224 Deborah Serani, "If It Bleeds, It Leads: Understanding Fear-Based Media," Psychology Today 7 June 2011.
225 David Rifkin and Lee Casey, "Default on U.S. Debt Is Impossible," The Wall Street Journal, 20 Feb 2023.
226 James Galbraith, "The Debt Ceiling Is a Red Herring," project-syndicate.org, 10 Jan 2023.
227 James Bovard, "Why Presidents Want You Scared," Mises Institute, 31 Oct 2018.
228 "Federal Land Ownership: Overview and Data," Congressional Research Service, 21 Feb 2020.
229 "Federal Assets Above and Below Ground," Institute for Energy Research, 17 Jan 2013.
230 prosperousamerica.org
231 Stephen Bullock, Esq., "The Value of U.S. Patents," bullock.law, 10 Jan 2023.
232 "What is Fiat Money?" Money, 13 Feb 2023.
233 Christopher Waller, "Independence + Accountability: Why the Fed Is a Well-Designed Central Bank," Federal Reserve Bank of St Louis Review, October, 2011.
234 nasdaq.com

[235] investopedia.com
[236] R Salais, International Encyclopedia of the Social & Behavioral Sciences, 2001.
[237] tradingeconomics.com
[238] apnews.com
[239] zebpay.com
[240] "How does blockchain work?" onlinestanford.edu
[241] Eduardo Levy Yeyati and Sebastian Katz, "Cryptomania: The good, the bad, and the ugly," brookings.edu, 17 Oct 2022.
[242] Rachel Hartman, "Here's How Much Money You Could Lose if Social Security Goes Bankrupt," U.S. News,16 Aug 2023.
[243] Loris Konish, "71% of Americans are worried Social Security will run out of money in their lifetimes. Why experts say that won't happen," cnbc.com, 6 July 2021.
[244] irs.gov
[245] Ian Freckelton, "COVID-19: Fear, quackery, false representations and the law," International Journal of Law Psychiatry, 10 July 2020.
[246] Birdie Buckingham, "I Explored The Psychology Behind Fear Mongering In The Media," sourcepr.co.uk, 28 July 2021.
[247] Jamie Ducharme, "News Coverage of Coronavirus in 2020 is Very Different Than it Was For Ebola in 2018," Time Magazine, 7 Feb 2020.
[248] Brendan O'Neill, "Covid fearmongering has consequences too," The Spectator, 23 Dec 2021.
[249] James Dean, "Fear year: Pandemic politics made us anxious, but hardly safer," Cornell Chronicle, 15 Apr 2021.
[250] "Fear and Fear-Mongering," The Center for Free, Fair and Accountable Democracy, Sept 2019.
[251] Leonard Weiss, "Fear and Nuclear Terrorism," Stanford Center for International Security and Cooperation, 3 Mar 2015.
[252] collinsdictionary.com
[253] Francesco Casarella, "How 'Permabears' Make Money by Selling Fear," investing.com, 26 Jan 2023.
[254] thedecisionlab.com
[255] Ten Ke Xuan, "5 cognitive biases that could lose you money in the stock market," The Fifth Person, 30 May 2023.
[256] Vijay Pande, "A.I. fear-mongering won't make the world a better place, but a less hopeful one," Fortune, 13 June 2023.
[257] Andrea Moran. "7 Reasons A.I. Won't be Taking Your Job Anytime Soon," The Washington Post, 28 Jun 2023.
[258] Vijay Jayaraj, "The media's climate fearmongering doesn't help anyone," the hill.com, 01 Aug 2023.
[259] thelancet.com
[260] Bob Yirka, "Research finds evidence that reductions in sea ice are helping tree lines spread north," phys.org, 4 Mar 2024.
[261] Ibid # 38
[262] Judith Garber, "Drug advertisements that scare," Lown Institute, 23 Oct 2020.
[263] Kirk Waldroff, "Fear: A powerful motivator in elections," American Psychological Association, 13 Oct 2020.
[264] "The remarkable folly of 'defund the police," The Advocate-Messenger, 29 Jun 2020.
[265] Aaron Chalfin and Justin McCrary, "Are U.S. Cities Underpoliced?: Theory and Evidence, Department of Criminology, University of Pennsylvania, Oct 2015.
[266] Sen. John Thune, "Demonizing and Defunding Police Has Consequences," thune.senate.gov, 16 July 2021.

[267] Rep. Clay Higgins, "Higgins: Democrats' Push To Defund Police Caused Crime To Spike," clayhiggins.house.gov, 22 June 2022.
[268] Catherine Shoichet and Priscilla Alvarez, "Migrants are taking more risks to reach the US," cnn.com, 29 June 2022.
[269] investor.gov
[270] "Bernie Madoff's Ponzi Scheme," International Banker 29 Sep 2021.
[271] Karen Berman and Joe Knight, "What Did Bernard Madoff Do?" Harvard Business Review 30 Jun 2009.
[272] Ben Sales, "10 years after Madoff ripped off the Jewish world, a sort of happy ending," The Times of Israel 21 Dec 2018.
[273] lappinfoundation.org
[274] abcnews.com
[275] Jonathan Stempel, "Allen Stanford's Ponzi scheme recovery tops $1 billion," reuters.com 20 Sep 2021.
[276] Laurel Brubaker Calkins, "A $7 billion Ponzi scheme that busted 14 years ago just settled for $1.6 billion the day a trial was set to begin," Fortune 27 Feb 2023.
[277] "Former Ladue Financial Advisor Sentenced On Federal Fraud Charges," U.S. Attorney's Office, justice.gov 17 Oct 2013.
[278] "Stock Promoter Indicted for Conspiring to Commit Securities Fraud," U.S. Attorney's Office, District of Massachusetts, 2 Sep 2015.
[279] Brian Tayan, "The Wells Fargo Cross-Selling Scandal," Harvard Law School Forum on Corporate Governance, 6 Feb 2019.
[280] David Lazarus, Los Angeles Times 28 Jan 2022.
[281] Jack Kelly, "Wells Fargo Forced To Pay $3 Billion For The Bank's Fake Account Scandal," Forbes 24 Feb 2020.
[282] U.S. Dep't of Justice, justice.gov, 11 Feb 2020.
[283] Pratik Pandab, "Survivorship Bias & How Mutual Fund Companies Make Use Of It," medium.com 2 Aug 2020.
[284] "Survivor Bias in Hedge Funds," swfinstitute.org 27 Nov 2019.
[285] Adam Liptak and Kevin Draper, "Supreme Court Ruling Favors Sports Betting," The New York Times 14 May 2018.
[286] zerofox.com
[287] "Two Men Indicted For Allegedly Operating Multimillion Dollar Sports Betting Pyramid Scheme In Las Vegas," U.S. Attorney's Office, District of Nevada, 2 Nov 2020.
[288] Connor Richards, "Poker Pro Cory Zeidman Indicted for $25M Sports Betting 'Fraud Scheme," pokernews.com 25 May 2022.
[289] Jeff Edelstein, "A 'Madoff'-Like Sports Betting Scheme Leads To Arrest Of WSOP Bracelet Winner," sportshandle.com 26 May 2022.
[290] Pieter Gunst, "How Phone Scammers Try to Access Your Online Banking," nwcu.com 7 Oct 2019.
[291] Genevieve Waterman, "The Top 5 Financial Scams Targeting Older Adults," National Council on Aging, ncoa.org 27 July 0222.

[292] Anthony Aguilar, "Scammers Are Smart. You Have To Be Smarter," aura.com 5 Jan 2023.
[293] "Types Of SEC Whistleblower Cases: High Yield Investment Program Scams and Prime Bank Frauds," secwhistleblowerinformation.com
[294] "Investor Protection Guide: Micro-cap Stock Fraud ('Pump and Dump')," law.cornell.edu
[295] Financial Services and Markets Authority, fsma.be
[296] investor.gov
[297] investorclaims.com

---

[298] efinancemanagement.com
[299] Nate Raymond, "Ex-State Street executive pulled 'bait-and-switch' on clients: U.S. prosecutor," Reuters 25 June 2018.
[300] sec.gov 22 Dec 2004.
[301] ibid #32
[302] "Bond Fraud," nyccriminallawyer.com
[303] Vikki Davies, "What is the fixed-rate bond scam?" cybermagazine.com 07 July 2021.
[304] consumerinvestorresource.com
[305] SEC, Litigation Release. #19591, 06 Mar 2006.
[306] consumer.ftc.gov
[307] ftc.gov
[308] Amanda Hetler, "10 common cryptocurrency scams in 2023," techtarget.com 19 Apr 2023.
[309] Coryanne Hicks, "5 Crypto Scams To Watch Out For," Forbes, 3 Jan 2023.
[310] Steven Pressman, "On Financial Frauds and Their Causes," onlinelibrary.wiley.com 03 July 2006.
[311] "Scammed: why the rich, famous and experts get duped more often than you think," theconversation.com 2 Feb 2023.
[312] "Famous Celebrity Scams," cnbc.com 13 Swept 2013.
[313] gobankingrates.com
[314] financesonline.com
[315] National Council on Aging, ncoa.org
[316] David Rodeck, "What Is An Annuity?" Forbes 14 Dec 2022.
[317] kiplinger.com
[318] Kelly Anne Smith, "What Regulation Best Interest Means For Your Financial Advisor," Forbes 5 Mar 2021.
[319] "VA sales slump to lowest level in 25+ years, Wink Inc. reports," insurancenews.com 17 Mar 2023.
[320] Marc Lichtenfeld, "Why annuities are a bad idea for almost everyone," marketwatch.com 10 Aug 2018.
[321] Amelia Josephson, "Is a Variable Annuity a Good Idea?" smartasset.com 02 May 2023.
[322] money.cnn.com
[323] upcounsel.com
[324] contractscounsel.com
[325] Carrington Coleman, "SEC Clarifies Fiduciary Duty of Private Equity Fund Managers," lexology.com 22 Feb 2020.
[326] Kat Tretina, "How Fiduciary Duty Impacts Financial Advisors," Forbes 15 July 2022.
[327] investor.gov
[328] Rebecca Lake, "What Fiduciary Duty Means (and What It Doesn't)" smartasset.com 12 Jan 2023.
[329] kitces.com
[330] keirsuccess.com
[331] cfp.net
[332] ibid #5
[333] masterclass.com
[334] M.T.Wroblewski, "Why Is It Important in Business for Relationships to Be Based on Honesty, Trust, Fairness & Respect?" work.chron.com 04 Jan 2022.
[335] gfoa.org
[336] corporatefinanceinstitute.com

[337] "What is confidentiality in business?" juro.co 28 Oct 2022.
[338] Kimberlee Leonard, "Meaning of Professionalism and Work Ethic," smallbusiness.chron.com 06 Feb 2019.
[339] phys.org
[340] cfainstitute.org
[341] finra.org
[342] cfainstitute.org
[343] corporatefinanceinstitute.com
[344] tiaa.org
[345] investopedia.com
[346] fidelitycharitable.org
[347] hessverdon.com
[348] investopedia.com
[349] Robert A. Westley, "Planning with charitable lead trusts," thetaxadvisor.com 1 Dec 2021
[350] law.cornell.edu
[351] Lizzie Nealon, "What is An Irrevocable Life Insurance Trust?" Forbes 26 Dec 2022
[352] Leslie S. Laffie, "Intentionally Defective Grantor Trusts," Journal of Accountancy, 31 Dec 2002.
[353] "What Are Intentionally Defective Grantor Trusts?" trustandestateslawyers.com
[354] wealthspire.com
[355] Elaine Silvestrini, "Grantor Retained Annuity Trusts," annuity.org 5 Dec 2022.
[356] law.cornell.edu
[357] "2023 Estate, Gift, and GST Tax Changes," Shipman & Goodman LLP, 10 Jan 2023.
[358] glenmede.com
[359] "The Spousal Lifetime Access Trust: A Nearly Perfect Tool?" Law Offices of Ericson, Scalise & Mangan.
[360] schwab.com
[361] "How and why to build a bond ladder," fidelity.com 07 Sept 2021.
[362] "What Are Muni Bonds?" munibondsforamerica.com
[363] corporatefinanceinstitute.com
[364] "Diversified Arbitrage," AQR
[365] wallstreetprep.com
[366] Mark Mitchell and Todd Pulvino, "Characteristics of Risk and Return in Risk Arbitrage," Journal of Finance Dec 2001.
[367] Ibid #4
[368] AQR
[369] Paul H Schultz and Sophie Shive, Mispricing of Dual-Class Shares: Profit Opportunities, Arbitrage, and Trading," Bergen Meetings Paper, 29 Oct 2009.
[370] financedocbox.com
[371] cfastudyguide.com
[372] AQR
[373] Jean-Phillipe Bouchard, Julius Bonart, Jonathan Donier and Martin Gould, "The Impact of Metaorders," Cambridge University Press Feb 2018.
[374] Julian Klymochko, "The Art of SPAC Arbitrage," accelerateshares.com.
[375] "Why Do The Wealthy Invest in MultiFamily Real Estate?" achieveinvestmentgroup.com
[376] David Greene, "Why Real Estate Builds Wealth More Consistently," Forbes 27 Nov 2018.
[377] (NOI) measures an income-producing property's profitability before adding costs for financing and taxes.
[378] investopedia.com

[379] Brian Skrobonja, "How to grow Your Wealth Like the Real Estate Moguls Do," Kiplingers 19 Jun 2022.
[380] Daniel Sotiroff, "REITs Aren't a True Alternative," Morningstar.com 14 Aug 2019.
[381] Ben Carmona, "REITs, Funds, TICs, DSTs and Crowdfunding: What's the Difference?" perchwealth.com 15 Oct 2021.
[382] Anna Robaton, "Equinix: A Giant Behind the Scenes of the Digital Age," reit.com 24 July 2017.
[383] "1031 Exchange: A Ladder To Wealth," Southern California Exchange Services 7 Feb 2022.
[384] "Build Generational Wealth With 1031 Exchanges," semiretiredmd.com
[385] ibid #388
[386] investopedia.com
[387] wealthmanagement.com
[388] endowmentwm.com
[389] "Tenant in Common 1031 Exchanges Explained," 1031crowdfunding.com
[390] "TIC's For A Wealth Management Strategy," whiteoakswealth.com
[391] Dirk Schultze-Makuch, "The cosmos can kill us in many ways. But the James Webb Space Telescope can help save us," bigthink.com, 15 June, 2022.
[392] planetary.org
[393] thejakartapost.com
[394] science.nasa.gov
[395] ibid #397
[396] ibid #398
[397] Jacob Paul, "Nuclear blasts could be the only thing that can save humanity from asteroids," express.co.uk, 24 Jan 2023.
[398] webb.nasa.gov
[399] Patty-Jane Geller, "Missile Defense," heritage.org, 18 Oct 2022.
[400] Ronald Reagan, "Address to the Nation on National Security," 23 Mar 1983.
[401] James Abrahamson and Henry Cooper, "What Did We Get for Our $30-Billion Investment in SDI/BMD?" National Institute for Public Policy, September 1993.
[402] Iain Boyd, "Israel's Iron Dome air defense system works well," colorado.edu, 13 Oct 2023.
[403] "RSAF'S ASTER 30 Missile System," mindef.gov.sg, 29 Nov 2023.
[404] mbda-systems.com
[405] baesystems.com
[406] "ASTER Surface To Air Missile (Sea Viper)", thinkdefence.co.uk, 5 Nov 2022.
[407] missiledefenseadvocacy.org
[408] gao.gov
[409] Eric Lipton, "A.I. Brings the Robot Wingman to Aerial Combat," The New York Times, 27 Aug 2023.
[410] Matt Berg, "Killer robot swarms, an update," politico.com, 07 Feb 2023.
[411] "Swarm Robotics Market," marketsandmarkets.com.
[412] icanw.org
[413] Barry Pavel and Christian Trotti, "New Tech Will Erode Nuclear Deterrence. The US Must Adapt," defenseone.com, 4 Nov 2021.
[414] Aliza Chasan, "U.S. sets record for billion-dollar weather and climate disasters in 2023," CBS News, 11 Sept 2023.
[415] climate.gov
[416] Remi Lam, Alvaro Saanchez-Gonzalez et al, "Learning skillful medium-range global weather forecasting," Science, 14 Nov 2023.
[417] Dan Stillman, "Why your weather forecasts may soon become more accurate," Washington Post, 14 Nov 2023.

[418] ibm.com
[419] ecmwf.int
[420] Yolanda Botti-Lodovico, "Harnessing technology for pandemic preparedness demands system reform," Brookings, 18 Feb 2022.
[421] "Experts Outline Key Ways to Prevent the Next Pandemic," Columbia Mailman School of Health, 20 Dec 2022.
[422] Kiley Price, "3 ways to prevent the next pandemic with nature, according to science," conservation.org, 23 July 2020.
[423] pfizer.com
[424] "A New World: The Geopolitics of the Energy Transformation," Norwegian Ministry of Foreign Affairs, 2019.
[425] Nathan Kohlenberg, "Over a Barrel: Energy Exports as a Political Weapon," securingdemocracy.gmfus.org, 10 Jan 2022.
[426] "Is the US energy independent?" usafacts.org, 14 May 2023.
[427] "Energy as a tool of foreign policy of authoritarian states, in particular Russia," Study requested by the AFET committee, European Parliament, April 2018.
[428] Trine Villumsen Berling, Peer Schouten and Izabela Surwillo, "Renewable energy will lead to major shifts in geopolitical power," Danish Institute for International Studies, 4 Oct 2021.
[429] onepointsolutions.com
[430] Avi Shultz, "No Smoke, All Mirrors: Developing Next-Generation Heliostats," energy.gov, 7 Oct 2022.
[431] Gege Li, "Mega solar plant uses 170,000 mirrors to generate heat for electricity," newscientist.com, 13 May 2020.
[432] Tom Hartsfield, "Can these mirrors give us solar power at night?" freethink.com, 2 Sept 2021.
[433] chariotenergy.com
[434] blm.gov
[435] Darren Orf, "A Caldera in Nevada Now Has the Most Lithium in the World. Let the Gold Rush Begin," popularmechanics.com, 12 Sept 2023.
[436] Kristen Lawrence, "Tesla Secures Massive Megapack Order," thecooldown.com, 21 Dec 2023.
[437] Michelle Lewis, "The world's largest single-site solar farm just came online," electrek.co, 17 Nov 2023.
[438] "Over one million solar panels powering Australia's largest solar farm," The Queensland Cabinet and Ministerial Directory, 5 Par 2023.
[439] Susan Montoya Bryan, "Powered by wind, this $10B transmission line will carry more energy than the Hoover Dam," Associated Press, 4 Sept 2023.
[440] Julia Layton and Austin Henderson, "Disadvantages of Wind Energy: Do Wind Turbines Affect Health?" science.howstuffworks.com, 23 Sept 2023.
[441] "2022 Elevated Wind Energy to New Heights," energy.gov, 23 Jan 2023.
[442] Owais Ali, "Latest Developments in Wind Harvesting Technology," azocleantech.com, 24 Oct 2022.
[443] Katherine Blunt, "America's Power Grid Is Increasingly Unreliable," The Wall Street Journal, 18 Feb 2022.
[444] finance.yahoo.com
[445] Liz Moyer and Avi Salzman, "Nuclear Power Is Seeing a Resurgence Because of AI Demand," Barron's, 28 Mar 2024.
[446] elibrary.imf.org
[447] santander.com

[448] Eric Milstein and David Wessel, "What did the Fed do in response to the COVID-19 crisis?" Brookings, 17 Dec 2021.
[449] Tobias Adrian, Gita Gopinath and Pierre-Olivier Gourinchas, "Central Banks Can Fend Off Financial Turmoil and Still Fight Inflation," International Monetary Fund blog, 5 June 2023.
[450] wikipedia.com
[451] investopedia.com
[452] "Food for thought: Globalization's role in ending world hunger," World Economic Forum, 23 May 2022.
[453] Milton and Rose Friedman, "The Case for Free Trade," Hoover Institution, 30 Oct 1997.
[454] upgrad.com
[455] Matt Wing, "Artificial intelligence will … change the world," news.illinoisstate.edu, 3 Nov 2023.
[456] innodata.com
[457] Ryan Chacon, "Understanding AGI: The Future of Intelligence?" iotforall.com, 22 June 2023.
[458] innodata.com
[459] Cindy Gordon, "How General AI Will Eventually Reshape Everything," Forbes 30 Sept 2023.
[460] Tech Banters, "Exploring AGI and Generative AI, the AI Prodigies," medium.com, 19 Jun 2023.
[461] "Difficult To Decode: Alan Turing's Life And Its Implications," Harvard University Blog, 3 July 2012.
[462] "Artificial Intelligence: Will Computers Pass The Turing Test By 2029? Does It Matter?" Harvard University Blog, 3 July 2012.
[463] "The Chinese Room Argument," Stanford Encyclopedia of Philosophy, 20 Feb 2020.
[464] wikipedia.com
[465] Murray Shanahan, "The Technological Singularity," MIT Press, August 2015.
[466] ibid #470
[467] Brad Stone, "AI Leader Proposes a New Kind of Turing Test for Chatbots," Bloomberg, 20 June 2023.
[468] "Decoding the Codes: Difference between AI and Generative AI," techify-software.com, 12 June 2023.
[469] Cem Dilmegani, "Artificial Intelligence (AI): In-depth Guide for 2023," AI Multiple, 10 Apr 2023.
[470] Cindy Gordon, "How General AI Will Eventually Reshape Everything, Forbes, 30 Sept 2023.
[471] A. Merchant, S. Batzner, S.S. Schoenholz *et al.* "Scaling deep learning for materials discovery," Nature, 29 Nov 2023.
[472] Stephanie Pappas, "What is DeepMind?" livescience.com, 22 Nov 2022.
[473] June Kim, "Google DeepMind's new AI tool helped create more than 700 new materials," MIT Technology Review, 29 Nov 2023.
[474] Randy Bean, "Artificial General Intelligence (AGI) And The Coming Wave," Forbes, 24 Oct 2023.
[475] Brandon Evans, "Saudi Arabia plans to pour $40B into AI technology: report," seekingalpha.com, 19 Mar 2024.
[476] analyticsvidhya.com
[477] "AutoGPT, BabyAGI, Jarvis: State of Artificial General Intelligence & Autonomous AI in 2023," unleashing.ai, 5 May 2023.

[478] Thomas Davenport and Randy Bean, "Companies Are Making Serious Money With AI," MIT Sloan Management Review, 17 Geb 2022.
[479] Will Daniel, "The A.I. boom will boost corporate profits 30% or more over the next decade, according to a Goldman Sachs senior strategist," finance.yahoo.com, 18 May 2023.
[480] finance.yahoo.com
[481] Michael Walker and James Tierney Jr, "How Can Companies Turn AI Promise into Profits?," alliancebernstein.com, 6 Sept 2023.
[482] mckinsey.com
[483] grandviewresearch.com
[484] Alyssa Schroer, "31 Examples of AI in Finance," builtin.com, 16 Oct 2023.
[485] Mihir Desai, "What the Finance Industry Tells Us About the Future of AI," Harvard Business Review, 9 Aug 2023.
[486] investopedia.com
[487] "Artificial Intelligence in Financial Services: Applications and benefits of AI in finance," insiderintelligence.com, 2 Jan 2023.
[488] onlinedegrees.sandiego.edu
[489] "Artificial Intelligence Market Size, Share & Trends Analysis Report By Solution, By Technology (Deep Learning, Machine Learning), By End-use, By Region, And Segment Forecasts, 2023 – 2030," grandviewresearch.com, 2023.
[490] "Generative AI could raise global GDP by 7%," goldmansachs.com, 5 Apr 2023.
[491] David Pierce, "Google launches Gemini, the AI model it hopes will take down GPT-4," theverge.com, 6 Dec 2023.
[492] androidauthority.com
[493] Michael Madden, "Google's Gemini: is the new AI model really better than ChatGPT?" theconversation.com, 15 Dec 2023.
[494] John Terra, "The Future of Robotics: How Robots Will Transform Our Lives," simplilearn.com, 6 Nov 2023.
[495] Jijo Malayil, "In a first, humanoid robot Sophia delivers commencement speech in New York," interestingengineering.com, 17 May 2024.
[496] zenbo.asus.com
[497] "7 Latest Innovations in Robotics," ECPI University, 2023.
[498] wevolver.com
[499] Jyoti Mann, "An advanced humanoid robot says it can simulate dreams to help it learn about the world," businessinsider.com, 11 Oct 2023.
[500] universal-robots.com
[501] Laura Ross, "8 Examples of Cobots in Everyday Life," thomasnet.com, 2 May 2023.
[502] Harshini, "Top 10 Breakthroughs in Robotics: Advancements and Applications," analyticsinsight.net, 22 June 2023.
[503] Don Basile, "Why 'soft robots' have NASA, doctors, and tech whizzes so excited," Fortune, 1 Jan 2021.
[504] "Databases, Tables & Calculators by Subject," U.S. Bureau of Labor Statistics, 30 Aug 2023; "How Robots Will Redefine Competitiveness," Boston Consulting Group, 23 Sept 2015.
[505] Jonathan Tarud, "7 Recent AI Developments: Artificial Intelligence News," koombea.com, 14 June 2023.
[506] Eric Ralls, "Robots can now learn to accomplish any task by watching videos or observing people," earth.com, 20 June 2023.
[507] "What are the most important advances in AI?" Stanford University, 2023.
[508] Emma Roth, "Boston Dynamics turned its robot dog into a talking tour guide with ChatGPT," theverge.com, 26 Oct 2023.

[509] "What are the most important advances in AI?" Stanford.edu, 2021.
[510] "World's First Fully Autonomous AI-Powered Restaurant to Open in Pasadena," pasadenanow.com, 6 Dec 2023.
[511] Jeremy Nolan, "A Look at Robots in Everyday Life," bairesdev.com.
[512] builtin.com
[513] Dave Dabbah, "Why Companies Should Invest In Robotic Process Automation," spiceworks.com, 18 Jan 2023.
[514] businessinsider.com
[515] electrek.co
[516] "Research: How Finance Professionals really feel about Automation," tradeshift.com, 23 May 2022.
[517] Jeanne Sahadi, "Why do we work 9 to 5? The history of the eight-hour workday," cnn.com, 9 Sept 2023.
[518] Matteo Colombo, "Should Wall Street move to a four-day trading week? seekingalpha.com, 27 Feb 2023.
[519] Todd Pittinsky, "Taking Care With Caregiving Robots," technologyandsociety.org, 23 Sept 2022.
[520] "33 Industries Other Than Auto That Driverless Cars Could Turn Upside Down," cbinsights.com, 20 Sep 2018.
[521] Jan Wienrich, "Autonomous Driving: The Steps to Self-Driving Vehicles," zf.com.
[522] Knut Sauer, "How Far Are We From Level 5 Autonomy?" blog.guardknox.com, 14 Dec 2022.
[523] Alyssa Altman, "The race to Level 5 will be won through collaboration," Automotive World, 10 Jan 2022.
[524] "Understanding the Levels of Autonomy Part II: Level 3 to Level 5," torc.ai, 3 June 2022.
[525] Marie Baca, "Why Geofencing Will Enable L5," semiengineering.com, 19 Sept 2022.
[526] tomorow.bio.
[527] Wilfred Chan, "Two hours of sitting in your car going nowhere: New York's unique parking rules are back," The Guardian, 6 July 2022.
[528] Stephen Rivers, "Tesla's Full Self-Driving Matches Waymo Skills Despite Far Less Hardware," carscoops.com, 17 July 2023.
[529] softwaretesting.news.
[530] William Poor, "Lidar remains the secret sauce for truly autonomous cars," theverge.com, 28 June 2023.
[531] Edd Gent, "Tesla Places Big Bet on Vision-Only Self-Driving," spectrum.ieee.org, 16 July 2021.
[532] Stephen Rivers, "Tesla's AI-Powered FSD v12 Reviews Reveal Highs And Lows," carscoops.com, 2 Feb 2024.
[533] neptune.ai.
[534] rosenbaueramerica.com.
[535] "How Tesla will transition from Modular to End-To-End Deep Learning," thinkautonomous.ai, 15 Sept 2023.
[536] Edd Gent, "Tesla Places Big Bet on Vision-Only Self-Driving," spectrum.ieee.org, 16 July 2021.
[537] Frits Klaver, "The economic and social impacts of fully AVs," compact.nl, Jan 2021.
[538] Nidhi Kalra, "What AVs Could Mean for American Workers," 29 Aug 2017.
[539] Suhasini Gadam, "What Kind Of Jobs Are Self-Driving Cars Going To Create?" Medium, 26 Jun 2018.
[540] techhq.com.

[541] Joann Muller, "Autonomous cars could help millions of disabled Americans find jobs, study finds," axios.com, 17 May 2023.
[542] Jeremy Bowman, "Driverless Cars Will Impact These 5 Industries," fool.com, 9 Aug 2018.
[543] askthemanager.com.
[544] Zachary Shahan, "NVIDIA's Autonomous Driving Tech Leadership a Feature at CES," cleantechnica.com, 8 Jan 2024.
[545] gotquestions.org
[546] "Aging changes in organs - tissue – cells," mountsinai.org
[547] The Sinclair Lab, Harvard Medical School.
[548] "Why we age according to David Sinclair," nuchido.com, 20 July 2022.
[549] Alan Miller, "What is Methylation and Why Should You Care About It?" thorne.com. 25 Sept 2021.
[550] "Rejuvenation treatments appear to be moving to the clinic," lifespan.io, 31 Oct 2023.
[551] cancercenter.com
[552] Mark Fischetti and Jen Christiansen, "Our Bodies Replace Billions of Cells Every Day," Scientific American, 1 Apr 2021.
[553] Brittany Gibson, "7 Immortal Animals That Can Basically Live Forever," Reader's Digest, 14 Feb 2023.
[554] Meghan Jones, "Meet the Most Indestructible Species on the Planet.
[555] National Institute of General Medical Sciences
[556] mountsinai.org
[557] "What Is A Point Mutation?" genetargeting.com, 8 Feb 2021.
[558] D Craig Wilcox, et al, "Genetic determinants of exceptional human longevity: insights from the Okinawa Centenarian Study," ncbi.nlm.nih.gov, * Dec 2006.
[559] "Is longevity determined by genetics?" medlineplus.gov, 11 July 2022.
[560] "Why People in "Blue Zones" Live Longer Than the Rest of the World," healthline.com 29 Sep 2023.
[561] Dan Buettner and Sam Skemp, "Blue Zones," National Library of Medicine, 7 july 2016.
[562] Swapnil N Rajpathak, Yingend Liu, Orit Ben-David, Saritha Reddy, et al, "Lifestyle factors of people with exceptional longevity," National Library of Medicine, 3 Aug 2011.
[563] Richard Faragher and Nir Barzilai, "Genetics: exploring why some people live beyond 100 years," World Economic Forum, 6 Dec 2021.
[564] Jabr, "How Long Can We Live?"
[565] Megan Molteni, "As billionaires race to fund anti-aging projects, a much-discussed trial goes overlooked," statnews.com 9 Aug 2022.
[566] National Library of Medicine
[567] R Fakoor, F Ladhak, A Nazi and M Huber, "Using deep learning to enhance cancer diagnosis and classification," a conference presentation at the 30th International Conference on Machine Learning, 2013.
[568] A Vial, D Stirling, M Field et al. "The role of deep learning and radiomic feature extraction in cancer-specific predictive modelling: a review." *Transl Cancer Res* 2018;7:803–16.
[569] Thomas Davenport and Ravi Kalakota, "The potential for artificial intelligence in healthcare," National Library of Medicine, 6 Jun 2019.
[570] "Towards AI-driven longevity research: An overview," frontiersin.org 1 Mar 2023.
[571] Maria Isaballa, "What AI Technology Is Doing for Longevity Now," lifespan.io 26 Apr 2023.

[572] Cheng Peng, Xi Yang *et al*, "A study of generative large language model for medical research and healthcare," Nature, 16 Nov 2023.
[573] William Haseltine, "Medical Text Written By Artificial Intelligence Outperforms Doctors," Forbes, 15 Dec 2023.
[574] "Can AI help scientists slow the aging process?" Northeastern Global News, 12 May 2023.
[575] Mark Mattson, "Dietary Factors, Hormesis and Health," National Library of Medicine, 1 Sep 2007.
[576] "Everything to Know About Your Circadian Rhythm," healthline.com
[577] "Active phase calorie restriction enhances longevity, UT Southwestern neuroscience study reveals," UT Southwestern Medical Center, 5 May 2022.
[578] hsph.harvard.edu
[579] hopkinsmedicine.org
[580] Sarah Achleithner, "Does intermittent fasting improve longevity?" elo.health.
[581] "Intermittent fasting may help you live longer," neurosciencenews.com 27 Dec 2019.
[582] Dr. Joe Schwarcz, "What is Hormesis?" McGill Office for Science and Society, 24 Jan 2020.
[583] youthandearth.com
[584] [584] Nir Barzilai, Jill Crandall, Stephen Kritchevsky and Mark Espeland, "Metformin as a Tool to Target Aging," National Library of Medicine,10 May 2018.
[585] "The start-ups seeking a cure for old age," Financial Times, 1 Jan 2023.
[586] Mikhail Blagosklonny, "Aging and immortality: quasi-programmed senescence and its pharmacologic inhibition." *Cell Cycle*. 2006; 5:2087–102.
[587] Mikhail Blagosklonny, "Rapamycin for longevity: opinion articles," National Library of Medicine, 15 Oct 2019.
[588] novoslabs.co
[589] Rebekah Harding, "How Longevity Experts Use Intermittent Fasting," honehealth.com 14 Jun 2023.
[590] "Chemically induced reprogramming to reverse cellular aging," Aging, 2023, Vol 15, No 13.
[591] Mark Mattson, "Dietary Factors, Hormesis and Health," National Library of Medicine, 1 Sep 2007.
[592] Chrissy Sexton, ""Fountain of Youth" pill created by Harvard scientists reverses aging," earth.com 29 July 2023.
[593] National Library of Medicine
[594] Eleanor Garth, "Spermidine: Benefits, side-effects, science and research," longevity.technology, 28 Oct 2022.
[595] "What to know about peptides for health," Medical News Today, 16 Aug 2023.
[596] Khushwant Bhullar and Jianping Wu, "Dietary peptides in aging: Evidence and prospects," Science Direct, Mar 2020.
[597] "Longevity & Anti-Aging," myadvitam.com
[598] verywellhealth.com
[599] Rena Christina Tabata, "How AI Could Predict Medical Conditions And Revive The Healthcare System," Forbes 25 Jan 2022.
[600] Breck Dumas, "Chelsea Clinton's VC firm invests in startup that uses AI to accelerate drug development," Fox Business, 9 Nov 2023.
[601] "Stem Cells" What They Are and What they Do," Mayo Clinic Staff, mayoclinic.org
[602] Louis Cona, "Stem Cell Therapy: A Comprehensive Overview (2023)," Da Vinci Wellness Center, 6 Nov 2023.
[603] Nicholas Wade, "Turning Back the Clock on Aging Cells," Yale School of Medicine, 24 Mar 2020.

[604] Eleanor Garth, "Resetting cells to a youthful regenerative state," Longevity Technology, 7 Dec 2020.
[605] "Harvard Medical School Scientists Reverse Age-Related Vision Loss, Eye Damage from Glaucoma in Mice," Mass General Brigham, 2 dec 2020.
[606] Chris Curwen, "Our Longevity Futures," Growing Life, 4 Mar 2021.
[607] "What are genome editing and CRISPR-Cas9?" medlineplus.gov
[608] "CRISPR: A technology that can be used to edit genes," newscientist.com
[609] Allison Gatlin, "Crispr Surges After Winning The First-Ever Approval For A CRISPR-Based Gene-Editing Drug," Investor's Business Daily, 16 Nov 2023.
[610] Joseph Walker, "FDA Approves World's First Crispr Gene-Editing Drug for Sickle-Cell Disease," The Wall Street Journal, 8 Dec 2023.
[611] James Farrell, "FDA Approves New CRISPR Gene-Editing Treatment," Forbes 16 Jan 2024.
[612] Amanda Mah, "Genome Editing Techniques: The Tools That Enable Scientists to Alter the Genetic Code," synthego.com, 13 Jun 2022.
[613] "What are genome editing and gene therapy?" genomicseducation.hee.nhs.uk
[614] ibid #612
[615] Eleanor Laise, "Eli Lilly gene therapy allows child born deaf to hear, clinical trial shows," morningstar.com, 23 Jan 2024.
[616] mayoclinic.org
[617] "Gene Therapy and Genetic Engineering," University of Missouri School of Medicine.
[618] pennmedicine.org
[619] Jim Daley, "Four Success Stories in Gene Therapy," Scientific American, Nov 2021.
[620] Jeremy Hengst and Jong Yun, *xPharm: The Comprehensive Pharmacology Reference*, 2007.
[621] A M Hedgecoe, *Encyclopedia of Applied Ethics*, 2012.
[622] Nicholas Sauderson, "*Emery and Rimoin's Principles and Practice of Medical Genetics,*" 2013.
[623] "Scientists Use Gene-Editing Technology to Produce First Calf Resistant to Major Viral Disease," U.S. Department of Agriculture, ars.usda.gov, 24 July 2023.
[624] Jianfeng Lan, Jarod A Rollins, Xiao Zang et al, "Translational Regulation of Non-autonomous Mitochondrial Stress Response Promotes Longevity," Cell Reports cell.com, 23 July 2019.
[625] Dan Satherley, "Mutations could let humans live for 500 years," newshub.co.nz, 9 Aug 2023.
[626] Ferris Jabr, "How Long Can We Live?" The New York Times, 15 June, 2023.
[627] "New technique makes gene editing at scale possible in animals," University of Oregon, 2 Nov 2022.
[628] Mario Aguilera, "Scientists Slow Aging by Engineering Longevity in Cells," UC San Diego Today, 27 Apre 2023.
[629] Olivia Lowden, "Human Microchipping: The Benefits and Disadvantages," blog.bccresearch.com, 21 Dec 2022.
[630] "The rise of microchipping: are we ready for technology to get under the skin?" theguardian.com, 8 Nov 2019.
[631] Maddy Savage, "Thousands Of Swedes Are Inserting Microchips Under Their Skin," npr.org, 22 Oct 2018.
[632] Ahmed Banafa, "Technology Under Your Skin: 3 Challenges of Microchip Implants," bbvaopenmind.com, 5 Apr 2021.
[633] Sarah Ghormley, "The History of the Human Microchip," medium.com, 19 Sept 2021.

[634] "The technology, devices, and benefits of remote patient monitoring in the healthcare industry," insiderintelligence.com, 19 Jan 2023.
[635] Tuan Minh Tran, "Microchip Implants in Healthcare: When Fiction Comes to Life," fptsoftware.com, 21 July 2023.
[636] Kian Soleymani, "A Fictional Reality: Human Microchipping," gnnguidepost.org, 16 Oct 2023.
[637] ocrportal.hhs.gov
[638] Professor Surjo Soekadar, "Pioneering research: Non-invasive brain stimulation with superior accuracy," eurekalert.org, 24 July 2023.
[639] Jo Craven McGinty, "Inside the Operating Room: Doctors Test a Revolutionary Brain-Computer Implant," The Wall Street Journal, 22 Mar 2024.
[640] Rolfe Winkler, "Elon Musk Says Neuralink Has Implanted Brain Chip in Human," The Wall Street Journal, 29 Jan 2024.
[641] seekingalpha.com
[642] "Musk's Neuralink to start human trial of brain implant for paralysis patients," Reuters, 20 Sept 2023.
[643] Ashley Capoot, "Neuralink competitor Precision Neuroscience conducts its first clinical study to map human brain signals," cnbc.com, 23 June 2023.
[644] Emily Mullin, "People Let a Startup Put a Brain Implant in Their Skull—for 15 Minutes," wired.com, 6 June 2023.
[645] Mehul Reuben Das, "Biotech firm beats Elon Musk's Neuralink, has implanted brain chips in 50 people for ailments," firstpost.com, 1 May 2023.
[646] Ashley Capoot, "Brain implant startup backed by Bezos and Gates is testing mind-controlled computing on humans," cnbc.com, 18 Feb 2023.
[647] Andrea Park, "Sci-fi no more: Synchron implants mind-reading device in first US patient in paralysis trial," fiercebiotech.com, 19 July 2022.
[648] Daniel Gilbert, "The race to beat Elon Musk to put chips in people's brains," The Washington Post, 3 Mar 2023.
[649] Sam John, "We've been connecting brains to computers longer than you'd expect. These 3 companies are leading the way," theconversation.com, 26 Mar 2023.
[650] Sarah Sarsby, "Pioneering assistive headband that acts as a "head mouse" can integrate with wide range of tech," attoday.co.uk, 9 Aug 2023.
[651] iberdrola.com
[652] massdevice.com
[653] Romain Fonsegrives, "US Woman Receives Revolutionary Brain Implant For OCD And Epilepsy," sciencealert.com, 5 Feb 20204.
[654] Anthony Cuthbertson, "Paralysed man feeds himself for first time in 30 years with robot arms plugged into brain," independent.co.uk, 30 June 2022.
[655] "Brain-computer interface enables woman with severe paralysis to speak through digital avatar," news-mwedical.net, 24 Aug 2023.
[656] Dr Mark van Rijmenam, "The mind-bending world of brain-computer interfaces: how the technology will change humanity," thedigitalspeaker.com, 20 Sept 2023.
[657] "Microchip Links Brain, Spine and Body, Allowing Paralyzed Man to Move and Feel," neurosciencenews.com, 2 Aug 2023.
[658] Rolfe Winkler, "Elon Musk's Neuralink Shows First Patient Using Its Brain Implant," The Wall Street Journal, 20 Mar 2024.
[659] Brooke Becher, "Brain Computer Interfaces (BCI) Explained," builtin.com, 25 July 2023.
[660] Mahdi Akhavan, "Possible risks in using brain-computer interfaces," open.mit.edu.
[661] traent.com
[662] who.int

[663] newsroom.accenture.com
[664] Thomas Aichner, "The economic argument for hiring people with disabilities," nature.com, 22 Jan 2021.
[665] "Economic Impact Of Disability Travel Reaches $58.7 Billion, PR Newswire, 28 Oct 2020.
[666] verywellmind.com
[667] positivepsychology.com
[668] ibave.weebly.com
[669] Oxford Languages
[670] study.com
[671] princeton.edu
[672] scribbr.com
[673] britannica.com
[674] "The Sources of Knowledge," risussite.wordpress.com
[675] A.G. Esposito and P.J. Bauer, "Going beyond the lesson: Self-generating new factual knowledge in the classroom." Journal of Experimental Child Psychology, 3 Sept 2016.
[676] K.W. Fischer and T.R. Bidel, "Dynamic development of action and thought" Handbook of Child Psychology, 2006 John Wiley & Sons.
National Academies of Sciences, Engineering, and Medicine. 2018. How People Learn II: Learners, Contexts, and Cultures. Washington, DC: The National Academies Press. https://doi.org/10.17226/24783.
[677] J.G. Greeno, A.M. Collins and L.B. Resnick, "Cognition and Learning," Handbook of Educational Psychology, 1996, Macmillan.
National Academies of Sciences, Engineering, and Medicine. 2018. How People Learn II: Learners, Contexts, and Cultures. Washington, DC: The National Academies Press. https://doi.org/10.17226/24783.
[678] stackpack.com
[679] Marguerite Ward, "How each of these 5 highly-successful people overcame their quarter-life crisis," cnbc.com, 22 June 2017.

www.ingramcontent.com/pod-product-compliance
Lightning Source LLC
LaVergne TN
LVHW020414220926
848484LV00018B/2578/J